The Market Makers

The Market Makers

How Retailers are Reshaping the Global Economy

Edited by
Gary G. Hamilton, Misha Petrovic, and Benjamin Senauer

OXFORD
UNIVERSITY PRESS

OXFORD
UNIVERSITY PRESS

Great Clarendon Street, Oxford OX2 6DP

Oxford University Press is a department of the University of Oxford.
It furthers the University's objective of excellence in research, scholarship,
and education by publishing worldwide in

Oxford New York

Auckland Cape Town Dar es Salaam Hong Kong Karachi
Kuala Lumpur Madrid Melbourne Mexico City Nairobi
New Delhi Shanghai Taipei Toronto

With offices in

Argentina Austria Brazil Chile Czech Republic France Greece
Guatemala Hungary Italy Japan Poland Portugal Singapore
South Korea Switzerland Thailand Turkey Ukraine Vietnam

Oxford is a registered trade mark of Oxford University Press
in the UK and in certain other countries

Published in the United States
by Oxford University Press Inc., New York

© Oxford University Press 2011

The moral rights of the authors have been asserted
Database right Oxford University Press (maker)

First published 2011

British Library Cataloguing in Publication Data
Data available

Library of Congress Cataloging in Publication Data
Data available

Typeset by SPI Publisher Services, Pondicherry, India
Printed in Great Britain
on acid-free paper by
MPG Books Group, Bodmin and King's Lynn

ISBN 978-0-19-959017-9

1 3 5 7 9 10 8 6 4 2

Acknowledgments

First and foremost, we want to acknowledge the support and encouragement of the Alfred P. Sloan Foundation, and in particular Gail Pesyna, the Program Officer for Sloan's Industry Studies Program, and Frank Giarratani, Professor of Economics, University of Pittsburgh, and Director of the Center for Industry Studies. Throughout the process, they have both been exceedingly helpful in making this book possible.

The idea for the book emerged out of a Sloan-sponsored workshop that was held on June 7–8, 2004, at the University of Washington. The workshop focused on "the role of intermediaries in global value chains." Robert Feenstra and Gary Hamilton had emphasized the importance of this topic in their book *Emergent Economies, Divergent Paths: Economic Organization and International Trade in South Korea and Taiwan* (2006), but they also recognized that relatively little research had been done on the topic. In an effort to work out the implications of intermediaries (mainly retailers, merchandisers, and trading companies) in international trade, Hamilton, along with Suresh Kotha and Misha Petrovic, organized a workshop that pulled together many of the leading researchers in the USA working on retailing and global trade. During this workshop, Hamilton and Petrovic introduced the market-making perspective, which, as discussed in Chapter 1 of this book, is an analytic approach centered on the institutional arrangements that structure and facilitate market transactions. The idea of intermediaries as market-makers provided a collective focus that allowed workshop participants working on diverse topics to converge on a core theme: the global significance of large retailers.

Building on the enthusiasm generated from the first workshop, Hamilton, Petrovic, and Senauer received additional support from the Sloan Foundation to hold a second workshop in order to prepare this book. We used the second workshop, held in Boston, on April 26 and 27, 2007, to present early drafts of some of the chapters and to revise the book's contents to reflect the ongoing research of the group.

We wish to acknowledge a number of people who contributed to and commented on the proceedings of the first workshop, but who did not contribute chapters to the current volume: Robert Feenstra (Economics, University of California, Davis), Frank Giarratani (Economics, University of

Pittsburgh), Greg Magnan (Albers School of Business, Seattle University), Mary Ann Odegaard (School of Business, University of Washington), and Thomas E. Reifer (Institute for Research on the World System, University of California, Riverside). In addition, at the first workshop, we benefited greatly from industry spokespersons who helped clarify the role of intermediaries in value chains: James Ayers (CGR Management Consultants), Kristina Erickson (Boeing Corporation), Kal Raman (Drugstore.com), Kim Suchomel (Costco), and Herman Uscategui (Starbucks).

Hamilton and Petrovic also wish to acknowledge the support of the Rockefeller Foundation, and in particular Katherine McFate, then a program officer at the Rockefeller Foundation, for funding some of the research on which our chapters are based.

Finally, we want to thank David Musson at Oxford University Press, who heard about our workshop and encouraged us to write this book. His help came at just the right time, and for that we are grateful. We also want to thank Emma Lambert, also at Oxford University Press, who helped us prepare the manuscript for publication.

Contents

Contents

List of Figures

List of Tables

Abbreviations

A&P	Great Atlantic and Pacific
AGOA	African Growth and Opportunity Act
ARPA	Advanced Research Projects Agency
BIOS	board-level input/output system
BOA	Bank of America
C&C	cash and carry
CAD	computer-aided design
CNC	computer numerically controlled
CPU	central processing unit
D2S	design to store
DC	distribution center
EAN	European Article Number
ECR	Efficent Consumer Response
EDI	electronic data interchange
EDLP	every day low pricing
ELS	Extra Long Staple
FPL	Field, Palmer, and Leiter
ERP	Economic Recovery Program
FDI	foreign direct investment
FLA	Fair Labor Association
FTP	File Transfer Protocol
GMA	Grocery Manufacturers of America
GVC	global value chain
HVAC	heating, ventilation, and air conditioning
IBEC	International Basic Economy Corporation
IBT	International Brotherhood of Teamsters
ICC	Interstate Commerce Commission
IDC	International Data Corporation
IDS	Integrated Distribution Services

Abbreviations

ILWU	International Longshore and Warehouse Union
IP	Internet Protocol
ISO	International Standards Organization
ITGLWF	International Textiles, Garment and Leathers Workers Federation
MFA	Multi-Fiber Agreement
MNC	multinational corporation
NAFC	National Association of Food Chains
NBI	National Bank Americard, Inc.
NGO	non-governmental organization
NIC	newly industrializing country
NIST	National Institute of Science and Technology
OBM	original brand manufacturer
ODM	original design manufacturer
ODM/CM	original design manufacturer/contact manufacturer
OEM	original equipment manufacturer
PC	personal computer
PMA	Pacific Maritime Association
POS	point of sale(s)
PPP	purchasing power parity
RFD	rural free delivery
RFID	radio-frequency identification
SHV	Steenkolen Handelsvereniging
SI	systems integrator
SKU	stock-keeping unit
SMEs	small and medium-sized enterprises
TCP	Transmission Control Protocol
TEU	20-foot equivalent unit
TSUSA	Tariff Schedule of the United States Annotated
TWC	The Waterfront Coalition
UPC	Universal Product Code
USDA NASS	US Department of Agriculture, National Agricultural Statistics Service
VAR	value-added reseller
VMI	vendor-managed inventory
WCWC	West Coast Waterfront Coalition
WTO	World Trade Organization
WWW	World Wide Web

Contributors

Frederick H. Abernathy is Abbott and James Lawrence Research Professor of Engineering and Gordon McKay Research Professor of Mechanical Engineering and Director of the Sloan Foundation Center on Textiles and Apparel, Harvard University. Abernathy is the co-author of *A Stitch in Time: Lean Retailing and the Transformation of Manufacturing: Lessons from the Apparel and Textile Industries* (1999), the authoritative book on the textile industry in the late twentieth century and the book introducing the concept of "lean retailing."

Richard P. Appelbaum is Professor of Sociology and Director of the Center for Global Studies, University of California, Santa Barbara. Appelbaum published extensively in the areas of social theory, urban sociology, public policy, the globalization of business, and the sociology of work and labor. He is currently engaged in a multi-disciplinary study of supply-chain networks in the Asian-Pacific Rim.

Sandip Basu is Assistant Professor of Management in the College of Business and Economics, California State University, Hayward. His current research includes work on corporate entrepreneurship, innovation, and new venture creation.

Edna Bonacich is Professor Emeritus of Sociology and Ethnic Studies at the University of California, Riverside. She is the author and editor of numerous books related to retailing, including *Global Production: The Apparel Industry in the Pacific Rim* (1994), *Behind the Label: Inequality in the Los Angeles Apparel Industry* (with Richard Appelbaum) (2000), and the important, recently published book *Getting the Goods: Ports, Labor, and the Logistics Revolution* (2008).

Jason Dedrick is Associate Professor in the School of Information Studies at Syracuse University. He, along with Kenneth Kraemer, is one of the world's leading experts on the computing industry and the author of many articles and books on the topic, including *Asia's Computer Challenge: Threat or Opportunity for the United States and the World?* (with Kenneth L. Kraemer) (1998).

Gary Gereffi is Professor of Sociology and Director of the Center on Globalization, Governance, and Competitiveness at Duke University. He is the developer of "global commodity chain" analysis and one of the world's leading authorities on global supply chains. He is the author of many books and articles on the topic, including *The New Offshoring of Jobs and Global Development* (2006).

Gary G. Hamilton is a Professor of Sociology and of International Studies at the University of Washington. He is an author of numerous articles and books, including most recently *Emergent Economies: Divergent Paths, Economic Organization and*

International Trade in South Korea and Taiwan (with Robert Feenstra) (2006) and *Commerce and Capitalism in Chinese Societies* (2006).

John Humphrey is a Professorial Fellow at the Institute of Development Studies, University of Sussex. He has published widely on current trends in globalization and has researched extensively on global value chains, economic governance, and standards.

Cheng-shu Kao is Professor of Sociology at Tunghai University in Taiwan. He is also Vice Chairman of the Board of Trustees at Feng-Chia University in Taiwan. He is the founding director and a continuing associate of the Institute of East Asian Societies and Economies at Tunghai University, which is the location of the world's most extensive archive of interviews with Taiwanese businesspeople. He is the author of many books and articles, including most recently *The Boss's Wife* (1999, in Chinese).

Suresh Kotha is Douglas E. Olesen/Battelle Excellence Chair in Entrepreneurship and Professor of Management and Organization at the Michael G. Foster School of Business at the University of Washington. He is a leading authority on e-commerce and the author of many articles and book chapters on this and related topics.

Kenneth Kraemer is Research Professor in the Paul Merage School of Business. He is also Associate Director of the Center for Research on Information Technology and Organizations (CRITO), as well as Co-Director of the Personal Computing Industry Center at the University of California, Irvine. He is the author and co-author of many books, including *Asia's Computer Challenge: Threat or Opportunity for the United States and the World?* (1998), *Global E-Commerce: Impacts of National Environment and Policy* (2006), and *Computerization Movements* (2008).

Misha Petrovic is an Assistant Professor of Sociology at the National University of Singapore. His dissertation, "Market Makers and Market Making: The Evolution of Consumer Goods Markets in the United States, 1870–2000" (University of Washington, 2005), is a pioneering study of the market-making perspective applied to the United States.

Thomas Reardon has been a Professor in the Department of Agricultural, Food, and Resource Economics at Michigan State University since January 1992; from, 1984 to 1991 he was with the International Food Policy Research Institute. His research focuses on links between agri-food industry transformation and food security in Asia. He has worked extensively on the "supermarket revolution," transforming horticultural and dairy product supply chains, and novel development strategies to link small farmers to dynamic markets. He was an invitee to the World Economic Forum (WEF) at Davos in 2009 and is a member of the WEF's Global Alliance Council for Food Security, as well as a member of the expert panel on food security and agricultural development for the Chicago Council on Global Affairs.

Benjamin Senauer is a Professor of Applied Economics at the University of Minnesota and a past Co-Director of the Food Industry Center with the Sloan Foundation Industries Study Program. He is one of the foremost experts on food retailing and food policy. His numerous publications include the books *Food Trends and the Changing*

Consumer (1991) and *Ending Hunger in Our Lifetime: Globalization and Food Security* (2003).

Timothy Sturgeon is Senior Research Affiliate at the Massachusetts Institute of Technology's Industrial Performance Center. He is a leading authority on global value chains and on the evolution of global industries. He is the author of many articles on the topic and co-editor (with Momoko Kawakami) of *The Dynamics of Local Learning in Global Value Chains: Experiences from East Asia* (2010).

Anthony P. Volpe is a senior research associate at the Harvard Center for Textile and Apparel Research. His latest work centers on the role of analytics in retail environments. He is currently a Global Product Manager in the retail division of SAS institute, Inc.

Michael Wortmann is currently in the School of Management, University of Surrey, UK. He is a researcher in the Social Science Research Center in Berlin and at FAST e.V., a research and consulting organization he co-founded in 1986. He is one of the foremost specialists on the retail industry in Europe and has written many articles on the topic.

Introduction

Gary G. Hamilton and Misha Petrovic

The transformation of retailing in the last half of the twentieth century substantially changed the global economy. This transformation is both obvious and largely unrecognized. It is obvious, because the transformation is a part of our everyday lives. In the United States, in 1954, there were only 500 shopping centers across the country, most of which by today's standard were minuscule. After a change in tax laws in 1955 allowing for accelerated depreciation on commercial construction, shopping centers in the USA jumped to 7,600 by 1964 and accounted for 30 percent of US retail sales (Hanchett 1996). By 2006, the shopping centers in the USA alone approached 50,000, many of which are gargantuan.[1] Moreover, this expansion has happened not just in the United States, but throughout the world. In fact, the largest shopping centers are no longer in the USA, but are scattered around the globe. Many of the newest and largest of them are now in Asia.

The obviousness of the shopping-center boom and other similar changes in the retail landscape is matched only by how few scholars recognize its significance for the global economy. Most economists and economic analysts continue to use equilibrium models to interpret aggregated economic data and ignore qualitative changes that have occurred over time. They see the severe global crisis of 2007–9 in terms of recurring business cycles, and compare this crisis to the ones that occurred in the 1980s or even in the 1930s in order to predict its course. Although such comparisons are warranted, it is the structural differences in how the economy is organized and not the apparent similarities that are most telling and ought to be examined the most thoroughly.

One of the biggest differences between the global economy throughout much of the twentieth century and the global economy in the first decade of the twenty-first century is the extent to which the latter is organized by retailers and through retailing. The expansion of shopping centers is just the tip of an iceberg. Underpinning this expansion is the dominance of large retailers. In 1963, large retailers, each operating a hundred or more stores, accounted for just under 20 percent of US retail sales; in 2002, their share was almost 60 percent (US Bureau of the Census, various years). In sectors as varied as electronics, drug stores, books, office supplies, and general merchandise, the four largest retailers have over a 50 percent share of the US market. Best Buy, Costco, Barnes & Noble, Home Depot, and Staples—to name a few—are amongst such national-level operators that dominate their respective retail sectors. The spread of chain stores and the huge market share they command are a global trend as well. The ten largest retailers in the world had combined sales of well over US$1 trillion, around 10 percent of the world's total, in 2007 (Deloitte 2009: 66).

These are amazing numbers, especially when one considers the absolute size and the unique character of the retail sector. Large global retailers of food and general merchandise typically deal with thousands of suppliers from many different industries and with millions of individual consumers. They also manage vast organizational networks consisting of hundreds, or even thousands, of stores, and many warehouses, buying offices, distribution centers, and processing facilities scattered around the globe. This multitude of diverse roles and tasks creates a potential for exercising a considerable influence on the shape of the global economy, but also means that efficient large retailers were slower to develop and more reluctant to expand to international markets than their manufacturing counterparts.

In the early decades of industrial capitalism, large manufacturers of consumer goods and large retailers rarely interacted with each other. Early advances in mechanization and transportation allowed manufacturers to benefit from economies of scale; they located factories in strategic locations, enlarged those factories to fit market conditions, and distributed their products as far as they could extend the market for their goods. As a result, many manufacturing sectors, such as those for cars, gasoline, home appliances, tobacco, and packaged and processed food, rapidly became more concentrated as their market reach widened. Large manufacturers started specialized marketing departments, organized distribution of their products, and often exercised a considerable market power over small and localized retailers that sold their products.

In other industries, such as printing, apparel and footwear, furniture and housewares, and most perishables, the available technology did not allow for concentrated mass manufacturing, and there it was often a large retailer who took the incentive in organizing the distribution, and occasionally even the production of goods (Scranton 1994, 1999). This bifurcation led, in the early years of US capitalism, to the establishment of two parallel ways of marketing consumer goods, one based on the links between large manufacturers and small dealers, and the other on the links between large retailers and small suppliers. Although these two types of marketing developed at the same time, between 1890 and 1930 in the USA, and somewhat later in the leading European economies, by the mid-twentieth century the one led by large manufacturers became recognized everywhere as dominant. This was due partly to the climate of economic planning and regulation that favored the large producers, itself a consequence of the Great Depression and the war effort, but also to the greater ease with which large manufacturers expanded globally. Between the early 1950s and the late 1970s, domestically as well as globally, large manufacturers were arguably the main driving force of the rapidly globalizing economy.[2]

All that has now changed. By the end of the twentieth century, large retailers had replaced large manufacturers as the key organizers of the world economy. This transformation, we suggest, amounts to a retail revolution on the global scale.

The Retail Revolution

The expression "retail revolution" is certainly not new. It has been used many times for everything from the introduction of the first department stores, chain stores, and supermarkets, to the post-Second World War adoption of US retail formats in Europe and Japan, to the more recent technological advances in retailing and international expansion of large retailers. All of these, however, saw the retail revolution as the process limited to the retail "industry" itself. When Bluestone and his colleagues (1981), for instance, titled their investigation of the transformation in the US department store sector *The Retail Revolution*, they focused on the processes of the "industrialization of retailing," characterized by the adoption of new technologies and corporate managerial hierarchies, the emergence of giant firms (such as Sears and J. C. Penney's) that were then "about to buy out or drive out their competition" (Bluestone et al. 1981: 143) and the concomitant changes in retail labor.[3] The US retail sector, they emphasized, was about to catch up with the developments that had been present in manufacturing for many decades.

In our view, the retail revolution should be understood as a more fundamental transformation in the organization of the overall global economy, the transformation that continues to change not only the world of retailing, or even the relative power between retailers and their suppliers, but also the shape of international trade, economic development, product worlds, and consumption practices.

The rest of this volume is dedicated to addressing various aspects of this transformation. Here we summarize some of the main trends from the 1950s to the first decades of the twenty-first century that helped propel what was initially a limited change of the US retail landscape into a major force of the global economy.

The first such trend, already indicated above, was the phenomenal growth of large retailers. The growth has been predicated on the convergence of major retail innovations—self-service, broad product mix, and chain-store replication—toward a standard business model adopted by retailers in many different sectors. The revolution started in the USA, in the late 1950s and early 1960s, based on the application of the supermarket model to general merchandise and specialty retailing and on the dramatic expansion of retail space in shopping centers. Some of its protagonists and major beneficiaries were already established operators, such as Sears and J. C. Penney's, Woolworth's and Kresge's, A&P (Atlantic and Pacific), Safeway and Albertsons, May and Federated department stores. But the change in retail formats also created opportunities for new specialty stores, such as The Limited (founded in 1963), CVS Caremark (1963), The Gap (1969), Best Buy (1977), Home Depot (1978), Costco (1983), and Staples (1986). Wal-Mart, Kmart, and Target, the big three of discount general merchandising, all started their operations in 1962, as did Kohl's. As the US retail formats spread abroad (see Petrovic, Chapter 3 this volume), similar transformations occurred in Western Europe and Japan, and then in a number of other economies, bringing to the fore new efficient operators, such as Carrefour, Tesco, Metro, and Aldi. This new generation of retailers would eventually converge on a portfolio of standardized retail formats, and come to dominate global retail markets.

The second major trend has been the blurring of boundaries between manufacturers, brand-name merchandisers, and retailers, as all of them increasingly saw marketing as their core organizational activity and competence. Before the 1960s, most brand-name merchandisers were also manufacturers who promoted, often through extensive advertising, the products that they actually made. In the 1970s, however, this pattern gave way to brand-name merchandisers that sourced from original equipment manufacturers (OEMs) most if not all of the goods sold under their brand name. Nike (1972), Ralph Lauren, and The Limited were amongst the first and most well-known merchandisers to do so, but the list of these factory-less brand-name merchandisers is now quite long. Most of them never had factories in the first place, while some of them, such as Schwinn bicycles, Eddie Bauer clothes, RCA TVs, began as manufacturers, but by the 1980s had closed all or most of their factories and simply became designers and merchandisers of products made by contract manufacturers. By the late 1980s, this same pattern of shifting from manufacturing to merchandising also swept through consumer electronics. Dell, a factory-less brand-name merchandiser and now one of the world's largest sellers of brand-name computers, established its business only in

1984. Dell's chief competitors in the area of personal computers, IBM, Hewlett Packard, and Compaq, all began as PC manufacturers and ended as merchandisers relying on contract manufacturing.

The third major trend concerns various momentous changes in retail technology, what Abernathy and his colleagues (1999; Chapter 2 this volume) refer to as "lean retailing." At the core of this transformation is the application of information technology to all aspects of selling products, from tracking consumer purchases to managing inventories and supply chains. One of the best examples of such technologies is the Universal Product Code (UPC). Supermarkets and food firms jointly developed bar codes and scanning devices in the mid-1970s. In the early 1980s, Wal-Mart and Kmart were amongst the first retailers to expand UPC to include non-food items, which enabled them to develop computerized inventory systems. Most other firms, large and small, followed suit later in the decade, so that, by the 1990s, UPC had become nearly universal. From the mid-1980s on, the spreading use of bar codes allowed a transformation in logistics, including containerization, shipping, warehousing, stocking, and tracking consumer choices from point-of-sales information.

Technological changes pushed retailers into the front category of technology adopters and users. By allowing them directly to access and track consumer demand at the checkout counter, new information and communication technologies gave retailers the means to refashion the relations with their suppliers. Before the 1980s, business practitioners conceptualized the distribution of manufactured goods from the viewpoint of manufacturers, as "distribution channels." After the 1980s, they coined new terminology to conceptualize the distribution of goods from the perspective of the retailer: "supply chains." With the help of information technology, retailers began to practice "supply-chain management," which is another way of saying that they created price-sensitive networks of firms that turned manufacturing and logistics into organizational extensions of retailing (Feenstra and Hamilton 2006: 233).

The increasing concentration at the retail end largely results from the national and international proliferation of chain stores that sell more or less the same set of products everywhere the companies establish their retail outlets. The proliferation of chain stores creates a tremendous intermediary demand (that is, the demand generated by the big buyers) for logistical and manufacturing solutions that can supply each outlet with exactly those goods required to restock their inventories. This intermediary demand always extends beyond the boundaries of individual firms to incorporate all other firms with which the specific retail firms do business. The networks of firms organized around the intermediary demand for products makes manufacturers and logistics providers into "vendors," into mere suppliers of goods and services that the "big-box" retailers "buy" for their customers.

The fourth and perhaps the most important aspect of the retail revolution is the fact that the goods that American and European consumers buy have been increasingly sourced from suppliers located outside the United States and Europe, particularly from East Asia. As we describe in Part III (see especially Hamilton and Kao, Chapter 6 this volume), starting in the mid-1960s there was a dramatic increase in US imports of select categories of consumer goods. Before 1965, imported goods represented a negligible part of US consumption, but by the late 1970s they came to dominate consumption of many common categories of consumer goods, from apparel and toys to electronics and, increasingly, motorcycles and cars. From the very first beginnings of this trend, these consumer goods came predominately from East Asia. This trend, which continues today, has had dire consequences for US-based manufacturing of non-durable consumer goods, but was at the same time a major factor in the development of manufacturing competences of Asian firms and, by implication, in the general economic growth of Asian economies. The ability of US, and soon after also European, retailers to find alternative sources of supply and weaken the competitive position of domestic brands increased the relative power of retailers over manufacturers.

The final aspect of the global retail revolution is the transformation of consumption.[4] The role of large retailers in globalizing consumption patterns has been largely ignored in favor of more striking references to McDonaldization and other similar putative processes of the globalization of American brands, products, and popular culture. We believe that the transformation of consumption brought about by the large retailers has been both more subtle and ultimately more consequential than what such examples centered on particular companies and products suggest. The issue is one not of homogeneity versue diversity, globalization and localization, but rather of the global convergence toward certain types of retail markets, product worlds, and expectations of choice.

This convergence has increasingly created new types of consumers, as well as an array of new types of retailers that cater to these consumers. Retailers have been able to create new consumer markets throughout the world, not simply because they offer cheaper prices, for that is usually not the case, but rather because they promise a new way of life for people who come to see themselves in a new light.

Social scientists have known for a long time that people consume what they do as a means of conveying to others a sense of who they are as individuals. Thorstein Veblen, in *The Theory of the Leisure Class* (1899), was the first social scientist to develop a demand-driven theory of the economy. He showed that the logic of consumption was to convey a sense of self-worth to others by means of making invidious distinctions. People who regard themselves as privileged in one way or another will use status-marking objects and actions as a way to establish their distinctiveness. For Veblen (1899), writing in the Gilded Age, this distinctiveness was based on a class identity, and to establish oneself in the upper class was to create an image of non-utilitarian consumption of goods and time, which is what he called "conspicuous consumption" and "conspicuous leisure."

A long line of sociologists have substantiated Veblen's insights: consumption and stratification go hand in hand. But more recent researchers (e.g., Holt 1997) have also qualified these insights by showing that class stratification is not what it used to be. When asked, almost everyone in the US with any means whatsoever put themselves into the middle class. Although the actual items of consumption vary greatly from person to person, the invidiousness attached to objects and actions cannot be comfortably ranked by class position. Instead of class, objects and actions increasingly attach themselves to lifestyles, which are only indirectly associated with class and income. Today, lifestyles, not class, are the vehicles of self-representation and also of stratification (Holt 1997).

The core of this phenomenon is to see that retailers today, in whatever business, have entered into a virtual, and sometimes an actual, conversation with their customers. Customers discover who they are by exploring what is being offered to them, and, once those identities form and once those identities signify a lifestyle filled with ideal and material goods, retailers strive to supply those goods, and in so doing expand the lifestyle. Demand-driven retailing responds to buying. What is bought gets made, and more and more of it, establishing a feedback loop.

What only the very rich could afford to do in Veblen's time has now become available, throughout the world, to people of a wide range of income categories. Instead of being synonymous with class, lifestyles themselves become stratified according to one's level of income. Eating foie gras in Paris and bird's nest soup in Hong Kong, playing golf at Pebble Beach and doing yoga at Borobudur, climbing the Matterhorn, and snorkeling off the Great Barrier Reef—all these are conspicuous activities that people can do today, even with modest incomes. And the very rich may not even have the most fun anymore. Only the very poor and dispossessed get left out, and the knowledge of their exclusion makes their plight all the more unbearable. For everyone else, an array of lifestyles is there for the choosing. Select the lifestyle that suits you, refine that lifestyle in terms of reachable goals, Google those goals on the Web, and, presto, here they are: travel agents to help you arrange your trip, retailers to give you a price and a delivery date for the objects you want to buy, clubs to join to help you become sophisticated consumers of that activity, even friends and potential friends with whom to enjoy your way of life.

This is not Veblen's world, but it is the world we live in today, a variegated and expanding world of diverse lifestyles and identities that go with them.

However anachronistic they may be, these lifestyles and identities are necessarily contemporary ones. They are up to date precisely because retailers and other purveyors provide the necessary accoutrements to establish a contemporary way of life. Without these retailers, a particular lifestyle might be difficult if not impossible to establish: difficult to find the right stuff, difficult to find others to associate with, difficult even to know about. Demand-driven retailing helps define and fill out lifestyles that would hardly exist otherwise.

It is also clear that, outside Europe and the United States, the feedback loop between retailers and the new consumers has helped to create new identities out of the apparent convergence that so many people have observed. Music, movies, the Internet, technology hardware and software, vacations and tourism, strategic English, standardized national languages, houses that call for interior decoration, cuisines that require specialized kitchenware, occupations that necessitate a standardized education—the list of convergences go on and on. But what this listing obscures is the fact that these are the very media of differentiation.

Demand-driven retailing allows consumers to create distinct worlds out of standardized points of entry. The youth of each country use cell phones to text to their friends and create their own rap songs; in turn, both media relay to the audience what it means to be young and in a particular place. Bollywood helps Indians to understand who they are or might be, a fact that can be shared with movie-goers around the world, who in turn can understand who they are not. Google and other Internet search engines adapt to each locale, as well as to differentiate amongst locales, and Google and the other search engines are strictly speaking demand driven; they rely on information fed by its users.

The standardization of entry points encourages cultural differentiation, encourages the formation of new worlds filled with new identities to explore. Mathews and Lui (2001) show, in their fine collection on consumerism in Hong Kong, that shopping in Hong Kong has become a way of life, not a Western way of life, but a new Hong Konger way of life. Chua, in *Life Is Not Complete without Shopping* (2003), makes the same argument for Singapore. In both locations, a unique consumer culture has emerged, including styles of clothing, home decor, movies, and food. Mona Abaza (2001) lets us see that shopping malls in Cairo offer a new space for Egyptians, not as Westerners, but as Egyptians forging new identities to fit the times, for women who are finding a space away from Islamic restrictions, for couples who can look into each other's eyes longingly and without shame. In *Golden Arches East: McDonald's in East Asia*, James Watson and colleagues (2006) look at variations in how customers in different Asian societies respond to McDonald's, and make it clear that there is nothing uniform in the diffusion of McDonald's in Asia. Like everything else, McDonaldization is a source of differentiation, the globalization of differentiation.

Large Retailers and their Impact on the Global Economy

The retail revolution today engulfs the world economy. Despite the obviousness of this transformation, and despite the fact that consumers experience its effects every day, there has been very little research and very little writing that explore the dimensions and effects of global retailing. To be sure, Wal-Mart has been in the news and under the pen of many writers, often bitterly criticized for its employment practices and for its ability to drive out local retailers from the communities in which it builds new stores, and occasionally praised as a champion of efficiency and consumer well-being (Bianco 2006; Fishman 2006; Lichtenstein 2006, 2009). While somewhat overshadowed by this focus on Wal-Mart, other large US retailers—such as the rapidly growing Costco, Target, Home Depot, Lowe's, Walgreen's, and Best Buy; e-commerce leaders such as Amazon, eBay and Dell; even those less stellar performers such as Sears and Kmart, and Federated and May Department Stores;[5] and supermarket chains such as Kroger, Albertsons, and Safeway—have also contributed to the recent wave of interest in retailing and retailers. In Europe, the spotlight has been on European retail giants, such as Carrefour, Tesco, Metro, Schwarz, and Aldi and their efforts to integrate the EU retail market, expand internationally, and meet the competitive challenge posed by the ultimately unsuccessful entrance of Wal-Mart into Germany and its successful move into Great Britain.

This reportage, however, addresses only a small piece of what is a much larger and much more complex phenomenon, a veritable transformation of global markets for consumer goods, and of the global economy as a whole.

Market making

The chapters in this book analyze the scope and effects of the world's largest retailers in terms of their market-making activities. By the term "market making" we mean something that is often overlooked in economic analysis but is very important for the analysis of economic development and globalization: large retailers "make" the markets for those products that they sell. Often in fierce competition with each other, retailers assiduously calculate how to generate, channel, and capture consumers' demand. They locate store sites and establish websites, select the mix of goods and services, set prices and plan promotions, advertise and manage manufacturers' and their own brands, process and facilitate thousands of consumer transactions. In doing this, retailers create and expand consumer goods markets, and shape consumers' preferences and behavior.

Large retailers do not only make consumer markets; they also make "supplier markets." Capturing sizable shares of the actual consumer markets for products, large retailers gain commanding positions to structure and organize suppliers for the products they sell. Conventional thinking describes retailers as middlemen, the passive conduit between manufacturers and consumers. The retail revolution, however, has made retailers proactive agents in designing products, organizing suppliers, and even shaping consumers' behavior. As brand-name merchandiser Apple Computers did for the iPod, retailers often create whole new markets—on both the consumer and the supplier side. Understanding this fact allows one to track the changing role that manufacturers have had in the emerging system of global markets. For most consumer goods, the manufacturer has become a contingent supplier of the goods it makes, one of many firms that could manufacture comparable goods. The markets in final goods, in turn, structure the markets for intermediate and primary goods.

By being able to establish markets for the final goods they sell directly to consumers, large retailers also shape global markets for many other goods and services as well. Their decisions on which manufacturers to select, where those manufacturers are to be located, what exact products the manufacturers should make, under what conditions the manufacturers will make and package and deliver these products, and what price retailers will pay the manufacturers for all these goods and services are amongst the most significant factors that shape the contemporary global economy. The concentration of global manufacturing in East Asia, the rise of huge contract manufacturers, the development of global logistics—these are but a few of the cascading effects of the retail revolution that we will explore in this book.

Size and concentration

The largest global retailers are very large indeed. From 2002 on, Wal-Mart has often topped the list of the world's largest companies (measured by revenue size), edging out the oil giants Exxon Mobil and Shell Oil. Nine other retailers (Carrefour, Home Depot, Metro, Ahold, Schwarz, Tesco, Kroger, Costco, and Target), although smaller than Wal-Mart, have also found their way into the top one hundred largest global companies over the last five years of the decade, and are consistently ranked amongst the largest firms in their home countries. These firms are also amongst the largest private employers in their home countries, with Wal-Mart being the largest in the world.

The global spread and huge size of modern retailers are new things. Until the 1980s, retail sectors in most countries were highly fragmented; most retail

Table 0.1. Retail concentration in grocery trade, select economies, 2005 (%)

Country	% share of top five retail firms	Country	% share of top five retail firms
Finland	90	Netherlands	62
Australia	83	United Kingdom	59
Ireland	80	Italy	35
Germany	70	United States	34
France	70	Japan	11
Spain	65	China	6

Sources: Planet Retail, Euromonitor, authors' estimates.

stores were small, locally owned shops, and large chain operators were more an exception than the rule. More recently, with the phenomenal growth of Wal-Mart and "category killers" in the USA, and with the consolidation of the European retail market, mostly by German and French retailers, concentration in global retailing has been rapidly increasing. In some smaller European economies, a few major retailers came to dominate large parts of the overall retail sector. Table 0.1 shows the proportion of the grocery trade, traditionally the largest retail sector, controlled by the five largest firms in select developed economies and China.

The absolute size of the US market has so far precluded the levels of concentration reached in smaller economies. In the comparable-sized EU-15 market, the concentration ratio is around 25 percent, while in the Asia-Oceania region, it is no more than 13 percent. However, if the huge and diverse retail sector is further divided into subsections, the concentration ratios are much higher. In the United States, as Table 0.2 shows, some of the major retail sectors, including the "general-merchandise" sector (corresponding to the last two rows of Table 0.2), exhibit very high concentration ratios. In each of these sectors, there are "category killers," such as Home Depot and Lowe's, or CVS and Walgreen's, which dominate the category. Moreover, the share of general merchandisers, such as Wal-Mart and Costco, in the sales of apparel, consumer electronics, and groceries is often higher than that of the major specialty retailers.

This trend of increasing retail concentration is particularly significant in some smaller economies around the world that have recently deregulated their retail markets and opened them to foreign investment. These economies have seen astonishing increases in retail concentration take place during a very short period of time (Reardon et al. 2007; see also Chapter 10 this volume). For instance, the market share of top-ten food retailers in Greece grew from 18.5 percent in 1990 to 72 percent in 1999, and in the Czech Republic, from less than 10 percent in 1993 to over 50 percent in 2005.

Table 0.2. Retail concentration, market share of top firms, United States, 2002

Sector	Four largest firms	Twenty largest firms
Total retail	11	23
Electronic shopping	29	51
Clothing stores	28	52
Grocery stores	31	55
Health and personal care	46	60
Electronics and appliance	44	61
Shoe stores	40	68
Book stores	66	74
Office supplies	78	81
Home improvement centers	91	93
Department stores	72	99
Discount stores, warehouse, supercenters	94	99

Source: US Bureau of the Census (2002).

The impact on retail structures

What is the impact of the rapid increase in size and market share of the largest retailers on the rest of the retail sector? First, there are concerns about the changing competitive structure of the sector, including issues of market power, collusion, anti-competitive practices, and the decline of consumer choice. When measured at a national, let alone the global level, retail concentration is still relatively low compared to the concentration in most manufacturing sectors. However, competition between retailers takes place not within an abstract space of a retail "industry," but in local markets, and it is not unusual for such markets to be dominated by a few large retailers. Oligopolistic competition can be very intense, but it also creates opportunities for price collusion and other forms of anti-competitive behavior. Neverthe-less, there is little evidence of a decline in retail competition in developed economies; if anything, the low profit margins of the largest global retailers, their cost-reduction focus, and their success in entering new markets, all point to intensification rather than a decline of competition. There is even less evidence that the increase in retail concentration has led to higher prices for consumers, although this issue continues to be monitored and investigated by various government agencies.

The second concern regarding the impact of big retailing business refers to the competitive threat that large retailers pose to small ones. This concern goes well beyond the issues of competition and efficiency. Throughout the world, small retailing establishments represent the most numerous form of small business. As shown in Table 0.3, even in the most developed economies, characterized by the domination of large operators and by relatively low

Table 0.3. Number and density of retail establishments, 2001

	Total retail firms (000s)	Total retail establishments (000s)	Retail establishments per 1,000 inhabitants
United States	444.5	694.3	2.5
Canada	57.6	110.3	3.6
Germany	268.5	412.9	5.0
United Kingdom	231.5	308.5	5.2
France	319.5	368.1	6.2
Turkey	514.3	517.8	7.9
Japan	1,215.0	1,222.1	9.6
Brazil	1,154.7	1,660.3	10.0
Mexico	1015.7	1091.0	10.9
India	10,585.5	11,165.0	11.0
Italy	653.1	749.4	13.0
China	16,875.4	20,287.2	15.9
Spain	548.2	685.5	17.4
Greece	167.6	188.1	17.8

Note: These numbers do not include gasoline stations and car dealerships.
Sources: Euromonitor (2002).

density of retail establishments, most retail firms operate only a single store. In the US retail sector, arguably the most advanced in the world, almost 80 percent of retail establishments have fewer than ten employees, accounting for 15 percent of all firms of that size in the economy.

Small retailing businesses often serve as a substitute for social welfare mechanisms, especially in developing countries, with a high proportion of self-employed, underemployed, and part-time workers. In addition, the large number of retail proprietors and entrepreneurs and their embeddedness in local communities give small retailers a measure of social and political importance that often exceeds the lobbying power of the big retailers. Hence, in most developed countries, the government regulation of retail competition typically includes measures that specifically protect small retailers from the competitive threat posed by the large retailers. These measures take the form of price regulations, strict zoning and development laws, limits on operating hours, and so on. Ostensibly, they sacrifice a degree of efficiency that comes with the expansion of the big retailing business in favor of alternative goals such as consumer convenience and equity, preservation of local communities, and environmental protection. However, just as in developing countries where similar measures are defended more directly in terms of the protection of domestic retail sector against foreign corporations, the impact of these regulations on consumers' welfare is at best ambivalent, and often negative, thus favoring the special interests of small retailers over those of the consumer majority.

Large retailers and their suppliers

The impact of large retailers is not limited to the retailing sector. Since the late 1970s, the early phase of what we described above as the retail revolution, an increasing number of industry observers have been noticing the shift in market power from manufacturers to retailers.[6] Large retailers, it is argued, are increasingly able to squeeze their suppliers and induce various forms of concessions. These concessions range from direct price discounts to large buyers, to shelf fees and trade promotions. Several purported causes for this power shift have been identified, including the already noted increase in retail size and concentration, technological advances that allow retailers to use point-of-sale data directly to assess consumer preferences, the decrease in effectiveness of mass media as marketing channels, and the rapid globalization of consumer goods industries. In addition to getting better purchasing terms on branded consumer goods, large retailers have also benefited from being able to procure an increasing amount of competitive private labels (store brands) in most major categories of consumer products. Store brands bring higher margins to retailers and enhance their negotiating power in dealing with the manufacturers of branded goods. At the same time, since the suppliers of store brands are typically smaller than the brand manufacturers and operate in highly competitive markets for undifferentiated products, they also have less negotiating power in the marketing channel.

The shift of marketing-channel power toward retailers has also led to the far-reaching reorganization of the structure of supply chains. As Chapter 7 shows, as retailers and brand-name marketers take more responsibility in organizing and controlling their suppliers, the orientation of supply-chain management shifts from production innovations and distribution efficiency to quick and flexible adjustments in response to the changes in consumer demand. The traditional distinction in marketing literature between push and pull marketing, both conceived as manufacturers' strategies, has gradually given way to a more general conceptualization of marketing channels as driven either by manufacturers' push or by consumers' pull, the latter type being, in fact, governed by the retailer, who has privileged access to the data about consumer demand.[7] In terms of logistics and operational efficiency, retail-driven chains are often seen as more responsive and transparent, better able to control stock levels, and characterized by less adversarial relations between manufacturers and retailers. The concepts such as "just in time," "quick response," and "efficient consumer response" signify this reorientation in supply-chain collaboration and management.

The distinction between retail-driven and manufacturer-driven supply chains has also been used extensively in the global commodity chain, or value-chain, approach, in order to describe different forms of global "production networks." Gereffi (1994b) emphasized the importance of large global buyers, both retailers and brand-name marketers, in the formation and control of global interorganizational networks, particularly in labor-intensive consumer goods industries such as apparel, toys, furniture, and some sectors of consumer electronics. Buyer-driven chains are characterized by decentralized production networks, flexible specialization, and the asymmetry of power between large buyers from developed economies and their smaller suppliers, located mainly in developing countries. Subsequent research in this tradition has highlighted the variety of interorganizational relations in global production networks, and in particular the empirical importance of "modular production networks" (Sturgeon 2002; Gereffi, Humphrey, and Sturgeon 2005; Bair 2009) based on loose contractual relationships and the relative autonomy of large OEMs from their retail customers.

Technological change and productivity

Besides increasing market power and interorganizational control over their smaller competitors and suppliers, the big retailers have also been a major driving force in the adoption and diffusion of technological and managerial change. Since the 1980s, rationalization initiatives and technology adoption pressures—from bar codes and scanning devices, to electronic data interchange, direct store delivery, and quick replenishment, to integrated logistics solutions and vendor-managed inventory—have increasingly flowed from large retailers to their suppliers. Large retailers were not the pioneers of developing and using new technologies, including the information technology that was the most dominant "general purpose technology" of the second half of the twentieth century; the latter's implementation in manufacturing predates the first retailing applications by almost two decades (Cortada 2004). However, once the changes in retailing reached a critical mass, which in the USA occurred in the early 1980s, the sector was not only profoundly transformed; it also induced substantial further changes in the wholesaling, transportation and logistics, and manufacturing industries.[8] While grocery retailers led the way in the early adoption of point-of-sale technology, including scanning devices and bar coding, retailers and brand marketers of apparel were the first to implement just-in-time methods and electronic data interchange, thus driving the diffusion of technological innovation amongst their suppliers (Abernathy et al. 1999; Chapter 2 this volume). By the mid-1980s, both types of technological developments converged in the hands of large general merchandisers, which emerged as the main driving force in the integration and reorganization of retailing and supply chains.

By the 1990s, these new, "lean retailers" had already garnered enough size and momentum for the productivity gains to become apparent at the aggregate level of the retail industry, as well as in wholesaling and logistics. US retailers led the way, a fact highlighted by a series of McKinsey Global Institute studies on sector-level productivity in developed economies. These studies, summarized by Lewis (2004), suggest that one of the main reasons behind the robust productivity growth that the US economy has largely enjoyed since the mid-1990s has been the ability of large US retailers, led by Wal-Mart, to restructure the retail industry as well as a number of related sectors. Retailing and wholesaling sectors contributed about half of the US productivity growth acceleration in the second half of the 1990s; Wal-Mart alone was responsible for 4 percent of this growth, and the competitive pressure it exerted on other retailers, as well as on wholesalers and suppliers, accounted for about twice as much.

Leading European retailers, such as Carrefour, Tesco, and Metro, have similar levels of productivity as Wal-Mart and other large US retailers, and were also amongst the early adopters of new technologies. Yet, hampered by restrictive regulations, European retailers influenced their respective national retail sectors less than did US retailers, and their recent expansion has been due mainly to their aggressive pursuit of internationalization opportunities. As a result, while the productivity growth in information- technology-intensive industries, such as automobiles, industrial machines, computers, and consumer electronics, has been equal or higher in the EU than in the USA, the productivity growth rate of distributive trades remains much lower (Denis, McMorrow, and Röger 2004).

The productivity-enhancing effects of large retailers' drive for efficiency are felt globally, even when those retailers themselves operate in only a handful of countries. Most large retailers source their products globally, and so their productivity gains create spillover effects in their supply chains. Global sourcing predates the globalization of retailing and has already played a major role in the development of export-led, or, to use a more appropriate term introduced by Feenstra and Hamilton (2006), "demand-responsive" economies. The "Asian Miracle," certainly the most striking example of economic success in the twentieth century, was to a large extent induced and supported by the efforts of US retailers to generate, channel, and organize "intermediate demand," thus creating global economic linkages between American consumers and Asian manufacturers. This demand-responsive development did not, of course, stay limited to the export-oriented consumer goods industries, as it triggered a cascading series of changes through sectors producing intermediate inputs, logistics, financial and business services, and so on.

The resulting transformation of the overall economy, including the processes of industrial upgrading and the emergence of the elaborate division of labor between East Asian economies, has also changed the social fabric of Asian societies and the geopolitical situation in the Pacific region. The Asian Miracle also often served as a role model for development policies in other parts of the world, although with much more modest results. As a consequence, a country's degree of economic development became almost synonymous with the ability of its export-oriented industries to produce technologically sophisticated, high value-added goods.

Impact on labor markets

Big retailers are also big employers. Wal-Mart alone employs more workers than the five leading global car-makers, General Motors, Ford, Daimler Chrysler, Toyota, and Volkswagen, combined. Overall, the retail sector accounts for about 13 percent of private-sector employment in the EU and almost 20 percent in the USA. In developing countries, the share of retail employment is typically lower, accounting, for instance, for just over 5 percent in China and around 10 percent in India. In most economies, a major share of the retail workforce is either employed in small retail firms or self-employed. In the EU, the proportion of retail employees working for "micro-enterprises" (fewer than ten employees) ranges from over 70 percent in Italy and Poland, to less than 30 percent in the United Kingdom, Netherlands, and Germany; in the USA, the estimated proportion is around 20 percent.[9] The rise of big retail chains has generally led not only to a decline in the share of small business employment and self-employment, but also to an overall increase in retail employment, both in absolute terms and in relation to the rest of the economy.

Retailers also tend to employ fewer skilled workers and pay lower wages than their counterparts from other industries. This trend is especially visible in the USA, where a high overall level of income is combined with a relatively low minimum wage and the domination of large retailers to create a significant concentration of low-paid workers in the retailing sector. These types of employment generate major concerns about the shift in the overall labor market from higher-wage, typically unionized, full-time manufacturing jobs toward low-wage, low-benefits, part-time retail jobs. These concerns notwithstanding, the ability of large US retailers to create new jobs at a time when the rest of the economy, and in particular the manufacturing sector, had not experienced stagnant or declining labor markets, had been a major factor in keeping the overall unemployment rate at an acceptable level and easing the structural adjustments in the economy. At the same time, the sluggish domestic expansion of major European retailers, induced partly by restrictive regulation, played a role in the maintenance of higher unemployment rates in their domestic economies.

17

As with market power and productivity, the impact of large retailers on labor markets is not limited to the retail sector. While a part of the shift from manufacturing to retail jobs may be attributed to expected, and perhaps unavoidable, structural adjustments in a developed service economy, US retailers are also playing a causal role in the decline of domestic manufacturing employment by their relentless pursuit of cost reduction and their global sourcing strategies. The outsourcing of manufacturing, and, increasingly, of service-sector jobs, has played a prominent part in recent public debates about competitiveness and the long-term prospects of the American economy. It is evident that large retailers are amongst the drivers of this process, as their relations with their suppliers provide a major mechanism through which the forces of global competition induce structural changes in local economies.

Impact on consumers

As we mentioned above, the effect of large retailers on consumers and their shopping and consumption patterns is quite obvious and quite pervasive; yet it has attracted somewhat less attention than the other effects discussed so far. The fact that large modern retailers bring lower prices to the consumer is well established and separable from the concerns about anti-competitive practices and local price discrimination. The role of large retailers in standardizing retail formats, product assortments, and shopping experience is less well documented, partly because these effects are more difficult to measure. The global diffusion of modern retailing formats is perhaps the most observable of these effects. Supermarkets, convenience stores, and fast-food restaurants have been successful in many different socio-cultural contexts and at various levels of economic development. Large "combination stores" selling general merchandise and groceries under the same roof, shopping malls, and big-box specialty stores ("category killers") are less universally adopted, but the main reason for their slower diffusion seems to be restrictive regulation rather than the lack of consumer acceptance.

The standardization and global diffusion of retail formats go hand in hand with the standardization of products and product assortments. Even when most products are sourced locally, as is generally the case in food retailing, large global retailers are able to benefit from the procurement of global brands and from the standardization of the merchandise mix. Outside the realm of cars, consumer electronics, and a few luxury items, there are few brands that are truly global, and this facilitates the attempts of large retailers to promote globally their own store brands, and, even more importantly, to turn themselves into globally recognized brands.

All of this does not just standardize the ways of meeting the demand for consumer goods, but also helps define and change this demand. It is somewhat ironic that, because of the efforts of a whole generation of historians, we know more about the role of the early modern retailers, above all department stores, in creating various forms of mass consumption in Europe and the USA of the eighteenth and nineteenth centuries than about how contemporary mass retailers shape consumer behavior around the world. Early modern retailers, mass marketers, and advertisers redefined the context and meaning of shopping, and educated the consumer about new goods and new techniques of consumption. This process continues unabated today, and on a much broader scale. The transformation of developing nations such as China and India into consumer societies must be considered one of the most profound and far-reaching social processes that will define the twenty-first century, just as the emergence of the first mass consumer society in the USA in the early 1900s, and the adoption of its main features by West European countries after the Second World War, defined the dynamics of the twentieth century.

At the same time, the talk about "consumer power," one of the buzzwords of the current marketing research, only obscures the fact that contemporary retailers play the same role as their predecessors, creating markets and shaping consumer behavior and attitudes; indeed, the current era of "consumer-driven marketing" is hardly an exception in the long history of mass marketing of consumer goods. Retailers, as well as the producers of consumer goods, have always expended a major share of their marketing efforts on figuring out consumers' preferences, and have also always tried actively to shape these preferences. New information technologies have certainly enhanced their ability to perform the former task and shifted the competitive advantage to those firms who can access and analyze vast streams of point-of-sales (POS) data. Still, technological advances do not make the efforts to shape consumer preferences and behavior less important, let alone obsolete. If anything, the ability quickly and efficiently to gather information about consumer demand for particular products has enabled all major players in consumer goods markets to intensify the efforts to shape this demand by managing product life cycles, consumption complementarities, sales promotions, and other marketing strategies in more sophisticated and elaborate ways. Similarly, while the argument can be made that new contexts of shopping, such as Internet-based retailing, allow consumers to gather product and price information, compare retailers, and avoid impulse buying to a much higher degree than ever before, it can also be argued that these opportunities are created within an overall context of markets and product worlds of increased complexity (see, e.g., Rezabakhsh et al. 2006 for a general discussion of the "consumer power" thesis).

Overall impact on economic development

The retail revolution has changed and continues to change the organization of the global economy. That is the conclusion that runs through this book. Our analysis shows that these changes brought on by the retail revolution are both pervasive and decisive. They are pervasive because retailing has changed both developed and developing economies, though in somewhat different ways. As we explain in the following chapters, large retailers are now able, directly and indirectly, to create and maintain both consumer and supplier markets. After the 1960s, as US and European retailers began more intensively to focus their selling efforts in their relatively wealthy consumer home markets, they also began, with equal intensity, to develop supplier markets in some of the least developed areas of the world to provide them with the goods that they would sell to their customers. The simultaneous growth of a global logistic infrastructure allowed these retailers to perfect the strategy of maximizing their leverage in both types of markets at the same time, and in the process to create both competent suppliers at one end and interested consumers at the other.

As competition amongst large retailers increased, this strategy continued to evolve over the remaining decades of the twentieth century and drove a global economic reorganization. Step by step, the locus of manufacturing shifted from the developed to the developing economies at the same time that developed economies began to split between high-end professions and low- and medium-level jobs in service and retailing.[10] Both the well-developed and the rapidly developing economies became increasingly demand responsive; both became integrated into a global economy reorganized around supply chains.

These changes in the global economy have been not only widespread, but also critically important for the rapid economic development that is occurring today in China and India, as well as in other locations around the world. The creation of supplier markets in East and South East Asia from the late 1960s on (namely, in Japan, Taiwan, South Korea, Hong Kong, and Singapore), which in the years after the Second World War were amongst the poorest countries in the world, began a process that led to the industrialization of these countries and to a steady increase in the standard of living for most of their citizens. These people have now become investors and consumers in their own right, and, throughout these countries, global retailers, some locally and some foreign owned, have opened new consumer markets.

As people in these economies became wealthier and as currencies in these countries appreciated, core contract manufacturers in these East Asian economies moved all or part of their production offshore. Within a decade or so, many of these contract manufacturers had moved portions of their business to China, where they became the leading investors in China's export-oriented manufacturing and were instrumental in driving China toward industrialization. The decade after China's membership in the World Trade Organization was a period when exports grew at an unprecedented rate of nearly 25 percent per year, and during this period over 50 percent of China's exports flowed out of factories wholly or partially owned by non-Chinese nationals (Blonigen and Ma 2010; Feenstra and Wei 2010). Most of these exports are from contract manufacturers.

China is now the world's second largest economy, still well behind the USA, but moving ahead of Japan. The expansion of export-oriented contract manufacturing in China is the primary reason China has grown so rapidly. In fact, as Blonigen and Ma (2010) show, exports from foreign-invested firms have increased rather than decreased since 2000, which is a clear indication that contract manufacturing is driving China's export expansion, and the growth in global retailing is driving the growth in contract manufacturing.

We show in this book that the reason global retailing has grown so rapidly since the late 1980s is because large retailers have dramatically increased their international business. Large retailers are opening stores around the world, especially in developing markets. New consumer markets are being tested, new suppliers and new supply lines are being created, and new product worlds are being established where they did not exist before. The global recession that started in 2007 caused an abrupt drop in exports from China, but this decline quickly turned around. As always occurs during post-Second World War recessions, consumers buy what they need at the cheapest possible prices. Discount retailers do well in recessions compared to their upmarket competitors, and in this recession retailers such as Wal-Mart and Costco in the USA and Carrefour and Aldi in Europe continued to thrive. For example, Wal-Mart's international division alone accounted for over $90 billion in sales in 2008, a more than 50 percent increase in two years.

In the post-Second World War era, global trade imbalances appear, on the surface, to be imbalances in production, on the one side, and consumption, on the other side. In the early twenty-first century, the global trade imbalance is seen in terms of too much production in China, and too much consumption in the USA. Seeing this imbalance as a problem of market equilibrium, economists argue that at some point trade needs to equal out. But, if we examine the underlying mechanism that is driving international trade, there is no reason to believe that a tendency toward equilibrium is a characteristic of international trade today, let alone that it will be "restored" at some point in the future. Retailers and merchandisers, not central banks, manage supply chains, and in so doing help to determine the balance of trade between nations. Macroeconomic levers, such as interest rates and the relative value of currency, may influence where contract manufacturers locate their factories and where retailers source their goods. Social insurance and welfare policies may affect how much consumers spend and on what types of goods. But it is always the role of market makers to create and organize markets, on both the consumer's and the supplier's side, and thus they play the decisive role in organizing the global economy. Insofar as the most important of these market makers today are to be found amongst the ranks of large retailers and merchandisers, they are the key to understanding and perhaps also to resolving the problems of imbalances in the global economy. Whether their actions will lead to the decrease in trade imbalances, by, say, developing and expanding domestic demand in China and other major developing economies, or will continue to exacerbate the trends of the last couple of decades, remains to be seen. What is certain is the fact that retailers will have a large and growing impact on global development for a long time to come.

Overview of the Book

The four parts of this book survey the dimensions and effects of the rise of global retailing. The two chapters in Part One provide the theoretical and historical background to understand the ongoing global retail revolution. In Chapter 1, Petrovic and Hamilton outline the market-making perspective. They argue that conventional economic analysis routinely misses the importance of markets as marketplaces, as institutionalized locations where transactions occur, and of market making as an organized process of intermediation, a process linking sellers of goods and services with buyers of the same. Without markets and without firms whose specialty is creating and maintaining marketplaces, the core feature of all capitalist economies—namely, the exchange of goods and services—would seem difficult, if not impossible, to analyze, and yet modern economic analysis pays scant attention to such phenomena and so pays little attention to retailing as an important economic activity. This chapter corrects this deficiency by providing the conceptual dimensions of the market-making perceptive.

In Chapter 2, Abernathy and Volpe demonstrate the impact of technological innovations, both as they enable retailing, such as the effect of containerized shipping on global sourcing, and as transforming factors, such as the impact of information technology in the development of lean retailing techniques. These technological innovations have had profound effects on many dimensions of retailing, including merchandising (that is, product mix and variety), retail formats, services offered (including payment), and supply-chain management and sourcing strategies. Most of these major technological innovations have generally occurred in other sectors of the economy, but retailers have been able to utilize them for their own advantage, either directly or indirectly, in selling products. Some examples include the development of the railroads and improved ocean transportation, which allowed retailers efficiently to expand the geography of their supply base. The shopping-mall and big-box retailers were dependent on the automobile and the interstate highway system, to bring them both their customers and their products. Innovations such as bar codes and checkout scanning, plus payment by credit or debit cards, would be impossible without the revolutionary changes in computer hardware and software.

The three chapters in Part Two examine the development and institutionalization of consumer markets. In Chapter 3, Petrovic addresses American retail formats and their global diffusion. All major formats that characterize contemporary retailing, from supermarkets, shopping malls and big-box stores to gas stations, convenience stores, and fast-food restaurants, originated in the USA and then spread around the world. The first part of the chapter deals with the origins and evolution of these formats within the US context. After discussing the evolution and the limits of the department store, the only major retail format that was developed simultaneously on both sides of the Atlantic, the chapter delves into the interwar period and the two major "retail revolutions" that shaped modern retailing throughout the twentieth century: the proliferation of chain stores and the introduction of a large self-service store, the supermarket. Petrovic emphasizes the continuities between major retail formats—the supermarket as the department store for food, the discount store as the hard-goods supermarket, the mall as the planned suburban mix of the department store and specialty store—and their convergence toward the modern big-box chain-store format.

The second section of Chapter 3 deals with the spread of American retail formats, first to Western Europe, then to Japan, and then, from the 1970s, throughout the world. The Americanization of global retail, somewhat ironically, has rarely been carried out, at least until very recently, by American retailers. Instead, it was mostly the local retailers who adopted and adapted American methods to their local economies and regulatory environments. During the first, limited phase of internationalization, the most successful of such operators from Western Europe introduced modern retail formats throughout Western Europe, but also to Latin America, Eastern Europe, and Asia. The newest phase of retail globalization, from 1990 on, is characterized by widespread and systemic adoption of modern retail formats in developing economies as well as by accelerated internationalization of major retail players. Still, as is repeatedly emphasized in the chapter, even the largest global retailers have achieved only a limited presence outside their home region, and thus we can expect the process of retail globalization only to increase in scope and importance in the coming decades.

In Chapter 4, Wortmann examines European retailing and its global expansion. Within the European Union, retail markets are still highly fragmented in many respects. The national retail systems in Europe are significantly different from one another, not only because of differences in consumer preferences, but also because of variations in regulations affecting retailing. The most rapid transformation in retailing in the opening decade of the twenty-first century has occurred in Eastern Europe, in many cases with West European retailers playing a leading role. Many of the changes in Europe mirror those in the USA, with the development of self-service, larger store-size formats, horizontal expansion, and retailer-led efficiency gains in the supply chain. However, in no European country are these changes as advanced as in the USA. The higher level of regulation not only hampers these changes, but modifies them, leading to new innovations and dynamics in some cases.

Wortmann focuses on retailing in four major countries. In France and Great Britain retailing regulation has been relatively weak, so many of the trends have materialized to a much greater extent than in Italy, which has very rigid regulations. Germany is somewhere in between, attempting to limit store size, but not merchandising practices, which has led to the growth of small-store hard discounters, such as Aldi. In part because of the limited opportunities to expand domestically, some of the major European retailers have been leaders in the global expansion of retailing. The chapter includes case studies of some of the major European retail innovators, such as Carrefour, Aldi, Metro, and Tesco, as well as a general overview of the internationalization efforts of European retailers.

The effects of the more recent technological changes, the development of the Internet and of overnight delivery services, are described by Kotha and Basu in Chapter 5. The Internet and online retailing have given rise to new retailing formats for selling traditional products, such as in the case of books and Amazon.com. In addition, these new technologies have generated new forms of market making. Perhaps the best and most successful example is eBay.com, which brings together millions of buyers and sellers in a cyber marketplace. Online shopping has also impacted incumbent retailers, whether they see the Internet as just another marketing channel or a new approach to retailing. Some existing retailers, such as Wal-Mart, are trying largely to use an online presence to leverage their physical assets, but that could change in the future. Online retailers are still in the process of discovering what works and what does not. Broadband connectivity has given a major boost to online retailing. The next stage, just beginning to emerge, may be global online retailing. Finally, the easy availability of information on the Internet, especially with the development of sophisticated search engines, such as Google, has helped create more knowledgeable consumers. Even if they do not buy online, by using the Internet, many consumers are now much better informed than in the past. When potential customers who have searched on the Internet come into automobile dealerships, they may literally know as much about the car models and pricing as the salesperson.

The four chapters in Part Three examine the continuing development of global supplier markets and the formation of global retail supply chains led by large retailers and brand-name merchandisers. In the first chapter in the part, Chapter 6, "Supplier Markets and the Asian Miracle: The Rise of Demand-Responsive Economies," Hamilton and Kao demonstrate that the industrialization of East Asia that started in the late 1960s and that is known as the "Asian Miracle" is most accurately seen as the widespread development of supplier markets for mostly American brand-name merchandisers and retailers. Asia's export-driven industrialization quickly led to the development of "demand-responsive economies." Using Taiwan as an example, the authors show, step by step and industry by industry, how, through the actions of big buyers, Asian economies in the 1970s and 1980s became organized backwards from the development of consumer markets in the USA to the creation of supplier markets for consumer goods in East Asia. Using extensive interview data from Taiwanese business people, the authors present a number of case studies showing the process of economic integration (and disintegration) around the development of supplier markets. Such supply-chain-driven economies are the essence of the demand-responsive economies that emerged in East Asia in the second half of the twentieth century and that are characteristic of economies around the world today.

In Chapter 7, "Global Logistics, Global Labor," Bonacich and Hamilton explain the crucial role played by logistics providers in creating the supply chains of global retailers. Goods produced in Asia and elsewhere via global sourcing must be moved to the United States in a timely manner. To meet this need, a complex logistics system has developed, which includes everything from infrastructure to logistics management. Some retailers have large internal logistics management departments. Others rely on third-party companies that specialize in logistics. Global sourcing has been dependent on the simultaneous development of crucial supporting actors, including ocean shipping, railroads, the trucking industry, air freight companies, and warehousing operations. A key factor has been the evolution of inter-modal transportation systems that can move containerized shipments quickly from Asia and elsewhere to points throughout the USA and Europe.

The development of a global logistics infrastructure has made retailers' management of their supply chains a global reality. Because of their tremendous volume, and concomitant power, large retailers have played a major role in shaping the development of global economies, including, most importantly, China, which has become the world's leading exporter of consumer goods. Through their management of supply chains, retailers are able to put tremendous pressure on their suppliers to achieve flexible production and cost controls. This pressure translates in company-level policies that directly influence wages and working conditions for employees in manufacturing and logistical service alike.

In Chapter 8, "Making the Global Supply Base," Sturgeon, Humphrey, and Gereffi analyze the co-evolutionary character of market making, in which the initial trials with global sourcing in the 1970s and 1980s by a few retailers helped spur the development of an increasingly competent group of contract manufacturers mainly located in East Asia. These contractors acquired the capabilities necessary to produce products to the specifications of leading firms in the West. Some of the early deals were made directly with Asian manufacturers, whereas others relied on Asian intermediaries (for example, trading firms) to organize and coordinate production in Asia. These early moves provided both an example and a ready-made supply base for other retailers and branded marketers, not yet engaged in global sourcing.

The increasing competence of these contract manufacturers also dovetailed with a trend toward outsourcing by manufacturing firms in the USA, including leading companies in technology-intensive sectors such as electronics, accelerating the creation of a global supply base of contract manufacturers. In the 1990s, as retailers and brand-name merchandisers passed more responsibility on to contract manufacturers for process development, material sourcing, and even some aspects of product design, the global supply base began to be populated by large, "full-package" contractors with a full range of capabilities. Today, the depth and breadth of the global manufacturing supply base, along with new Internet-based tools for buyer–supplier matchmaking and operational coordination, may be opening a new stage in the development of global sourcing.

In Chapter 9, "Transnational Contractors in East Asia," Appelbaum examines a subset of these contract manufacturers in much greater detail. The trends just discussed in Chapter 8 have given rise to a few giant transnational contractors, based primarily in Hong Kong, Taiwan, South Korea, and China, that operate factories throughout the world. The emergence of these giant transnational contractors portends a dramatic shift in the organizational power within global supply chains, which may provide a counterweight to the growing power of large retailers. Global supply networks have typically been buyer driven, with large retailers and branded manufacturers playing the central role in their creation and coordination. Most of the contractors have been small, reinforcing their vulnerability to big buyers. However, this situation is changing with the emergence of large contract manufacturers. This chapter examines several examples of these giant contract manufacturers. The Taiwanese multinational Nien Hsing Textiles is the world's largest manufacturer of denim fabrics and denim garments. With a customer base that includes most of the major designer brands, Nien Hsing Textiles has factories in

Taiwan, Mexico, Nicaragua, and Lesotho. Yue Yuen/Pou Chen, based in Hong Kong and Taiwan, with a global workforce of 242,000 employees, is the world's largest maker of branded athletic and casual footwear. Its dominance shapes the relative bargaining power it has with such major brand-name merchandisers as Nike and Reebok. Increasingly, large contractors, and not the retailers, manage the supply chain. Their emergence, along with the pressure of lean retailing for cost cutting and quick response, is also compelling retailers to shift critical functions such as inventory management to these giant contract suppliers. China's rise as an industrial power may further change global supply-chain dynamics, with synergies arising from its supplier clusters, investment in the next generation of technologies, and the rapid growth of its domestic retail chains.

The two chapters in Part Four detail the multiple linkages between retailing and manufacturing for two very different industries. In Chapter 9, "The Global Spread of Modern Food Retailing," Senauer and Reardon examine the global transformation in the food industries and grocery retailing. Historically, some of the original global market makers were merchants trading agricultural commodities, and such companies remained dominant until the mid-twentieth century. In the period after the Second World War, major food manufacturers, such as Coca Cola, Kellogg, and Nestle, became leaders in the creation of multinational consumer markets for their products. In the last quarter of the twentieth century, food retailers, including food service operators, began to play a major role in creating global consumer and supplier markets. The fast-food companies, a uniquely American format, led the global market making. McDonald's, which in 2010 operates in some 120 countries, excels at the creation of consumer markets for its format, offering a mix of products and service, which in many of the countries it has entered literally did not exist previously. At the same time, it has created a supplier base in many of these countries.

Consumers have now become accustomed to having fresh fruits and vegetables year around and exotic food products from abroad, thanks to global sourcing. A small number of European companies, including Carrefour, Ahold, and Metro, along with Wal-Mart, are dominating the international expansion of food retailers. The spread of supermarkets in developing countries, typically regional chains, but also major global retailers, is having a profound impact on their agricultural systems. It is reshaping the supply chain for locally sourced products, all the way back to the farm level. Supermarket chains want to deal with a small number of reliable suppliers, not hundreds of small peasant farmers. A contractual arrangement is frequently established with a few "preferred suppliers" who can meet their standards.

In Chapter 10, "Market Making in the Personal-Computer Industry," Kraemer and Dedrick analyze a similar transformation in the personal-computer (PC) industry. In the traditional structure of the PC industry, PCs were marketed through a variety of channels from direct sales forces, to corporate resellers and electronic superstores. The connection between the PC manufacturer and the final consumer was weak (via advertising) or non-existent. In the mid-1990s, a major shift began in the US market toward direct sales of PCs, led by Dell Computer, which allowed PC-makers better to match demand and supply. Dell Computers pioneered a new type of PC-maker, which was basically an assembler of parts made by contract manufacturers and assembled according to the consumers' specifications. This approach cut out the distributor and retailer, putting the PC-maker/brand-name merchandiser in the role of market maker. Direct sales accounted for over half of all PC sales by 2005, dominating the corporate market and augmented by the consumer acceptance of e-commerce. The direct sales model has made smaller inroads outside the USA.

By 2007 there were three major retail models in the US PC consumer market. The first is the traditional indirect model and the second is the PC-maker as retailer. The third, which might be called the retailer as PC-maker, includes the private-label brands sold by some retailers, such as Wal-Mart and CompUSA, and local "white-box" makers that sell primarily to small businesses. In terms of impacts on suppliers, PC-makers have adopted just-in-time practices and moved to vendor-owned inventory to reduce costs. As PC firms have focused on retailing and marketing, they have outsourced even new product development to a contingent of original design manufactures, mostly in Asia.

Part One

The Market Makers:
A General Perspective

1

Retailers as Market Makers

Misha Petrovic and Gary G. Hamilton

Introduction

When we think of capitalist economies, we think of organizations, or of markets, but rarely of both together. On the one hand, modern capitalism seems to be all about large organizations—big corporations and powerful states—and the impact of their decisions on our lives. On the other hand, modern capitalism is also seen as consisting of markets, self-organizing entities that emerge spontaneously, without anyone's command or authority, from the actions of many independent actors. The major actors of the capitalist economy may be, and typically are, powerful and highly organized; yet the basic economic structure within which they act is understood, both descriptively and normatively, as spontaneous and self-organizing.

The opposition between markets and organizations shows up in many economic theories. For example, when theorists conceptualize communist and capitalist economies in the abstract, they cast them as polar opposites. The former is described as a command economy, in which the state makes decisions about the allocations of goods and services, and markets play no role; the latter, as consisting entirely of self-organizing markets with no imposed organization, as a "market economy" where all buyers and all sellers decide, by means of prices, which and at what cost goods and services will be available. Similarly, transaction-cost theorists (e.g., Coase 1937; Williamson 1975) divide the geography of capitalist economies into "markets" and "hierarchies," a division that led one economist (Bowles 1986: 352) to characterize the transaction-cost theorists' view of "the capitalist economy as a multiplicity of mini-command economies operating in a sea of market exchanges."

The perceived absence or presence of imposed organization in markets is, of course, an artifact of the theories used to understand economies. These theories require that "organization" and "market" be set in opposition to each other, with the market derived from Adam Smith's conception of the "invisible hand," and with organization cast as the "visible hand" (A. D. Chandler 1977) by which the wills of owners and managers are exercised.

In these and many other examples, the term "market organization" is an oxymoron, a situation where more of one leads to less of the other. The subject matter of industrial organization, a subfield in economics, is a good example of how these two words do not get along. The primary topics of interest in this subfield are actions of organizations, states, and firms that impede or otherwise corrupt the "normal" operations of self-organizing markets. The result is the economics of "imperfect competition" whereby strategic organizational action leads to "market failure." Organizations' attempts to act on, rather than strictly within, self-organizing, competitive markets naturally lead to problems, inefficiencies, and suboptimal outcomes.

The market-making perspective introduced in this volume seeks to eliminate this artificial opposition between organization and market, by bringing in the ideas of market making and market makers. In this perspective, markets are not simple, spontaneously occurring, self-organizing structures. Rather, they are made, maintained, and reproduced by economic actors, typically large firms, that act as market makers. The results of their actions are the markets of the modern economy—institutionally complex, consciously generated structures that enable and facilitate large numbers of transactions between large numbers of diverse trading partners.

Our perspective thus shifts from abstract, purely conceptual markets of standard economic theory, depicted by hypothetical supply-and-demand curves, to retail stores, stock exchanges, trading companies, showroom floors, all places where transactions occur, and to the institutional arrangements that facilitate those transactions. It also shifts from looking at organizations as either irrelevant for or detrimental to the functioning of the market, to understanding their crucial role in making market transactions possible.

Economic theorists, of one type or another, have been little interested in market making and market makers. This disinterest is a result of two deeply ingrained habits of thought in economic analysis. The first one, the *equilibrium bias*, we have already hinted at above. It treats markets as simple, spontaneously emerging mechanisms of exchange and thus does not allow for the ideas that markets could be institutionally complex and need to be consciously created and maintained. In fact, markets are treated as non-institutions, as paradigmatic examples of the celebrated "invisible hand" that operates automatically and should be protected from being tampered with. In such a perspective, market making can refer to little more than guaranteeing the rules of the game, by the exchange parties themselves or by an external legal–political authority, and perhaps regulating certain irrational behaviors of economic actors.

The equilibrium bias has often been identified and criticized for its theoretical shortcomings and policy implications. The other type of bias, although as commonly espoused in economic analysis and no less detrimental to the understanding of markets, is less well recognized.[1] We refer to it as the "productionist" bias, since it is based on the belief that markets are a somewhat epiphenomenal aspect of the economy when compared to the fundamental economic reality of production. The productionist bias does not deny the possibility of market making in general, but rather deprives it of economic significance. The main activity of firms, it contends, is to produce valuable goods and services. The way those are procured in the market, and the activities involved in such a procurement, are peripheral and incidental to what the "real" economy is about.

The two types of bias may seem barely related, or even opposed to each other. However, in the history of economic analysis they have often gone hand in hand, partly because they have both chosen to ignore the institutional aspects of markets and market making. Ever since Adam Smith wrote about the pin factory and about the natural laws of supply and demand in *The Wealth of Nations* (1977 [1776]), most economists have assumed that firms are about the organization of production and that markets, for better or worse, are self-organizing. The coexistence of the two biases was predicated on the division of labor that produced a mutual lack of interest in each other's models. A theorist enthralled by the idea of spontaneous, automatic competitive markets will in principle have little interest in the specifics of organizational activity, yet would still be likely to see production as the core concern of the firm and market making as at best an imperfection and at worst an attempt to tamper with the invisible hand of the market.[2] Similarly, a theorist who sees the economy as a system of production will have little interest in exploring the details of the "distribution realm" and will probably accept that in complex modern economies markets are effective, if not necessarily perfect, mechanisms for the distribution of goods and services.[3]

Even when the two biases were at odds with each other, this only strengthened their prejudice against market making. For instance, a relatively strong belief by some productionist theorists that the market system is an inefficient mechanism of distribution, to be supplanted by some version of a "planned" economy, zeroes in on market-making activities such as pricing and advertising as the best example of everything that is wrong with markets. On the equilibrium side, transaction-cost theorists reject the view of the firm as a production function, preferring to represent it instead as an alternative and complement to the market system; yet this market-and-hierarchy approach never broaches the issue of firms as market makers.

Both types of bias, thus, render market making irrelevant if not outright harmful: a market imperfection or market tampering in equilibrium theories;

an appendage to or wastage of production in productionist ones. We will discuss these biases throughout this chapter as an alternative to the market-making viewpoint.[4]

Mass Production and Mass Selling:
The Origins of the Productionist Bias

It is an open question which of the two aspects of the creation of the modern economy is more important: mass production or mass selling.[5] One thing is certain, however; each depends on the existence of the other, and for this reason, they both developed concurrently. However, a lot more has been written about mass production than about mass selling. In the initial burst of industrialization in the nineteenth century, the factory system was so new and so instrumental in changing the organization of work that mass production got the lion's share of the attention. When Karl Marx joined Friedrich Engels to write *The Communist Manifesto* (1849), the smoke stacks of England's factories were what seemed to be the most important part of capitalism, and so they wrote about the emergence of new forms of production and labor, which resulted, they believed, in vastly cheaper prices of goods that people everywhere, if they had those products in front of them, would obviously want to buy. But Marx and Engels did not discuss the selling part of the equation; that was assumed to be unproblematic. Later, when Marx wrote his tome *Das Kapital* (1867), he did not talk about selling there either. In the "Preface" to the first German edition, Marx said he studied the factory system in England because that is where the "iron laws" of capitalism were being worked out, but he did not go to Latin America or India or South East Asia to see how English textiles were being peddled aggressively by British, Indian, and Chinese merchants. Obviously, for Marx the laws of capitalism were laws about the organization of mass production and not of mass selling.

Marx and Engels were not the only ones to concentrate on making rather than selling goods, for most other writers have done the same. Factory production, however, was only half of the matter. With new forms of production in the nineteenth century came the necessity to remake existing markets and to find new markets, both of which in turn fostered more production. But which came first, markets or factories? This is a chicken-and-egg question. It is clear, however, that British colonialism was in full bloom before the textile factories in England's heartland reinvented themselves through mechanization and expanded their production to meet the merchants' demand for more and more goods. And for many years, well into the nineteenth century, the markets for English textiles and other English products expanded. From the very beginning, the markets for selling those products were vastly more developed and more complexly organized than the factories making them,[6] but, in the eyes of nineteenth-century observers, the more tangible factory production seemed far more amazing and more revolutionary in every way than selling goods.

The productionist view of the economy became even more dominant by the end of the nineteenth century.[7] In the second half of the nineteenth century, large industrial enterprises emerged in nearly every sector of production and played a central role in the expansion of national economies. These enterprises were at the forefront of capital formation and productivity growth. They were the leaders in the utilization of science and technology, and the electrical and internal-combustion machines that these firms invented, used, and sold captured people's imagination. These machines, marveled worldly wise Henry Adams (1973 [1918]) in the opening years of the twentieth century, were "dynamos," "symbols of infinity," signs of a limitless future.

To be sure, the techniques employed in mass selling even if less dramatic were no less elaborate. Most of the selling that occurred in the early years of European and American capitalism made use of organizational forms that preceded the development of large mechanized factories. English and Scottish trading companies and merchant houses (Chapman 1992; Jones 2000), ethnic merchant groups (such as those organized by Chinese (Hao 1986; Suehiro 1989) and Indians (Markovits 2000, 2008), who followed British colonialism around the world), and various types of specialized wholesalers organized much of the selling to general stores and specialty shops, which in turn sold to final consumers.

In the second half of the nineteenth century, a major new market format, the department store, emerged in the European and American urban centers, attracting enormous crowds and capturing the imagination of that generation of urban dwellers, many of them recent migrants from the countryside (see Petrovic, Chapter 3 this volume). For those who could not access department stores on a regular basis, mail-order businesses, some operated by department stores, and some, especially in the United States, as independent operations, brought the new world of modern, mass-produced consumer goods straight to the home through their detailed, lavishly illustrated catalogs. By the early twentieth century, department stores such as Bon Marché, Macy's, and Harrods, and mail-order catalogs such as those for Sears and Montgomery Ward's, rivaled in size and organizational complexity the biggest manufacturing operations of the time, and were certainly more visible to the masses of urban residents. The pervasive productionist bias, however, made most economic observers of the time downplay the innovativeness and importance of these mass retailers. The selling activities of mass manufacturers, and their innovations in advertising, marketing, pricing, franchising, and so on, also received little attention.

While we cannot survey in detail the entire history of market organization in this volume, the important point is that the markets for buying and selling goods and services have always been organized in some way by innovative, entrepreneurial, and most often large-size market makers. The growth and changes in these markets are essential aspects of the development of global capitalism as we know it today, but they are rarely analyzed in this context. The market-making perspective is a way to pay close attention to the changing organization of mass buying and selling and the actors that effect such a change. This perspective targets the institutional contexts in which transactions take place and the strategies the chief players in those markets use to attempt to structure the opportunities for buying and selling. The institutions, strategies, and players themselves all co-evolve, and it is this co-evolving mix that is the primary subject matter of the market-making perspective. The perspective, therefore, complements, but also expands beyond, the preoccupation with analyzing the organization of industrial enterprises. The evolution of mass production has been described in detail by a generation of business historians, following A. D. Chandler's pioneering work on *The Visible Hand* (1977).[8] However, without understanding the organization of mass selling, this preoccupation with mass production is the sound of one hand clapping.

The Idea of Market Making

Market making is a concept rarely used in general economic analysis. It is, however, a specialized term used to analyze the role of traders (a brokerage firm, a bank) in organized financial markets (O'Hara 1995; Abolafia 1996). The trader, the so-called "market maker," is the intermediary between those who want to sell and those who want to buy specific stocks or commodities. The trader provides the necessary connections and liquidity to "make the market." As their assigned duty, market makers maintain both sides of the market and prevent the market from stalling because of insufficient supply or demand at any given moment. Without this institutionalized role in such an institutionalized setting as the stock market, large numbers of transactions would be difficult, if not impossible, to arrange. Market makers, intermediaries in an institutionalized setting, make these exchanges possible.

Daniel Spulber (1996, 1998) extended the use of this idea of intermediaries and market making to formulate a more general theory of economic activity. Using transaction-cost theory, Spulber sees market making as a process of intermediation that is ubiquitous in the larger economy. In all kinds of settings, market makers reduce the cost of exchange between potential buyers and sellers by creating market structures: "Intermediaries seek out suppliers, find and encourage buyers, select buy and sell prices, define the terms of transactions, manage the payments and record keeping for transactions and hold inventories to provide liquidity or availability of goods and services" (Spulber 1996: 135).

According to Spulber, intermediation encompasses most activities in retailing, wholesaling, and financial sectors, as well as a substantial proportion of those in business service and manufacturing sectors. He calculates that intermediation accounts for somewhere between one-quarter and one-third of the US gross domestic product.[9]

Clower and Howitt (1996: 24), approaching the issue from a post-Keynesian perspective, describe market making in even broader terms:[10]

> Trading opportunities are given not randomly by nature, or forced upon agents by "authority," but given instead by business firms: wholesalers, retailers, brokers, jobbers, manufacturers, banks, commodity exchanges, auction houses, employment agencies, mail order businesses, shopping malls, newspaper publishers, accountants, doctors, lawyers . . . [These types of firms] find it profitable to organize markets in such a way as to make trading relatively convenient and inexpensive for other transactors.

Most of this previous conceptual work on market making aims to broaden the economist's concept of markets, but still keep the resulting conceptualization within a conventional economic framework. With the market-making perspective that we propose, this same idea of market making is expanded yet further in order to examine categories of economic activities that the more standard approaches do not adequately analyze, including global retailing and the economic changes that have resulted from these activities.

Market making refers, thus, quite literally, to the activity of creating and maintaining markets (that is, trading opportunities) for oneself and one's trading partners. Market making includes a number of routine business activities, such as pricing and contracting, finding and retaining trading partners, and getting products into and through the market. But it also involves an element of *institutional entrepreneurship*, of finding and implementing novel ways of facilitating trade through intermediation, and this is what distinguishes market making from the standard notion of marketing.[11]

Retailers as market makers

The claim that retailers are market makers may sound all too obvious, since one of the most visible functions of retailing is to create and maintain marketplaces. Retailers choose store locations, display and advertise goods, set prices and provide transaction facilities, and perform many other tasks directed toward creating convenient trading opportunities for consumers. By and large, however, mainstream economic analysis has ignored such market-making activities, preferring instead to describe markets as abstract spaces where supply meets the demand, and where trading opportunities, along with the rules and mechanisms of trading, emerge spontaneously out of the necessity for exchange.

In the modern economy, markets neither emerge spontaneously, nor equilibrate automatically. Marketing and market making are difficult, costly, and time-consuming activities that most firms, of whatever type, have to do. This includes the so-called industrial, or manufacturing, firms, as US automobile manufacturers have learned time and again. Retailers, however, not only create and maintain markets, but also intermediate amongst multiple and quite diverse markets. In their role of integrating many supplier and consumer markets, for a large array of diverse products and services, they become market integration specialists, and it is in this role, as increasingly all encompassing and efficient market integrators, that retailers have transformed the global economy.

To understand this role, it is useful to contrast the more conventional productionist view of retailers with their role in the market-making perspective. Many analysts view retailers, not as market makers, but rather as conduits for goods being passed from manufacturers to consumers. Normally called marketing or distribution channels, these conduits depict the organization of the economy from the viewpoint of manufacturers. A number of years ago, Hollander (1964: 18) described these conduits as follows:

> We often think of a marketing channel as a sort of "bucket brigade" that passes goods from manufacturers to consumers. Moreover, we can easily come to think of that brigade as if it were composed of a limited number of institutional types who perform relatively standardized duties and who are represented by little boxes bearing the conventional letters "M," "W," "R," and "C" for manufacturer, wholesaler, retailer, and consumer.

Although highly stylized, this depiction captures the essence of the conventional view of retailers. The retailers' position in this linear progression always comes later in time and in importance to the "fundamental" process of actually making goods. More importantly, in this orderly flow of goods, there is an implicit theory of markets as being functional to the operation of the chain, with markets occurring at points where goods supposedly change hands. Manufacturers buy inputs, make a product, and sell that product to wholesalers, who in turn sell the product to retailers, who then "clear" the channel when they sell those products to final consumers. In this portrayal, manufacturers play the pivotal role of being the buyers of inputs who creatively combine those inputs to make a product that is in turn sold to final consumers. Market making is an unimportant activity along the chain, and instead represents primarily the final consumers' demand for the manufacturers' products.

If we conceptualize the economy in this fashion, then marketing and market making become synonymous and largely the responsibility of manufacturers who make products and of brand-name merchandisers (for example, Nike) who promote them.[12] Distribution channels and supply chains become, conceptually, the same thing. The role of retailer is reduced to that of service provider, the supplier of locations where particular goods can be purchased, the last link in a long chain of transfers that ends with the final buyer. This portrayal assumes that the primary transaction in this lineal chain continues to be the exchange between manufacturer and final consumer; all the rest are merely transfers with a suitable mark-up for costs incurred (for example, transportation costs) plus a suitable profit. This assumption maintains the fiction that the overall chain can be represented conceptually and parsimoniously by a supply and demand curve.

This is a productionist narrative of how economies work. Within this narrative, there is an implicit critique of merchants and retailers as sometimes less than honest and often greedy purveyors of products. This characterization suggests that retailers' organizations are less than efficient and, at times, obstruct "normal" market forces through promoting cut-throat competition and then selling goods at levels above or even below their "true price" merely to drive out competition.[13] Considering the pervasiveness of this account and of the distrust of retailers implicit in it, we should not be surprised that retailing has received scant interest from most economic observers of whatever discipline who are interested only in the "real" foundations of the economy.

The market-making perspective provides another account of the same set of activities told from the point of view of selling rather than making products. The productionist version divides market players into singular functional roles that efficiently link the supply (that is, the manufacturer) with the demand (that is, the final consumer) for a good. By contrast, the market-making perspective recognizes that markets and market making come in a remarkable variety of types and levels of complexity; that market-making activities occur at numerous points along the chain; that nearly every market player engages in multiple roles; and that the link between supply and demand is a function of market making and market makers, a link that is not well represented by a supply and demand curve and equilibrating markets.

The multiplicity and complexity of markets and market roles

A firm's primary business classification is often misleading. Although most manufacturers do not sell directly to final consumers, they still engage in advertising and other sales promotions, and most of them have marketing departments. Most large retailers typically engage in wholesaling activities, and occasionally also in product development and manufacturing. Brand-name merchandisers (for example, Nike) are typically listed as manufacturers when what they do is to specialize in product development and marketing, but not in manufacturing or retailing. Other firms develop core competence in managing and marketing portfolios of brands, without entering product development and manufacturing activities. Still others, such as McDonald's and Starbucks, operate primarily as "replicators" of business formats (Winter and Szulanski 2001). In order to analyze market making, therefore, we must replace the standard distinction between manufacturing, wholesale, and retail firms by a series of distinctions based on the complexity of markets in which firms sell their products, as well as on their specific capacities and competences in making those markets.

The first, and most basic, distinction is between two types of markets in which firms buy and sell. On the one hand, there are inter-firm markets, often called supplier or industrial markets, in which firms (for example, DuPont) sell goods or services only to other firms, but not to individual consumers. On the other hand, there are consumer markets in which firms also, or exclusively, sell directly to final consumers (for example, Wal-Mart). The latter category, which includes retailing firms, deals on average with more complex markets, since consumer markets involve a larger number of trading partners (their customers) whose demand is less rationalized, less predictable, and harder to ascertain.

The second distinction is between firms that market their products to final consumers only in limited ways—for instance, through media advertising and sales promotions—and those firms that mount "full package" selling operations in consumer markets, such as retail stores, restaurants, and hotels. There are many examples of firms (for example, Intel, Kraft Foods) in the former category that are able to create and maintain consumer markets, even though they do not sell directly to consumers.

The third distinction refers to the breadth of products sold, separating firms that sell only a limited range of products defined by production or consumption complementarities, from those that sell a broad range and variety of products. The former category includes some specialty retailers, but also firms such as Microsoft, Dell, and Nike, as well as car dealerships, gasoline stations, retail banks, personal service providers, and so on. The latter category contains general retailers, such as supermarkets, hypermarkets, and department stores, but also many "category killers" whose merchandise assortment, although somewhat specialized, still typically includes thousands of different products (e.g., Best Buy).

Finally, a distinction can be made between firms that buy from few suppliers, typically from large wholesalers, and those that deal with a large number and variety of suppliers. Unlike the previous distinctions, this last one refers strictly to inter-firm (supplier) markets, rather than consumer markets, and captures the tendency of large general retailers to bypass traditional wholesalers in favor of dealing directly with other types of suppliers.

How Retailers Make Markets

In addition to these distinctions based on the complexity of markets in which a firm operates, we can also distinguish between market makers and market takers—that is, between those firms that assume the primary responsibility for making one or more of the markets in which they trade, and those that mostly accept exchange institutions created by someone else. Retailers always play a role of intermediaries and market integrators; they connect both supplier and consumer markets, typically for a large number of different products. That fact alone, however, does not make them market makers.

Before the twentieth century, with few exceptions, most retailers were modestly sized, locally owned stores that received most of their inventory from much larger wholesalers.[14] These retail stores were market takers; they operated within the framework that other powerful actors established. These actors included, by the standards of the day, large industrial firms making consumer products and an array of well-connected and territorially ambitious wholesalers that sold many of these and other products to small stores. Although these retail stores may have held, in remote locations, something close to a monopoly position in relation to consumers, in relation to suppliers, they were strictly market takers.

Such a structure persisted in most supplier markets for consumer goods until recently. In the USA, where we find the earliest examples of the growth of mass retailers, by the Second World War we can already distinguish two parallel systems of selling consumer goods, one linking large "producers" with small sellers, the other linking large sellers (such as Sears and A&P) to small producers. By 1940, both accounted for about one-third of the total sales of consumer goods in the USA. The domination of manufacturers and wholesalers still persists, however, in many other economies, including Japan, the world's second largest retail market.

On the global level, however, the large retail chains of today, such as Wal-Mart, Tesco, Carrefour, and Home Depot, are major market makers in both their supplier and their consumer markets. Through their intermediary roles, these retail chains connect thousands of suppliers with millions of consumers. These retail chains are, however, not conduits; they are not passive vessels used to pass goods along to consumers. They are, instead, the main players in the game, several times larger than any consumer goods manufacturers, and they earn their prominence by being specialists in connecting supplier and consumer markets. These mass retailers use their leverage (that is, market power) in one market to enhance their leverage in other markets. They use their connections with suppliers to deliver just the right products at the right price for their customers. They use their access to a huge number of customers and potential customers to select and specify the products they sell and to extract the best deals from the suppliers of those products. This leverage from intermediation and market integration augments their capacity to make both consumer and supplier markets. However, the ability to make these two types of markets calls for very different market-making strategies in each market.

Consumer markets

Retailers of all types compete for consumers, and one of the ways that they compete is in their ability to create a particular kind of marketplace where particular kinds of products are sold. Retailers offer consumers ready-made market mechanisms that facilitate exchange. These mechanisms come in bundles or packages or formats that represent institutionalized market structures. A supermarket, a fast-food restaurant, a warehouse club, and a convenience store are all examples of such standardized formats for obtaining food. Retailers in each of these categories are market makers who assemble together market mechanisms (pricing, advertising, product assortment) that match their own competences with a perceived consumer environment.

In consumer markets, market making is, in the first instance, a competition amongst and within market formats. Such market-making activities may include competition within a well-recognized market category, such as price or service competition between two supermarkets, or competition between different market formats, such as the competition between, say, supermarkets, warehouse clubs, and convenience stores. As Schumpeter (1950: 85) put it, referring to early twentieth-century retailing: "In the case of retail trade the competition that matters arises not from additional shops of the same type, but from the department stores, the chain store, the mail order house and the supermarket."

The competition "that matters," then, is not about varying a few attributes at the time, but rather is about devising "new ways of organizing things, new sales–cost relationships, new methods of selling" (Bliss 1960: 72). This variety of competing marketplace formats has resulted in big waves of innovation and "creative destruction," but, at any one point in time, multiple competing formats coexist simply because the basis of competition is not, strictly speaking, just about price. Warehouse clubs (Costco, Sam's Club) and convenience stores (7-Eleven, AmPm) sell some of the same products, but do not compete with each other in terms of price for those products. 7-Eleven, for example, taps a market of people looking for convenience or, perhaps, of people needing a place to "hang out."

Price competition is less important between than within formats. But, even within formats, competition is primarily between retailers (that is, market makers) and not products. For example, price competition between super-markets commonly takes the form of some offering "everyday low price" and others subscribing to a "hi–low" pricing strategy involving low margins on sales items and high margins on other goods.[15] Although couched in terms of prices, this, in reality, is a competition that applies less to products individually than to the retailers themselves.

The competition within market formats may also emphasize the range of products being sold, or the level of service, rather than price, as the main competitive tool. This kind of "horizontal" competition also exists between very different types of markets. For example, a large supermarket, such as Whole Foods, which offers a wide selection of organic products, may be competing with a small grocery store, with a large chain like Wal-Mart, but also with a neighborhood restaurant or an antique shop. Although it does not sell similar products and services as the latter two, Whole Foods may, for example, draw consumers away from other locations, or it may even capture a larger portion of the consumer's budget, thus shifting the structure of preferences for specific goods and services.

Another very significant strategy in making consumer markets arises between manufacturers (or merchandisers) of branded consumer goods and retailers who sell these goods. The former typically advertise their goods directly to the consumer and thus engage in market-making activities in consumer markets. The latter may prefer to stock a different brand, including their own store brand,[16] but are compelled, at the same time, to offer those brands for which consumers may have developed preferences based on mer-chandisers' advertisements. By offering their private-label goods at a slightly lower price, retailers hope to create a multiple-product market for their own brand, as well as to place a ceiling on the price that manufacturers and merchandisers want for the brand-name goods that they sell to retailers.

While retailers try to create a marketplace that is in some sense unique, they also share many market mechanisms that retailers commonly use. This mix of unique and common elements is what creates the condition for competition. Each seller tries to persuade consumers—by its pricing, product assortment, store location, service, and many other elements—to shop in a specific way that best suits the seller's competence in selling. Because sellers are likely to adopt organizational innovations from each other, they are also likely to emulate each other's market-making strategies. The most common forms of competition, then, include a large degree of emulation combined with strategic differentiation on just a few dimensions. As a consequence, stores within the same format that compete directly with each other typically resemble each other.

Consumer markets are extremely competitive, more so today than ever before. The range of formats and the range of selling strategies within formats have increasingly made market making into highly specialized sets of activities that have grown ever more sophisticated and complex. In whatever formats they use, retailers must continually adapt to constantly changing technological environments and consumer trends. They are persistently challenged to make new markets, as well as to retain existing markets. More importantly, to compete effectively in consumer markets, all large and even modestly large retailers must also be concerned with making supplier markets as well.

Supplier markets

Unlike the horizontal competition in consumer markets, the competition in supplier markets is typically referred to as being "vertical." Competition in supplier markets is a struggle amongst trading partners to define a market structure for mutual exchange, a struggle to locate and refine the terms for cooperation. This is competition amongst firms having different positions in a supply chain, between, say, a manufacturer, a trading company, and a retailer. The idea of verticality (for example, upstream and downstream) derives from a production-centered image of the economy and does not capture the complex firm and inter-firm structures that emerge in supplier markets and that we discuss in Part Three of this book. Although rejecting the specific notion of verticality, we shall nonetheless retain the label of vertical competition in order to emphasize that such competitive relations often generate power inequality amongst trading partners. In horizontal competition, since they do not interact directly with each other, competitors do not have a position of authority in relation to each other. In vertical competition between, for instance, a retailer and its suppliers, one party in an exchange can directly assert its market power to define the contractual foundations for exchange.

Economists conventionally define market power in terms of the firm's relative share of the market and its concomitant ability to influence the market price for the product it is buying or selling. As noted above, this definition makes market power into a market imperfection, a distortion from the ideal type of perfectly competitive market where no market player, by definition, can have (more than an infinitesimally small amount of) market power. In distorted markets, firms having high market power can exert various types of price and non-price pressures on their suppliers and customers, and can also easily enter collusive agreements, tacit or explicit, with other such firms, thus forming a cartel.

Such a definition not only presumes that, in the absence of market power, markets would be "naturally" balanced between manufacturer's supply and consumer's demand, but also misses the type of market power intrinsic in market making. Only when market power is defined more broadly as the ability to shape the exchange structure—that is, as *market-making power*—does the notion of vertical competition become subsumed under a more coherent framework of market-making competition. The competition within supply chains is rarely limited to bargaining over the price of a predefined homogenous good. In fact, price may be relatively unimportant. The struggle also typically involves bargaining over issues such as how and when the product will be delivered, who will take the responsibility for packaging and presentation, advertising and warranty provisions, and even what the product itself should consist of. Given this complexity, it should not be surprising that trading partners compete not only to determine the outcomes of market negotiations, but also over the right to set the rules and mechanisms by which these outcomes are typically determined.

Market-making power, then, can be defined as the power to impose organization on the market, the power to define the shape of the market for oneself and one's trading partners. This outcome of market making can be thought of more generally as "market organization." Market organization is typically more complex than simply the organization of one's supply or distribution channels. Even in the same industry, supply chains vary in many ways, and at each link there are usually multiple players that can deliver comparable goods or services. For instance, on the one hand, large retailers, as well as brand-name merchandisers, typically line up many manufacturers to make such products as apparel or footwear. By being able to pick and choose amongst a number of manufacturers, trading companies, and logistic firms for particular goods or services, large retailers and merchandisers are able to influence, if not set, the terms (including price) for market exchanges, not only for themselves, but also potentially for other players in the market as well. On the other hand, manufacturers typically try to negotiate with multiple retailers, thereby diversifying market outlets for their products.

Market institutions

Competition and cooperation between various firms in inter-firm markets, as well as between retailers in consumer markets, result in the creation of a highly sophisticated and complex institutional framework within which buying and selling of consumer goods occurs in the modern economy. Various elements of such an institutional framework define and stabilize expectations of market participants and structure market transactions. Market makers, however innovative and powerful, always operate within these structures, even as they strive to shape and change them to suit their own organizational competences.

We can distinguish amongst the elements of the institutional structure of consumer goods markets by identifying their connections and closeness to market transactions. Some institutions are directly related to market transactions: money, credit, and other institutions related to exchange; location, shape, facilities, and other elements of marketplaces (stores, shopping centers) where transactions occur; standardized goods and services, their combination into product lines and types, branding, advertising, and other institutions related to products being sold. Typical ways of combining these market institutions lead to institutionalization of retail market formats (for example, supermarket, department store) and categories (for example, grocery retailers, general merchandisers, fashion retailers) that can be emulated and replicated. All these institutions are made and reproduced by actions of many market makers; yet they also provide the essential context in which market makers' capacities and strategies evolve, and in which they compete with each other for market-making power.

Other types of institutions, while not related directly and exclusively to market transactions, are essential in enabling market making to occur and market institutions to function. These include technologies involved in producing, transporting, and delivering goods to stores as well as those that enable stores to operate efficiently, and consumers to have access to those stores. As Abernathy and Volpe (Chapter 2 this volume) demonstrate, such technological inventions that we take for granted today were often developed for purposes other than retailing, and then adapted with great success to retailing. The post-1980s transformation of the global economy, led by major retailers, is based on major technological advances we can see today in most stores, such as bar codes, scanning devices, and computerized inventory systems, but also, as described in Chapter 7, by the development of distant ports, containerized shipping, and other elements of global logistics.

Of equal importance are institutions that shape consumer motivations and behavior. The retailing rule of thumb is that people rationally buy what they socially desire. Social desirability is directly related to highly localized dimensions of social class, status, and lifestyle, which are in turn directly shaped by various institutions, from the family and local community to mass media, education, and politics. Consumers become competent market participants mainly by participating in the market, but they also bring to the market many other traits. Retailers and brand-name merchandisers, through analyzing POS information, have increasingly been able to tap into these dimensions and thereby to establish market-making feedback loops between themselves and their customers. Manufacturers increasingly find themselves outside these feedback loops and, therefore, find it necessary to connect themselves to consumers through the organization of retailing, which often involves redefining themselves as "vendors," as participants in retailers' supplier markets. Increasingly, the primary form of producing consumer goods, contract manufacturing, is, by definition, outside the loop.

Various institutions related to business organization and management, as well as to inter-firm relations, are another major aspect of the institutional environment of the markets. The evolution of firms is to a great degree shaped by their participation in markets and their ability to act as market makers. Yet firms also need to develop competences in many other realms, from research and development to technologies of production, to management of human resources, to dealing with legal, political, and other environments. In this regard, we side with the growing literature on evolutionary and competence approaches to the firm (Nelson and Winter 1982; Prahalad and Hamel 1990). Although these approaches rarely recognize the strategic significance of competence in market making, we see them as complementary to the market-making perspective, as they illuminate other key aspects of firms' performance and evolution.

Finally, market institutions are embedded in legal and political institutions, on several different levels, from local to state levels, and beyond, to international contexts. While most contemporary economic theories, given their equilibrium bias, tend to ignore both market organization and market institutions, they do allow for the crucial role of the state in creating a legal framework that ensures property rights and enforces contracts, regulating certain less-than-rational behavior in markets and ensuring fair competition, and promoting trade amongst nations—all this, in theory, in order to encourage entrepreneurial initiative and to allow open and competitive markets to flourish spontaneously. Similarly, in productionist models, the state *is* the primary institution that supports and coordinates strategic industries, develops and controls human capital (including managing the demands of labor), and provides the necessary infrastructure for competitiveness, innovation, and economic growth.

The market-making perspective acknowledges the importance of the state and its policies, yet sees it as only one of the market-making organizations. The state often acts directly as a market maker, by controlling major enterprises or whole strategic sectors, and thus structuring market transactions within a large part of the economy. At other times, its influence on market institutions is less direct, if not less consequential. As discussed in Part Two, government regulations, or the lack thereof, shape the development of specific retailing formats and facilities, and often define the relations between retailers and their suppliers. However, according to the market-making perspective, the state's power to make markets and influence market makers is always limited by the institutional complexity of markets and the degree of entrepreneurship and competence needed for market-making success. The more complex the markets, the more limited the state capacity to make them "from above." This complexity is why direct state control or ownership of the retail sector almost always fails to deliver, especially when compared to the state's role in purely "industrial" sectors such as resource extraction (oil, mining) or the provision of basic infrastructure (power, telecommunications).

Conclusion: Institutional Changes and the Co-Evolution of Market Players

As they create market institutions out of the tools available to them in their time and place, and in order to suit their organizational capacities, market makers impose new organization on markets. The development and spread of market institutions continually reconstruct the relationship between buyers and sellers and thereby redefine the extent of the market.

In the following chapters, we examine such a co-evolution of market institutions, marketable products, market participants and market-making strategies. In Part Two, we address the evolution of consumer markets; in Part Three, we trace the evolution of supplier markets; and in Part Four, we present case studies combining both types of markets. By co-evolution, we mean that institutions, products, participants, and strategies are all linked in a framework of mutual causation. This framework of mutual causation is not obvious in the abstract world of modern equilibrium economics, where *homo economicus* has a constant presence across time and space, where firms are seen as production functions or contract structures and not as actors, and where all markets, whenever and wherever found, differ only in how close they approach the "perfect" model of pure competition. Nor is this framework of mutual causation relevant for the productionist narratives, where production, and the forces that shape production, are the only true factors in the evolution of the economy. In contrast to these conventional approaches, we view all these aspects of markets and market making as being in a constant process of invention and re-invention.

For example, as Petrovic makes clear in Chapter 3, the institutionalization of the supermarket format in the first half of the twentieth century necessitated that manufacturers and retailers alike develop new strategies for selling products, that these products be reimagined and redesigned, and that consumers start seeing themselves and the act of shopping in a different light. The co-evolution of all these aspects of self-service shopping created an institutionalized package that entrepreneurs could move across the retailing spectrum, from food to clothes, to hardware, to consumer electronics, to scrambled merchandising. This same institutionalized package, in turn, allowed a few of the most successful firms to impose a new organization on, and create new boundaries for, capitalist supplier and consumer markets for all types of goods.

Usually, such changes are incremental and remain that way, but occasionally these incremental changes are so transformative that they fundamentally alter the organization of national economies. The global development of modern retail markets and of giant retailers that make those markets, in the post-Second World War era, has been one of those transformative processes that led to the emergence of the contemporary global economy.

Large multinational retailers arrived at the global scene late. This should not be surprising, given that the complexity of markets they operate delayed their growth and is still placing limits on their expansion. We can hardly imagine a Wal-Mart, Tesco, or Carrefour that would command the same share of the global retail market for groceries and general merchandise as Toyota, Exxon Mobil, or even Dell Computers do in their respective sectors. Likewise, many types of industrial and financial markets are far more integrated and more globalized than retail markets.

However, the recent transformation of retailing worldwide has been profound, as it has led to the rapid spread of the main retail formats and the emergence of the first global retailers. Since the 1980s, retail market makers have also exerted an unprecedented influence on the organization of many other industries, becoming thus the leading force in structuring global supply chains and other inter-firm relations. Moreover, the globalization of retailing represents the main link through which consumers worldwide are increasingly drawn into participating in the modern economy and its ever evolving world of goods and services. All of this, we believe, indicates a new phase in the evolution of the global economy, one that we may be justified in calling "the age of global retailers."

2

Technology and Public Policy: The Preconditions for the Retail Revolution

Frederick H. Abernathy and Anthony P. Volpe

Introduction

Many people living in Boston, Massachusetts, visit the Mall at Chestnut Hill for their upmarket shopping. The Mall is located at the crossroads of Route 9 and Hammond Pond Parkway in Newton, one of the many upscale western suburbs of Boston. The Mall follows the merchants' dictum of locating stores where it is easy for customers to drive to and park, with attractive merchandise to make their visit a pleasant experience.

The Mall at Chestnut Hill is the present-day embodiment of the nineteenth and early twentieth-century department store updated with ample parking for today's suburban shoppers. Richard Woodward (2007) of the *New York Times* suggests that the present-day mall is but a modernized version of the Paris arcades of the 1820s and 1830s, which he describes as follows:

> Diminutive cathedrals to commerce and leisure, the arcades offered unheard of amenities to the emerging class of bourgeois consumers. Gas lighting, heated shelter from rain and mud, a panoply of goods and services in a contained space, cafes and restaurants where you could rest and observe fellow lingerers—these were a decided plus over the shopping experience of hunting and gathering all around town.

The Mall at Chestnut Hill has the conventional two large anchor stores at either end; in this case both anchors are Bloomingdale's stores specializing in different products at opposite ends of the two-storey enclosed atrium. Parking spaces surround the Mall, and additional spaces are provided in a multi-storey parking structure with a convenient covered bridge to the Mall. Beyond the Bloomingdale anchors there are fifty-five other individual stores ranging from

Brooks Brothers, Coach, Ann Taylor, Barneys New York, Sur La Table, and Apple Inc., to banks, three restaurants, and many small specialty shops. Shoppers might have done pre-shopping on the Internet before coming to the mall, some might have come in response to an advertisement sent to them by mail, while others come just to have a good time enjoying the eye candy and having lunch with a friend to cap off the outing. A few simply come and sit in the overstuffed chairs in the lobby and watch the other shoppers.

Almost all shoppers come to the Mall with just a credit card—avoiding carrying large amounts of cash—so that they can purchase whatever they fancy, provided it is within their credit limit. When they enter the Mall, they are probably unaware of the amount of technology and its sophistication needed to keep the Mall and the stores running. Most of the technology is hidden from view by careful design—the stores are providing an enticing atmosphere with attractively displayed merchandise, not their back-office technology. Technology is certainly visible in the Apple store, selling Apple computers, iPhones, and iPods, along with the peripherals that make the iPod the world's most widely used MP3 player. But even here the WiFi system connecting the displayed items to the Internet is happily running quietly in the background throughout the store. Almost all of the technology necessary for modern retailing was invented or developed outside the retail industry for other applications or purposes. Over time, forward-looking merchants saw in various technological advances an opportunity to enhance the retail shopping experience, create new retail channels, and provide efficiently new and more varied products. They adapted these technologies for use in their stores and operations, forever altering the retail environment. In this way, technology has become critical to modern retail market making.

Retail market makers who have exploited technology have done so in two distinct ways. First, technology has been the basis for developing new retail channels that are both pleasing and convenient for customers. This includes enhancing traditional brick-and-mortar stores, as well as new channels such as e-commerce, and Internet boutiques. Second, market makers have used new technology to create more efficient supply channels expanding products for retail selections, and to improve their organizational function. The technology has put new products from around the world into retail stores and expanded consumer choices at reasonable prices. This chapter will examine the most prominent technologies responsible for today's retail marketplace.

In later sections of this chapter we will trace the development of several early disruptive technologies that have changed the face of American retailing and manufacturing. We will start with the push of the railroad into the West in the 1860s and the birth of mail-order market making by Montgomery Ward's in 1872. Then we will look at the effect of that most disruptive transportation technology—the automobile—on big city retailing and the beginning of suburban shopping, lead first by Sears, Roebuck and Co. in the 1920s. In 1956 two other important disruptive technologies were introduced, one quietly and the other with all of the fanfare of an Act of Congress pushed by the then President Dwight Eisenhower. The first of these two technologies was the shipping container, as well as the container ships that transport material around the world very economically; the other is the US interstate highway system, which was so important in providing Wal-Mart, as well as other big-box retailers, with locations for stores during their rapid expansion during the 1960s and 1970s. By being amongst the first in the 1980s to use bar-code identifiers and the Internet for ordering, Wal-Mart revolutionized supply chains and subsequently expanded its stores to become the world largest retailer. Ports for container ships, railroads, and interstate highway connections are the basic triad of modern intermodal transportation of global commerce. But first we will review some of the important contemporary technologies, working partially in the background, that make modern retail shopping so attractive to customers and so transformative to the global economy.

Technology and Retail Channels

Stores

Much of the ease of use and general pleasantness of current retail channels can be attributed to technology and the creative merchants who found novel ways to employ it. The most obvious retail channels are the physical store fronts reached from sidewalks, plazas, and shopping malls. The Mall at Chestnut Hill is just such an example; this type of marketplace leverages technology to create the most enjoyable customer experience possible. Consider the heating, ventilation, and air-conditioning (HVAC) systems that keep the air fresh and free of unpleasant odors, and maintain the humidity at acceptable levels, and the temperature at an ideal value for the season. HVAC was invented by Willis Carrier in 1902. His motivation was to control the humidity of a printing plant where he worked. Paper and cardboard change their dimensions as they gain or lose moisture. Carrier realized that controlling the humidity would stabilize the dimensions of paper, so that different colors applied sequentially at different times would dry quickly and would register properly.

It was a long time before air conditioning was widely used. One of the authors of this chapter (FHA) still remembers vividly the first time he experienced air conditioning; it was the unexpected and unexplained physical shock at going from inside an air-conditioned restaurant out onto the very hot St Louis railroad station platform in the summer of 1936. Nowadays we would all be shocked if we were to go into a store in the summertime and find there was no air conditioning; it would probably be our last visit. In fifty or sixty years the disruptive technology of air conditioning has gone from a memorable experience to ubiquity. And that is the nature of most disruptive technologies that are part of the standard retail environment.

Some technologies diffuse more rapidly—electric lighting, for example. Edison first commercialized distributed electrical lighting in 1882. Less than fifty years later, the construction of new power plants, fixtures, and bulbs had led to electricity replacing gas and oil lighting in US cities and suburbs. John Wanamaker, an important market-maker innovator in US retailing, installed electrical lighting in his department store in Philadelphia in 1879 (Gibbons 1926: i. 218–19), having already installed arc lighting in outside window displays in 1878. Soon after Edison's demonstration of the system of electrical lighting, Wanamaker went to Menlo Park, New Jersey, to visit Edison at his research and development laboratory, and arranged for DC motors to power ventilation fans in his stores, long before air was "conditioned."

Along the way, it was necessary for public policy to provide enabling legislation creating local and state building codes to ensure human safety when electrical power was installed and used. We will see this time and time again: public policy—national, local, or both—is necessary for the broad diffusion of a new technology. We allow one electric power company to have a monopoly of the means of distributing power to our homes. Imagine the mess if there were multiple sets of power poles belonging to different companies competing for our business. Some standards are set by an industry; the typical standard screw base of an incandescent bulb—called the Edison base—is just one example. It is true that there are several different light-bulb bases, but most are for special lighting fixtures. It would be a household nightmare if every manufacturer of lighting fixtures required a special bulb base.[1]

In addition to lighting and air conditioning the elevator and the escalator are two other common electrical devices in every modern multi-storey retail building. Both were invented for other purposes: Elisha Otis invented a steam-powered elevator with safety features in 1853 to move freight; modern elevators are now powered by electricity and controlled by elaborate computer systems along with greatly enhanced safety features from those possible in the 1853 patent for the elevator.[2]

Jesse Reno invented the escalator in 1892 as an electrically powered conveyor belt for moving people at Coney Island, New York. Harrods installed an escalator in their already famous store in London amid great fanfare just two years later. People movers were and are always important for retailers trying to make it as painless as possible for customers to reach the upper floors without the arduous climb of stairs. By 1900, department stores of ten storeys became common in the big cities of the USA, because growing land prices and increasing population made large vertical retail spaces economically viable. Structural steel, electric lighting, electric elevators, and electrically powered ventilation made tall buildings possible. John Wanamaker, the famous merchant of the nineteenth and early twentieth centuries, had a three-storey auditorium seating 1,300 people built into his new New York store in 1907 (Gibbons 1926: ii. 109–10). In 1911 he topped all that had gone before by installing the world's "finest organ in the world" in the lavishly decorated marble-clad 149-foot-high Grand Court of his new 1911 building in Center City, Philadelphia. Macy's now owns the store, and the organ has been refurbished and expanded to 28,543 tubes (Whitney 2007). The store manager, James Kenny, reports: "Every lunch time, people hear the organ and feel good—and people are in a mind to shop when they're feeling good. It is the ultimate feel-good experience." Visionary merchants such as Wanamaker quickly adopted new technology to make the shopping experience inviting: concerts, restaurants, and tearooms were added for shoppers' convenience and enjoyment.

Charge cards and credit

Besides providing a more comfortable marketplace, technology has been adopted to change retail channels in other ways. In particular, the emergence of credit cards has provided consumers with cash-less convenience, means for greater impulse buying, increased buying power, and opportunities to shop in new retail markets, including catalogs, e-commerce stores, such as Amazon, and more.

American retailers have been making new markets around issuing credit since this nation's founding. By 1924, consumers relied on financing for about 75 percent of their vehicle purchases (Calder 1999: 158). Large mail-order stores and catalog companies, most notably Montgomery Ward's and Sears, Roebuck and Co., provided a variety of exotic "buy-now, pay-later" schemes that played a prominent role in the early success of these retail giants (Calder 1999: 200). While the concepts of credit and revolving debt unquestionably drove important new markets and retail channels, the physical credit card has been creatively leveraged in market making as well. The impressive new retail formats and merchandising possibilities afforded by plastic were made possible only after an impressive array of technological advances had been borrowed from a variety of industries.

In 1914, Western Union offered its preferred business customers metal charge cards to be used in lieu of cash (MacDonald and Gastmann 2001: 227). Payment was expected upon invoicing, so the initial attraction was convenience rather than credit. A number of travel and entertainment chains followed suit. In an effort to consolidate the number of charge cards required by a business traveler, Frank McNamara and two friends in 1950 started a credit organization, the Diners Club, that issued 200 cards (paper, not plastic), which could be used in twenty-seven restaurants throughout New York; the card was gradually accepted by retailers nationwide, becoming Diners Club International (Evans 2005: 53). This general-purpose card, which came to signify membership in Diners Club International, grew nationwide.

In 1959, San Francisco-based Bank of America (BOA) put its own spin on the charge card by offering card-holders immediate, pre-approved credit. The BankAmericard became the first nationally recognized bank card and spawned the credit-card industry, as we know it. Merchants funded the nationwide network by paying a fee for each transaction, a practice that took some getting used to. Customers were permitted to pay for their purchases in monthly installments, incurring a finance charge on the outstanding balance. This type of agreement provided card-holders with an enhancement beyond the simple convenience of a charge card; it gave them purchasing power beyond their immediate means. This is a critical element in today's retail market.

BankAmericard eventually grew into Visa by 1976, while MasterCharge, the forerunner to Mastercard, began as a competing network in 1967. The existence of distinct, unconnected networks, high interchange fees, and a general lack of standards continued to hamper merchant acceptance. In turn, consumer adoption was also slow, and a vicious circle would have to be overcome.

The most significant step toward improving credit cards for both merchants and buyers would come from reducing the overall time and cost to approve a purchase and conduct the corresponding transactions between the various agents. In 1970, it could take over five minutes for a merchant to gain an authorization code by telephoning the issuing bank and reading the account and purchase information. At closing, the merchant would capture the day's sales only by submitting to his acquiring bank the paper sales drafts, each with recorded authorization and signature. These would ultimately have to be settled with the appropriate issuing banks. Naturally, this caused enormous workloads for banks, which charged high fees back to the merchant, and errors were frequent.

The overall approval and transaction process was significantly aided in the next three decades by merging a series of new technologies. First, in 1960, the London Transit Authority began encoding data on cards via magnetic strip. Then, in a separate development early that same decade, Bell Labs created touch-tone dialing. This made long-distance calling faster and cheaper. Equally important, touch tone opened the door for automated telephoning via computer systems, which would come nearly twenty years later. This critical advance could take place only after early generation data modems invented for US air defense systems in the 1950s evolved into the "smart modems" of today. Released in 1981 by Hayes Communications, "smart modems" could transmit at 300 digital bits per second, and for the first time serve as a dialer by translating digital computer commands directly into the analog telephone network. It should be noted that the adoption of international standards to ensure accurate data exchange between modems was crucial in advancing this technology.

The credit industry, led by National BankAmericard, Inc. (NBI),[3] leveraged these technologies to automate the data-exchange process by developing a fully electronic authorization system, which they called Base I (Mandell 1990: 62). An electronic card reader/dial terminal at the point of sale (POS) could pull critical information from the "Magstripe," including the issuing bank's phone number, the account number, and the expiration date; then place a call answered by a computer; pass purchase information via touch tone; and accept an authorization code—all in less than a minute. On the receiving end, increasingly efficient databases could compare the queried purchase amount to the customer's available credit balance, and, if the charge was approved, place immediate holds on the account. NBI's success with Base I in automating the authorization process led to the development of Base II. This complementary touch-tone system allowed merchants to capture sales electronically at the day's end, eliminating the need to deposit mountains of paper for processing at the acquiring bank. Acquiring fees were reduced and accuracy was improved throughout the credit system. As a result, merchant acceptance of credit cards continued to grow.

Beyond these benefits, electronic transaction networks also opened the door to 24/7 credit-card use and Internet retailing. No longer constrained by banking hours, merchants were able to secure authorizations around the clock. From the consumer's perspective, plastic became a preferred substitute for cash, day and night, on both weekdays and weekends. Encryption techniques allow secure credit-card transactions online, and electronic signature has become widely accepted. The result has been exciting new markets and retail channels.

Next-generation POS systems are already being used in novel retail applications. Broadband lines and the Internet are permitting more real-time fraud detection routines at the POS, without a noticeable increase in transaction time. A growing number of chains use electronic signature pads to facilitate credit-card use, eliminating the need for cashier identification. These rely on LCD touch-screen technology. Symbol Technologies, now a subsidiary of Motorola, is well known for its handheld POS terminals. Associates at Apple Stores use these wireless devices to process customer credit-card purchases on the spot, using IEEE 802.11 wireless protocols for speed and security. Never needing to enter a checkout line enhances shoppers' overall store experience. Rental car companies use the same technology to close agreements within moments of a customer returning a vehicle. Not only is a credit card preferred; it is expected.

Not surprisingly, legislation has been and will remain crucial in the marriage of retail market making and credit cards. To date it has been most pivotal in protecting card-holding consumers. The landmark 1968 Consumer Credit Protection Act, which included the Truth in Lending Act, dictates that all terms be clearly disclosed to card applicants in a common language. It also limits a cardholder's liability to $50 per unauthorized charge in cases of loss and theft, provided such events are reported within two days (15 U.S.C. § 1643 (a)(1)(B)). A host of other legislation is constantly being updated to protect consumers from unfair practices of credit-card issuers. Laws meant to protect merchants, particularly small businesses, have received considerable attention. These tend to focus on controlling the merchant fees, which are negotiable between a merchant and its acquiring bank. Finally, standardization continues to bolster modern credit-card use, which is so pivotal in today's evolving retail environment. Because of the prevalence of POS scanning, card dimensions are governed by the International Standards Organization (ISO) 7810 guideline. Smart-chip technology used in many newer cards follows ISO 7816, and radio-frequency identification (RFID) chips are governed by ISO 14443.

Total credit-card purchases reached $2.2 trillion in 2007 in the USA alone.[4] Essentially, all Internet commerce is transacted with credit cards or their derivatives. While this impressive volume has been driven partially by convenience and purchasing power, it can also be attributed to an ever-expanding set of global markets accessed through a wider array of retail channels.

Bar codes and product identification

A final contemporary technology that dramatically improves physical retailing in several ways is the bar code printed on every retail item. While this breakthrough has enabled faster checkout, more reliable pricing, and more dynamic markdown and promotion strategies, it was developed by the retail food market industry and their suppliers simply to increase the efficiency of the checkout at the front end of food stores.

In the early 1970s, at the dawning of the new computer and robotics age, people in manufacturing and retailing were aware of the need for electronic systems that could recognize a machine part for manufacturing assembly or assist in checkout in food stores. Each group approached the problem in a different way. The manufacturers' approach was first to capture a digital photo as a step in recognizing a desired part. One of this chapter's authors (FHA) was on a review panel at the National Bureau of Standards (now called the National Institute of Science and Technology (NIST)) viewing attempts being made to solve this recognition problem. The researchers had selected a box of cornflakes of a particular size as a representative target object. By scanning laser beams onto the box in several directions and looking at the scattered signal, they hoped to determine the size of the box. Other techniques were being explored to recognize the name of the manufacturer; in this case it was Kellogg. It is not easy to teach a computer system to find the name of the manufacturer amongst all the writing on a breakfast food carton. So their first attempts were just to recognize the K of the name, which is always positioned prominently on the carton.

At the time, no one on the review panel was aware that the food market retailers and their suppliers were already solving this problem in a beautifully simple way, and without direct help from government of any level. Their work resulted in the Universal Product Code (UPC), and its twelve numerical digit bar code symbol that identifies the manufacturer and allows an exact description of the item. The focus of the group was solely on improving the efficiency of supermarket checkout. It did not anticipate that it was about to create the tool that would allow the entire retail supply chain to be rationalized. Alfred D. Chandler Jr, writing on the jacket of the definitive book on the history of the development of the bar code and the supermarket scanners systems, *Revolution at the Checkout Counter: The Explosion of the Bar Code*, said:

> This book tells in intriguing detail the almost unknown history of the coming of the Universal Product Code (UPC)—an innovation that has transformed the process of distribution and production as profoundly as the coming of the railroad and the telegraph did more than a century ago. The book is essential reading for an understanding of the evolution and impact of today's information revolution. (Brown 1997)

The bar code in the form that we all know, and the Universal Code Council that administers the allocation of codes to manufacturers, were the product of an initial meeting in 1969 of the Administrative Systems Committee of the Grocery Manufacturers of America (GMA) and their counterparts in the food market industry, the National Association of Food Chains (NAFC), to discuss a product code for the food market industries. There was a general belief that a machine-readable product code would increase substantially the productivity of the front end of supermarkets. It was envisioned that each item offered for sale would be marked with a code identifying the manufacturer and uniquely describing the product. The code would be read by a scan system at the checkout; the computer system would then rapidly look up from internal files the name of the manufacturer, the product description, and the price. Individual tagging of each item (item pricing) would no longer be needed for checkout, and the labor cost saving from eliminating item pricing would be available to finance the scanning equipment.

The motivation of grocery firms for such a system is obvious, while that of the grocery manufacturers was equally pressing, if not as direct. There was talk in Europe and in the USA that several high-tech firms were developing product codes and scanning systems. The grocery manufacturers were worried that, if a "universal code" were not developed and implemented across the industry, some of the larger chains would select an identification code for their products and then pressure their suppliers to use it on all the products shipped to their stores. Such requirements would introduce huge inefficiencies in suppliers' product inventories and might result in Federal Trade Commission objections that a manufacturer was providing services to one retailer not available to others—something not allowed under the law.[5] The way forward then was clear: develop one product identification symbol and encourage all food product manufacturers to provide it on their products. A reasonable code for the retailer was one that could be scanned at the checkout counter or read by a wand or entered in a register system by a clerk at a store without the necessary technology. Naturally the scanning equipment would have to be priced so that the hard saving from using the system would pay for the equipment in a few years.

John T. Dunlop and Jan Rivkin (1997) describe the general economic and technology conditions in the USA when the Universal Product Code (UPC) was being developed. During the time of the UPC development, Dunlop had been the Director of the Cost of Living Council appointed by President Nixon to attempt to rein in the then raging national inflationary increases in the cost of living. At that time the food industry was anxious to gain control of costs, and product codes were one step in that direction. Their book also documents the penetration of UPC bar codes into almost every product category in the retail sector. By 1994, Food & Beverage had gone from being 100 percent of all registrations to only about 28 percent of registrations; the remaining registrations were in twenty-one different sectors, from Audio & Video to Health & Beauty Aids. This diffusion into the overall retail sector was not anticipated in 1969 at the first meeting of the principals of food manufacturers and chain-store grocery operators; nor was it foreseen as late as June 1974, when the first item bearing the UPC code, a package of Wrigley's gum, passed through the checkout scanner of the Marsh's Supermarket in Troy, Ohio.

From the beginning the groups sponsoring the development of the UPC aimed for a *symbol* code that would be in the public domain. They finally came up with a twelve-digit bar code, which grew to fourteen digits in 2005 and can now be found on virtually everything that we buy. Today the decision to choose a series of bars surrounded by a white border to represent a series of digits may seem an obvious one—obvious because it is simple and has been so successful. Frozen-food products with small ice crystals on the package can be scanned as well as a crumpled bag of pretzels or potato chips. We see how easily the bar symbols can be machine scanned when we do it ourselves at the self-checkout counters at the local food and home improvement stores.

Clerks at big-box stores can now easily scan bags of lawn fertilizer with portable wands that automatically sweep a red laser diode light beam across the bars. The light reflected back to the wand creates a corresponding bright and dark pattern on its receiver element, allowing internal deduction of the numerical code that is printed on the base of the symbol. From the sophisticated fundamental structure of the light and dark bars of the code, it is possible for scan systems to distinguish the first digits—the manufacturer code—from the last digits allocated to the item description, even when the code is scanned backwards.

We have to admire the courage of the group from the GMA and NAFC meeting in 1969: they set out to devise a product code and scanning system for the food market industry by engaging the attention of the US electronic industry. At the time they must have been encouraged by the 1969 moon landing to believe that something seemingly as simple as codes and scanning systems could be developed. The 1960s was after all the era of the laser, the third generation of computers, and integrated circuits (H. B. O. Davis 1985: 140–5). The committee used its knowledge of the food industry wisely to insist that detailed requirements for printing code labels be drawn up and tested on actual products. Scanning trials were insisted on for assurance that the codes could be successfully read 999 times out of 1,000 under normal conditions at food markets. In the competition between the bull's eye code of RCA and the rectangular code of IBM, the winner was the latter's rectangular bar code with its specified clear surround.

It is hard to imagine now that the adoption of UPC at the checkout counter was initially rather slow. The necessary scanning and computer equipment then available was deemed very costly. Some food chains were worried that not all food store product manufacturers would voluntarily adopt the UPC code, making some item pricing of products necessary and thereby diminishing labor cost saving and making scanning systems uneconomical. In fact some states had consumer laws requiring individual price markings on each item in the store, as Massachusetts still does.

By 1984, ten years after the first package of gum had passed a scanner in March's supermarket, only 33 percent of supermarkets had scanners (Haberman 2001: 27). But a tipping point was soon reached, and bar-code scanners appeared in nearly every store. In the 1992 presidential campaign, the *New York Times*, the *Washington Post*, and many other national publications ran stories about President George H. W. Bush's apparent wonderment upon seeing a new supermarket scanner operating at a National Grocers' Association convention in Orlando, Florida (Brinkley 1992). Whether the President was really seeing a scanner for the first time is not the point of the story for us now.

It is, rather, that by 1992 almost all newspaper readers were familiar with bar codes and scanners in food stores; hence the President's reaction suggested that he was out of touch with everyday life in the country. Today bar codes and scanners are near universal in mass retailing, not only in the USA, but around the world. As consumers, we typically see only a few aspects of the use of bar codes. For example, the item description that accompanies the sales price on the printed sales receipts for every retail purchase comes from bar-code look-up tables. Later in this chapter we will address the role of bar codes in improving the efficiency of product supply chains and the prominent role Wal-Mart has played in driving this process.

A succession of disruptive technologies has transformed retailing from the general stores away from the city supplied by manufacturers in the cities to the multiple overlapping forms of retailing we have today. First we begin by visiting the history of early disruptive technologies, the railroad that gave us mail-order retailing, and then the automobile that led to suburban mall retailing. We will then explain how the disruptive technologies of bar codes and the Internet, coupled with containers and container shipping, railroads, and trucking, have helped to revolutionize worldwide product sourcing. In 1956, when container shipping started and Congress passed and President Eisenhower signed the bill starting the Interstate highway system, no one saw how these two events would change where goods would be manufactured. These events allowed electronic and other manufacturers to create new markets for parts and assembly that would never have existed without these disruptive shipping technologies.

Early Disruptive Technologies

Railroad expansion to the West and mail order

We are all aware that railroads bring merchandise from factories and ports to freight yards and then to trucks that deliver the merchandise to the retail stores. While the role of the railroad in allowing the West to be settled is well known, the railroad's role in the introduction of mail-order merchandising is perhaps just as important to retailing yet less widely recognized. In 1850 the railroads in the USA were principally located on the East Coast; by 1860 they were branching out to the Midwest and connecting the manufacturing centers in upper New York State with large markets along the East Coast. In 1850 there were already over 9,000 miles of railroads, and within the next decade this network had expanded by a factor of three (Solomon 2001: 29). This westward expansion made Chicago the focal point of the intercontinental rail system and, consequently, an important merchandising center. By 1860 more than a dozen rail lines connected Chicago with the East and with points in Indiana,

Illinois, Ohio, and further west (Soloman 2001: 40). Because of the railroad and the corresponding westward expansion of the US population, Chicago became a dynamic and important city, growing from an estimated population of only 100 in 1830, to 29,963 in 1850, to 298, 977 in 1870, to 503,185 in 1880, and to 1,099,850 in 1890.[6] By 1872, Chicago had many retail establishments catering to the local demand for clothing and practical items of everyday use. In 1872, a young clerk with an entrepreneurial spirit named Montgomery Ward was working for the prominent and expanding store Field, Palmer, and Leiter (FPL). The "Field" partner of FPL was the Marshall Field whose fame in Chicago as a merchant grew to allow him to open the then largest department store in the world on State Street in Chicago in 1907. As a clerk for FPL, Montgomery Ward traveled by train and horse and buggy to service the country stores that were the major clients of FPL.

> He found that the country store, with its pot-bellied stove and cracker barrel, was a snug place for farmers to sit and swap gossip on stormy days. But it was not so comfortable for the farmer when he went to the counter to buy goods. Prices were high and the choice of goods small. When the farmer complained, the storekeeper pointed out that he had to buy what the wholesaler offered at the prices set by the wholesaler. The farmer could take it or leave it and, since the storekeeper usually was the only merchant in the area, the farmer had to take it. (Latham 1972: 3)

Ward understood the farmers' and the shop owners' dilemma. The long chain from manufacturer to wholesaler, to jobber, and finally to the retailer at the crossroad store had too many steps in the supply chain, each step marking up the product to cover its costs. He conceived of direct mail-order sales. He would be located in Chicago close to manufacturers and wholesalers; and by combining many mail orders together he could buy in bulk at a discount and sell directly to the farmers. He would write a catalog with detailed listing of the items for sale, at a fixed price, with a money-back guarantee if the customers were not satisfied with the merchandise. Ward began with two partners and just $1,600 in August 1872. An early catalog listed 163 items, ranging from yard goods of flannel and jeans fabric to an ostrich plume. In time, the catalogue expanded to contain more than 130,000 items in 1967 (Latham 1972: 91).

There is always a problem of locating potential customers, and the early mail-order company was no exception. There was certainly no easy way to find listings of people in the farming communities in the rural west. Ward solved this problem by sending his catalog—in the beginning really just a list of items offered with their price—to the local Granges. The first local Granges, founded as the National Grange of the Patrons of Husbandry in 1867, were established as social and educational organizations but rapidly became political organizations for the voice of the Western farmers to protest against the abuses of the day. Ward was familiar with Granges from his sales trips in the farm communities for FLT. Ward encouraged the local Granges to aggregate their members' orders and send a single order to Montgomery Ward, who would ship the order to the nearest rail station c/o the Grange. Since the minimum rail shipping order then was 100 pounds, this aggregation of individual orders minimized the shipping cost to the farmers. The high cost of rail shipments was always a concern to the farmers, both for the things they purchased and for shipping their farm products to markets. The railroads at this time had monopoly control of shipping to and from the rural farms. The farmers, through their Granges, lobbied successfully in 1887 for a federal law establishing the Interstate Commerce Commission (ICC) to regulate railroad shipping rates.

At that time postal mail was delivered only to the nearest post office. Direct rural delivery to the home was years off; free city delivery of mail would come only in 1863. The consumers' cost of mail-ordered items is the sum of the merchants' selling price and the cost of delivery. Even after the ICC had regulated freight rates, farmers complained that they were poorly and expensively served. Merchandise could be shipped by freight at a cost by weight and distance, with a 100-pound minimum charge; by express with one of the many express companies with unregulated rates; and by US Post, with a 4-pound limit. Post was by far the cheapest, but not many orders could meet the low weight limit. And for all three modes of shipment the package was delivered only to the post office or train station. In many communities the rail station was the post office and often the general store as well. If a farmer bought from Ward's, his local merchant and postmaster would know. But farmers often needed credit at the general store to buy essential items before the harvest, and they had reason to worry that buying from Ward's might jeopardize their credit.

The local merchants in the rural communities did not take kindly to their customers going around them to Ward's for dry goods and other staples of farm life, but they could not match the prices offered by Ward. As Ward's volume of business expanded, prices would fall because of Ward's volume discounts from manufacturers. Ward's prices in 1878 were lower than they had been in 1872 (Latham 1972: 10). Every few years the volume of business expanded, forcing Ward to move to ever-larger quarters along with expanded catalog offerings. Ward offered almost everything: from farm machinery, saddles and harnesses, to fine fashions for the ladies. Business grew, and by 1908 Ward's mail-order house in Chicago contained more than 2 million square feet of space, with other service centers in other Western cities.

While Ward's was expanding, competition grew. Sears, Roebuck and Co. grew from Richard Sears's small operation of selling watches to other rail station agents in 1886 into a firm with a large general catalog in 1896. This was also the year that rural free delivery (RFD) was first tried in a few regions of the country on a very limited experimental basis. The sales of both Ward's and Sears were constrained because of the inflated expense of shipping orders to rural customers. John Wanamaker, the famous Philadelphia merchant, appointed Post Master General in 1889 in the Benjamin Harrison administration, tried without success to obtain Congress's approval in 1891 for an expanded RFD. In 1890, 1891, and 1892 Wanamaker (Gibbons 1926: i. 282–3) also sought permission for the Postal Service to offer parcel post, without success.[7] When he was asked: "Mr. Wanamaker, why can you not inaugurate parcels post?" He answered: "There are five insurmountable obstacles: first is the American Express Company; second, the United States Express Company; third, the Adams Express Company; fourth, the Wells-Fargo Express Company; fifth, the Southern Express Company" (Gibbons 1926: i. 283).

Parcels Post became an official activity of the Postal Service only in 1913, with approximately 300 million parcels handled in the first six months. The weight limit was upped from the original 4 to 11 pounds, with increases to 20 pounds soon after (National Postal Museum 2008). The Parcel Post weight limit in 2010 is 70 pounds, but other delivery systems such as UPS allow heavier and larger packages.

The coming of suburban living

With most mail-order delivery problems solved and the US population expanding, the future appeared bright for Ward's and Sears, Roebuck and Co., the two biggest mail-order firms, but a new disruptive technology was already on its way. It was the internal combustion engine and the widespread use of automobiles. Henry Ford alone sold more than 15,000,000 Model T cars between 1908 and 1927, when their production stopped, with most sales going to the home market of 106 million citizens in 1920 to a bit over 123 million in 1930. Few in retailing saw the implications of the automobile and the massive building of local roads. General Robert Wood was one of the exceptions. He joined Ward's in 1919 and quickly was promoted from his initial position of merchandising manager to that of vice president. He was a West Point graduate who had served in the US army quartermaster corps in the First World War and had been promoted to Brigadier General by the war's end. From then on he was called General Wood. He thought strategically about the future of mail-order retailing, observing that, with increases in farm productivity, people were moving to the cities and the suburbs, and that their automobiles enabled them to live in the suburbs and drive to downtown department stores. He believed that people in the cities and suburbs would prefer to shop in retail stores rather than buying by mail. In a retail store they could actually touch the fabric and try on apparel before purchasing, or get the feel of a hammer or wrench. This was not possible in a mail-order-only business.

General Wood was unable to convince Ward's management of the validity of his vision for retail merchandising—Ward's probably believed that it should stick to its core competencies—mail-order retailing. Wood left Ward's in 1924 and went to Sears, first as head of factory operations. Sears's first retail store experiment followed in 1925 and was a huge success, leading to a dramatic expansion of retail stores. By 1928 Sears had opened 192 retail stores, and General Wood was promoted to president. General Wood imagined Sears retail stores would carry both hard and soft goods and be located not in the center of the city but near its perimeter, with easy access by car. He believed that people in the suburbs would always need shoes and hammers. By 1931 Sears had more than 350 retail establishments in addition to its thriving mail-order business. Ward's soon followed the Sears retailing approach and opened its own stores, generally in small towns, but it was never able to catch up with Sears and closed for good in 2001.

Modern Disruptive Technologies

The years of the Great Depression and the Second World War saw a few major changes in retailing technology, linked to the rise of supermarkets and the completely new world of packaged consumer goods and retail hardware these new self-service stores required (see Petrovic, Chapter 3 this volume). But in 1956 two seemingly disconnected events occurred that were to have profound effects on modern retailing and global sourcing of retail products: the inter-state highway system and the shipping container.

The interstate highway system

Certainly, when Congress passed the Federal-Aid Highway Act of 1956, no one could have foreseen clearly the future economic impact of the program that was designed to build 41,000 miles of broad and wide interstate highways. Perhaps President Eisenhower, the strongest backer of the Act, came closest when saying of the highway-building program in his memoirs: "More than any single action by the government...this one would change the face of America...Its impact on the American economy—the jobs it would open up—was beyond calculation" (McNichol 2006: 107). It is now difficult to realize that as recently as 1953 only 53 percent of the 3,000,000 miles of US highways—many just two lanes at best—were paved (McNichol 2006: 103).

President Eisenhower came by his understanding of the importance of paved highways from his long military career. First, in 1919 he was part of a three-mile-long convoy of US Army vehicles—cargo trucks, ambulances, four kitchen trailers, and so on. It was undertaken in July 1919, just after the First World War, to highlight the need for better highways for defense. It took the convoy two months to make the 3,000-mile trip across the country, over half the distance on unpaved roads. Then again in the Second World War, General Eisenhower saw at first hand the value of the Autobahn to the German army. When he became president, he proposed building the interstate highway system as necessary for national defense, a very significant public policy undertaking.

The US Interstate Highway system opened the Midwest and South to road transportation. The original system plan was to link all the state capitals by interstate highways, and in time most were. The interstate highways improved local and state highways, and the expansion of the US fleet of cars and light trucks allowed people living in America to have great mobility. Sam Walton understood this and built his stores on the inexpensive land near local crossroads. He turned rural and suburban locations to his advantage. Governments paid for the roads that brought customers to his doors, and allowed trailer-loads of goods from US and overseas factories to be brought quickly and easily, first to the distribution centers and then on to his stores.

Montgomery Ward in the nineteenth century used the then new disruptive technology of railroads to introduce mail-order retailing and achieve a comparative advantage with the local merchants located at rural crossroads. Then Sears, Roebuck and Co. combined mail-order retailing with urban stores for suburban customers with cars in the 1920s and achieved a competitive advantage over Wards. Sam Walton, after beginning his retailing empire in small rural communities, used the disruptive technology of the US modern highway system to provide low-cost locations that encouraged a range of urban, suburban, and rural customers to drive their cars and light trucks to his stores. Great locations in combination with forward-looking supply-chain practices, advanced technology of distribution centers, mainframe computers, bar codes, and tight inventory control through technology allowed Wal-Mart to grow to be the largest US retailer by 1990. Naturally other factors and business practices were important to the growth of Wal-Mart; we have mentioned only a few of the technological contributors to Walton's success.

Shipping containers

The second great disruptive innovation of 1956 was the birth of shipping with ocean-going containers. There have been articles in our newspapers for decades about the importance of intermodal transportation hubs bringing subway, rail, and surface bus service together at city centers. For the global flow of manufactured goods and produce, the ocean link with rail and trucking has been the most difficult to achieve, and it took most of the post-Second World War era to succeed.

Ocean-going containers, like most technological innovations important to retailing, did not begin with the goal of improving the way goods are shipped across the oceans. Rather, it all began when Malcom McLean, the owner of one of the largest trucking firms in the US in the early 1950s, attempted to find a cheaper way to ship products to New York from the South. Because the Interstate Commerce Commission (ICC) set trucking rates for all firms, a persistent focus on reducing operating costs was a primary path to higher profits and further expansion. In 1953 McLean had the revolutionary idea of sending his trailer trucks from North Carolina to New York and Boston by putting them on old Second World War cargo ships. The ICC had jurisdiction over costal shipping and had allowed shipping rates to be significantly lower than highway trailer shipping because water way shipping was slower. McLean was the only person who saw the value of this rate discrepancy, and he moved to take advantage of it. The Port of New York Authority was looking to expand its activities and welcomed McLean to create a terminal at the Newark docks. McLean first thought to send trailers onto the ships, then trailers without their wheels, and finally special containers designed to allow them to be stacked and lifted from and onto trailers at each end of the sea trip. The first test of this final concept was held in April 1956 with the sailing of a converted Second World War tanker, the *Ideal-X*.

The first voyage was from Port Newark to Houston with fifty-eight containers on board. Special extra-large dockside cranes had to be placed on shore to load and unload the 33-foot containers, but the trip was a great success. And, as Levinson (2006: 52) wrote:

> For McLean, though, the real triumph came only when the costs were tallied. Loading loose cargo on a medium-size cargo ship cost $5.83 per ton in 1956. McLean's experts pegged the cost of loading the *Ideal-X* at 15.8 cents per ton. With numbers like that, the container seemed to have a future.

The entrepreneurial energy, drive, and skill required by McLean to make this into a successful venture is described in detail in Marc Levinson's marvelous, insightful, and heavily documented book, *The Box* (2006).

In 1956 few might have been willing to bet that McLean and others would be able to overcome the objections of the International Longshoremen's and Warehousemen's Union, the various port authorities, the ICC, the railroads, and the local communities that had to allow the huge areas needed for current intermodal port facilities. But succeed they did, and now the biggest ports in the world are no longer London or New York. Singapore, Shanghai, and Hong Kong are the top three in terms of containers handled per year. According to the list of busiest container ports, in 2007 Singapore was reported to have handled 27,000,000 TEUs (20-foot equivalent units).[8]

The two largest US ports, Los Angeles and Long Beach, were numbers 13 and 15 on the list of the busiest container ports in 2007; New York/New Jersey was number 19 with less than 20 percent of the volume of Singapore. The port facilities to handle millions of containers per year can only be called gigantic. The cranes that lift the containers from the ship one at a time must be able to lift the 30,480 kg of a fully loaded container and place it on a trailer that drives on the roadway between the legs of the crane.

In 2008 the largest ship in the worldwide container fleet was the *Emma Maersk*, a part of the Maersk Line fleet.[9] The ship is 397 meters long and 56 meters wide. It can carry 10,500 TEUs, according to the company, but others list the capacity as 15,200 TEUs. The weight of the ship is about 1.5 times the weight of a modern USA aircraft carrier. The ship has 1,000 plugs for refrigerated containers, making it possible to ship vast quantities of meat and produce around the world. This class of vessel expends just 1 kWh of energy to transport one ton a distance of 66 kilometers; a jumbo jet, in comparison, could transport only one ton of cargo 0.5 kilometers on 1 kWh of energy. In other words, the largest and newest ocean-going container vessel is 132 times as efficient in using energy to transport cargo as a modern airplane carrying freight. The ship requires a crew of only thirteen, making the operating cost very low. Worldwide shipment by container continued to expand, rising from 137.2 million TEUs in 1995 to 417 million TEUs in 2006, while the share of shipping to and from the US ports fell from 16.3 percent in 1995 to only 11.1 percent in 2006 (US Department of Transportation 2008).

Railroads, trailer trucks, shipping containers, and standardization

The shipping revolution caused by containers has allowed a corresponding revolution in retail sourcing. The impact on retailing would have been greatly diminished if it were not for the intermodal transportation facilities at major US ports. McLean recognized this at the very beginning of the container revolution in 1956. Port Newark/Elizabeth has rail and road connections, and a part of his original plan was to take his trailers off the ships at the port and put them on the New Jersey Turnpike, at its nearby ramp. Rail connections to Port Newark predated McLean's container activity. In 1953, when McLean was planning at first to ship truck trailers to Newark, he did not consider the Port of New York. Connections to highways from New York City are poor and it takes time to get out of the city, and time is money for shippers using any mode of transportation. For that reason, container shipping is done at Port Newark and at the adjacent Elizabeth Marine Terminal in New Jersey. From the Port, containers can be sent by trucks on the highway or put on special railcars that can carry ISO containers double stacked.

Having containers that meet international standards requires dimensional, strength, openings, and capacity standards. Perhaps the most important standards for container shipping are the details of corner posts, with their special block at each end with holes at specified locations allowing the crane to connect with the container. The ISO corner blocks mean that cranes at container ports anywhere in the world can lower a frame over the container and engage the container after the operator has flipped a switch. Only internationally agreed upon standards make it possible to have ISO containers loaded and unloaded with a standard fixture on the crane. ISO containers can be stacked one upon another with the load properly supported, and shipped double stacked on special low-slung rail cars.

There are other ISO features that allow special forklifts to move containers around in the storage area and to stack them on rail cars. The electrical connections on a refrigerated container must be in the same specified place to allow electrical connection on board ship and on ground transportation. Global transportation requires that containers must be essentially interchangeable in all important features except for the name and identification code painted on the outside. Getting agreement on all these container features took decades of discussion and persuasion. Some firms surrendered patent rights to make it possible for the "best" design to be adopted as the standard. Without standards of both hardware and documentation, the current smooth international flow of goods would not be possible.

Without standards for containers and for communications, the present intensity of international sourcing of products would be unlikely. The international trade agreement worked out under the auspices of the World Trade Organization (WTO) has removed many of the import quotas on entire categories of manufactured products. For example, the WTO trade agreement removed quotas on apparel and textile imports from all WTO member countries on January 1, 2005. With the ISO standards in place for containers, imports into the USA have expanded, despite remaining import tariffs. Exports of textiles and apparel from South Asia flow into the USA on container ships and then move onto railcars or trucks at large intermodal ports. They are carried on trucks to their final destination, most likely on interstate highways. For long-distance shipping, the containers are generally stacked two high on trains. This shipping of goods of all kinds happens without the product being touched by human hands from the factory in South Asia or the farm in Chile to the nearby retail store. The present volume of global product sourcing has been made possible in large part because of international standards of all sorts of systems: hardware, software, electronics, commercial laws, and clear communications back and forth along the entire sourcing channel. International trade benefits from vast prior investments in multi-purpose infrastructures.

Technology and Supply Channels

Bar codes, Internet, lean retailing

We have just described how products can be efficiently shipped from anywhere in the world to retail stores in the USA, but we have not mentioned how the stores are able to manage inventory efficiently and to order products from remote suppliers. The primary tools for modern supply-chain management are products' bar codes, electronic data interchange (EDI), and the Internet coupled with modern computer networks. Again, most of these technologies were not developed for market-making purposes.

The Internet, now an indispensable part of all our lives, was begun in 1969 by the Department of Defense's office of Advanced Research Projects Agency (ARPA) as a project for researchers at one place to communicate with computers at another place. This led to the development of a communication network called ARPAnet. Soon after interconnection was achieved, researchers realized that messages could be sent, resulting in the creation of email. Then, in the span of a few years, methods and standards for transferring files electronically were created and called FTP (File Transfer Protocol) and before that IP (Internet Protocol) and TCP (Transmission Control Protocol). These initials are still with us, and many more have since been added. Researchers created all this to send messages to colleagues who had access to the ARPAnet. In 1986 the National Science Foundation created a high-speed network, first connecting just supercomputers and university sites. In December 2007, there were 383,702,883 Internet users in all of the Americas and 1,408 million users worldwide (Internet World Stats 2008). The Internet became an essential tool of everyday communication in just a decade; now few would willingly give up the Internet.

The development of bar codes has been discussed earlier in this chapter. In this section the focus is not on the role of bar codes at the checkout counter but rather on their unique role in inventory and supply-chain management. As mentioned before, bar codes were slow to diffuse into general retailing for a number of reasons. Chief amongst them were: (1) scanner systems were expensive and suited only for the checkout at supermarkets; (2) there was no incentive for non-food product manufacturers to purchase code identifications and to put the code on each item they made; and (3) general retailers did not at first see any hard savings from adopting bar codes and scanners. These objections were overcome by the willingness of the food product manufacturers, which were a part of the original industrial group, to affix bar codes on their entire product lines. Initially it was Heinz Company's leadership, under the direction of its CEO R. Burt Gookin, who was the chairman of the Ad Hoc Committee that led the development of Universal Product Codes, that assured the cooperation of other food product manufacturers (Brown 1997: 42).

Food markets developed bar codes and scanners to increase the efficiency at the front end of their stores—the checkout counters—and reap hard saving from eliminating the item pricing in the states and communities that allowed simply shelf pricing. Department stores and boutiques did not have checkout counters, but mass merchants such as Kmart and Wal-Mart did. Moreover, mass merchants and department stores faced more daunting inventory tasks than did food stores, because of the low rate of yearly turnover of their inventory. Trying to gain additional control over their inventories, the two Marts were the first to try using bar codes. Their successful adoption and continued advancement of this technology prompted other retailers to follow suit.[10]

The mass merchants had another far-reaching plan to recover the capital cost of the bar-code scanner systems, and that was to shift some of their inventory risk to their suppliers. First Kmart in 1983, and soon after Wal-Mart in 1987, began to demand that their apparel suppliers affix bar codes on each item of apparel they supplied. Naturally, apparel manufacturers objected, saying that they did not need to do it for all of their customers and asking why they should do it for Kmart or Wal-Mart alone. There was the question as to who was going to pay for this new service. The Marts told their apparel suppliers that they, the manufacturers, were going to bear the cost; they must treat it simply as a cost of doing business with them. The Marts were very important and highly valued customers, even though the manufacturers' margins were smaller with them than with their other customers. Manufacturers of branded merchandise and private-label products reluctantly complied, and so mandatory bar coding came first to the apparel retail trade, expanding to other types of goods after that.

Bar codes and retailers' POS data from electronic cash registers made it possible to have accurate real-time inventory status. Inventory control is important for any retailer, but especially for department stores. Food stores might have 40,000 stock-keeping units (SKUs), while department stores might have 500,000 to several million. Macy's on New York City's 34th Street might have two or three million SKUs. The scale of the inventory problem is immense. Great university research libraries might have several million different books or SKUs on their shelves, but for a store it is important to know how many units they have of each SKU. A single volume of a given book is generally enough for a library, but more than one T-shirt of a given size is absolutely essential for the store. To meet expected demand with an adequate number of units across an entire apparel collection is a staggering task. Over 10 percent of material in the classic book on retailing used at the Harvard Business School in the late 1930s is devoted to Merchandise Control (McNair, Gragg, and Teele 1937: 211–62), the term used then for inventory control. If a food store has sold all its cans of a particular kind of soup, it can often get more in the next-day delivery from a chain's warehouse/distribution center, where the necessary inventory of high turnover items is carried for next-day delivery. Most food stores' items outside of produce are, in fact, replenishable items. That is not the case for department stores: only a fraction of their items are replenishable. Before bar codes and lean retailing, a department store might need to carry a substantial inventory of popular basic items such as jeans and underwear on the shelves of the store, in the back room, and in the central warehouse/distribution center. This is no longer the case.

Modern lean retailing requires detailed and complex relationships between a retailer and each of his suppliers of basic items (Abernathy et al. 1999). The retailer's central computer places orders with a supplier's computers on Sunday evening for a specified number of units of each SKU for each store in the area served by that retailer's distribution center. The manufacturer must pick and pack the order for each store, placing the items in a carton for each store, with the correct bar-coded shipping label. The code on the shipping container is a scannable bar code but not in the UPC format. The code on the carton designates the particular store for which it is intended. All the cartons for the many stores are loaded onto a trailer for delivery to the retailer's distribution center. Each distribution center might service 100 or more individual stores.

A trailer backs into a specified loading dock of the distribution center at a time prespecified, to the minute. A portion of the distribution center's power-driven conveyor system extends into the manufacturer's trailer, and the driver unloads the cartons onto the conveyor. As a given carton moves along the power-driven conveyors, laser beams scan the five visible surfaces of the carton looking for the bar code containing the precise code to allow automatic sorting. Gates automatically switch the carton onto the trailer designated for that store. More automated paperwork is actually done than has been just described; for example, there must be an open-to-buy order from the retailer to the manufacturer, etc., before any shipment will be accepted. The checking, verifying, and recording that at one time was all hand paper work is now accomplished with bar codes, laser scans, and computers. Cartons go from the manufacturer's distribution center to the designated store's trailer without human intervention except for loading on and off the conveyor on opposite sides of the distribution center. Products are not stored in a distribution center; rather they are automatically transferred from the supplier trailers to the retailer trailers. A distribution center might have 100 or more docks on each side of a long narrow building; suppliers' trailers on one side of the building and retailers' delivery trailers on the other. Such distribution centers allow supplies to be "cross docked"—to go from the manufacturer's trailer to the appropriate merchant's trailers without human intervention.

Lean retailing and weekly replenishment of the basic items sold during the past week has shifted the risk of carrying inventory that did not sell from the retailer to the manufacturer of basic apparel. Manufacturers in turn minimize their inventory risk by maintaining short supply lines. Consequently most T-shirts, undergarments, and jeans sold in the USA are reorders and assembled in North America, while most fashion garments represent single orders and come from Asia. Communication in this global industry is rarely by surface mail; rather it is done electronically as electronic data interchange (EDI), a vast system of formats for interchanging data electronically.[11] EDI documents generally contain the same information that would normally be found in the paper documents that were used for the same organizational function. For example, an EDI 940 ship-from-warehouse order is used by a manufacturer to tell its warehouse to ship products to a designated retailer. It typically has a "ship to" address, "bill to" address, a list of product numbers (usually UPC codes), and quantities. It may have other information if the parties agree to include it.

EDI and UPC codes avoid the ambiguity and misunderstanding that plagued supply and retail industries before there were codes and electronic communication standards. Although there is one EDI standard in the USA and another internationally, the adoption of standards in general has increased the efficiency of the industry enormously. The old days, before bar codes, are described in the book celebrating the twenty-fifth anniversary of the development of the UPC called *Twenty Five Years behind Bars* (Haberman 2001). A chapter titled "Scanning's Silver Celebration" by John E. Nelson (Haberman 2001: 26–7) describes what it was like for food retailers and manufacturers:

> The retailers do have memories. They remember the armies of stock clerks stamping prices on every candy bar, and then restamping them when the next sale came along—every one of them! They remember the checkout clerks trying to read the handwritten pricing on those packages of T-bone steak, and reading $1.45 instead of $4.45, and losing three dollars on every sale. And they remember taking endless inventories; filling out paper reorder pads so that they'd know how much to reorder; and the huge amount of counting that went on as merchandise was received in the stores. All that tedious effort! . . . And the manufacturers remember. They remember receiving all those paper orders through the mail. Processing the returns and reductions when we didn't ship exactly what the customer had asked

for because we couldn't keep track of all customers' numbering schemes, and we transcribed those orders incorrectly as they came in the door. And remember how difficult it was to track all of the inventory in our warehouses as it was picked and loaded onto our customer's trucks?

New tools for the market makers

At the beginning of the Second World War the federal government encouraged manufacturers to disperse their factory plants as a defense strategy. For strategic reasons, after the war, the US government expanded quotas for textile and apparel products from the low-wage countries of South Korea, Taiwan, Japan, and Hong Kong (but not China.) As described in Chapter 6, business people in these countries took advantage of this opportunity, and in collaboration with retailers they developed the capability of designing and sewing fashion garments for the US market. These countries combined low factory wages with reduced costs of container shipping to create a comparative cost advantage in textiles and apparel. Visionary entrepreneurs of these countries became the new suppliers for buyers from US department and discount stores. They became what are now called "full package dealers." They began by offering to find desired fabric and sewing factories to produce fashion designed in the USA. With the Internet, the details of the complete design with photographs and parts layout were sent instantaneously from the USA to South Asia's full package dealers. The emailed information contained not only pictures of model garments, but also the details of the layout of the individual pattern pieces ready for cutting. The Internet and its associated software created a fully integrated information supply channel (see Abernathy et al.1999: ch. 14, "Suppliers in a Lean World: Firm and Industry Performance in an Integrated Channel," 263–80).

The last piece of information technology integrating the ultimate customers to worldwide markets, and linking manufacturers together with all their vendors, is the World Wide Web. Like most of the technologies mentioned in this chapter, the Web was not invented to help retailers or other market makers. Rather it was invented by Sir (now) J. Timothy Berners-Lee, an English researcher at the European laboratory for particle physics in Geneva (CERN). This Internet-based tool was invented to allow researchers at CERN to share complex files, including hypermedia—that is, text, graphics, video, and so on. Berners-Lee did not file for a patent, making his invention available to all, and this spirit of openness has no doubt contributed to the explosive growth of the Web. He was knighted by Queen Elizabeth II of England for his invention, and in 2007 he received the highest US award for technology, the Charles Stark Draper Prize of the American National Academy of Engineering.

The Internet, along with high-speed broadband communication networks, fast microprocessors, and the software search engines the Internet has spawned—such as Google and Yahoo—allow Internet-users to find very detailed product information before making a purchase. Many websites allow consumers, at their computers, to price-shop branded merchandise at retail, mail-order, and e-commerce stores. Consumers can now look on the Web at manufacturers catalogues, find lost product instruction manuals, and become nearly the economists' old ideal of "the informed consumer."

Most corporations and other organizations worldwide maintain websites to provide information to the public and to allow authorized personnel easy access to proprietary information. The size of the Web is growing with explosive speed, as new uses continue to be developed. You can search the Web to discover the current number of individual websites and find several estimates putting the number over 100 million and the number of individual pages to be several billion. Certainly the market makers described in later chapters all find their activities enhanced by ready access from their computers and cell phones to the ever-expanding Web. Our shopping opportunities have been expanded by the nearly limitless offerings of items, old and new, on eBay or from Amazon.

It is impossible to anticipate what new technology will be developed that will impact retailing, but this chapter gives example after example of technologies developed for one purpose that were later incorporated into retailing. We can, however, confidently assume that new technology will be invented that will change retailing in important ways. New laws will be passed from time to time that impact on retailing in one form or another, and retailers will respond, just as they have in the past. New paradigms of market making will be developed that, like the market makers described in this book, were not on the horizon just a few decades ago. We can be certain only that changes will come.

Part Two
Making Consumer Markets

3

US Retailing and its Global Diffusion

Misha Petrovic

Introduction

In 1953, the Italian business consultant Ezio Diotallevi described to his American colleagues the main reason why the concept of self-service could not succeed in Italy:

> How would our public react to the mute coldness of a [self-service] store in which there is a complete lack of the cordial incentive to buy and the exciting stimulus of discussion and where the psycho-economic aspect of buying and selling is reduced to a dialogue—and a silent one at that—between the buyer and the inanimate goods. (Report on the A.T. 45/157 USA Mission, Sept.–Oct. 1953, 29, quoted in R. T. Davis 1959: 44)

His opinion, apart from its rhetorical flourish, was not unusual amongst West European businessmen and policy experts. The European housewife, they reasoned, would neither put up with the impersonal shopping environment of the American-style supermarket, nor accept standardized, pre-packaged, canned, and frozen items in place of the variety of fresh products available in traditional European stores and open markets (Dunn 1962). Moreover, even if she did want to convert to such an unfamiliar method of buying, this would have had little practical consequence: the lack of the supporting infrastructure, the limited size of retail stores and of living quarters, the low rate of ownership of cars and refrigerators, and the absence of a sizable middle class, all conspired against adopting an American style of consumption.

Only a few years later, in the late 1950s, a "self-service revolution" swept through most of Western Europe. Between 1953 and 1959, the number of self-service stores increased from 229 to 1,663 in France, from 119 to 1,785 in the Netherlands, and from 203 to 17,132 in West Germany (Henksmeier 1960).

Even in Italy, where the adoption of self-service did not take off until the late 1960s, its slow spread could be traced to highly restrictive municipal regulations and the lobbying efforts of small retailers rather than to the alleged lack of acceptance by consumers (Sternquist and Kacker 1994).

> The self-service revolution of the 1950s was not the first time that a marketing concept that originated in the USA spread to Europe. By the beginning of the twentieth century the USA lead in advertising, selling, and other mass-marketing techniques was already obvious to many European observers, and since that time the flow of marketing innovations across the Atlantic has been mostly unidirectional. The elements of American consumer markets were at the same time envied and celebrated, detested and reviled, but most of them eventually found their place in the evolving European consumer society. Only in the years after the Second World War, however, did the US model of consumer society become the obvious and most visible standard of global modernity. The "American way of life," with its emphasis on the mass ownership of cars and appliances and mass consumption of standardized and affordable goods, emerged as the immediate target of modernization efforts for West European nations, and, a decade later, for Japan as well. It also became a major weapon in the Cold-War propaganda, where the deficiencies of the Soviet system were most plainly visible in its failure to deliver attractive consumer goods to its own population, let alone export them to the rest of the world. (M. I. Goldman 1960; De Grazia 2005)

Driven by economic and political reasons, and promoted by a set of government agencies, productivity missions, NGOs, trade associations, and entrepreneurial businessmen, the diffusion of marketing innovations from the USA intensified rapidly during the 1950s and 1960s, transforming Western Europe and Japan into economies of mass consumption and setting tangible standards of development and modernity for developing economies. Along with the new techniques of corporate advertising, brand promotions, direct selling, marketing research, and so on, also came innovations in retail formats. With the exception of the department store, whose early forms developed independently on both sides of the Atlantic, all other major formats that characterize contemporary retailing, from supermarkets, shopping malls, and big-box stores to gas stations, convenience stores, and fast-food restaurants, originated in the USA.[1]

The process of "Americanization" that transformed Western European and Japanese retailing continues even today with the adoption of new waves of retail innovation, the most recent example being e-retailing. It has also spread beyond the small number of developed economies, reaching Latin America, Southern Europe, and the Asian tigers in the 1980s and rapidly becoming global in the 1990s. Indeed, the recent transformation of retailing in China, Russia, South East Asia, and, to a lesser extent, India signifies a whole new stage in the evolution of consumption, since for the first time the majority of the world population has access, though still limited, to the world of modern goods and services.

While the processes of globalization of modern retailing and of the spread of the "American model" have largely been one and the same, they have rarely involved, at least until very recently, direct internationalization efforts by American retailers. Compared to most other sectors, retailing shows a surprising lack of concentration and of the global reach typical of most major multinational firms. Out of the top forty largest retailers in the world, each with annual sales of over $20 billion in 2008, over half operate only in their headquarters' country, or in a small number of neighboring countries (Deloitte 2009). This limited reach is particularly characteristic for US retailers. Fifteen out of the top forty global retailers are headquartered in the USA, but only three of those have operations outside North America.[2] The globalization of retailing, insofar as it involves direct investment and the concomitant replication of stores and concepts by large multinational retailers, is still in its early stages. The story presented in this chapter, accordingly, follows two parallel strands. One of them deals with the global spread of modern, "Americanized" formats of consumer goods markets; the other, with the somewhat limited role that major multinational retailers have played in making and replicating those markets across national and regional borders.

Today, there exists a considerable literature on the globalization of retailing, but most of it is focused either on the internationalization strategies of retail firms or on changes and reactions within national retail sectors. This chapter has a different focus: on how the market-making efforts of retailers transformed consumer goods markets around the world.[3] In line with the rest of the book, it examines those market makers that are commonly described as retailers—that is, those that sell goods and services directly to consumers through owned or franchised outlets. These retailers are the "full package" market makers of consumer goods markets, compared to those engaging in consumer marketing but not operating retail stores, such as many consumer goods manufacturers and brand-name managers, or those selling consumer services but not goods, such as retail banks, hotels, airlines, and amusement parks. The two latter groups are obviously highly visible in the contemporary global economy, contain many of the world's largest firms, and have played a major role in the development of global consumer markets. Despite following only one thread of the overall complex process of making, maintaining, emulating, and replicating consumer markets, limiting one's attention to retailers has a distinct advantage of focusing on the most complex type of such markets, in which selling a wide variety of goods and services is combined with the direct contact with the consumer.

The first part of the chapter describes the emergence and evolution of the standardized "packages" of market mechanisms in the USA. Replication and diffusion of these packages, or retail formats—from the early twentieth-century department store and variety store to the modern shopping centers, superstores and e-retailers—played a major role in creating and organizing the world's most developed system of consumer goods markets. The second part describes four successive waves of the diffusion of those formats outside the USA. The chapter concludes with a discussion of the potential future trajectories of retail globalization.

American Retail Formats

Department stores: the first modern retail format

Modern retailing emerged in the major urban centers of Europe and the USA in the second half of the nineteenth century. The story of its development is inextricably linked to one of the most influential institutions of nineteenth-century capitalism: the department store (Barth 1980; Crossick and Jaumain 1999). Department stores were amongst the largest businesses of the nineteenth century in terms of employment, capitalization, and sales, and certainly the most visible ones, with millions of consumers visiting their downtown stores every day. They were on the forefront of innovation in the use of new technologies, logistics, and management, and their organizational complexity rivaled and often exceeded that of manufacturing enterprises. By their drive to "eliminate the middlemen" and source their merchandise from a broad range of suppliers, department stores effected a substantial reorganization of supplier markets in their main lines of trade, and generated new challenges and opportunities for the small shopkeeper. Yet perhaps their biggest impact was in creating a distinctly modern culture of consumption through putting together a set of new, innovative techniques of selling to the consumer (Hower 1943; M. B. Miller 1981).

DEPARTMENT STORES AS MARKET MAKERS
Amongst those innovations, the most obvious and most frequently noted by contemporaries were new ways of attracting customers. Monumental stores with beautiful window displays, located in central urban districts, invited the consumer to participate in the new spectacle of consumption (Leach 1993). The principle of free entrance, with no obligation to buy, was by itself a major attraction, and was supplemented by aggressive advertising and ostentatious publicity. Once inside the store, the spectacle continued, with marble floors and pillars, archways, rotundas and grand staircases, chandeliers, ornate carpets and decorations, all framing displays of goods meticulously arranged on glass shelves and showcases. Department stores typically spread over several

floors, each divided into numerous departments, and had well-appointed salons, writing and smoking rooms, restrooms and restaurants. They offered, and indeed defined, the setting for respectable middle-class sociability, their leisure and rest facilities inviting a new, relaxed approach to shopping. In contrast to traditional shops, department stores made it possible for a wide range of customers to spend hours browsing goods and comparing prices without having to engage in direct communication with sales clerks or to feel a pressure to buy. This was particularly welcomed by women, who now had a safe and socially approved public space of their own (Rappaport 2000), aptly described as "the ladies paradise" in Émile Zola's eponymous novel *Au bonheur des dames* (1992 [1883]), the first and still the most famous literary celebration of the world of the department store.

The grandeur of the department store's architecture and interiors was matched by the breadth and quality of its merchandise. The second set of distinctly modern mechanisms of selling consumer goods deployed by the department stores dealt with the world of goods, their organization, and their presentation.[4] Most department stores started as drapery stores and gradually expanded their lines to include ready-to-wear clothing, housewares, toiletries, books and stationery, sporting goods, furniture and appliances, fine foods, and so on, until they covered most of the types of consumer goods available at the time. Even in smaller department stores, the breadth and depth of merchandise lines were much higher than in any other type of shop, ranging from handcrafted and imported goods to mass-produced and standardized ones, which were, unlike in traditional bazaars and general stores, systematically organized and displayed in separate departments. Clearly posted prices and accessible merchandise displays allowed shoppers to learn about different goods and judge their value, including a large number of new fashions and new lines of merchandise. Some of the largest department stores supplemented their in-store merchandising with a thriving mail-order business, their catalogs serving as guides to fashion and encyclopedias of modern goods.[5]

Finally, if and when the consumer decided to buy, department stores offered a set of market mechanisms specially geared toward facilitating the transaction. Fixed and posted prices not only reduced the transaction costs associated with bargaining, but also minimized price discrimination and the potential for embarrassment in asking. At the same time, they encouraged budgeting and planning of purchases and eased the comparison between goods. Department stores pioneered modern pricing and price promotion techniques, such as odd number pricing, bargain and clearance sales, multiproduct pricing, and the use of "loss leaders." They had liberal policies of returns and refunds, and often provided services such as wrapping of parcels and home delivery, free of charge (Hower 1943; Pasdermadjian 1954).

Put together, the innovations in these three basic categories of market mechanisms—dealing, respectively, with attracting customers, managing products, and effecting a transaction—defined the department store as the first modern retail format. The debate amongst historians as to who should be credited with creating the first exemplars of such a format has been a long and involved one. Boucicaut's Bon Marché store in Paris, which by the end of the 1850s sold a wide range of goods in separate departments, has often been identified as the first department store (e.g., Nystrom 1917; Pasdermadjian 1954); some American historians have claimed primacy for the New York City's Macy's (Hower 1943) and Stewart's (Resseguie 1965); and others have pointed out to even earlier similar developments in Britain and Japan (Fukami 1953; Hughes 1958). As with most other types of retail formats, the defining features of the department store are a matter of convention, rather than of a clear-cut empirical type, and it has been easy to trace examples of some such features back to the retail environments of the early nineteenth and even the eighteenth centuries (Walsh 1999). At the same time, through the process of mutual borrowing and emulation of successful policies, several typical features of department stores did converge by the late nineteenth century to create the well-defined and recognizable retail format described above.

French department stores, most prominently the Bon Marché whose name was used for numerous stores throughout Europe (as well as in Seattle, USA), but also the Louvre, Samaritaine, and Le Printemps, defined the format for Europeans in the late nineteenth, and often well into the twentieth centuries. American department stores, already the biggest and most successful in the world by the turn of the century, were also often emulated on the other side of the Atlantic and in Japan. After the First World War, in line with the spread of the new American model of organizing business, they also became the main source of innovation in "scientific" selling, personnel training, and management (Chessel 1999). In comparison, British stores were late developers and somewhat less inclined to use the most modern marketing methods, and German, Swiss, and Belgian stores lagged further behind in terms of merchandise assortment and management.[6] But national differences amongst the largest department stores were secondary to their similarities, and the flow of marketing innovations had not yet become as concentrated and unidirectional as it would in the years after the Second World War.

Unlike the supermarket, the gas station, the shopping mall, and the fast-food restaurant, the department store never exemplified the peculiarly American model of making consumer markets. Its role in establishing this model, however, was crucial, as it defined the essential principles as well as major dilemmas of twentieth-century retailing. American retailers applied these principles and tackled these dilemmas faster and more effectively than European ones, and, as a result, the somewhat similar national retailing structures of the early 1900s came to be widely different by the end of the Second World War. Department stores based their success on selling a wide range of goods to a wide range of consumers and making the buying process streamlined and easy. They utilized economies of scale in purchasing, and were ready to experiment with new methods of marketing and management. These features placed them at the center of the movement to create new mass markets for consumption goods and would continue to define such a movement throughout the twentieth century, long after department stores themselves had lost their central position to supermarkets, shopping malls, and big-box stores.

As they evolved from drapery stores to fashion houses to true general merchandisers, department stores managed to redefine the world of goods for their customers. Even if they never truly democratized the world of consumption, as most of their wares were priced out of the reach of most people most of the time, they did democratize the access to the world of goods, through creating new habits of browsing and shopping. In the market based on specialized small shops, where the process of buying was highly interactional, and thus embedded in social custom and status distinctions, the world of goods remained highly segmented. The department store managed to reorganize large parts of this world, putting an ever broader range of goods on the single continuum of affordability. Consumers who would have never dared to enter a piano store or inquire about a price of a cashmere shawl in an upscale specialty shop, could now see pianos and cashmere shawls alongside thousands of other products in the department store, each with a clear and posted price, and contemplate saving for one, especially if they could find them on one of the seasonal sales or clearance events.

THE LIMITS OF THE DEPARTMENT STORE FORMAT

The department store of the early twentieth century, however, also faced two major limits to further expansion. First, not even the largest department store could keep up with the rapidly expanding world of mass-produced and mass-advertised goods. The largest downtown stores of the early twentieth century already had up to one million square feet of selling space, several times as much as today's hypermarkets and only a few percent less than the biggest department stores of today. Urban congestion, the increasing value of downtown property, the unwillingness of customers to go beyond a certain number of floors, all combined to limit further physical expansion. The department store had to become increasingly selective about its merchandise mix, even while trying to maintain its reputation as the general merchandiser. In the process, many department stores, especially the ones that were well established in major urban centers, became increasingly focused on displaying fashion and novelty items and competed with each other less on price and more through offering an ever-expanding range of free services. They took the "high road" that would gradually transform them into high-margin high-service specialty stores, often with many leased departments selling branded goods. This type of retail format would survive throughout the twentieth century, with well-known names such as Macy's and Nordstrom's, Harrods and Debenhams, Galeries Lafayette and Le Printemps, Isetan and Takashimaya still active today, but it will never again play such a central role in consumer goods markets as it did at the beginning of the twentieth century.

The other, "low road," which consisted of selecting a smaller range of cheaper, standardized goods and selling them at low margins but with a high turnover, might have looked much less promising to the established department store operators at the time. Yet, it gradually became established as the core of all developed retailing systems and remains so today, represented by retail giants such as Wal-Mart, Carrefour, and Tesco. In the USA, this path was initially taken by variety stores, such as Woolworth's, Grant's, and Kresge's, and small grocery stores selling packaged goods such as A&P, Kroger, and Safeway; it was then successfully emulated and expanded by "junior" department stores such as J. C. Penney's, and mail-order catalogs turned into store operators such as Sears and Montgomery Ward's.

The secret of these retailers' success was not in their focus on a range of merchandise that was somehow more central and more representative of consumer taste than that of upscale department stores. In fact, such a merchandise mix evolved only gradually and was defined by the main operators' success as much as being the precondition of such a success. Rather, the main advantage of these retailers was in their ability to address the second major limit of the department store expansion: standardizing the market and bringing it closer to the consumer through a rapid replication of outlets. The early twentieth-century US department store was too large, too idiosyncratic, and too embedded in its downtown surroundings to be easily replicated. A few large downtown stores tried to overcome these limits by opening smaller suburban branches. Others financed or acquired department stores in smaller towns. Yet the real success of department store replication had to await the maturation of planned shopping centers in the 1960s, and by that time department stores had already been relegated to a peripheral role in the American landscape of consumer goods markets. In contrast, the ability of the variety and grocery-store operators to replicate rapidly their more modest stores, and thus bring their market format to a much broader range of consumers, enabled them to assume a central place in making consumer goods markets, first in the USA, and then around the world.

Replicating markets: the chain-store revolution

The origins of the chain-store format in American retailing can be traced back to the early 1860s, when A&P (originally The Great American Tea Company, from 1869 The Great Atlantic and Pacific Tea Company) opened a number of stores in New York (Lebhar 1963).[7] In 1900, A&P already operated 200 stores, and by 1910 it had 372. The only other US chain-store operator that reached a substantial size before 1910 was Woolworth's, which operated a large chain of five-and-dime (variety) stores.[8] Between 1910 and 1930, however, the number of chain stores grew at a rapid pace. The 1929 Census of Business reports almost 160,000 chain stores in operation, accounting for almost 11 percent of all retail outlets and 22 percent of sales.[9] These stores had, on average, two to three times larger revenues than their independent counterparts, and 5–10 percent lower prices (Barger 1955). More than 15,000 were managed by A&P alone, which by then had become the world's largest retailer, with more than $1 billion in sales. Other giant chains had developed in variety, grocery, and general-merchandise retailing, but the penetration of the chain-store format was not limited to these sectors. A substantial proportion of sales of apparel stores (28.2 percent), shoe stores (45.6 percent), and home-appliance stores (32.3 percent) was also captured by chain-store operators, which, although not matching the absolute size of industry leaders, were based on the same organizational and marketing principles.

GROCERY CHAIN STORES

In the grocery sector the chain-store format spread early and to a greater extent. In 1929, there were more than 53,000 grocery stores operated by chains in the USA, about 17 percent of the total number of grocery stores in the country, and they captured 39 percent of grocery sales. The chain-store revolution in the grocery sector did not generate as dramatic changes in the context and experience of shopping as the department store had done in the nineteenth century. A typical A&P or Kroger grocery store was cleaner, better lit, slightly larger, more orderly and attractive than its non-chain counterpart, but it was not radically different in its pricing, location, advertising, and product-management policies (Nystrom 1930).[10] Its prices were usually lower than those of its competitors, but it also offered fewer services such as delivery, credit, and telephone orders, and had a more narrow—if well-planned and properly stocked—merchandise assortment. The importance of chain stores for making markets for consumer goods was not in providing brand new types of market mechanisms, but rather in standardizing the existing ones. Chain grocery stores were centrally located, standardized in appearance, merchandise assortment, and selling policies, and able to secure good locations and high coverage density. In 1934, when the total number of grocery chain stores had already somewhat declined from its 1930 peak, there were still 417 A&P stores in Buffalo, NY, 300 in Cleveland, 289 in Newark, NJ, and 104 in Providence, RI, in addition to 695 stores in Chicago and 370 in Detroit. In the same year, Safeway operated 504 stores in Los Angeles, 262 in San Francisco, and 107 in Denver, while American Stores had 721 stores in Philadelphia alone (Zimmerman 1939).

The standardization of chain-store elements and policies was achieved through the weeding-out of unprofitable and badly managed stores as well as through strict operating instructions and manuals and frequent inspection. The importance of standardization can be understood only in relation to the high turnover rates of retail stores in general, and grocery stores in particular. Lebow (1948: 13) estimated that:

> In the first 39 years of this century, some 16 million businesses opened their doors and in the same 39 years, over 14 million closed up. All but a small fraction of these were small businesses and all but a tiny percentage were engaged in distribution. For the past 50 years only seven out of ten grocers have reached their second year and only four out of ten reach their fourth year.

In such a context, the standardization of store appearance and policies of chain stores suggested strength and stability, not only because these stores failed less often, but also because, when they did, they were soon replaced by identical stores in nearby locations.

GENERAL-MERCHANDISE CHAINS

Variety chains evolved from the humble beginnings of small-town five-and-dime stores of the late nineteenth century. In these stores every item cost either 5 or 10 cents, and the assortment depended on whatever bargains the store owner could secure from wholesalers. Catering to the small-town residents and immigrant masses in large port cities, five-and-dime stores became known in the 1880s as the poor person's department stores (Raucher 1991). By the turn of the century, a few of these stores had expanded rapidly by adopting the chain-store format. Woolworth's, the largest such chain, operated more than 600 stores in 1910, and was the second biggest retailer in the nation after Sears. By 1920, most five-and-dime stores (but not Woolworth's) adopted the moniker of "limited price variety stores" as they sold an increasing proportion of higher priced articles. In 1929, 89 percent of the variety-store sales was captured by chain-store operators, with more than half of this accounted for by just two major operators, Woolworth's and S. S. Kresge. Variety stores had a large impact on the reorganization of the world of products. They pushed further the logic of selling "affordables," not just by selling cheap articles but by helping mass consumers recognize an increasing variety of products as affordable and comparable in price. The marketing strategy of the limited price range encouraged frequent shopping, assisted planning and budgeting of purchases, and further streamlined mechanisms of transaction.

Similar to variety chains, but with a distinct assortment of merchandise that emphasized cheap "soft" goods, was J. C. Penney's. James Cash Penney, the founder of the store, opened his first cash-only dry goods store named Golden Rule in 1902 in Kemmerer, WY, a mining town of 1,000 residents (Mahoney and Sloane 1966). The company changed its name to Penney's in 1912, and rapidly expanded throughout Western mining and agricultural towns. In 1929, there were 1,395 Penney stores with combined sales of $210 million, yet the chain retained its small-town orientation—more than half of its stores were in towns of 5,000 or fewer people (Raucher 1991).

The variety store, and the "junior department store" such as Penney's, successfully combined a relatively broad range of general merchandise with quick replication of markets. Their experience certainly helped two retail giants of the time—Sears and Montgomery Ward's—to branch out from a mail-order catalog business into store retailing. They were forced to do so by the limited expansion opportunities in the shrinking rural markets they catered to. Sears started opening several categories of general-merchandise stores in 1925, some almost as large as a department store, some as small as a typical variety store; Ward's followed in 1926 (Hoge 1988). The efficient purchasing operations, warehousing, and logistics system serving their existing mail-order operations, and the well-established brand name, eased the transition to store-based retailing, and by 1930 Sears derived a majority of sales revenue from its 350 stores (Emmet and Jeuck 1950). The merchandise mix, however, was difficult to establish and manage, and both companies spent the best part of the interwar period honing their store retailing skills.

CAR DEALERS AND GAS STATIONS
While the impact of the chain-store revolution on grocery and general-merchandise sectors is well established, its impact on the buying of cars and gasoline, the two main new consumer products of the first half of the twentieth century, is rarely addressed in the same vein. Yet the problems facing market makers in markets for cars and gasoline were quite similar to those facing market makers in markets for groceries, apparel, and appliances (T. G. Marx 1985; Dicke 1992). Mass manufacturers of cars faced an inefficient, traditional distribution system, dominated by wholesalers, and attempted to reorganize it through integrating forward into distribution and marketing. They needed a large number of marketing outlets, and the rapid expansion of these outlets created major financial, organizational, and logistics problems. The number of car dealerships expanded quickly in the 1920s, peaked around 1930, and then gradually declined. A few major operators controlled most of these dealerships and were responsible for the standardization of their

features. A similar process can be observed in the gasoline industry, with an exception that the peak in the number of outlets was not reached until the late 1930s.

Despite the legal differences that separate the franchise system, such as Ford's or Shell's, from the chain-store system of fully owned outlets, such as Sears's or A&P's, the similarities in their organizational development are obvious, and the simultaneity of this development striking. Moreover, the fully owned retail chains and the franchised dealership systems were more similar during the 1920s than ever before or since, since the former had rather less control over their outlets, and the latter rather more, than in the later period. The main distinction between the two types of "chain systems" was not so much in the organization of their operations, as in their basic merchandising strategies. The chains controlled by mass retailers were inherently multi-product markets, and the increase in the average number and breadth of products they carried continues to the present day. The mass-manufacturer-controlled chains, on the other hand, emphasized only a narrow line of technologically similar or purchase-complementary products, and the general tendency has been toward standardizing this line around a single major brand.

THE FRANCHISE BOOM: CONVENIENCE STORES,
FAST-FOOD RESTAURANTS, AND MOTELS
While manufacturer-organized franchises dominated the early years of franchising, the 1930s saw a rapid spread of the business model into retailing and food service. From Rexall drugstores and Ben Franklin variety stores to Howard Johnson and Dairy Queen ice-cream parlors, franchised outlets were becoming increasingly common in America's pre-Second World War consumer markets. However, the real franchising boom occurred in the early post-war period, with Dairy Queen (1945), McDonald's (1954), KFC (1954), Best Western (1946), Holiday Inn (1952), and similar franchisors transforming the food service and hospitality industries (Jakle, Sculle, and Rogers 1996; Jakle and Sculle 1999). Their strategy was similar to the one that drove the earlier franchise efforts: combining a narrow line of products (goods and/or services), tightly controlled through branding and standardizing, with a rapid replication of consumer markets.

Franchising was also the key to the success of the Southland Corporation, with its chain of 7-Eleven convenience stores. Southland began experimenting with franchising in 1963, rapidly expanding from a regional chain of 1,000 stores to a national network of more than 3,500 stores in 1969. It also played a major role in bundling the convenience store and the gas station in the late 1960s, thus developing another major format of the US retail landscape (Sparks 1996).

THE CHAIN-STORE AGE

By 1930, it was clear that American retailing had entered the "chain-store age" and that its future lay in the hands of big corporations (Lebhar 1963). The big retailers benefited from the economies of scale in management, distribution, and retail services and were best positioned to implement organizational innovations that drove down operating expenses. Their massive buying power enabled them to obtain discounts on quantity buying, as well as tax breaks and the financial backing of Wall Street. For manufacturers, especially smaller ones that did not attempt to integrate forward into wholesaling (or direct selling), these large retailers represented efficient and predictable channels of distribution. The prevalence of chain-store operators in large sectors of consumer markets also meant that marketing innovations could be adopted and diffused quickly, thus unifying and standardizing previously segmented markets.

Many firms that developed a successful strategy of replication in this early period remained dominant in US retailing throughout the rest of the century. Three of these, Kroger, Safeway, and Acme Markets (American Stores, Albertsons) are large grocery chains, and another two, Sears and J. C. Penney, were amongst the first chain-store operators in the general-merchandise sector. Kmart traces it origins to Kresge, another major variety chain of the early part of the century. The main new entrants between 1930 and 1990 on this exclusive list were department store chains, Federated, Allied, May, and Dayton Hudson (the parent of Target), indicating the somewhat later development of the chain-store format in this sector. Perhaps even more striking than the longevity of large retail chain-store operators is the fact that today five out of the ten largest US companies (and eight out of the top ten global ones) are car makers and oil companies, just as they were in the 1920s, when they adopted their own franchised version of the chain format.[11]

The American model: supermarkets, shopping malls, and big-box stores

From the consumer's perspective, the chain stores of the 1930s remained quite different from the chain stores the US consumer patronizes today. They were small, with a somewhat haphazard and narrow assortment of products, and they allowed the consumer only a limited access to merchandise, which was displayed behind the counters and handled by store clerks. As long as the merchandise assortment remained limited and purchasing habits and interactions standardized by local customs, this was rarely seen as a problem. Yet the next transformation of consumer goods markets depended on successfully combining the principles of large size and easy access to a broad range of products, as pioneered by the department store, with fast replication and centralized control skills of the chain-store operators.

By the early 1960s, the main elements of this transformation had been established in American retailing, creating a set of retail formats that, in most aspects, would be recognizable today. Small chain grocery stores were replaced by large, self-service supermarkets. Large planned shopping centers offered a proper home to both general merchandise and specialty chain-store operators, and gave a new lease on life to the department store. And, some of the most successful general merchandisers and specialty-store operators that did not participate in the shopping-center boom developed the free-standing big-box store format. Apart from their differences, all three formats were based on combining strategies of scrambled merchandising, a dramatic increase in size, and simplification and standardization of the selling process, most notably through "self-service." All of them were also highly replicable and, as they spread throughout the American landscape, they for the first time crossed that critical threshold at which there were enough modern retailers in contact with each other to assure rapid adoption of innovations.

THE RISE OF THE SUPERMARKET

In 1930, the average chain grocery store in the USA was three times larger than an independent one. In 1960, the ratio increased to ten to one. Throughout this period, A&P remained the world's biggest retailer, and one of the world's biggest companies of any kind. A typical A&P store of 1960, however, bore little resemblance to its 1930 ancestor. The number of A&P stores declined during this period from almost 16,000 to 4,400, while the sales per store increased ten times in constant dollars (Zimmerman 1955). The force behind this transformation was the new retailing format that emerged during the early 1930s: the supermarket.

While the first grocery stores that arguably could qualify as "supermarkets" were opened in the 1920s in California and Texas, by operators such as Ralph's, Alpha Beta Food, and Weingarten's, it was the phenomenal success of the New York-based King Cullen (1930) and Big Bear (1932) stores that started the national supermarket revolution (Zimmerman 1955; Longstreth 1999). Their success paved the way for other independent supermarkets, and between 1932 and 1937 their number grew from 300 to more than 3,000, and their presence from 6 to 47 states. At this time, large grocery chain operators, such as A&P, Safeway, and Kroger, started converting their stores into supermarkets, and by 1953 supermarkets had become the dominant force in grocery retailing. A survey in this year found 17,500 supermarkets, about 6 percent of the total number of grocery stores in the USA, capturing 48 percent of total grocery sales (Zimmerman 1955). By 1960, the number of supermarkets was reaching its saturation point of about 30,000, as they captured almost 70 percent of all grocery sales. Within thirty years, the format went from a few independent suburban stores to capturing most of the sales in the biggest retail sector (Bucklin 1967).

The supermarket format spread faster and more intensely than any type of consumer goods market did before. One of the secrets of its success was in its high replicability. Once big chain-store operators entered the field, it became clear that, despite the relatively high set-up costs of opening a supermarket, the format was fairly easy to replicate, to a large extent because of its self-service character. Despite the common preconception, supermarkets did not employ significantly fewer employees than regular grocery stores, controlling, of course, for difference in size. The main reason was that the new technology of self-service, while requiring less labor directly employed in sales, initially demanded more labor for stocking, pricing, arranging displays, and so on. These functions, however, could be more easily rationalized than the diffuse competences of a grocery clerk, and their performance depended less on acquired skills and experience. Finding thousands of competent store managers was a daunting task for large chain-store operators, and making them follow the company's policies was even more difficult (Adelman 1966). The transition to the supermarket format reduced the number of stores, and greatly rationalized and standardized their operating procedures.

THE DEPARTMENT STORE FOR FOOD

From the consumer's perspective, the attraction of the supermarket was easy to understand. The typical 1950s supermarket was a very large, well-organized, brightly lit store, in a convenient location and with ample parking space, which carried a broad selection of various merchandise at fairly low prices. In this sense it represented, rather directly, an application of the early department store format to grocery retailing, offering one-stop shopping for necessities. Just as department stores did in the late nineteenth century, the supermarket of the late 1930s provided a novel context of consumption, with open display shelves, large open refrigerated cases, standardized price tags, clear and broad walkways, shopping carts, and cash registers. Most of the equipment used by supermarkets was new and designed specifically for self-service selling. This also required a new store layout. Ideally, the supermarket operator wanted customers to pass all displays before they reached the cash register. Early marketing research in supermarkets revealed the importance of "impulse buying"—that is, of various types of purchases on which the customer decides while in the store.[12] This opened up a whole new realm of marketing efforts that, not unlike those in the department store, relied on displays, signs and cues, merchandise arrangement, and store layout to induce the consumer to buy a greater variety of goods and in greater quantities than ever before.

Given their self-service nature, supermarkets provided a particularly fitting laboratory for observing consumer behavior. An early study, for example, noticed the shoppers' tendency to move along the periphery of the market, "like mice scurrying along the walls;" another observed that most customers gravitate toward the right side of the market (Zimmerman 1955). Different layout plans, from radically arranged aisles to placing promotions and "pure-impulse" items in the front of the store, were designed to respond to, as well as to modify, observed consumer behavior.

Supermarkets were also amongst the biggest advertisers of this period. The low price appeal of the first supermarkets was supported by their heavy emphasis on price advertising in local newspapers. By the early 1950s supermarkets were not only by far the largest category of retail advertisers, but their total advertising outlays exceeded those of all national food manufacturers—themselves the heaviest brand advertisers of all industries—combined (Zimmerman 1955). The parallel between early supermarkets and early department stores could also easily be drawn in regard to their promotion strategies. On a smaller scale than the department store, but with the same intent and often with the same zeal, supermarkets organized contests and promotions, free giveaways, and public events such as parades and concerts; some of them even housed art exhibitions and public-library branches on the premises.

SCRAMBLED MERCHANDISING AND PRODUCT MANAGEMENT
The organization of the supermarket also had a major influence on the nature of the products stocked. Self-service shopping required products that are properly and attractively packaged and clearly labeled. Such products—mostly canned, bottled, and packaged groceries but also increasingly toiletries and household goods—had been available from manufacturers and sold in grocery stores since the early years of the twentieth century (Tedlow 1990; Strasser 1995). Many of them, however, had to be adapted for self-service selling—packaged in different sizes and with more attractive labels including more information and advertising on the packaging. Moreover, since supermarkets included a much wider range of products than other grocery stores (typically meat, produce, dairy, and frozen foods departments, but also drugs, house-wares, bakery and delicatessen, magazines, toys, and stationery), they exerted pressure on a broad range of consumer goods industries to create new products that were ready for the self-service-style selling.

Early independent supermarkets often sold a variety of non-food merchandise, typically in leased departments. Big Bear, for instance, sold auto accessories, paints, radios, hardware, drugs and cosmetics, and operated a soda fountain and a small restaurant. Large chains generally eschewed such a haphazard strategy of scrambled merchandising, and refused to rely on concessionaire or leasing arrangements. Nevertheless, they also pursued expansion into non-food lines, if much more cautiously. Health and beauty aids, magazines, books and stationery, toys, soft goods, housewares, and cleaning products, all found their way into supermarkets in the 1930s and 1940s, and in 1954 a study of non-food merchandising found the majority of supermarkets carrying extensive lines of these products (*Super Market Merchandising* 1954).

SELF-SERVICE AS SELF-SELLING

In addition to size, location, and store appeal, and the breadth of the merchandise mix, the supermarket's other major draw for the consumer was its emphasis on self-service. The idea of a self-service grocery store had been tried to some degree many times before, most famously in Clarence H. Saunders's franchised Piggly Wiggly stores.[13] The synergies achieved by combining the self-service format with store size and a broad merchandise assortment surprised even the most enthusiastic early operators of supermarkets, let alone the more conservative chain-store operators. The less sales service they were offered, and the greater the variety of merchandise, the more consumers bought on each trip to the supermarket. And this rule held for non-food as much as for food items, for packaged articles as much as for produce, and even, as A&P and Safeway were soon to find out, for store brands as for nationally advertised ones. At the beginning of the supermarket development it was often assumed that the success of self-service represented little more than the trade-off consumers were willing to make between retail service and low prices. Only gradually did it become clear that, for most customers, self-service meant better service. Early surveys of consumer behavior show that the freedom from high-pressure selling and the "leisure of choice" figured quite prominently in consumers' preference for shopping at supermarkets (Regan 1963; Bucklin 1972). Shorter queues were another major advantage of the supermarket. Although initially viewed with suspicion, by the late 1930s self-service was already considered a convenience, rather than a matter of necessity, and was featured prominently in supermarkets' advertising (Zimmerman 1955).

The adoption of self-service signified the transition from the focus on interactional aspects of selling, defined as a diffuse set of retail services provided by store clerks, to a focus on creating and improving the features of the marketplace. Now to a large extent it was the consumer who performed traditional "selling services" for herself, searching for products, and comparing their prices, quality, and characteristics; yet these activities were performed in a new type of market structure defined and controlled more than ever by the retailer. The commitment to the self-service format also led supermarkets to reorganize the physical aspect of the store—the architecture, signs, entrances, fixtures, displays, shopping carts, checkout points, and so on—in a way that would be emulated by most "discount" retailers. In this context, the rise of general-merchandise discounters in the USA, from the early leaders such as Korvette and Vornado, to the 1960s creations such as Kmart, Target, Woolco, and Wal-Mart, represented little more than an adaptation of supermarkets' retailing strategies to an assortment of products—apparel, luggage, home furnishings, toys—traditionally sold in department stores (McNair and May 1976).

THE MALL

Shopping centers may be the most ubiquitous aspect of the contemporary retail landscape in the USA. Loosely defined as clusters of retail stores, planned, owned, and managed as a unit, they capture more than half of all non-automotive retail sales and employ one in every fifteen Americans (Cohen 2002). Depending on the definition, there were anywhere between 60,000 and 100,000 shopping centers in the USA in 2008, ranging from small-scale neighborhood centers (strip malls) to super-regional malls often exceeding a million square feet of retail space. Although the history of planned retail centers in the USA goes back to the late 1920s, the shopping center boom that would transform American retailing started only in the mid-1950s, and was closely related to the government tax policy (the Accelerated Depreciation Act of 1954), making development of large centers a particularly attractive business proposition for real-estate developers, including the financial giants such as Prudential and Equitable (Hanchett 1996, 2000). In 1955, there were still only about twenty large regional shopping centers in the USA, all of them of the open-air variety. In 1956, Victor Gruen built the first fully enclosed shopping mall, Southdale near Minneapolis, which featured what was to become the classic mall format with two department stores as anchors and a two-level parking space (see Hardwick 2004). By the end of that year the number of large centers in operation had more than doubled. Ten years later, there were nearly 400 such shopping malls in the USA, and "the mall" as the largest, most visible, and, arguably, most innovative shopping-center format had become not only the favorite leisure destination for most Americans but also a new form of community center for suburbs and small towns.

The interaction between large institutional investors, enterprising developers, and major chain-store operators brought about the standardization of the development process as well as of the shape of America's new marketplaces. For enterprising retailers in all major sectors, this offered vast opportunities for expansion with advantages of modern infrastructure, on favorable lease terms, and in environments more hospitable than traditional downtown shopping districts. At the same time, the growth opportunities created by new shopping centers were clearly stacked in favor of large stores over the smaller ones, and chain-store operators over the independents.

In terms of the structure and performance of the American retailing sector, the rise of the shopping mall had three major effects. First, it gave a new lease on life to the declining department store sector of the 1950s, and led to a major organizational transformation and growth of chain department store operators such as Allied, Federated, and May Department Stores. Second, it led to the rapid growth and merchandise assortment upgrading of the so-called mass merchandisers, Sears and Penney's and, with somewhat less success, Ward's. These two categories of general-merchandise retailers became major innovators in customer service, including store organization and displays, advertising, and consumer credit; as well as in inventory management and organization of supply chains. They also played an instrumental role in shaping the discount sector after 1960, both as entrepreneurs (for example, Dayton Hudson's Target, J. C. Penney's Treasure Island) and as organizational models. Moreover, they became the pioneers in the creation of global supply chains, by opening a number of purchasing offices in East and South East Asia, starting from the late 1960s (Hollander 1970; Gereffi 1994b). Finally, the expansion of the shopping mall also provided a major opportunity, mainly from the mid-1970s, for the rapid expansion of innovative apparel retailers such as Gap and The Limited, and for many other types of specialty chain retailers.

On the consumer side, shopping malls provided new marketplaces where one could enjoy the convenience of easy access, ample parking space, and comparison shopping. The ultimate triumph of scrambled merchandising, shopping malls represented an expansion of the traditional downtown department store, with a similar emphasis on fashion and home furnishings combined with various services. Yet they had major advantages over the chaotic and often rapidly declining downtown areas. The mall was a controlled, secure, climatized, and clean shopping environment. Parking and store access was easy, the interior design unified and full of visual clues, from lighting to store signs, that encouraged spending. Grouping similar stores together facilitated comparison shopping, and various entertainment, food, and services venues made the shopping trip more enjoyable.

THE BIG-BOX STORE

Large "regional" shopping malls were the most visible and attractive parts of the new retail landscape, but they captured only about one-third of the shopping center sales. The rest went to smaller neighborhood and community shopping centers. The former were typically anchored by a supermarket or a drugstore, the latter by a junior, or discount department store. Discount department stores, such as Kmart, were a format that evolved from the 1950s hard-good discounters, such as Korvette and Vornado, that sold a limited line of national brands merchandise below the manufacturer recommended list price. During the early 1960s, many major chains, most of them department or variety store operators, entered the ranks of discounters. In 1962 alone, more than twenty retail chains started discount operations, prompting *Fortune* magazine to publish a comprehensive study of the new trend, spanning four issues of the magazine and titled "The Distribution Upheaval" (Lebhar 1963). As the leaders in cost-cutting and labor-saving innovations that passed a considerable share of those savings on to the consumer, discounters were a highly undesirable competition to established department stores, and the latter often used their clout to ban the "price cutters" from shopping malls. This led to the development of the standard free-standing big-box store, oftentimes loosely incorporated into a roadside shopping center, along with a few smaller service and retail shops.

On the consumer side, the format itself was hardly new; in fact, it represented little more than the application of the supermarket model to non-grocery retailing. What was new, however, and what paralleled the other two massive transformations of American consumer markets brought about by supermarkets and shopping centers, was how rapidly the discounting format was adopted in the broadly defined general-merchandise sector and also how rapidly, once the adoption had reached critical mass in the early 1970s, those new discounters emerged as the leaders in technological and market-making innovation. By 1990, the Big Three of the general-merchandise discounters, Wal-Mart, Kmart, and Target, had joined the exclusive list of the top ten US retailers. The following year, Wal-Mart surpassed Sears as the largest American retailer, only the third retailer in eighty years to occupy that spot.

By the late 1960s, the American system of consumer goods markets was beginning to approach the degree of concentration of major chain-store operators that would make the rapid diffusion of market innovations possible. At the same time, the absolute size of the market ensured that few chains had nationwide presence and that there was little direct competition between major operators. In 1991, when it became the biggest retailer in the world, Wal-Mart still operated in only twenty-eight US states, and almost exclusively in small towns (Vance and Scott 1994). Major supermarket operators also remained mostly regional, the revenue share of the top twenty firms in grocery retailing approaching 50 percent only by the end of the century. This situation created little pressure on American retailers to pursue international expansion; it also enabled the most efficient retailers to grow very fast, as they wrestled the sales out of the hands of the least efficient competition first. In 1967, chain stores captured just under 50 percent of the total retail sales in general merchandise and food. By 2002, this figure had risen to nearly 80 percent. Yet the sales share of the ten largest US retailers rose only slightly in the same period, most of this increase being due to the phenomenal growth of Wal-Mart, thus indicating that a fairly large number of chain retailers managed to grow at the expense of traditional stores.

US consumer goods markets, 1970–2010

The post-1960s trends in making mass markets for consumer goods in the USA could be seen as the continuation and maturation of retail format innovations from the previous period, rather than as radically new developments.[14] The elements of the big-box, self-service marketplace developed by supermarkets and big-box discounters, had, by the early 1980s, diffused into most categories of merchandising. Discounters established themselves as the dominant type of retailing format, in fact so successfully that by the late 1980s the notion of discounting lost any distinct meaning and was replaced by notions such as "everyday low price," on the one hand, and "off-price" and "deep discount-ing," on the other. New discounting formats such as off-price retailers, ware-house clubs, and limited price (dollar) stores joined the general-merchandise discounters of the 1960s (*DSN Retailing Today* 2002). The big-box retailing concept was successfully applied to specialty retailing, first in clothing, toys, and electronics, and then in office products (including computers), home improvement stores, sporting goods, and other categories. At the same time, the general trend toward scrambled merchandising in what was increasingly referred to as "fast-moving consumer goods" led to further blurring of retail categories. Supermarkets and drugstores, warehouse clubs and general mass merchandisers all developed overlapping merchandise assortments geared toward one-stop shopping and convenience.

Shopping centers continued to expand their presence, got even bigger, moved back to long-neglected downtown retail cores, and added an increasing number of side attractions. By the late 1980s, the emergence of outlet malls and power centers indicated further convergence between the big-box store and shopping center concepts. The introduction of self-service in gasoline retailing in the late 1960s started a new trend of integrating convenience stores and gas station formats. In such outlets, gasoline retailing provided minimal margins but major drawing power, and the real profits were derived from the sales of convenience goods.

In the most recent decades, perhaps the biggest transformation of the US consumer market landscape was effected by the emergence of Wal-Mart's supercenters in the 1990s. Those giant stores for the first time successfully combined retailing of groceries and general merchandise. Such a late adoption of this integrated format, compared to the European-style hypermarkets, was, somewhat paradoxically, due to the higher level of development of American consumer markets. Many original hard-good discounters of the 1950s had leased grocery departments; a few supermarkets experimented with an extensive range of non-food products as early as the 1930s. Various "combo" stores, some even larger than today's Wal-Mart supercenters, had been tried throughout the postwar decades, but few of them survived, Portland's Fred Meyer (merged in 1998 with Kroger) being one of the most successful ones. The size of the world of consumer products in the USA, and the high level of development of various retail formats, made it extremely difficult to find a proper merchandise mix that would encourage one-stop shopping and yet would not appear too narrow and too random.

Wal-Mart succeeded where most of its predecessors failed, partly because it could already count on customer loyalty, being the biggest retailer in the USA, and partly because of its strategy of placing its stores in smaller towns and suburbs, where the competition was weaker. In only fifteen years, between 1991 and 2006, the number of Wal-Mart supercenters went from 6 to almost 2,000, and they captured over 10 percent of all non-automotive retail sales in the USA. The rapid ascendance of Wal-Mart supercenters, as well as of similar stores by Target, and warehouse clubs by Costco and Sam's Club (operated by Wal-Mart) brought about the integration of the general-merchandise, specialty retailing, grocery and drugs sectors, changing the nature of retail competition in the USA. The consolidation in these sectors left only a handful of major competitors with a lion's share of the market.

American Retail Formats: The Waves of Diffusion

American retail formats developed in the context of the overall system of consumer markets and marketing, and, even more broadly, in the context of the evolution of the American consumer society. While this process was, to a great degree, independent from retail developments elsewhere, it was also shaped by the general evolution of the American economy and its position in the world economy. In retrospect, the adoption of American retail formats around the world, in different socioeconomic contexts and with little direct internationalization effort of American retailers, has been quite remarkable. Whether this process should be described as one of Americanization or modernization seems less important than the fact that it was typically not a consequence of other elements of the economy and society achieving a certain level of development, and then, in turn, providing the basis for retail innovations. Rather, new consumer goods markets were often introduced directly into the traditional fabric of the economy. They had major disruptive effects on such a fabric and, at the same time, played a catalytic role for the development of other modern economic institutions.

While the consequences were revolutionary, the process itself has been quite gradual. Until just two decades ago, only a minority of the world population had access to modern consumer markets, and even today there are few retailers that have a truly global reach. The reasons for this relate to the complexity of consumer goods markets. In general, the more complex markets, in terms of numbers and diversity of products (goods and services, and the ways to combine them), trading partners, and transaction mechanisms, are more difficult to emulate and replicate. Consumer goods markets, given that they involve complex packages of goods and services, many diverse trading partners, and disparate transactions, are typically more difficult to replicate than business-to-business markets, those for services only, and those where transactions are few and highly standardized.

Within the overall process of the global diffusion of modern retailing practices, there are several distinct types. The diffusion of separate market mechanisms or marketing techniques is the most common one, and the easiest to achieve. The departmental organization of a large store, the concept of self-service, centralized checkouts and cash registers, and online browsing for consumer goods, are all examples of some elements of consumer goods markets that have traveled exceptionally well. The diffusion of full retail formats has also been widespread, but until recently limited to simpler markets, such as those for fast food, cars and gasoline, or luxury items. Within these categories of goods, the firms that tightly control product management in supply markets, through branding, design, and even through performing manufacturing activities, are typically in a better position to replicate consumer markets for their products than the firms that engage exclusively in retailing. Yet their growth is also limited by the scope of their merchandise assortment. On the other hand, the firms that sell many different types of products not only cannot afford to organize the production and design of all such products, but are also limited by the difficulties of replicating retail outlets. The process of the international adoption of the supermarket format, described in the following sections, provides a good example of the difficulties and obstacles related to emulation, let alone replication, of more complex market formats.

The process of internationalization, understood as the replication of outlets in another country, is another type of diffusion of modern retailing, and it presents additional problems to the retailer. Amongst those, the differences between national "consumer cultures," while often highly visible, might not be the most significant factor. Regulatory contexts, organization of supplier markets, and the increased complexity of organizational structure and management are typically more important.

The aggregate result of the diffusion and replication of market mechanisms and formats by many individual retailers is the emergence of local systems of consumer goods markets. Such systems do not always, or even commonly, emerge at the national level, although governments' regulatory efforts and the way in which official statistics are generated, suggest that this is the case. More commonly, the diffusion, replication, and competition processes are local, or subnational, and sometimes they are transnational or even global in character. The process of forming such systems of consumer goods markets is initially limited to the emergence of a few modern firms that deploy and promote modern retailing methods. Once these firms reach a certain critical size and visibility, the recognition and subsequent diffusion of best practices between firms is accelerated and the formats standardized. Center–periphery structures emerge to channel the flow of innovation to other areas and less innovative firms. Direct competition between leading retailers usually develops quite late, but has major consequences in terms of the integration of the market system. Competitive threats, whether actual or potential, lead not only to the further standardization of most successful formats, but also to the proliferation of complementary formats—that is, to formats that support and co-evolve with each other. Thus the rise of large suburban supermarkets may encourage the development of a dense network of small convenience stores, one-stop shopping co-evolves with fast-food chains, and so on.

The first wave, 1900–1945: limited diffusion

By the opening decades of the twentieth century, the USA had already established itself as the economic role model for the rest of the world. While European and Asian observers were initially fascinated mostly by American techniques of mass production and scientific management, the methods of what was increasingly referred to as "distribution" were also observed and emulated. Before the Second World War, the spread of knowledge about the US retailing models went mainly through informal channels, from the individual entrepreneurs' visits to the USA to transatlantic networks of department stores operators. Occasionally, an accomplished American retailer would move to Europe, bringing about new marketing methods. Perhaps the most famous example of this was that of Gordon Selfridge, who was the leading man of Chicago's Marshall Fields, the largest department store in the world, when in 1906 he decided to move to London. There he opened an American-style department store, introducing modern advertising and merchandising methods, which were then rapidly adopted by his more established West End competitors (Honeycombe 1984; Rappaport 1995). Even more exceptional were direct attempts to replicate American retail formats abroad, the only prominent example being Woolworth's variety stores in the UK (from 1909), and Germany (1927).

During this period the adoption of American retailing methods was typically limited to separate market mechanisms and techniques within the general department store format. By the end of this period, department stores were present in most of Western and Central Europe, in Japan, China, and Australia (MacPherson 1998; Coles 1999; Crossick and Jaumain 1999; Miller and Merrilees 2004). The Soviet Union also had its GUM department stores from 1921 on, and there were many outposts and emulations of metropolitan department stores, catering to colonial elites in far-reaching corners of colonial empires, from South Africa to Iraq to Singapore (Hollander 1970). Diffusion and borrowing were ubiquitous: Tokyo's Mitsukoshi store was modeled on Philadelphia's Wannamakers, Hong Kong and Shanghai department stores owned by Chinese entrepreneurs were based on British stores in China and American in Hawaii (Moeran 1998; Yen 1998). In many non-Western stores, most of the merchandise originally came from the West. However, as one of the dominant symbols of modernity of that era, the department store lent itself well to appropriation by diverse modernization projects, including anti-Western ones. Sun Yat Sen saw Chinese department stores as an important part of the project of national renewal (Young 1998), and Soviet GUMs were expected to assist the goals of socialist revolution (Hilton 2004). Department stores everywhere showcased the world of modern consumer goods. In many places, they also acted as major agents of change in the broader system of consumer goods markets. Such a role, however, was always limited to major urban centers by the difficulties of replicating the department store format.

At the same time, the typical chain store of the time, just as in the presupermarket era in the USA, remained small and unexceptional from the consumer standpoint, despite having a major role in reorganizing and modernizing supply chains. Chain grocery stores were quite common in Britain in the late nineteenth century, and the development of "multiple shops" there was, in fact, ahead of the USA (Jefferys 1954). However, one particular type of the chain store, the "limited-price" (five-and-dime) variety store, was recognized everywhere as an American invention and was consciously emulated in Europe. Variety stores spread quickly to Britain, where Woolworth's operated after 1909 and Marks and Spencer had "penny bazaars" from the 1880s. In continental Europe they were introduced much later, by Tietz (1926) and Woolworth's (1927) in Germany, and by Audiberts, as a direct imitation of Woolworth's, in 1927 in France, and the following year in Belgium (De Grazia 2005). Unlike in the USA and Britain, major department store operators often took the lead in starting the chains of this new retail format. This pattern was to be typical in many other countries and in later stages of the global diffusion of various American retail formats. While the original innovation might have come from small firms, the large modern retailers often took the lead in exploiting its potential.

The second wave, 1945–1970: big-box retailing comes to Europe and Japan

In contrast to the first wave of diffusion of American retail formats, the second wave was generated by a more concerted effort by various organizations, most notably US productivity missions and assistance agencies, but also private organizations such as Rockefeller's International Basic Economy Corporation (IBEC) (see Broehl 1968), firms such as National Cash Registry, trade associations, and enterprising retailers.

In the war-ravaged economies of Western Europe, most of the effort under the US-organized Economic Recovery Program (ERP), better known as the Marshall Plan, was initially focused on distributing American-made staple goods and rebuilding the infrastructure in order to alleviate "hunger, poverty, desperation and chaos."[15] With the intensification of the Cold War, especially from 1950 on, the productivity aspect became paramount, and a part of enhancing productivity concerned the dismal state of "distribution" (Schröter 2005).

SUPERMARKETS

The initial attempts to modernize European distribution by using the American model focused on the introduction of separate market mechanisms, most notably self-service (Henksmeier 1960; Dawson 1981). The supermarket was the first US retail format to be systematically introduced, and the slow spread of supermarkets shows how complex and often difficult was the process of adoption of full retail formats (see A. Goldman 1981; Goldman, Ramaswami, and Krider 2002; Shaw, Curth, and Alexander 2004). The supermarket, just as the planned shopping center and the big-box store, evolved in a context characterized by widespread ownership of automobiles, cheap suburban land made available for retail stores and amenities, as well as large storage and refrigeration facilities at consumers' homes. None of these conditions was particularly well satisfied in the Western European urban centers of the 1950s, and even less so in Japan. Supermarkets also required a large number of well-established and marketed brands of pre-packaged, standardized consumer products, and a broad range of new technologies of packaging, display, and delivery. For an entrepreneur, starting a supermarket entailed a high capital investment in the store and its fixtures, from refrigerated cabinets to checkouts. It also necessitated a change in mindset, since it involved training and supervising a different type of labor, and engaging in different marketing and selling techniques. Licensing restrictions, government regulations, high taxes, and the animosity of small retailers all presented further obstacles, making the required investment for opening a supermarket three times higher in Europe than in the USA (Schröter 2004).

As a result, the main appeal of the supermarket format as it was introduced in the USA—that is, offering low prices for staple branded goods—was not present in Europe, where supermarket prices were often higher than in small shops and open markets and the merchandise mix unfamiliar. The fact that the supermarket succeeded at all was due to persistent efforts of major market innovators, only some of which were established retail chains. It was also due to the fact that it was a distinctly American type of market, and thus it symbolized modernity and a high standard of living for a generation of European consumers. The traditional shopping and consuming habits of European consumers, initially considered the main obstacle in adopting the format, have thus proven to be much less significant, as they changed quickly in response to the presence of new types of markets.

Despite the trade statistics showing the supermarket revolution of the early 1960s in Western Europe and Japan, the American-style supermarket format was adopted only gradually and partially. The adoption of the self-service principle was generally easy and quick, but the pricing, store size, and merchandise mix aspects were adopted only much later and to a lesser degree. While the first supermarkets emerged in Europe in the late 1950s, the size and product assortment of American supermarkets have not been approached even today. A typical American supermarket of the 1960s sold up to 5,000 different products using a selling space of more than 1,500 square meters; by 2000, the average floor space had tripled and the number of products had increased to 45,000. An average German or French supermarket in 1960 sold no more than 1,000 items, and by 2000 it had reached 800–1,000 square meters with an assortment of up to 7,000 items. The introduction of self-service, packaging, and preprocessing in the meat and produce departments also represented a major problem, and was not standardized until the 1970s (Schröter 2005).

These trends were even more pronounced in Japan. Although a few large size (400–600 square meters) self-service grocery stores emerged in Japan in the late 1950s, the introduction of open refrigerator consoles and the selling of pre-packaged meats and produce did not take off until the early 1980s. As a result, the number of small specialty stores in Japan continued to increase until 1985, and the 1950s and 1960s supermarket pioneers soon shifted their operations toward the "superstore" format, which, similar to European hyper-markets, sold extensive lines of non-grocery items (Meyer-Ohle 2003; Takaoka and Kikkawa 2004).

The difficulties of matching the American supermarket format in size, merchandise assortment, and pricing policies gave rise to several adaptations of the format. One was the development of the hypermarket, a combination store selling a large proportion of non-groceries. The latter commanded higher margins than grocery products, and thus compensated for the inefficiencies of the grocery departments.[16] In Europe, with a rapidly emerging middle class starved of modern consumer goods, the standard merchandise assortment in such stores was much easier to establish than in the USA. Another variation on the supermarket format, particularly successful in Germany, was the so-called hard-discount store, which gave up the size and merchandise assortment for the strict emphasis on self-service and low prices. The first examples of such a format emerged in Germany between 1954 and 1956, as a direct emulation of the US "box" discount store. The format was later perfected independently by Aldi (Schröter 2005; Wortmann, Chapter 4 this volume) and then copied by other German operators such as Lidl.

SHOPPING CENTERS

In comparison to the development of the supermarket, the spread of the shopping center in Europe involved fewer problems and modifications. This was the result of the much larger size of such undertakings, which were often actively supported by local governments, developed by established architectural and construction firms, and underwritten by major institutional investors, all of which had substantial access to the skills and knowledge accumulated by their American counterparts. The first such planned shopping centers in Europe were developed in the 1960s, including the first examples of large-scale "regional" shopping malls of American style and size, such as Elephant and Castle in London (1965), Europa Center in Berlin (1965), and Parly II near Versailles (1969). Unlike in the USA, many of these shopping centers were built within the existing urban area, rather than on its outskirts, as a part of the effort to revitalize urban neighborhoods. In the UK and France, the activity peaked in the 1970s, and by the end of that decade, the best European shopping-center developers were matching the US ones in sophistication if not in size.

By 1970, then, the retail landscape in Europe started to resemble that of the USA, although only in isolated pockets. Modern gas stations became ubiquitous, as did smaller self-service stores. Large supermarkets and hypermarkets were dotted around new suburban areas, while planned shopping centers and revamped department stores provided shopping attractions within urban cores. Perhaps more importantly, the most successful European operators had developed skills and capacities to operate stores that nearly matched US size, assortment, and operational efficiency, and those operators would become one of the major forces in the globalization of retailing in the following period.

LOW LEVELS OF INTERNATIONALIZATION

Throughout this period, the successful, if limited, international diffusion of US retail formats stood in sharp contrast to the lack of internationalization of retail operations. Woolworth's maintained and expanded its prewar variety store network, and in 1965 operated 1,100 stores in Britain, 277 in Canada, 112 in West Germany, and 10 in Mexico. The world's largest retailer, Sears, operated 41 retail stores in Brazil, Colombia, Mexico, Peru, and Venezuela. Safeway, the largest of the US supermarket operators, entered the UK in 1962, Australia in 1963, and Germany in 1964. Yet these isolated examples only underscore the relative lack of internationalization efforts in the period. Then, as much as today, large US retailers of food and general merchandise rarely looked for expansion opportunities abroad because of the virtually unlimited opportunities for growth in the domestic market. European retailers, on the other hand, had much more limited growth opportunities at home; but they had not yet developed the critical size and organizational competence for international expansion.

The third wave, 1970–1990: internationalizing and modernizing

RAPID INTERNATIONALIZATION

While the first two periods of the diffusion of the US retail models had established a regular channel for the flow of retail innovations between best practices in the USA and leading operators in Europe, it was only in the 1970s that the spread of retail innovations was bolstered by the direct internationalization actions of leading retailers. US franchise operations were the first and most successful in this drive. Operating relatively small markets, in terms of product assortment and store size, and capitalizing on a strong product brand name, fast-food operators, motel chains, and car rental and automotive service companies were amongst the pioneers, rapidly entering new countries and replicating outlets.[17] KFC entered Britain in 1965, the first US fast-food operator in Europe. McDonald's followed in 1971, entering the Netherlands and Germany, and also Japan and Australia in the same year. 7-Eleven's decision to enter Japan in 1973, by franchising its convenience stores to the domestic retailer Ito Yokado, resulted in one of the most fascinating cases of retail internationalization. The Japanese operator expanded and perfected the format while adapting it to the local conditions, and in a rare case of "reciprocal internationalization" bought the controlling stake in the parent corporation in 1995 (Sparks 1996). By the first decade of the twenty-first century, the Seven-I Holdings Company became not only the biggest operator of convenience stores in the world, with over 34,000 owned and franchised outlets, but also one of the largest, most global, and most innovative world retailers.

Amongst the retailers with more general assortments, the European ones were the pioneers in crossing borders, most commonly within the emerging European common market, but also in the USA, Latin America, and East Asia. This was a result of several "push" factors, such as restrictive regulation in their home countries, the limited size of the home market (especially in smaller economies such as the Netherlands and Belgium), increased local competition, and the negative economic environment of the late 1970s (Sternquist and Kacker 1994). While their expansion abroad was a mark of their growing organizational size and capabilities, many of the early expansion efforts were unsuccessful and resulted in quick retreats. Carrefour entered seven European countries in the 1970s but succeeded in only one, Spain; however, its entries in Brazil (1975) and Argentina (1982) were more successful, even if initial growth was slow and cautious (S. Burt 1994; Dupuis, Choi, and Larke 2006). The expansion of European retailers into the US market was particularly impressive, so much so that at one point almost 20 percent of the US grocery sales on the East Coast were controlled by operators headquartered in Europe. However, many of these operations have been divested in the meantime.

Specialty retailers also joined the internationalization effort. Amongst the first were fashion and luxury items retailers operating relatively small outlets with limited assortments and strong brand names. Laura Ashley, Benetton, and Gap successfully managed to internationalize the merchandise assortment based on private-label merchandise, as did IKEA, perhaps the first successful specialty big-box retailer (Prime 1999). Amongst the specialty retailers selling manufacturer advertised brands, Toys "R" Us has been a particularly visible example of internationalization.

MODERN FORMS OF RETAILING

While the internationalization of retailing proceeded only slowly between 1970 and 1990, there was a more intense trend of the integration of consumer goods markets in developed countries. Everywhere within Western Europe the proportion of retail sales controlled by large chain stores increased substantially, and American-style retail formats, from supermarkets to big-box stores and shopping centers, established a firm foothold. This trend has been more observable in smaller economies than in larger ones. At the same time, the integration of the US domestic market, across various regions, has been faster than the integration of the similar-sized "common" European market, where cultural and regulatory barriers slowed down the expansion of major operators. The reduction of the role of independent retailers (small shop owners) proceeded the furthest in the two biggest European economies, Germany and the UK. At the same time, Italy and Spain remained dominated by traditional retailing, and Eastern Europe, still behind the Iron Curtain, remained untouched by modern marketing methods.

The adoption of American retail formats was not limited to Western Europe. It was also happening in Japan, although more gradually, as well as in a few major urban centers in Latin America. In Japan, while the official statistics show the rapid development of "general superstores" and "food superstores" in this period, those stores rarely resembled Western-style supermarkets and general discounters in their size, assortment of goods, or operational efficiency. The best operators, such as Kansai supermarkets, closely emulated American selling techniques, yet the combination of the seller's market, due to the rapidly expanding purchasing power of Japanese consumers, the highly restrictive regulations, and the power of wholesalers stalled the modernization of Japanese retail (Meyer-Ohle 2003).

One peculiarity of Japanese consumer markets was the rapid adoption and further development of the convenience store format. After Ito Yokado had introduced 7-Eleven stores in Japan in 1973, as the franchisor of the US Southland Corporation, other major Japanese retailers soon followed suit, Daiei with Lawson, and the Seibu Group with Family Mart. The format evolved rapidly in Japan, establishing a dense network of city center locations, as opposed to the US roadside ones, offering a more extensive assortment of fresh merchandise and prepared food, and often assuming price leadership. An extensive range of services was added in the 1980s, and today convenience stores remain the most modern and efficient retail operators in Japan.

The fourth wave, 1990–2010: making global markets

GLOBALIZATION OF FORMATS

Only in the period since 1990 has the true globalization of American retail formats taken place worldwide. To a great degree this has been a result of the actions of major retail firms, most of them from Europe and Japan, which have, since the early 1990s, undertaken a more focused and successful project of global expansion. Perhaps the most visible form of such an expansion was the spread of supermarkets in the developing world. The successive waves of supermarket diffusion are well documented (Senauer and Reardon, Chapter 10 this volume). In a very short period, sometimes in less than ten years, the percentage of food sales through supermarkets and hypermarkets went from 10–20 percent to more than 50 percent in countries as diverse as the Czech Republic, Poland, Greece, Taiwan, South Korea, Thailand, the Philippines, Costa Rica, and South Africa. In China, the largest developing market, the first supermarkets emerged only in 1990. In 2007, there were more than 50,000 supermarkets in operation, and, while they still captured only 20 percent of total food sales nationwide, they approached a 50 percent share in major urban centers.

At the same time, there was a boom in the development of shopping centers. Planned shopping centers, and in particular large regional malls, became a standard feature of many urban centers, and not just in developed countries. Indeed, out of the world's ten largest shopping centers today, eight are in Asia, and all but two of them opened since 2004.[18] Many large shopping centers in developing countries have major discounters and hypermarkets, rather than department stores, as anchor tenants, and others dispense with the very idea of anchor tenants, reflecting the drawing power of major fashion and other specialty chain outlets. They are also often located close to city centers, and house major big-box specialty retailers, such as electronics and home improvement chains.

At the other end of the scale, convenience stores have spread through a large part of East Asia, capturing 12–14 percent of food retailing in Japan, Hong Kong, and Singapore, over 20 percent in Taiwan and rapidly growing in importance in China. The landscape of supermarkets and hypermarkets, shopping centers and big-box stores, gas stations and fast-food restaurants, is becoming increasingly standardized everywhere in developed countries and in most major urban centers in the developing world. South Asia, as well as large portions of sub-Saharan Africa, remain the last large frontiers for the spread of modern forms of retailing.

The latest wave of expansion of retail formats concerns e-commerce or Internet-based retailing. US firms were the early leaders, and the gap between Western Europe and the USA in 2000 was still quite large and seemingly expanding. The EU's investment in infrastructure closed this gap considerably in the next nine years (European Commission 2009), and the rapid spread of online retailing in East Asia and elsewhere in the developing world (see Rouibah, Khalil, and Hassanien 2009) is a good indicator of the decreasing time lag between the adoption of retail formats in the USA and then in the rest of the world in each subsequent wave of consumer market innovation.

MARKET MAKERS

After 1989, the understored, drab retail landscapes of Eastern Europe became major expansion targets of Western European retailers. By 2000, they were dominated by supermarkets and hypermarkets operated by Metro, Casino, Carrefour, Auchan, Tesco, Aldi, Lidl, and other leading Western chains, including a few local power players such as Slovenian Merkator. Southern Italy, Spain, Portugal, and Greece were all fully incorporated into the EU retail market during this period, and significant modernization occurred in smaller markets such as Macedonia, Albania, and Montenegro. The two large economies on the periphery of Europe, Turkey and Russia, managed to develop major domestic retail operators even while opening up their retail sector to foreign entry. The giant Russian retail market attracted retailers such as Metro, Auchan, and Spar Coop, but the domestic discount chains such as Pyaterochka and Kopeika, and supermarket/hypermarket operators such as Seventh Continent and Perekrestok, have so far been able to compete. In 2006, the merger of Perekrestok and Pyaterochka created the first Russian food retail giant, the X5 Retail group, with over $5 billion in revenues.

The consolidation of the European market for consumer goods remains largely an intra-European affair, since no general-merchandise retailer from the USA or Asia is, in 2010, operating in continental Europe. The same holds to a large degree for the other two major regional developed markets, the USA and East Asia. A few European retailers still have a strong presence in the retailing sector in the USA, most notably Belgian Delhaize and Dutch Royal Ahold, which derive a majority of their revenues from the supermarkets they acquired in the USA, as well as the German Aldi, which operates hard-discount stores as well as upscale supermarkets under the Trader Joe's name. However, other European-based retailers, including Carrefour, have pulled out of the US market, just as Wal-Mart did from Germany. In Japan, the presence of foreign general retailers is very low, Wal-Mart-owned Seiyu being the only case amongst the fifty largest operators. In South Korea and Taiwan, the two other major developed retail markets in Asia, Tesco (in partnership with Samsung) and Carrefour, respectively, do play a significant role, but other major operators are domestic.

The largest retailers in the world still operate almost exclusively in their home regions. Out of the top twenty world retailers, eleven do not operate at all outside their home region, and only five derive more than 10 percent of their sales from outside the region. The most global of these, Seven-I Holdings, headquartered in Japan, operates as an umbrella company for owned and franchised outlets around the world, and has a strong presence throughout Asia and in North America, but few stores in the European market. Carrefour, one of the most global general-merchandise retailers, derives 16 percent of revenues from its Latin American and Asian operations, and Tesco 13 percent from Asia and less than 1 percent from North America. Wal-Mart generates over $90 billion of sales and 26 percent of revenues from its international operations, but most of those are in Canada, Mexico, and the UK. The proportion of revenues from its extensive Latin American, and smaller, but rapidly expanding East Asian, operations is perhaps closer to 12 percent. Aldi has a strong presence in the USA, with 1,400 of its 9,000 stores, but operates no stores in Asia or Latin America.

The lack of truly global reach amongst the largest retailers does not show their lack of organizational capacities. After all, they are amongst the largest and most profitable companies in the world. They excel at operational efficiency and supply-chain management. Rather, it shows the difficulties inherent in the global replication of very complex markets. Moreover, their limited scope of operations is not the only indicator of these difficulties. Many of the large retailers that achieved considerable internationalization operate many formats under many retail store names, without true integration in branding, merchandise mix, pricing, and store image. At best, they achieve integration of the supply chain, and of organizational strategy, but rarely of market mechanisms in consumer goods markets. This is especially true for European retailers, which were typically pushed by their economic and regulatory environment to favor rapid expansion through acquisitions over organic growth. The weakness of such organizational strategy gets exposed only when they start competing with more focused and integrated rivals, and until recently the degree of such direct competition was quite low.

Big-box specialty stores do not fare much better in this respect. Two of the three largest US big-box specialty stores, Home Depot and Best Buy, are starting to expand beyond the North American market, by opening their first stores in China, while the third one, Lowe's, is satisfied with growth opportunities within North America. Ikea and Kingfisher, the two top European big-box specialty retailers, have more of a global presence, but still derive 82 percent and 78 percent of their sales, respectively, from the European market. An early example of a successful big-box store globalization is Toys "R" Us, which, despite its financial troubles in its home US market, maintains a strong presence in all major regions. Similar, more recent examples are the world's biggest retailer of video and computer games, the Game-Stop, and the largest retailer of office products, Staples.

The ability to replicate market formats in diverse environments is often achieved more easily by specialist retailers that operate small to medium-size stores. Most of them tightly control their supply chains by integrating back into design and manufacturing. Inditex, the owner of Zara, Bershka and a number of other brands and store concepts, Hennes and Mauritz, Gap (Old Navy, Banana Republic, and so on) and Limited Brands (Victoria's Secret, Bath and Body Works) are the largest firms in this category. Even more successful are leading managers of branded luxury items, such as jewelry, watches, haute couture, and spirits. The Dior-LVHM group, PPR, Richemont, and the eyewear specialist Luxottica all own large stables of brands and operate retail stores, concession stands, and licensed outlets around the world, most of them in major shopping centers and on the Main Street. The fact that operating retail stores hampers one's replication efforts becomes clear when comparing these companies with Nike and Adidas, which have similar organizational structures, supply-chain management and marketing features, with the major difference that they sell mostly through independent retail accounts. Nike operates nearly 700 retail outlets (50 percent of which are outside the USA), and Adidas almost 2,000, but they also distribute to tens of thousands of external retail firms. Both firms have achieved nearly global presence of their products.

Another category are the Internet retailers, such as Amazon and eBay, which, unhampered by the needs for physical retail outlets, can easily replicate their retail websites and thus enjoy access to the consumer limited only by the infrastructure and consumer interest. It is important to note, though, that even the most successful Internet retailers have not yet been able to achieve the consumer traffic of large general-merchandise retailers, let alone their revenues. Amazon.com and eBay, the two leading e-retailers, had over fifty million unique users in November 2008, during the peak of the shopping season. But Wal-Mart and Target websites attracted thirty-nine million and thirty-six million shoppers in the same period, and their physical stores several times as many. In general, almost half of the sales of the 100 largest e-retailers is captured by large retail chains' websites, and the rest is split between manufacturer and brand-name managers and the "pure" e-retailers. Ten of the top fifteen US e-retailing sites in 2008 were online outposts of major mass retailers.

Toward the Integration of Global Consumer Markets

The 250 largest world retailers captured over $3.6 trillion in retail sales in 2007, or more than one-third of the estimated world's total, and the top ten alone accounted for more than $1 trillion (Deloitte 2009). Nine of the top ten and almost 40 percent of the top 250 largest retailers operated markets that combined food and general-merchandise assortments, indicating an increasing integration of market formats around the cluster of supermarket, hypermarket, superstore, warehouse, and similar big-box, scrambled merchandising formats. While these large retailers still rarely compete directly with each other outside their home markets, they play a major role in making consumer and supplier markets around the world, and thus represent a key organizing force in today's global economy.

The global market for consumer goods should not be seen as a set of segmented, separate national markets, despite the regulatory attempts of many governments to limit the expansion of large retailers and, in particular, foreign ones, within their jurisdiction. Rather, the system of global consumer markets is being increasingly organized as an integrated center–periphery structure, where there is a steady flow of innovations from retailers in the core countries toward less-developed economies. The core economies' retailers are not only the most modern and efficient; they also collectively control the major share of consumer goods markets, thus enabling very rapid diffusion and replication of innovations and best practices.

Large retailers are often uniquely positioned to test new market mechanisms and store formats. While market innovations often start from small retail firms, once they achieve some success, they can be quickly adopted by large chains. The adoption of supermarkets by small-store grocery chains and the role European department stores played in starting single-price variety stores are some early examples of such a process. The adoption of online retailing by major general merchandisers and of health and organic foods by grocery retailers are amongst more recent examples. While most large retailers have the advantage of organizational size and complexity in trying out new market mechanisms, those that are also well integrated in organizational terms, and have effective control of supply chains and retail formats (from pricing to merchandise assortment to store image), can generally react to market changes and adopt innovations most quickly.

The emerging global system of consumer goods markets is not organized just as a center–periphery structure, radiating from the large and most innovative retailers outwards, but also along the lines of functional differentiation. In functional terms, the center of the retailing world is increasingly organized along the retail format of large stores that sell "fast-moving consumer goods," or "general merchandise and food" lines at low prices. The composition of the merchandise assortment within this category is constantly changing as it defines the world of necessary, affordable, and, increasingly, disposable, goods in the developing world. Apart from groceries, drugs and cosmetics, home furnishings and apparel, this can now include some furniture, appliances, electronics, multimedia, books, sporting goods, toys, tools, hardware, and auto parts, and even basic services, gasoline, and fast food.

Functional differentiation means not only that different stores sell different types of goods (indeed, this might be much less the case in contemporary integrated markets than before), but also that retail formats develop complementary features. Along the core, "one-stop-shopping" formats arise specialty retailers for fashion and apparel, often grouped together in shopping malls: home improvement, electronics, and furniture specialists; bookstores, sporting goods and outdoor gear stores, and so on. In the areas underserved by hypermarkets and supercenters, superettes and convenience stores provide a narrower, highly selective version of the basic goods and services assortment, but increasingly with the same level of operational efficiency and marketing competence as the big stores. Around the core of price leadership, usually defined as a "low price format," arise complementary promotional pricing techniques.

On the global level, we still see a few major areas that are not being reached and transformed by modern retailing practices. However, since the beginning of the new century, most of the world markets for consumer goods are being organized and integrated by large, modern retailers. As we have seen on the more circumscribed, regional scale, the presence of such retailers is the first phase in the transformation of local markets for consumer goods. The second step is reaching a threshold market revenue share of modern retailers, often no more than 10–20 percent, at which the diffusion of practices and replication of modern markets becomes faster and more routine. Direct competition between major market makers presents the next transformative step, as it encourages integration and functional differentiation of consumer goods markets.

These steps have been achieved within the centers of the three major regions, in North America, the EU, and Japan (with South Korea), but not between those regions. In China, for instance, only a few major urban centers have crossed the threshold of the adoption of modern retail formats, and there the expansion of consumer markets and the entrance of new players have been as rapid as regulatory authorities allow. The vast world of several million small-town and rural stores is only now slowly being transformed by modern retailing. In India, the process has barely started, even in urban centers. Within the next twenty years, India is poised to become one of the five largest consumer markets in the world. The retailing transformation this process requires will be enormous, on an even grander scale than what is currently happening in China.

In the USA, the processes of diffusion and replication of successful types of market formats within each major retail sector, and, then, the integration of different retail sectors took the larger part of the twentieth century. The diffusion of those formats to the rest of the world has initially been quite slow, yet the pace has increased in each subsequent wave. Moreover, different elements of the American model have been adopted in different regions at a different pace, without the need to replicate the evolutionary path of the US system of consumer goods markets. We have seen this in the case of Western Europe, where several modern formats were adopted concurrently after the Second World War, and even more clearly in some recent transformations, such as in South Korea in the 1990s and in China a decade later.

Will the further evolution of consumer goods markets around the world follow the American model? The answer to this question must remain ambivalent, and not only because of the author's reluctance to talk about the future of a rapidly evolving institutional realm. On the one hand, it is likely that the spread of standard American formats, from the supermarket and shopping center, to the fast-food outlet and convenience store, will continue for at least several more decades. A large proportion of the global population is still without access to such market formats, which remain powerful symbols of modernity; at the same time, the financial and organizational requirements of replicating large retail outlets on a global scale are enormous, and thus such a process will necessarily be gradual.

On the other hand, if we focus on the character of innovations and the best retailing practices, those are likely to become increasingly less "American." This does not mean that the USA will decline as one of the centers, perhaps even the major center, of retail innovations. After all, it is well poised to capitalize on having only minimal regulatory obstacles, efficient markets for investment capital, the most developed consumer society, and so on. Yet, as the largest market makers of consumer goods markets increasingly globalize their operations, they will be able to source for innovations and deploy them globally. Those innovations are therefore likely to bear very little sign of their national origin and socioeconomic context. And, with the rise of substantial middle-income consumer classes in developing countries, the spread of such innovations will be increasingly dependent less on the general level of national economic development, and more on other factors such as market opportunities and regulatory frameworks. In this sense, then, the emerging global system of consumer goods markets, created and organized by large global market makers, is bound to move beyond the domination of American retailing formats.

4

Globalization of European Retailing

Michael Wortmann

Introduction

Most of the technological developments and market formats described in other chapters of this book have also been adopted in Europe during the fifty years after the Second World War. Bar codes and scanner checkouts have been introduced; the size of stores has become larger and larger, big boxes at newly constructed greenfield sites have appeared, and so have shopping centers; market power is increasingly concentrated in a few companies, amongst them Carrefour, Aldi, Metro, and Tesco.

This is not astonishing: living standards in most West European countries had caught up with those in the United States during the first three post-Second World War decades. More and more families owned cars to drive to the stores of their preference, and they had refrigerators to store their purchases. After the fall of the Iron Curtain, at least some of the Central and East European countries are also catching up, although their development departs from a different starting point.

Even though it is debatable whether US and European consumption patterns are becoming increasingly similar, many US branded products can be found in European supermarkets: Kellogg's corn flakes, Mars candy bars, Heinz ketchup, Colgate toothpaste, P&G's Pampers, or 3M's Scotch tapes. All these products are produced at the European factories of US consumer goods manufacturers. Other products like Mattel's Barbie dolls are being sourced from Asia—just like Nike or Timberland shoes, which might even be manufactured by the same factories as those of their European competitors like Adidas or Puma.

Obviously, several elements of retail development follow global trends, and many of them have been pioneered in the USA as the most advanced economy of the world, where—which is important, as we shall see shortly—retail development was only marginally restricted by government regulation. European development has frequently followed the American lead. The spread of supermarkets using self-service (and shopping carts) in Western Europe gained momentum only in the 1950s.[1] European retail entrepreneurs frequently traveled to the USA in order to learn more about the latest retail innovations (Schröter 2005). Amongst them was the German Hugo Mann, who set up one of the first German big out-of-town variety stores in 1958, which started the Wertkauf chain and which later, in 1997, was taken over by Wal-Mart. Also amongst those traveling to the USA were the founders of Carrefour, Tesco, and Metro and many other founders and leading managers of today's biggest European retailers.

Compared to the spread of retail innovation through cross-border learning and copying (Alexander, Shaw, and Curth 2005), the impact of US retail chains expanding their store operations into Europe was more limited. Woolworth's had entered the UK in 1909, where it had developed into the biggest chain store until the 1950s; it later (1927) also entered Germany. Safeway opened its first store in the UK in 1962 and quickly developed into one of the UK's leading grocery chains. Another US company, Gem International, had opened two stores in the 1950s—one of them with premises of 70,000 square feet, a dimension unknown in Europe at that time. These stores were taken over by a (then) small supermarket chain, Asda, in 1965, which concentrated its further growth on larger stores (Whysall 2005), until it was taken over by Wal-Mart in 1999.

In the 1970s, when supermarkets had become the dominant form of grocery retailing in most of Western Europe, new technologies, especially ICT (information and communication technology) but also container shipping, started to have an impact on retailing. Introducing these new technologies, European retailers again followed those in the USA—but this time much faster. An agreement between US and European transport organizations on the standardization of inter-modal containers was reached in 1970. The American Universal Product Code (UPC) from 1973 was adopted into the European Article Number (EAN) system only five years later; and the first European scanner checkout was introduced by the Austrian retailer Billa in 1979.

While many basic developmental trends in retailing are global, there are at the same time striking differences between single European countries. In many respects Europe still has a highly fragmented retail market. This is due not only to differences in consumer taste, but also to very different retail traditions and different forms of retail-specific regulation, which are part of distinct national business systems. These differences relate to store formats, ownership structures, and the types and sizes of companies and groups. This again has implications for retailers' market-making capabilities and strategies of internationalization—the internationalization of store operations as well as the globalization of sourcing.

The biggest European retailers of today, such as Carrefour, Metro, Tesco, and Aldi, started their modern big-box, self-service operations in the 1960s, just like their US counterparts (Wal-Mart, Kmart). Operating in smaller and less-specialized markets, they tended to fill their big-box stores with a more diverse mix of goods (hypermarkets), or to keep the merchandise mix limited and the stores small, and to emphasize rapid turnover (hard discounters). Some of them, such as Metro, avoided restrictive regulations by adopting the "cash and carry" wholesaling format. As a result, even today, most large European retailers exhibit a greater variety of formats and retail fascias (store brand names) than their US counterparts. While this enabled the top operators to acquire a wide range of market-making capabilities, it also led to occasional problems of formulating integrated company strategies and promoting the company image. More generally, the degree of retail specialization within the EU remains lower than in the USA, with top European specialty retailers (fashion, electronics, DIY) only recently starting to match the size and market-making capabilities of their US counterparts.

The absence of the large-scale involvement of US retailers in European markets meant that European market makers took the responsibility of modernizing and integrating their domestic markets. While adopting major market-making innovations in direct contact with US agencies and retail operators, European retailers adapted those to local conditions and created distinct versions of retail formats that they were later able to export to other parts of the world. In the major economies of the north-west, from the Scandinavian countries and the UK to France and Germany, this process was mostly endogenous. The retail markets of Southern (Italy, Portugal, Spain, Greece) and Eastern Europe, in contrast, were developed mostly by the French, German, and British retail operators. The degree of fragmentation still present within the EU provides a good example of the difficulties of integrating complex (retail) markets for consumer goods, especially in the presence of restrictive local regulations.

The limited size of domestic markets and strict retail regulations also led large European retailers to pursue internationalization earlier and in a more sustained manner. While many of the early attempts at internationalization, even when limited to cross-border expansion, ended up as failures (see, for instance, the section on Carrefour below), the early internationalization leaders acquired the valuable experience of making markets in different economic and social contexts, which enabled them to seize opportunities during the global retail internationalization wave of the 1990s. With a few exceptions, European retailers' forays into North American markets failed; yet their expansion into Latin America was often quite successful, and the more recent wave of entering major Asian markets showcases the advantages of accumulated internationalization experience.

This chapter starts with an analysis of retail development in the four biggest West European economies: the UK, France, Germany, and Italy. These economies are well suited to exemplify the different retail structures that have developed within Western Europe. The following sections present case studies of the internationalization of four of the largest European grocery retailers, Carrefour, Aldi, Metro, and Tesco. The chapter concludes with a more general analysis of internationalization patterns of large European grocery retailers.

Grocery Retailing in the UK, France, Germany, and Italy

The various retail innovations and new retail formats, most of them originating in the United States, met very different environments when US multinationals tried to transfer them to their affiliates in Europe or when European retail entrepreneurs tried to implement them in their home countries. Retail structures were quite different to start with, and established retailers, especially small traditional retailers, had a very different position in the market and were differently organized and differently embedded in their country-specific social and political environments. Thus, the reactions of established retailers, but also of consumers, city planners, and politicians, toward change and modernization in the retail industry, and especially toward big-box retailing, differed significantly. This led to different patterns of retail modernization and to quite different structures of the retail industries in the single European countries.

The UK in the 1950s was still Europe's most advanced economy, and, thus, the UK led the supermarket revolution in Europe, introducing self-service and increasing the size of stores, which became increasingly organized as chains. In addition, the UK economy traditionally had a liberal regulatory environment, and the development of new retail formats went relatively unrestricted.[2] Increased competition was supported by the difficulties of enforcement and finally the abolishment of resale price maintenance in 1964, increasing the pressure on retailers to modernize store formats and ownership structures (Guy 2007). Supermarket chains quickly developed, amongst them Sainsbury's and Tesco. In addition, the UK was most open to foreign investment, which—because of cultural and language proximity—came especially from the USA (Godley and Fletcher 2001). The US supermarket chain Safeway was one of the first entrants into the UK market in 1962 (Shaw and Alexander 2006).

In France, retail change started somewhat more slowly than in the UK, but eventually became more of a true retail revolution. This began in 1963, when

Carrefour set up the first *hypermarché* at a road intersection (literally: *carrefour*) in the outskirts of Paris. It had a total sales area of 2,500 square meters, 12 checkout counters, and 400 parking spaces. At that time it was considered huge. But Carrefour's third store in 1966 was 9,500 square meters, carried 20,000 SKUs, and had 2,000 parking spaces (Lhermie 2003). These hypermarkets were designed for one-stop shopping of car-borne customers, combining the assortments of a grocery and a variety store (about 50:50).[3] In a situation where supermarkets were not yet well established, the hypermarkets of Carrefour, Auchan, and others did not face much competition in the French market.

In contrast to the UK and France, Italy has a long tradition of 'social protectionism' for small shopkeepers (J. Morris 1999). Restrictive retail regulation had been introduced in 1926, and was in place, with a slight modification in 1971, until the late 1990s. Special licenses (quotas), issued by the local authorities specifically for different food as well as non-food retail categories, limited the amount and type of retail space for every store. This regulation effectively protected the holders of such licenses: independent shopkeepers, which were sometimes organized in buying groups or voluntary chains. The development of supermarkets or other larger and more modern retail formats, as well as concentration processes and the formation of chain stores, were considerably hampered. Amongst those few retailers that were able to introduce self-service stores were the consumer cooperatives, which had formed a national association in 1947 that later became Coop Italia.

Germany too has a strong tradition of social protection of all kinds of small (*Mittelstand*) entrepreneurs, including shopkeepers. The economic crisis of the early 1930s in particular led to measures protecting shopkeepers from competition. These measures were extended by the Nazi government through the 1933 Retail Protection Law (*Einzelhandelsschutzgesetz*), which restricted the opening of new shops. Consumer cooperatives, single-price or penny stores, and department stores were declared 'undesirable' formats. Several of these restrictions were in place until the mid-1950s; other restrictions following similar intentions were in place until 1965 (Berekoven 1986; Winkler 1991; Scheybani 1996). The strong position of independent shopkeepers in the German retail market as well as in the political arena was also supported by their organization into retailers' cooperatives. The two largest, Edeka and Rewe, had been founded in 1907 and 1926 respectively. Originally, their combined buying power was directed against wholesalers, which, at that time, were able to appropriate a large share of the profit along the value chain.

In the mid-1960s, when independent retailers as well as downtown department stores perceived new competition from large out-of-town stores, a new kind of protective regulation was established. The revised spatial planning (zoning) legislation of 1968[4] limited the construction of shopping centers and single large stores to city centers or special zones, which had to go through a complicated planning procedure, involving local as well as regional authorities. Further revisions of spatial planning legislation in 1977 and 1986 defined exact store sizes, finally effectively limiting the maximum sales area to about 800 square meters for most stores in most locations.[5] This regulation, on the one hand, gave established retailers some protection and, on the other, since it was much more flexible than the Italian regulation, allowed for retail modernization, while channeling it in a certain direction. It allowed smaller supermarkets as well as other new small retail formats, such as hard-discount stores, to develop (Wortmann 2004). The first hard-discount store was opened by Aldi in 1962. It combined a post-war-style store focusing on a very limited assortment presented in a no-frills environment with the self-service concept, which was becoming increasingly common at that time. Another store type favored by German special-planning legislation was large cash and carry (C&C) markets focused on business customers buying in bulk, like those of Metro, because they were legally defined as wholesalers rather than retailers.

The different patterns of retail regulation that were established during the first retail revolution—that is, the spread of self-service stores and the appearance of large formats—in the four countries analysed had a long-lasting impact on the subsequent development of their retail structures.

In the UK, supermarkets gradually grew larger and larger. In the late 1960s, the largest supermarkets were called superstores. Today, these are between 3,000 and 8,000 square meters, have parking lots, and are usually located outside city centers. Their assortment is—like that of supermarkets—concentrated in grocery products. Usually they carry only a very limited range of non-food products. Chains of superstores today are the dominant format in grocery retailing. Independent shopkeepers found it very difficult to respond to the new competition. Even though the number of those organized in voluntary chains increased from only 2 percent of all independent retailers in 1958 to 29 percent in 1968 (Hall 1971: 44), their market share remained marginal.

Besides supermarkets and superstores, formats similar to French hypermarkets combining food and non-food assortments developed very late. The Asda stores came closest to this format. In 1965 Asda had taken over two large out-of-town stores that had been opened by the US company Gem International in the late 1950s (Whysall 2005). From that time on Asda concentrated its further growth on big out-of-town stores, low prices, and a relatively large non-food assortment. This made it one of the UK's largest retailers. These characteristics of Asda's stores were quite similar to those of Wal-Mart's supercenters, which contributed to the ease of their acquisition by Wal-Mart in 1999. Other UK retailers entered the hypermarket segment relatively late. Tesco introduced its Tesco Extra store in 1997, after it had gained experience with large non-food assortments at its acquired Czech subsidiary (see below).

Despite the appearance of foreign hard discounters as well as Wal-Mart, superstores are the dominant form of grocery retailing in the UK today. Ownership of stores became more and more concentrated, partly because of mergers and acquisitions. In 1987 Argyll acquired the UK subsidiary of Safeway Inc., and in 2004 Argyll/Safeway was acquired by Morrisons, creating the UK's fourth largest grocery retailer, next to Tesco, Asda/Wal-Mart, and Sainsbury's. (See Table 4.1 for the top five retailers in selected countries.)

In France, supermarkets and especially hypermarkets have been gaining market share since the 1960s. A law, the *Loi Royer*, was passed in 1973 with the intention of restricting the establishment of new larger retail outlets requiring approval of special regional commissions for new larger stores (S. Burt 1984).[6] A further regulation, *Loi Raffarin*, was passed in 1996, requiring an authorization for all new stores of more than 300 square meters. The suspicion was that this was especially directed against the expansion of German hard discounters in France (Colla 2003: 47). But the effects of both laws remained very limited.[7] Associations of independent retailers, like in the UK, emerged only after the 1960s, but in France they became more important: E. Leclerc now organizes independent hypermarket owners, while Intermarché (ITM), separated from E. Leclerc in 1969 and also known as Les Mousquetaires, organizes smaller retailers running supermarkets of various sizes. Both groups are amongst France's biggest retailers today.

Table 4.1. Top-five national grocery retailers, four European countries, 2007

United Kingdom			Germany		
Store	Sales (€bn)[a]	No. of outlets	Store	Sales (€bn)[a]	No of outlets
Tesco	51.0	2,115	Edeka	35.8	9,602
Sainsbury's	28.2	823	Rewe	31.6	9,492
Asda	24.4	352	Metro	26.3	1,259
Morrisons	19.0	375	Schwarz	25.1	3,405
M&S	12.2	622	Aldi	21.5	4,232
France			Italy[b]		
Store	Sales (€bn)	No. of outlets	Store	Sales (€bn)	No of outlets
Carrefour	37.6	1,699	CoopItalia	11.8	1,331
E. Leclerc	28.2	561	Conad	7.7	2,789
Intermarché	26.9	3,103	Interdis	7.1	3,712
Auchan	18.4	533	Selex	7.0	2,781
Casino	17.9	8,397	Carrefour	6.3	1,533

[a] Local food and non-food sales.
[b] Italian data for 2006.
Note: figures sometimes refer to gross or net sales.
Source: EHI Retail Institute (2008).

Ultimately, hypermarkets have become the dominant retail format, with a market share, in 2010, of over 50 percent in French grocery retailing. The largest groups in this segment are Carrefour, which merged with Promodès in 1999 (see below), and Auchan, which acquired Docks de France in 1996, as well as the voluntary group E. Leclerc. The supermarket segment has become dominated by Casino and the buying association ITM.

In Italy, because of the very restrictive regulation, the traditional small-scale retail structure has been preserved to a great extent (Pellegrini 1996; Zander-ighi 2003; see Figure 4.1). The level of concentration is still very low today. Several buying groups, such as Conad, Selex, Interdis, Sisa, and Despar, running mainly small and mid-sized supermarkets, are amongst the ten largest Italian grocery retailers. The first place is held by the consumer cooperative Coop Italia, which had been a pioneer in the development of supermarkets, and today also runs hypermarkets.

In 1998, a new law, the *legge Bersani*, abolished the product-specific sales area quota, giving more power to the regional level urban planning authorities. New stores now need a permit only if they are over 1,500 square meters, and permits are no longer limited by quota, but have to be based on regional zoning plans (Potz 2002). This liberalization has enabled the further growth of hypermarkets in Italy, whose number has nearly doubled since 2000. Two of the dominant players in this segment are the French companies Carrefour and Auchan.

The most striking characteristic of German retail development has been the success of hard discounters. This format had been pioneered by Aldi in the

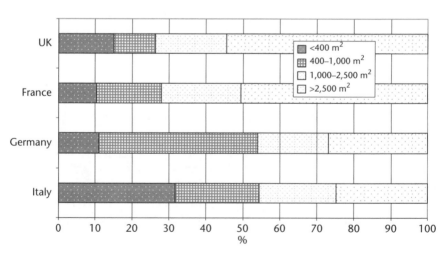

Figure 4.1. Grocery market share according to store size, four European countries, 2006
Source: Nielsen Company (2007); own careful estimates for small stores (<400 m²) in France, because original data omitted traditional stores.

1960s, but its overwhelming expansion began only in the 1970s, when Rewe, Tengelmann, the Schwarz Group (Lidl), and some other companies also developed their own hard-discount formats (Wortmann 2004). All these companies profited from the retail regulation that limited store size, and left other aspects, such as assortments, distribution centers, or ownership, unregulated. They were also supported by the abolishment of retail price maintenance in 1974. Since the 1980s, the hard discounters have slightly broadened their assortments, introducing dairy products, fresh produce, and meat. Even with a very limited assortment (between 600 and 1,600 SKUs), hard discounters have conquered over 40 percent of the German grocery market.

But, the two largest grocery retailers in Germany are still the buying groups Edeka and Rewe. Both have some thousand members, each which runs its own stores, usually supermarkets of various sizes. These groups increasingly operate as integrated systems, with a growing centralized steering capacity for assortments, prices, and store appearance. In addition, these groups run more and more stores that are owned by the groups' central headquarters. Rewe has invested considerably in the development and expansion of new retail formats, especially its hard-discount chain Penny. Edeka has grown recently through the takeover of the German voluntary chain Spar (then number seven in the German market) from the French ITM, which had been unable to run it successfully.

Another format that has developed quite successfully in Germany is the cash and carry (C&C) markets, where Metro is clearly the market leader. Through the takeover of the German stores from Wal-Mart, which had tried to enter the German market through two acquisitions in 1998–9, and the merger of these with its own chain of Real stores, Metro has become the biggest operator of large grocery stores in Germany. But stores with more than 5,000 square meters have a market share of only 13.5 percent in German grocery retailing, while stores with less than 800 square meters still capture over 50 percent; within this group, discounters with a total market share of over 40 percent have pushed all other kinds of small stores aside.

After having analyzed how the different patterns of retail development in the four biggest West European countries have been shaped by different general and retail-specific institutional legacies, we will now look more closely at how the different types of retailers that have developed under the different conditions in these countries have internationalized their operations.[8]

Carrefour

When Carrefour, then France's number two retailer, and Promodès, also amongst the top five, merged in 1999, they created the world's second largest retailer with a combined turnover of €54 billion. With this merger, Carrefour had become a truly multiple format retailer. While Carrefour had been the pioneer of the hypermarket and had realized 78 percent of its sales in these very large stores that combine food and non-food assortments, Promodès, originally a wholesale company, was stronger in supermarkets (37 percent), but also operated hypermarkets (42 percent) and other formats including hard-discount stores (7 percent). Both companies operated more than 9,000 stores in 26 countries.

Carrefour had been founded in 1959 by two entrepreneurs, Marcel Fournier and Louis Defforey, in Annecy in eastern France, where they opened a first supermarket at a crossroads (literally *carrefour*) in 1960.[9] At a time when there were only a very few self-service stores in France, this store became an immediate success; and its next supermarket already had a large parking lot. Following a trip to the United States, visits to several stores, and participation in seminars by the retail guru Trujillo in Dayton, Ohio, the two entrepreneurs invented a new store concept. The first hypermarket (*hypermarché*) was opened in Sainte-Geneviève-des-Bois, on the outskirts of Paris, in 1963. This store had a sales area of 2,500 square meters, 12 checkouts, and 400 parking spaces. Its assortment was concentrated in food, but it also carried a large range of non-food items. Carrefour's hypermarkets quickly became larger and larger. In the early 1970s the average store size was 10,000 square meters. The hypermarket that opened in 1972 south of Toulouse, with its 23,000 square meters, is still, in 2010, the largest hypermarket in Europe.[10] The additional floor space was increasingly used for an extended non-food assortment. Cheap land in commercial areas, accessible by highways, and a simple architecture reduced construction costs per square meter to one third of traditional supermarkets (Bell et al. 2004). Hypermarkets were to become the backbone of Carrefour's rapid growth. But Carrefour did not only establish its own outlets; the company also entered into partnerships and licensing agreements with several other companies, which set up hypermarkets under the Carrefour brand, amongst them Docks de France, Docks du Nord-Mielle (later Cora),[11] as well as Comptoirs Modernes and Promodès, which all operated their own hypermarket brands a few years later. The latter were to be merged into the new Carrefour more than two decades later (Lhermie 2003).

Internationalization began in 1969, one year before Carrefour was introduced at the Paris stock exchange. The first hypermarket abroad was opened in Belgium, in cooperation with Delhaize le Lion (which had a 70 percent share in the store).[12] Three stores were opened before Carrefour withdrew in 1978. The next country it entered was Switzerland: Carrefour held 25 percent in two hypermarkets; but sold its share in 1991. Great Britain followed in 1971, where four Carrefour hypermarkets were set up in cooperation with Dee (90 percent); here Carrefour withdrew in 1983.[13] In 1972 Carrefour entered

Italy; but, after opening two stores, it again withdrew. In Austria Carrefour opened a hypermarket (100 percent owned) at Shopping City Süd near Vienna in 1976, then Austria's largest food store; two years later Carrefour sold 51 percent and withdrew completely in 1990. The first Carrefour hypermarket in Germany was set up in cooperation with the German Stüssgen Group (60 percent) and the Belgian Delhaize le Lion (20 percent) in Mainz in 1977. Since further expansion failed, because of restrictive zoning policies, Carrefour withdrew less than two years later.

Only one of seven European market entries in the 1970s was to become successful: Spain. In a joint venture with Grupo Radar, which held 50 percent, the first hypermarket was opened in El Prat de Llobregat near Barcelona in 1973. In 1986, Carrefour took 100 percent in the company, which now operated under the name of Pryca (*precio y calidad*, price and quality). Shortly after Carrefour had introduced the new format into Spain, other French chains (amongst them Promodès (see below)) as well as Spanish companies followed (Cuesta 2004).

Carrefour's plans for internationalization were not limited to Europe. Carrefour was the first international grocery retailer to enter the Latin American market. In 1975 it set up its first hypermarket in Brazil. The first hypermarket in Argentina followed in 1982. Expansion in Latin America was very slow at first, as Carrefour experimented with the layout and the organization of its first stores (Bell et al. 2004); in 1985 there were still only ten stores. The operations in both countries were eventually to become very successful. Market entry into further Latin-American countries came much later. In Mexico Carrefour set up a joint venture with the local retail group Gigante, starting hypermarket operations in 1994. Four years later, Carrefour hypermarkets were also opened in Colombia, Chile, and, as a franchise, the Dominican Republic.

Carrefour also tried to enter the United States, opening its first outlet in 1988 in Philadelphia: a huge hypermarket, very similar to those it operated in France. At that time, Wal-Mart had already experimented with its own hypermarket format called Hypermart, which was very much a copy of Carrefour's French hypermarket outlets; and in the same year, 1988, Wal-Mart opened its first supercenter. A little later, Carrefour reacted by opening its second hypermarket in the United States, in Voorhees (NJ), this time somewhat smaller (and looking more like a warehouse club). Both stores were closed down in 1993, probably because of competition from nearby Wal-Mart stores.

At about the same time, Carrefour also turned to Asia and opened its first hypermarket in 1989 in Taiwan, in a joint venture with President Group, Taiwan's largest food manufacturer, which held 40 percent.[14] After Carrefour had set up a first hypermarket in Malaysia in 1994, also in cooperation with a local partner, other Asian countries quickly followed. In China, Carrefour began operations in 1995; and in 1996, it entered Thailand, South Korea, and Hong Kong; Singapore followed in 1997, and Indonesia in 1998. Within just five years, Carrefour had entered seven new Asian markets.

Parallel to this intercontinental expansion, Carrefour strengthened its position in its domestic and other European markets. An important step had been the creation in 1976 of a private "brand-free" or "no-name" label (*produits libre*) for a limited range of low-priced basic foods, offered in simple white packages. In 1978, after Aldi and others had firmly established the hard-discount format in Germany, Carrefour launched its own chain of hard-discount stores in France, called Ed. Attempts to enter the UK, Denmark, and Italy failed. A further step consolidating Carrefour's number one position in the French hypermarket segment was the acquisition of its smaller competitors, Euromarché and Montlaur, in 1991.

New attempts, after the failures in the 1970s, to enter European markets beyond France and Spain were made in 1993. Carrefour opened its first own hypermarket in Italy and also acquired Al Gran Sole, which owned four hypermarkets in the country. The same year, Carrefour set up its first hypermarket in Turkey in a joint venture with the second largest Turkish firm, the conglomerate Sabanci, which was also involved in joint ventures with food-processing firms such as Philip Morris Kraft and Danone (Tokatli and Eldener 2002). Finally, Carrefour's expansion into Eastern Europe began relatively late, when it opened its first hypermarket in Lodz, Poland, in 1997.

Paul-Auguste Halley, one of the founders of Promodès, the multinational retailer that merged with Carrefour in 1999, had been amongst the pioneers of the self-service concept in France when he opened some of the first supermarkets in the 1950s. Promodès itself was established through the merger of two wholesale companies in 1961. This tradition of wholesaling is also reflected in the operations of Promocash cash and carry markets, which started in 1965, and still operate today. In 1969, Promodès also began operating its supermarkets under the Champion banner; by the end of 1970 there were already 43 Champion supermarkets, and in 1990 there were over 350, most of them being franchised. Promodès had operated hypermarkets under a franchise agreement with Carrefour under the Carrefour banner since 1970, but the first hypermarket branded Continent was set up two years later, and Promodès's hypermarket sales grew at about the same speed as supermarket sales. Promodès also expanded its wholesale activities with neighborhood stores and convenience stores, which were franchised under the Shopi (1973) and 8 à Huit (1977) brands. Several acquisitions in the 1980s and 1990s also added to Promodès's domestic growth—amongst them 128 supermarkets from Primistères in 1988, Codec and Félix Potin convenience stores in 1990 and 1996, as well as Cattau from Tesco consisting of 7 hypermarkets, 73 supermarkets, and a few neighborhood stores in 1997 (see below).

Promodès undertook its first steps toward internationalization in 1975. It started to internationalize its hypermarket operations to two neighboring countries, Germany and Spain. In Germany, Promodès set up a joint venture with the German group Schaper, which held 60 percent. When Schaper merged with another German retailer, Asko, in 1988, the two partners split up. Some Continent hypermarkets were now rebranded by Asko as Real and later became part of Metro (see below), while some others were now owned 100 percent by Promodès. In 1990, Promodès in addition bought 47 Plaza hypermarkets from bankrupt Coop. But Promodès's hypermarket operations in Germany, which accounted for less than 5 percent of Promodès's total sales, never managed to achieve the size necessary to compete with its larger German competitors. After running into losses, Promodès withdrew from Germany in 1996, selling its Plaza hypermarkets to German Spar. In 1998 they were taken over by Wal-Mart and finally, in 2006, by Metro (see below).

Operations in Spain also started in 1975, and developed much better. Here Promodès also operated in a joint venture, but held a majority. The first Continent hypermarket was opened in Valencia in 1975—only two years after Carrefour had come to Barcelona. Some Champion supermarkets followed later. The Spanish base was also used in 1981 to enter neighboring Portugal, where Promodès opened hypermarkets in a joint venture with Sonae (Modelo-Continente).

Spain—and not its home country France—was also the place where Promodès started its own hard-discount chain in 1979, one year after Carrefour had started Ed discount in France. The discount concept of Día was not as "hard" as that of Aldi or Lidl: the stores, despite being significantly smaller, carried at least 1,600 SKUs, but, as the first hard-discount chain in Spain, it was to gain a dominant position in this growing segment of Spanish retailing. In the first half of the 1990s, the Día format was also transferred to several other countries. These attempts did not succeed in Italy and Promodès's own home country France, which Día left in 1996. But it was very successful in Portugal, where operations began in 1993 and were expanded in 1998 through the acquisition of the Portuguese discount chain Minipreço from French retailer Auchan, increasing the number of Promodès's hard-discount stores in Portugal by 125 to 300. In Greece, where Promodès had opened Continent hypermarkets since 1991, as well as in Turkey, where Día had started in 1999, Promodès also became the market leader in the discount segment. Día discount stores were also introduced into Argentina (1997), Brazil (2001), and China (2003).

Promodès also tried to enter the United States. In 1979–80 it acquired twenty-three supermarkets from Red Food Stores and tried to convert them into a more hypermarket-like format with a 50 percent non-food assortment. In 1983 it added forty supermarkets from Houchens. Later, Promodès also started several wholesale activities. But about ten years later Promodès left the United States, and sold its Red Food holdings to the Dutch retailer Ahold (1994).

Before the merger with Carrefour, the operations of Promodès were highly concentrated in France (63 percent of sales in 1987) and Spain (28.5 percent). Further European activities were concentrated in Italy, where Promodès had bought the supermarket chain GS (6 percent) (see below) and Greece (1.6 percent). In Taiwan, where a Continent hypermarket had opened in 1995, Promodès sold out to its local partner in 1998. Hypermarket operations in Indonesia, in cooperation with local partner Sinar Mas, were just about to start in 1998. Compared with Promodès, Carrefour, despite the fact that its two main markets were also France (57 percent of sales in 1998) and Spain (over 10 percent), was much more global, with operations in several Latin-American (23 percent) and Asian (6 percent) countries. But its business was concentrated in hypermarkets, while Promodès was much more diversified as regards formats.

In 1999, three years after French hypermarket giant Auchan had merged with Docks de France (Mammouth), and Metro had established itself as Europe's biggest retailer, and two years after Wal-Mart had entered the European stage, Carrefour and Promodès merged their activities. This new Carrefour was now Europe's largest and the world's second largest retailer. In addition to the merger, a large number of other companies in France and abroad were acquired between 1998 and 2000.

The most important was the acquisition of Comptoirs Modernes, a very old family business that had started a self-service store in France as early as 1949, and now consisted of 16 Carrefour branded hypermarkets, a chain of over 400 supermarkets (Stoc), and about 300 convenience stores (Comod; Marché Plus). Comptoirs Modernes had also been operating in Spain since 1988, where it had developed a group of over 100 supermarkets under various, frequently acquired brands, such as Maxor and Supeco. Promodès had also recently (1987) expanded its Spanish operations when it acquired a chain of 61 Simago supermarkets.

In addition to the strengthening of the new Carrefour's position in its two core markets, France and Spain, the group also expanded its activities into other European countries. In 2000 Carrefour bought Italian Gruppo GS, with which Promodès had cooperated since 1997, and which owned more than 20 hypermarkets, as well as networks of almost 300 supermarkets (two-thirds franchised) and over 500 convenience stores (DìperDì; mostly franchised). Carrefour was now operating 31 hypermarkets in Italy. Also in 2000 Carrefour re-entered the Belgian market, acquiring GB (Grand Basar) the country's leading retailer, in which Promodès had taken a minority share in 1998. GB operated 60 hypermarkets, as well as 73 integrated and 350 franchised supermarkets. In Greece, Carrefour set up a 50:50 joint venture with Marino-poulos, managed by Carrefour (in 2000). The company, operating 10 hyper-markets and 133 supermarkets, was the biggest retailer in Greece. The discounter Día was not integrated in this joint venture and expanded its business independently to 190 stores in 2000. In 2001 Carrefour took 40 percent in a joint venture with Maus Group in Switzerland; 11 Jumbo stores were converted to Carrefour hypermarkets.

This wave of acquisitions, which all occurred at about the same time as the merger of Carrefour and Promodès, gave the company a strong position in France and Spain, as well as in Belgium, Italy, and Greece. Because of its mix of formats, ranging from huge hypermarkets, supermarkets, to small (frequently franchised) convenience stores, operating in all countries, in some countries flanked by discount stores, Carrefour was able to react flexibly to customer needs as well as to regulatory demands, utilizing several cross-format syner-gies—for example, in sourcing and private-label development, or in logistics and distribution. From now on, a multi-format strategy was used not only in European core countries but also in transition and developing countries. Market entries and growth in many of these countries were again accelerated. But, based on its strategy to become the number one grocery retailer in every country where it operated, or at least to be amongst the top three, Carrefour—as in earlier decades—also retreated from a large number of countries where it was not possible to achieve this goal. In Europe, Carrefour withdrew—again—from Switzerland, and sold its hypermarkets in Portugal.

When Carrefour acquired Belgian GB in 2000, this company also operated 27 Globi supermarkets in Poland, which considerably strengthened the so far very weak position of Carrefour's hypermarkets in that country. Carrefour then opened many new outlets, including convenience stores and also so-called mini-hypermarkets. Finally, in 2007 it became the country's number one mass food retailer, when it took over 183 supermarkets and 15 hypermar-kets from Dutch Ahold. Carrefour also entered the Czech Republic (1998) and Slovakia (2000) by setting up new hypermarkets. But it was unable to grow successfully, and thus it decided to withdraw from the market. The Czech hypermarkets were sold to Tesco (see below).[15] A further Eastern European country that Carrefour entered was Romania. Here a French franchisee had first opened some hypermarkets (Hyparlo) in 1999. Five years later, Carrefour took control. The number one hypermarket group in the country finally broadened its activities by adding 21 supermarkets of the local chain Artima to its 11 hypermarkets at the end of 2007. In Turkey, Carrefour strengthened its position as number two retailer by buying Gima, the country's third largest supermarket chain, with 81 stores, as well as a chain of 45 discount stores in 2005.

Parallel to its merger with Promodès and the various European acquisitions, in Latin America Carrefour now added more supermarkets to its hypermarket business—also by acquisitions. In Brazil in 1998–9, it bought 6 local supermarket chains with a total of 85 stores, amongst them 23 stores of Lojas Americanas—the company that had been the joint-venture partner of Wal-Mart when it entered Brazil in 1994. Since 2001 Día discount stores have also operated in Brazil. In 2007, by acquiring 34 hypermarkets from Atacadao, Carrefour became Brazil's number one food retailer. In Argentina, Carrefour started Día operations in 1999, and by adding over 130 supermarkets of the leading local chain Norte to its 21 hypermarkets two years later became the number one grocery retailer in Argentina, too.

In contrast to these two countries, in Colombia, where Carrefour had set up its first hypermarket in 1998, the company grew only internally and, as of 2010, still operates only hypermarkets, which it has partly adapted to different kinds of neighborhoods. Here Carrefour is only the number two, far behind Casino. In two other Latin-American countries, Carrefour decided to leave: it sold its seven hypermarkets in Chile in 2004, and in 2005 a further twenty-nine hypermarkets in Mexico.

In Asia, Carrefour further expanded its hypermarket activities. In Taiwan the number of outlets was doubled from twenty-four (2000) to forty-eight (2007), which was only partly due to an agreement with Tesco, by which Carrefour traded its Czech hypermarkets for six hypermarkets in Taiwan. In Indonesia where Carrefour had opened its first hypermarket in 1998, in the middle of the Asian financial crisis, it has recently speeded up expansion, opening seventeen outlets in 2006–7 and buying a 75 percent stake in the local retailer Alfa Retailindo, which operated twenty-nine supermarkets of various sizes, in early 2008. These were the only acquisitions Carrefour made in Asia, where most of the growth so far had been generated internally.

In China in the beginning of the 2000s, Carrefour had serious problems with government authorities, resulting from the way it had operated its first hypermarkets. Carrefour's Chinese retail operations had been owned by joint-venture companies with different local partners in which Carrefour held only a minority, but these operating companies were linked by management contracts with additional joint-venture companies in which Carrefour owned a majority. This allowed Carrefour effectively to control its retail operations in China, bypassing restrictive legislation that did not allow majority ownership. Following some legal wrangling, public apologies by Carrefour, and—at the same time—a loosening of tight regulation, 89 hypermarkets were set up after 2002. By May 2008 Carrefour operated 113 hypermarkets all over the country, form Shenzhen to Harbin and from Shanghai to Urumqi. Attempts to add supermarkets to its Chinese stores were halted after two years. But the Día discount chain that started operations in 2003 has already grown to nearly 300 stores, concentrated in Shanghai and Beijing.

While Carrefour has managed to become the leading foreign retailer in Taiwan, Indonesia, and—at least for a time—China,[16] as well as in Singapore, where it operates two hypermarkets, it has been much less successful in Malaysia (twelve outlets) and Thailand, where its twenty-seven hypermarkets bring it only to fifth place amongst Thailand's grocery retailers. In Hong Kong, South Korea, and Japan, where again Carrefour was unable to become one of the leading retailers, it withdrew from the markets, by selling its stores to local companies or, in Japan, by franchising the stores out to Aeon, Japan's largest retailer.

By 2008 Carrefour was the second biggest retailer of the world; it was number one not only in Europe and its home country France but also in Spain, Belgium, and Greece, in Brazil and Argentina, in Taiwan and Indonesia; and number two in Italy, Poland, and Turkey, as well as being the second largest foreign-owned retailer in China. France accounted for 43.4 percent of total net sales of €108.6 billion; other European countries accounted for 39.1 percent, Latin-America for 11.1 percent, and Asia for 6.4 percent.

In 2008, 1,302 (in 2007: 1247) hypermarkets accounted for 59.0 percent of the group's total sales. The vast majority of these hypermarkets were located outside France (228): in Western Europe, Carrefour operated hypermarkets in Spain (168), Italy (69), Belgium (57), Greece and Cyprus (31), and Turkey (22). In Eastern Europe Carrefour's hypermarkets were located in Poland (78) and Romania (21). Its presence in Latin America was concentrated in Brazil (162), Argentina (67), and Colombia (59). And in East and South East Asia it was focused on China (134), Taiwan (59), Indonesia (37), Thailand (27), Malaysia (12), and Singapore (2). In addition, franchised outlets operated in Japan (7), nine Arab countries (27), and the Dominican Republic (1), as well as in French overseas departments and territories.

Supermarkets accounted for 23.6 percent of total sales, mostly under the Champion banner. This business is relatively less internationalized and still concentrated in Europe. In countries outside Europe, supermarkets have followed the expansion of hypermarkets. Out of 2,919 supermarkets, 1,001 were in France, 508 in Italy, 444 in Belgium, many operated by franchisees and licensees; others were in Greece and Cyprus (229), and in Poland (225), Turkey (125), and Spain (98). The few supermarkets outside Europe were concentrated in Argentina (112) and Brazil (39). Convenience stores, which are mostly franchised, are the least internationalized store type: of the 4,813 stores, over two-thirds were in France and most others in Italy (1,016), Belgium (191), and Greece and Cyprus (256).

Discount stores, accounting for 10.2 percent of the group's sales, are a very special case. While the discount business of Carrefour under the Ed banner, started in France in 1978, it has never been internationally successful, Promo-dès's Día format, which has been developed since 1979 in Spain, where Carrefour's discount division is headquartered, has been transferred to other Mediterranean countries and even to Latin America and China—adding on to the already established hypermarkets. In 2008 there were 22,796 Día stores in Spain, 914 Ed stores in France, 498 Minipreço stores in Portugal, 613 Día stores in Turkey, and 372 in Greece and Cyprus. Further Día stores are in Argentina (410), Brazil (327), and China (322).

Aldi

The brothers Karl and Theodor Albrecht ran their first shop, originally owned by their mother, in Essen in the Ruhr area from 1946.[17] Like many others in the early post-war period, this little store sold a very limited range of products. By 1950 the Albrechts had expanded and owned thirteen shops. It was in this period that they developed some central elements of their hard-discount retailing strategy. When the German economy recovered and an increasingly diversified range of products became available on the wholesale market, the Albrechts discovered that they could make a good business by sticking to the limited product range, since this allowed them to keep their costs low. In the early 1950s their shops concentrated on the fastest-moving articles and offered only one product of each kind. In total, only between 250 and 280 different products were offered. Besides helping to reduce purchase prices, since products could be bought in larger quantities, this improved the effi-ciency of sales work, since the lack of choice encouraged customers to decide quickly what to buy. As Karl Albrecht explained in 1953, the company "adhered to the principles of low prices as well as that of limited selection . . . we went so far as to exclude whole product categories. The reason? Turnover." There were no decorations, counters and shelves were kept very simple, and all products were visibly displayed for the customers. This helped to keep total sales costs down to 11 percent and personnel costs to between 3.1 percent and 3.7 percent of turnover. Advertising expenditure was less than 0.1 percent, since "all our promotions are put into discount prices."[18]

This concept allowed the Albrechts to expand dramatically. By 1960, the number of outlets had increased to 300. The following year, the two Albrecht brothers divided their business into two clearly separated areas, Nord and Süd, with Theo in the north and Karl in the south; this division was later extended to an agreed segmentation of foreign markets as well. The first "real" Aldi (Albrecht Discount) store opened in 1962 in the Ruhr-area city of Dortmund. It combined the principles described above with the new concept of self-service, which had slowly started to spread in Germany in the mid-1950s

(Henksmeier 1988). The first Aldi outlets had an average sales area of somewhere above 200 square meters and sold only a small assortment of 400 fast-moving packaged grocery products that could be easily (and cheaply) handled and stored. By 1974 there were already 1,000 Aldi stores in Germany.

Up to the present, Aldi has remained true to its original principles of concentrating on a limited number of high-sale, fast-moving goods, keeping in-store presentation of goods as simple as possible (products are left in their cardboard boxes or even on the palette), and reducing service to the minimum. The high turnover/space ratio and low store and personnel costs, which allow low sales margins, combined with the low cost of sourcing made possible by large-scale buying, enable Aldi to offer its products at very low prices. Almost all products sold at Aldi stores are private labels with fancy names made up like branded products. They are frequently sourced from mid-sized manufacturers that, while typically able to maintain reliable long-term supplier relationships, remain highly dependent on Aldi.

Aldi Nord and Süd are, in 2010, still family owned. They do not publish annual reports or any similar information and do not have public-relations departments. The internal ownership and management structures of the group are complex and inscrutable. Distribution and sales activities are organized in local companies consisting of forty or fifty stores grouped around their distribution center. This unit size also defines the minimum size for international activities (except for intra-EU border regions).

The international expansion of Aldi (Süd) started as early as 1967, when the company took over the small Austrian retail chain Hofer. Aldi transformed the stores to its own concept and used the Hofer stores as a platform for further growth. Austria is the only country where Aldi discount stores do not operate under the Aldi banner. Other neighboring countries were entered by Aldi Nord: the Netherlands in 1973 and Belgium in 1976, again by acquiring small local firms as starting platforms. The first stores in Denmark (1977) concluded the first phase of market entries into neighboring European countries. In all these countries Aldi was the first company to introduce the hard-discount concept. In Austria, the Netherlands, and Belgium Aldi was able to grow quickly, while in Denmark it was soon confronted with competition from Dansk Supermarked's own discount chain Netto, started in 1981.[19]

In 1976 Aldi Süd entered the United States. It acquired some fifty stores from Benner Tea of Iowa and remolded the stores to its own hard-discount concept, even though US stores are a bit larger and carry more products (about 1,400 regular SKUs) than the German original.[20] Since then, operations have spread continuously from Kansas to the East Coast, recently even down to Florida. Today, Aldi owns over 1,000 stores in 29 states. In 1979 Theo Albrecht from Aldi Nord made an investment that was very untypical for the company. He acquired the California-based retailer Trader Joe's. In stores of 1,500 square meters, it sold about 2,500–3,000 quality food items, many of them specialties with a gourmet touch. As in Aldi stores, about 80 percent of the items are private labels. Even though this company is managed quite independently from Aldi's hard-discount operations, there are certainly synergies, especially in sourcing European-style food products. Trader Joe's has developed extremely well and by 2009 operated over 300 stores in 23 states.

During the 1980s, partly in reaction to the emergence of competitors in Germany's discount segment, Aldi introduced some changes to its business model. It started to broaden its regular assortment, which until then had been limited to canned and dry foods, with new products: in particular, dairy products were introduced as well as fresh produce. The number of SKUs increased to over 600 at Aldi Nord and 700 at Aldi Süd. But the still limited range of products allowed Aldi to avoid costly investments in IT systems and scanner checkouts for a long time. These were installed only in the early 2000s. With this wider assortment Aldi competed not only with newly emerging discounters, such as Penny, Plus, and Lidl, which were all somewhat "softer," but also with traditional supermarkets.[21] In addition, Aldi, like other discounters, began to sell various non-food products, such as kitchenware, textiles, toys, or stationery products, and even TV sets and computers. Since Aldi stores, because of German regulations, cannot expand their store size, it is not possible to keep all these products in stock at the same time. Instead, they are sold as one-off special offers, which change once or twice a week. All these products are manufactured exclusively for Aldi, and are usually sourced through specialized importers. At Aldi, these products account for over 20 percent of total sales, making the company one of the top ten apparel retailers in Germany. Its special-offer computers have also become quite popular since the mid-1990s.

In 1988–90, in a second phase of internationalization, Aldi Nord entered France and Luxembourg, while Aldi Süd turned to the UK. In France, Aldi faced competition not only from local companies like Ed (Carrefour) or Leader Price (Casino) but also from Aldi's German arch rival Lidl, which entered France as its first foreign market in 1989 and has since become the number one discounter in the country. Faced with this situation, Aldi bought 74 Día stores from Promodès in 1996, an unusual step for Aldi, which usually prefers to grow internally. The UK also proved to be a difficult environment for Aldi— as for hard discounters in general, which have been unable to overcome their poor image in an environment of high brand awareness. Generally, the 1990s were characterized by the addition of further stores in those countries that Aldi had already entered, and by the expansion of Aldi Nord into Eastern Germany.

By the end of the 1990s, a third phase of internationalization began. In 1999 Aldi Süd expanded from the UK to Ireland, and in 2001 it turned to Australia, where its entry raised furious public debates. But Aldi was able to do well, even without acquiring a starting base in this faraway market. In 2002 Aldi Nord set up its first stores in Spain, where it had to struggle with Día as well as Lidl, which had already entered the market. A few stores were opened in Portugal, supplied from distribution centers in Spain. In 2005 Aldi Süd entered Switzerland, a non-EU market dominated by local supermarket chains and characterized by relatively high retail prices. In 2008 Aldi Süd entered Greece, where it was able to operate thirty-five stores.

Amongst the larger German discounters, Aldi was the last to enter Eastern Europe. In 2005 the first stores were opened in Slovenia, operating under the Hofer banner and managed from Austria. Austria was also used as a springboard to enter Hungary, where it proceeded to operate over fifty stores. Aldi Nord has also turned to Eastern Europe, opening a distribution center and some forty stores since 2008 in Poland.

By 2008 Aldi was operating about 8,500 stores worldwide, of which over 7,000 were in Europe, including 4,200 in Germany. About 80 percent of all Germans live within walking distance of an Aldi store, and at least 70 percent of all households use one of these stores at least 'occasionally'. In its home country, Aldi is the fifth biggest grocery retailer. And the company has a similarly strong position in Austria, Belgium, and the Netherlands. However, in other countries, such as the UK or Spain, it is not even amongst the top ten grocery retailers. In the USA Aldi, including Trader Joe's, ranks only at about the twentieth place. But this—seemingly—weak position in several host countries is no problem for Aldi and other hard discounters, as they can generate high cross-border synergies (see below).

Metro

The German retail conglomerate Metro AG was Europe's largest retailer until the 1999 merger between Carrefour and Promodès. Metro is active in a broad range of retail and trading activities, including food retailing in large stores under various brands, Galeria Kaufhof and Horten department stores, various specialized retail chains such as Media-Markt and Saturn (trading consumer electronics and home appliances), as well as a broad range of other activities, many of which have been divested since 1998.

The most important division were cash and carry outlets operating under the Metro and Makro brands in Germany as well as in seventeen other countries, contributing 40 percent to total sales at that time. The company Metro SB-Großmarkt was founded in 1963 by two established wholesale businessmen. One year later, Otto Beisheim became managing director and the company established its first self-service wholesale outlet in Mühlheim, in the heart of the Ruhr area. This self-service wholesale outlet operated on an area of 14,000 square meters catering to small retailers and other businesses. Even though the cash and carry concept, which had originated in the USA, had been introduced to Germany before, Metro, because of its financial resources, became by far the most successful company in this field. After 1967 the company was owned in equal parts by the families of Schmidt-Ruthenbeck, the co-founder, and Haniel, the owner of the huge trading company Franz Haniel & Cie., as well as its general manager Otto Beisheim. By 1970 there were already thirteen Metro cash and carry outlets in Germany. Their status as a wholesaler leaves C&C big boxes unaffected by restrictive German special planning regulation, which was to restrict other large retail formats.

Internationalization also started quite early. In 1968 Metro and the Dutch family-owned conglomerate Steenkolen Handelsvereniging (SHV) struck a partnership agreement to combine their forces on international markets. In some countries SHV would hold 60 percent and Metro 40 percent in operations under the Makro brand, while in other countries Metro would hold 60 percent and SHV 40 percent, and operations were to be branded Metro. The first outlet was opened the same year in Amsterdam. In 1970–1 further Makro stores followed in Belgium and the UK, while Metro stores were opened in Austria, Denmark, and France. With the opening of a Metro store in Italy and a Makro store in Spain in 1972, the first phase of foreign-market entries was completed. Only eight years after its first German cash and carry outlet, Metro operated outlets in nine European countries.

During the 1980s a long period of acquisitions and diversifications as well as corporate restructurings began, which ended only in 1998. By 1986 Metro gained a controlling interest in Kaufhof, one of four big German department store chains originating from the end of the nineteenth century, which also owned a chain of around 100 Kaufhalle variety stores. In 1994, Kaufhof acquired Horten department stores.[22] In the late 1980s, Kaufhof had also expanded into specialized non-food retailing; it acquired two chains of larger stores specializing in consumer electronics and household appliances, Media-Markt and Saturn, which were merged to form Media-Saturn-Holding in 1990. Other diversifications of Metro and Kaufhof turned to shoe stores (Reno), office equipment (Sigma), and a computer store franchise system (Vobis).

By 1993 Metro had step by step gained majority control in another big German retail conglomerate, the Asko group. Asko had started as a regional consumers' cooperative in the late nineteenth century, which was transformed into a stock-listed corporation in 1972 and had since grown through specializing in larger food stores (under the Basaar banner) while abandoning smaller ones. It had also acquired several grocery retail groups, which were themselves frequently the results of merger processes amongst smaller retail companies that had started to set up larger out-of-town stores in the 1960s, at a time when restrictive retail legislation had not yet been introduced. The large grocery store format developed in Germany is called *SB-Warenhaus*— literally: self-service warehouse. These stores are frequently referred to as hypermarkets, as we will do in this chapter, even though they are usually somewhat smaller than their French counterparts and carry only about 25–40 percent non-food products.[23]

One of the groups acquired by Asko was Schaper, which owned some cash and carry outlets, Extra supermarkets, as well as several hypermarket chains, such as Real, Esbella, and Continent (in cooperation with Promodès (see above)). Another group acquired in 1990 was Deutsche SB-Kauf. This company consisted of what was left over from another company, which until recently had been known as Coop AG and which still owned a large number of stores of various formats, sizes, and brands (Comet, Tip, and so on). Coop had developed from the merger of around a hundred local consumer cooperatives during the 1970s and 1980s, and had a very complicated and opaque ownership structure, including various trade unions as well as its own managers, frequently former trade unionists. Coop was dissolved in 1988, following one of Germany's greatest business scandals. Asko also engaged in a partnership with Massa Group, which like Asko was amongst the top ten German grocery retailers at that time. But Asko also ventured into new businesses: it established the DIY chain Praktiker, bought the apparel retailer Adler, which owned apparel factories in Germany, Sri Lanka, and South Korea, and took 50 percent in a chain of furniture stores.

In 1996 Metro merged its German cash and carry business, together with the various activities of Kaufhof and Asko, into the newly founded stock-listed Metro AG, which immediately became Europe's number one retailer. Former Metro general manager Beisheim, who had retired from active management in 1994, and the Schmidt-Ruthenbeck and Haniel families still owned the majority of this company through Metro Holding AG, which had been founded in Baar, Switzerland, several years previously—probably for tax reasons. The Metro and Makro cash and carry operations outside Germany were still held directly by this Swiss holding, together with the Dutch company SHV. In 1998, Metro bought all the shares of SHV in the joint European operations, and transferred their ownership to Metro AG. At that time, Metro had already started to set up its own (100 percent owned) cash and carry stores in China and Romania in 1996 (see below).

SHV kept its activities under the Makro cash and carry brand in Latin America and Asia. By 2009 SHV ran 72 outlets in Brazil, 19 in Argentina, 29 in Venezuela, and 13 in Colombia. In Asia, SHV had been active in Thailand, Indonesia, China, the Philippines, Malaysia, and South Korea. South Korean stores were sold to Wal-Mart in 1999, stores in Malaysia were sold to Tesco in 2007, while stores in the Philippines, China, and Indonesia were sold to local partners. In Thailand, by 2009, SHV was running about forty Makro cash and carry outlets; and a joint venture in Pakistan, started in 2006, operates another four stores.

Parallel to the integration of these various activities of Kaufhof and Asko, Metro also tried to get rid of several businesses defined as non-core: the apparel manufacturing and retailing activities of Adler, the variety stores of Kaufhalle, and some unprofitable department stores of Kaufhof, the participation in a furniture store chain, the grocery discount chain Tip, the computer store franchise Vobis, the shoe stores Reno, the office equipment stores Sigma, and several other companies, combining sales of nearly $10 billion, were transferred to a special holding company in which Metro held only 49 percent, and were to be sold whenever possible. The Sigma office equipment stores were, for example, sold to Staples. In 2005 Metro also divested its chain of Praktiker DIY stores, originally started by Asko in the 1970s. Praktiker had become the number four European DIY retailer, which had also entered Greece, Poland, Hungary, Turkey, Romania, and finally Bulgaria.

From 1998 on, Metro concentrated on four core businesses, integrated in four divisions: cash and carry (Metro, Makro), food retail (Real, Extra), non-food specialty stores (especially Media-Saturn), and department stores (Galeria Kaufhof). In these four business areas, brand integration and internationalization were pushed forward from the early 1990s. The department stores of Kaufhof and Horten were integrated under the Galeria Kaufhof concept and brand, while smaller and unprofitable stores were sold. In 2001, fifteen department stores of Inno in Belgium were added and subsequently also refurbished. Even though this seems a small step of internationalization, it is remarkable in the department-store business, where European companies rarely have left their home market.

The former Kaufhof subsidiary Media-Saturn-Holding became a true category killer in the fields of consumer electronics, information and telecommunication products, office equipment, as well as small and large electric appliances. It carried traditional European manufacturer brands, low-profile brands of specialized German importers as well as most international computer brands, and also Chinese Haier appliances; but there were no private labels. Store managers usually owned a participation of around 10 percent in the single stores and had some degree of autonomy concerning assortment, pricing, and even advertising. By the mid-1990s there were already 150 Media-Markt and Saturn stores in Germany, as well as a few stores in France (from 1989), Austria (1990), and Switzerland (1994). Hungary, Poland, and Spain followed soon after, and in 1999 Media World, a group with twenty-three stores, was acquired in Italy. Since 2000 the company has entered the Netherlands, Portugal, Greece, Sweden, Russia, Turkey, and Luxembourg. At the end of 2008, there were 768 Media-Markt and Saturn stores, about half of them in

Germany (367), 315 in Western Europe, and 86 in Eastern Europe. Stores also became much larger over time: average size grew from 2,500 square meters in 1998 to 3,100 square meters in 2007.

The various food retail chains that Metro had acquired through Asko were restructured from the early 1990s on. This ultimately led to the divestment of over 250 supermarkets to the German group Rewe in 2008, while the larger 162 hypermarkets, with an average size of 7,068 square meters, were consolidated under the Real banner chain, which was further expanded in 1998 with the acquisition of 94 Allkauf and 20 Kriegbaum stores. The Real chain was also internationalized. The first four stores abroad were opened in Poland in 1997, and the first Turkish store followed just one year later. After 2005 stores were also opened in Romania and Russia. In 2006 Metro also acquired nineteen Géant hypermarkets from the French retailer Casino in Poland. In the same year, Metro also acquired all eighty-five German Wal-Mart stores. Wal-Mart had entered the German market in 1997–8 when it took over the stores of Wertkauf and Eurospar. The reasons for its failure are probably manifold and cannot be discussed here, but it should be noted that the combined sales of Wal-Mart in Germany were only a fraction (little more than 10 percent in 2005) of Wal-Mart/Asda sales in the UK, stores—though large by German standards—were small for Wal-Mart, and the buying organizations of the two acquired chains were highly fragmented. In 2009, Real operated around 340 hypermarkets in Germany, 54 in Poland, 21 in Romania, 14 in Russia, 13 in Turkey, and 1 in Ukraine.

Amongst the four business divisions of Metro, cash and carry has always been the core and also the most internationalized. In Germany, most of the cash and carry markets that had been operated by various acquired companies were converted to the Metro cash and carry brand. By 2008, Metro had increased the number of cash and carry markets in Germany to 126, from about 50 in 1986.

By 1972, Metro, together with its Dutch Partner SHV, had set up outlets in eight European countries. The two partners then started a second round of internationalization, beginning in the Mediterranean in the early 1990s. Metro cash and carry markets were opened in Turkey, and Makro markets in Portugal, Morocco, and Greece, by 1992. In 1994 expansion turned toward Eastern Europe: the first stores were opened in Hungary (Metro) and Poland (Makro); the Czech Republic (Makro) followed in 1997. In 1996 Metro had also started fully owned operations in Romania.

Another country that Metro entered on its own was China. Here it partnered with Shanghai-based conglomerate Jinjiang Group, which took 40 percent in the operations. A first store was opened in Shanghai in 1996. This was a risky investment, because the Shanghai government licensed such new retail operations, knowing all the while that at that time the Chinese central government had not allowed foreign companies to hold a majority stake in retail companies (Wang and Zhang 2005). It did so only in 1998, and Metro received the first license for the operation of cash and carry outlets throughout China in 1999. This was welcomed by Metro as a breakthrough for accelerated expansion over the coming years. Metro has since expanded in the Shanghai area, but also all over Eastern and Central China. In China, Metro took some innovative measures. For example, it established training kitchens at its Shanghai and Beijing stores, whose mission—according to its website—is, on the one hand, to raise the level of service to professionals by increasing the product knowledge of Metro staff, "and on the other, through the training of cooking skills, [to] influence professionals and raise the awareness of Metro's profile" in China.[24] In 2006, Metro raised its stake in the Chinese operation to 90 percent.

After 1998 Metro entered a large number of Eastern European countries: Bulgaria, Slovakia, Croatia, Russia, Ukraine, Moldova, and Serbia. Besides China, selected Asian countries were also entered: Japan and Vietnam in 2002, India in 2003, Pakistan in 2007, and Kazakhstan in 2009. In Japan, Metro joined forces with the huge conglomerate Marubeni, which holds 20 percent in the new company.

Metro's most important division is also its most internationalized. In 2008, 655 Metro cash and carry outlets accounted for sales of €33 billion, just about half of total Metro group sales; only 17 percent thereof was realized by its 126 German outlets. Metro is the market leader in the cash and carry business, not only in Germany, but also in the UK (33 stores), France (91), and Italy (48), as well as in several other countries, such as Belgium (11), the Netherlands (17), Poland (29), Romania (24), Russia (48), Slovakia (5), Turkey (13), the Czech Republic (12), and in China (38).

Metro's food retailing business, with total sales of €11.6 billion, is much less internationalized. In Germany, in 2009, Metro's 343 Real stores were number two in the hypermarket business, behind Schwarz Group's Kaufland chain, while in Poland, Metro's 50 stores make it also number two, behind Tesco. The category specialist Media-Markt/Saturn, with its 768 stores and total sales of €19 billion is highly internationalized. It is the European market leader, ahead of British DSG International, former Dixons.

Today, Metro is the world's fourth biggest retailer, with total sales of over €68 billion. With 39 percent of these sales in Germany, nearly 35 percent in other Western European countries,[25] and nearly 25 percent in Eastern Europe, Metro is—despite its high degree of internationalization—a very European company; only 3 percent of its sales are outside Europe, in five Asian countries, including China, and Morocco.

Tesco

Jack Cohen started as a grocery market stall holder in London and opened his first store in 1929. By the end of the 1930s, there were already 100 Tesco stores, grouped around a modern food warehouse. During two trips to the United States before and after the Second World War, Cohen learned about the self-service concept.[26] After some experiments with this innovation in the UK, he opened a first self-service supermarket in 1956. Tesco was soon expanding by setting up new stores, but also through a large number of acquisitions, adding several hundred stores to its portfolio. By the late 1960s, the supermarket chain consisted of about 800 stores. Its supermarkets had also become larger and larger. In 1968, the first store was opened that was labeled a superstore; it extended over 4,000 square meters.

In the 1970s Tesco abolished trading stamps and started its "Operation Checkout" campaign, reducing prices to undercut those of its main competitors. The company also decided to close some 500 small stores and prioritized the development of large out-of-town superstores where parking was convenient and a higher volume of business could be generated. The 1980s saw the introduction of computerized checkouts as well as Tesco's own private labels for high-quality products, supplemented somewhat later—in reaction to foreign hard discounters entering the UK market—by the low-priced Tesco Value brand. In 2009 more than 10,000 Tesco branded SKUs account for 48 percent of total sales, the highest share of any full-assortment retailer in the European Union.

In the early 1980s Tesco had tried to establish its own chain of discount stores; but the forty-five outlets that had been established were sold after only four years of trial and error. Tesco, in cooperation with Marks & Spencer, also began to invest in greenfield shopping centers that held Tesco superstores as anchor stores. The first of these out-of-town shopping centers had a 6,100-square-meter Tesco superstore with 900 employees and 42 computerized checkout counters. By the beginning of the 1990s, Tesco had reduced the number of its stores to 371, 150 of which were superstores, which generated most of the company's sales and profits. And by 1994, after an acquisition of fifty-seven stores in Scotland and northern England, Tesco had become the number one grocery retailer in the UK. In the same year Tesco also started operating a new store format, the Tesco Express convenience stores.

Tesco's first steps toward internationalization came quite late in comparison to its main competitors. It started with Ireland in 1979; but the majority share taken in a local retail chain was divested seven years later. When Tesco took a majority in a regional retail chain in northern France in 1992, it was unable to use this as a springboard for further expansion; Tesco withdrew from France in

1997, selling its activities to Promodès. While these first two foreign investments directed toward neighboring mature retail markets had failed, Tesco's further expansion into the emerging markets of Eastern Europe and Asia were to become successful (Dawson, Larke, and Choi 2006).

In 1994 Tesco entered Hungary, acquiring the local Global supermarket chain with forty-three small stores for £15 million, and, one year later, it acquired Savia, a chain of thirty-six small supermarkets in Poland, for £8 million. In both cases Tesco used these companies to acquire some knowledge of the local markets including a pool of experienced managers that Tesco would later use for establishing its own large stores, while closing down the acquired ones.

The next countries to be entered were the Czech Republic and Slovakia. Here, Kmart from the USA had acquired thirteen department and variety stores from the former Czechoslovak government in 1992. Kmart's problems in the United States prompted the company to sell the six Kmart stores in the Czech Republic and the seven stores in Slovakia, most of which were quite profitable, to Tesco in 1996. With these acquisitions, Tesco was dealing for the first time with a broad range of non-food merchandise lines, and the company used the experience that it made with these stores as a starting point to depart radically from its established superstore format in the UK (Palmer 2005). Tesco had decided to develop its own hypermarket stores. This new format developed conjointly in the UK home market and in the distant markets of Eastern Europe. After a short period of experimentation, hypermarkets became the main driver of Tesco's growth in the new century.

In the UK, Tesco opened its first hypermarket in 1997 under the new banner of Tesco Extra. This store covered over 9,300 square meters, with one-quarter of the sales area occupied with non-food assortments. By the end of 1999 Tesco operated five hypermarkets in the UK. By the end of 2007 there were 166. The average size of Tesco's hypermarkets is now about 6,500 square meters, but at several of these stores non-food accounts for some 40 percent of sales space. Tesco's share in the UK non-food market has grown from about 1 percent to over 8 percent since 2000.[27]

In 1997 Tesco entered the Irish market for the second time, this time acquiring the supermarket businesses of Associated British Food (ABF), which had been the market leader both in the Republic of Ireland with seventy-five supermarkets and in Northern Ireland with thirty-four supermarkets. Since then store assortments have been expanded so that they now include clothing, household, entertainment, and other non-food ranges. A first Tesco Extra was opened in 2005. In 2003 Tesco entered Turkey, acquiring the local operator of five hypermarkets, Kipa, which had started operations ten years previously. Additional openings have increased the number of hypermarkets to twenty-six. Express convenience stores have also been added.

From the late 1990s, Tesco speeded up expansion in Eastern Europe. After it had acquired small companies in Hungary and Poland as local platforms, it focused its expansion on the hypermarket format, which it was just developing. In 1998 it opened its first own hypermarkets in Poland, and then in 2002 acquired thirteen hypermarkets (of 5,600–14,200 square meters) from Dohle. The German company had been the first to introduce hypermarkets into Poland in 1994. Then, in 2006, Tesco bought 146 soft discount stores from French Casino. In Hungary, Tesco mainly expanded by setting up new hypermarkets. Similarly, in the Czech Republic and in Slovakia, the acquired Kmart stores were transformed and additional hypermarkets were added. In the Czech Republic Tesco acquired eleven hypermarkets from Carrefour in 2005—in exchange for its outlets in Taiwan. In 2006, Tesco added twenty-seven supermarkets, bought from German Edeka, to its network.

Internationalization into Asia started in 1998 and right from the start concentrated mostly on hypermarkets. Thailand was the first country it entered; there it acquired a controlling interest in Lotus, then a chain of thirteen hypermarkets, part of the huge conglomerate Charoen Pokphand Group.[28] From this base, Tesco Lotus has built a very strong position made up of 420 stores trading across four formats, including 81 hypermarkets, 307 Express stores, and 32 supermarkets. In 1999, Tesco formed a joint venture with the South Korean conglomerate Samsung, which started with two Homeplus hypermarkets; several new stores have been opened every year since. In 2005, Tesco also acquired twelve hypermarkets from the Korean company Aram-Mart, and in 2008 Tesco bought thirty-six Homever stores, many of which were formerly Carrefour hypermarkets. The third Asian market entered was Taiwan, but here Tesco was unable to grow against strong competitors that had entered the market before, and thus it handed its six hypermarkets over to Carrefour in 2006.

In 2002, a joint venture with Malaysia's conglomerate Sime Darby—with Tesco holding 70 percent—opened its first three hypermarkets and slowly added more stores. In 2007, Tesco acquired eight Makro cash and carry stores from Dutch SHV, which retreated from the market. In 2004, Tesco entered the Chinese market by founding a 50:50 partnership with Ting Hsin International Group, which at that time operated twenty-five Hymall hypermarkets in the Shanghai area. Tesco soon increased its stake to 90 percent, and also opened further stores in the Beijing and Guangzhou regions. The first Tesco-branded store, called Tesco Legou, opened in Beijing in February 2007.

While market entry and initial growth in the four Asian emerging markets of Thailand, South Korea, Malaysia, and China were concentrated on hypermarkets, Tesco later added convenience Express stores to its networks. The latest country was China, where the first Express store was opened in Shanghai in 2008. In Japan, where Tesco acquired several smaller chains in 2003–5, the company concentrates on small stores, of a discount as well as convenience type. In its home market, too, Tesco has expanded the convenience store business, including the acquisition of over 800 T&S stores in 2003. Most recent internationalization plans are directed toward the United States. Since 2007 Tesco has built a few distribution centers and has opened over 100 stores in California, Arizona, and Nevada. This newly developed formula, called Fresh & Easy Neighborhood Market, combines discount and convenience elements (Lowe and Wrigley 2009).

Traditionally focused on supermarkets and superstores, Tesco has become a multi-format retailer. In particular, its hypermarket outlets, developed since the late 1990s in the UK and abroad, have allowed the company to triple its sales since 2000. Hypermarkets have allowed the company to expand its assortment into non-food, where growth rates far above the average have been achieved; hypermarkets have also been the central vehicle for expansion into emerging markets. In stark contrast to Carrefour, Tesco has concentrated its expansion abroad on a relatively small number of countries, and, after some failures in earlier decades, in recent years has withdrawn from only one country, Taiwan. Domestic sales still accounted for 70 percent of the 2008 total £59.4 million; in Ireland they add another 4 percent. But, taking into account that Tesco began internationalization quite late, it is remarkable that 64 percent of its sales space is abroad, most of which is in the four emerging markets in Asia as well as in five emerging markets in Eastern Europe and Turkey.

Internationalization of the Largest European Grocery Retailers

The sixteen leading European grocery retailers, as listed in Table 4.2, come from five European countries: Tesco, Sainsbury's, and Morrisons from the UK; Carrefour, Casino, Auchan, Leclerc, and Intermarché from France; Metro, Rewe, Schwarz Group, Aldi, Edeka, and Tengelmann from Germany; Ahold from the Netherlands, and the Delhaize Group from Belgium. Amongst these sixteen companies, only two do not have international store operations; these are the British superstore chains Sainsbury's and Morrisons. Three other groups show a very limited level of internationalization; these are all buying groups: the French voluntary group of independent hypermarkets Leclerc, the voluntary group of supermarkets Intermarché, and the German cooperative of supermarket owners Edeka. Intermarché had taken over the German voluntary group Spar, then Germany's seventh biggest grocery retail group,[29] with about 4,000 supermarkets; but in 2005 Spar was sold to Edeka. Edeka, too, has recently given up most of its international operations, which had been quite small anyway. The German Rewe is the only buying group amongst the top

Table 4.2. Top sixteen European grocery retailers, store count, 2007, and sales, 2008

	Store count Total	Home country	West Europe	East Europe	Other DCs	Latin America	Asian LDCs	Africa	Gross sales 2008 (€bn)
Carrefour	14,991	5,515	7,359	360	7	1,097	535	8	109.4
hypermarkets	1,163	218	323	83	7	256	260	5	
supermarkets	2,708	1,021	1,226	277	—	141	—	3	
convenience	4,800	3,245	1,491	—	—	—	—	—	
discount	6,166	897	4,299	—	—	695	275	—	
C&C	154	134	20	—	—	—	—	—	
Metro	2,221	1,259	598	305	3	0	49	7	79.2
hypermarkets	434	349	11	74	—	—	—	—	
C&C	615	122	276	158	3	—	49	7	
others	1,172	788	311	73	—	—	—	—	
Tesco[a]	3,729	2,115	167	580	178	—	689	—	74.5
hypermarkets	659	166	32	223	—	—	238	—	
others	3,017	1,949	135	357	125	—	451	—	
Schwarz Group[b]	7,980	3,360	3,850	770	—	—	—	—	59.0
hypermarkets	720	520	—	200	—	—	—	—	
discount	7,260	2,840	3,850	570	—	—	—	—	
Rewe	12,719	9,492	2,264	862	—	—	—	—	54.5
hypermarkets	27	—	22	5	—	—	—	—	
supermarkets	8,633	7,052	1,195	386	—	—	—	—	
discount	2,934	2,008	490	436	—	—	—	—	
C&C	98	45	22	31	—	—	—	—	
others	1027	389	635	3	—	—	—	—	
Aldi	8,550	4,200	2,850	50	1,450	—	—	—	50.3
discount	8,250	4,200	2,850	50	1,150	—	—	—	
Trader Joe's	300	—	—	—	300	—	—	—	

(continued)

Table 4.2. *(Continued)*

	Store count Total	Home country	West Europe	East Europe	Other DCs	Latin America	Asian LDCs	Africa	Gross sales 2008 (€bn)
Auchan	2,480	545	1,721	90	—	—	124	—	50.0
hypermarkets	435	128	119	64	—	—	124	—	
supermarkets	2,045	417	1,602	26	—	—	—	—	
Casino	9,556	8,119	315	—	—	959	114	49	46.2
hypermarkets	386	129	—	—	—	174	72	11	
supermarkets	1,416	709	315	—	—	342	25	25	
discount	718	489	—	—	—	225	4	—	
convenience, others	7,036	6,792	—	—	—	218	13	13	
Ahold	3,225	2,199	—	321	705	—	—	—	44.5
hypermarkets	96	25	—	71	—	—	—	—	
supermarkets	2,125	1,170	—	250	705	—	—	—	
others (Etos, Gall)	1,004	1,004	—	—	—	—	—	—	
Edeka	9,711	9,711	—	—	—	—	—	—	38.3
hypermarkets	186	186	—	—	—	—	—	—	
supermarkets	8,135	8,135	—	—	—	—	—	—	
discount	1,279	1,279	—	—	—	—	—	—	
C&C	111	111	—	—	—	—	—	—	
Leclerc[c]	609	540	50	19	—	—	—	—	35.1
hypermarkets	460	391	39	18	—	—	—	—	
supermarkets	131	131	—	—	—	—	—	—	
Intermarché	3,942	3,464	310	168	—	—	—	—	32.8
supermarkets	2,168	1,795	245	128	—	—	—	—	
convenience	305	305	—	—	—	—	—	—	
discount	410	407	3	—	—	—	—	—	
non-food	1,059	957	62	40	—	—	—	—	

Tengelmann	7,707	5,990	678	633	406	—	—	25.6
supermarkets	1,109	703	—	—	406	—	—	—
discount	3,819	2,912	361	546	—	—	—	—
non-food	2,779	2,375	317	87	—	—	—	—
Sainsbury's	788	788	—	—	—	—	—	25.6
supermarkets/superstores	490	490	—	—	—	—	—	—
convenience	298	298	—	—	—	—	—	—
Delhaize Group	2,539	738	153	22	1,570	—	56	20.0
supermarkets	2,539	738	153	22	1,570	—	56	—
Morrisons	375	375	—	—	—	—	—	20.0
superstores	222	222	—	—	—	—	—	—
supermarkets, others	153	153	—	—	—	—	—	—

[a] Feb. 23, 2008.
[b] early 2007.
[c] 2006/7 (estimates).

Note: Europe here is defined as Western Europe plus all new EU member states.

Sources: Store count: company information from annual reports, websites, and private communication. Gross sales: own calculations and estimates; Planet Retail.

sixteen with relevant international activities: these are concentrated in neighboring Austria, where it bought the market leader, the supermarket chain Billa, which is expanding into other neighboring countries; Rewe's discount chain Penny is also expanding abroad.

Three international grocery retailers amongst Europe's top sixteen are operating mainly with the supermarket format: Dutch Ahold, German Tengelmann, and Belgian Delhaize Group have concentrated much of their international growth in the United States, where they bought large supermarket chains in the 1970s and 1980s. In 1976 Tengelmann had bought a majority share in the then biggest supermarket chain of the USA, Great Atlantic and Pacific (A&P); attempts to internationalize the supermarket business in Europe through a series of acquisitions in the 1980s failed; and in 2007 its share in A&P was reduced to a minority when A&P merged with Pathmark. In 2008–9 Tengelmann also sold most of its discount operations (Plus); stores in Germany were sold to Edeka, and those in other European countries to various other companies; this left only a few stores in Austria and Romania in Tengelmann's possession. Ahold had acquired several supermarket chains in the USA, such as Bi-Lo (1977), Giant-Carlisle (1981), Tops Markets (1991), Stop & Shop (1996), or Giant Food (1998), and also expanded its supermarket activities—mostly by acquisitions—to Spain in 1976, and in the 1990s to Czechoslovakia, Poland, Malaysia, Thailand, Indonesia, Singapore, China, Brazil, and another eight Latin-American countries (Burt, Dawson, and Larke 2006). Since the late 1990s and especially after 2003, when the company was hit by a financial scandal, Ahold sold all these activities except its supermarket chains in the United States and its business in the Czech Republic and in Slovakia, which mainly consists of hypermarkets. Ahold, similar to Tesco, had introduced the hypermarket format to its home country, the Netherlands, only after it had operated hypermarkets abroad. The Belgian Delhaize Group had since 1974 acquired several supermarket chains in the United States, later renamed Food Lion; the company also expanded into Greece, buying Alfa-Beta (1992) and Trofo (2001), and also operates a few stores in Romania and Indonesia. Finally, besides Ahold, Delhaize Group, and Tengelmann, British Sainsbury's had also entered the United States, acquiring a controlling interest in Shaw's Supermarkets step by step between 1983 and 1987, but it withdrew in 2004. The expansion of European supermarkets outside the United States has been quite limited,[30] and concentrated in neighboring countries, such as Tesco in Ireland, Carrefour in Belgium, or Rewe in Austria; in emerging markets supermarkets are usually operated in addition to already existing hypermarkets (see below). Generally, the internationalization of the supermarket format has been achieved primarily through acquisitions.

In contrast to supermarket chains, discount chains, as well as operators of cash and carry markets, and—to a somewhat lesser extent—hypermarkets have internationalized primarily through internal expansion, opening up new outlets abroad (Zentes 1998). These companies possessed knowledge about operating a retail format that did not exist in the countries to which it was transferred; they had a competitive ownership-specific advantage (Dunning 1979, 2000)—that is, competencies developed in their home country environment that they could exploit through foreign direct investment.

Hard discounters such as Aldi and Schwarz Group's Lidl have concentrated their internationalization in Western Europe, although they later began to expand into Eastern Europe. Lidl's expansion abroad began much later than that of Aldi, when it opened its first stores in France in 1988, where it has 1,300 stores today and is the clear leader in grocery discount. In total, Lidl runs about 3,850 discount stores in sixteen West European countries, and about 600 in seven East European countries. The internationalization of the other German discounters, such as Plus (see above) and Penny (Rewe), have been much less advanced and are also concentrated in Western and Eastern Europe.

A somewhat different pattern is being followed by Carrefour's discount formula Día, which was developed in Spain and has been transferred mainly in the Mediterranean region but also to Brazil and Argentina, and even to China, where discount stores were added to already existing Carrefour hypermarkets. Aldi's discount stores in the United States and Australia are the only stand-alone discount operations outside Europe.

Discounters follow a uniform internationalization strategy using an identical shop formula and even selling the same products—mainly private label—in different national markets. In the case of Aldi, there is an overlap of 70 percent between the products offered in Spain and those sold in Germany (Gurdjian et al. 2000), which is very high, given a still fragmented European food market. This strategy has strong cost-saving effects, for example, in sourcing from suppliers, which improves the discounter's competitiveness in all countries, including the domestic German market. High cross-border synergies allow discounters to act in niches of their host countries and to operate profitably without being amongst the largest retailers in every country they enter. The high degree of cross-border integration and standardization can best be realized through internal growth abroad—that is, through setting up new clone-like operations rather than through big takeovers; subsidiaries abroad are usually 100 percent owned, allowing corporate headquarters full control of their foreign operations.

Unlike supermarket and discount retailers, hypermarket chains have concentrated their international expansion not in other industrialized countries, but in emerging markets (for Eastern Europe, see Table 4.3). Carrefour, the inventor of the hypermarket, has clearly also been the leader in its internationalization. While attempts to enter several developed retail markets in Europe and North America failed, expansion in less-developed retail markets

Table 4.3. The biggest grocery retailers, five Eastern European countries, 2006

Poland	Hungary	Czech Republic	Slovakia	Romania
Metro (DE)	Tesco (UK)	Schwarz (DE)	Coop Jednota (SK)	Metro (DE)
Jerónimo Martins (PO)	CBA (HU)	Ahold (NL)	Tesco (UK)	Rewe (DE)
Tesco (UK)	Metro[a] (DE)	Tesco (UK)	Metro (DE)	Carrefour (FR)
Carrefour (FR)	Co-op (HU)	Metro (DE)	Schwarz (DE)	CBA (HU)
Auchan (FR)	Reál (HU)	Rewe (DE)	Rewe (DE)	L. Delhaize (BE)

[a] In a joint venture, Metspa, with Spar Austria.

Source: EHI Retail Institute (2008).

has been very successful, first to Spain and Latin America, and later to Asia, Eastern Europe, and some other South European countries. Auchan has concentrated more on Southern Europe (Spain, Italy, and Portugal) as well as five Eastern European countries; it was only later that it started expansion into China (1999) and Taiwan. Casino, the leading supermarket chain in France, has concentrated its internationalization on hypermarkets (Géant) and runs over 250 hypermarkets in the emerging markets of Latin America (174) and Asia (72). Another French hypermarket chain, Cora, owned by Belgian Louis Delhaize,[31] has expanded into Hungary and Romania.

Tesco, the only internationalized British grocery retailer, has also concentrated its internationalization on hypermarkets, a format that was unknown to British retailing before Tesco's internationalization began. The two leading German hypermarket chains, Kaufland belonging to the Schwarz Group and Real belonging to Metro, are much less internationalized and have transferred their hypermarket formats to some East European countries. It is remarkable that over 75 percent of all non-domestic hypermarkets owned by the top sixteen companies (in 2007) are located in the emerging markets of Latin America (18 percent), Asia (28 percent), and Eastern Europe (30 percent); and, of those hypermarkets operating in other European countries, the majority is located in the less developed retail markets of Southern Europe.

Operators of hypermarkets usually aim to be amongst the top three or so retailers in each country they enter. In countries where they were unable to reach this goal after a few years of operation, they often sold their activities to local companies or, more frequently, to other European hypermarket companies (on international retail divestment, see Burt, Dawson, and Sparks 2004). Operators of hypermarkets can realize relatively few cross-border synergies and thus need to consolidate their activities in each country they enter. This is due to the fact that they have to adapt their operations and their assortment to different national environments—ranging from specific legal regulations to different consumer tastes.[32] Since, for their food departments, hypermarkets source a large share locally—according to companies' websites, over 80 percent or even 90 percent—these retailers have to gain market share in order to gain buying power vis-à-vis their suppliers and to be competitive. At the same time they are increasingly rationalizing their local supply chains.[33] In the business literature, such an international strategy is frequently called multinational or multi-domestic, while a strategy that standardizes and integrates across borders neglecting national particularities, as do grocery hard discounters, is labeled global (see Porter 1986; for the retail industry, see Salmon and Tordjman 1989).

However, for the non-food assortments of hypermarkets, which are to a large extent private-label ranges, the situation is somewhat different. While here ultimate buying decisions are made by central buyers working for the different subsidiaries in the single countries who know the different national consumer preferences, these buyers are supported by globally operating buying organizations. These usually have their head office in Hong Kong and branch offices in a large number of mostly Asian countries. Metro's Real hypermarkets are linked to Metro Group Buying, whose antecedents have operated in Hong Kong since the 1970s. Schwarz Group's Kaufland had been a member of the buying group Markant, whose subsidiary Markant Trading Organization Ltd operates in Hong Kong and Asia; in 2005, the company also set up its own Kaufland Hong Kong Ltd. Carrefour had set up its Hong Kong office in 1995; and the other French operators of hypermarkets, Auchan, Casino and Leclerc (Siplec), also have their own Hong Kong-based buying organizations in Asia. Tesco moved the headquarter of Tesco International Sourcing to Hong Kong in 2004; by 2009 "more than 60 percent of all clothing and 40 percent of other non-food products sold in Tesco's UK stores, as well as most of the non-food items sold in the 12 other countries Tesco operates in, are procured via the retailer's global sourcing office."[34] Thus while hypermarkets source most of their foods locally, their equally important non-food assortments are increasingly sourced on a global scale, allowing for some cross-border synergies—for example, when choosing, monitoring, and bargaining with suppliers.[35]

Hypermarkets seem to have been the ideal grocery retail format to enter the emerging markets of Eastern Europe, Latin America, and Asia, as well as the less-developed retail markets of Southern Europe.[36] One reason for hypermarkets being so suitable is that they can operate as stand-alone sites. Because of their size, hypermarkets do not need the support of distribution centers. These were usually set up only after a company had established at least a handful of hypermarket outlets in a certain country. In a third step, the established distribution infrastructures were then sometimes used to serve smaller stores, such as supermarkets, convenience stores, and also discount stores, which cannot operate standing alone.[37]

Internationalization patterns of retail companies from the four biggest Western European countries depend highly on the formats these companies operate. As we have seen, the development of retail formats has been shaped by retail regulations embedded in national general and retail-specific institutional traditions. In Italy, tight retail regulations did not allow the development of modern retail companies, and no internationally competitive retailers have developed there. Instead, Italy became a host country for foreign retailers, especially for hypermarket chains from France. In Germany, retail regulations limiting store size, originally intended to protect small independent retailers, have helped (as an unintended consequence) limited-assortment hard discounters to become the leading retail format in this country—a retail format that could also grow in niches in other developed retail markets. In the UK, where early and unrestricted retail modernization led to the gradual transformation of supermarkets into superstores, a format not fit for internationalization, Tesco remained the only British multinational retail company; it developed the hypermarket format only in the context of its internationalization. Finally, in France, the invention of the hypermarket at a time when supermarkets had not yet fully developed, as well as ineffective regulations, have made France home for the strong operators of hypermarkets, the format most appropriate for internationalization in the emerging markets of Eastern Europe, Asia, and Latin America.

5

Amazon and eBay: Online Retailers as Market Makers

Suresh Kotha and Sandip Basu

Introduction

Rapid technological change and the emergence of the World Wide Web (WWW) have enabled many new firms to rewrite the rules of doing business in different retail sectors of the US economy. Since the advent of the Netscape Corporation's browser software, Navigator, in December 1994, online retail sales have grown steadily. In 2007 the US Commerce Department indicated that online retail sales amounted to $108.7 billion in 2006, representing an increase of 23.5 percent over 2005. In contrast, US total retail sales in 2006 increased 5.8 percent from 2005 to reach a total of $3.9 trillion. In 2006, online retail sales accounted for 2.8 percent of total US retail sales, and were expected to double over the next few years.

There is now a large body of knowledge that highlights and discusses the Internet's growing universality, and its impact on society in general, and commerce in particular. It is oft-noted that the Internet signals a fundamental shift in the nature of competition in certain, if not all, industries (Armstrong and Hagel 1996; Grove 1996; Evans and Wurster 1997). To many observers, the Internet presents both an opportunity and a threat for commerce. On the one hand, it is perceived as a threat because it enables people and businesses to connect directly, thereby sidestepping intermediaries such as distributors and retailers (Gates 1995; Lohr 1997). Also, since the Internet has the potential fundamentally to alter the "economics of information" (Evan and Wurster, 1997), and the way information is communicated, it threatens incumbents in many retail sectors such as music retailing, travel, and book retailing, to name a few. Prior to the Internet, many firms in such retail sectors exploited the information asymmetries between buyers and sellers to make profits. The growing popularity of the Internet as a universal communications medium has reduced such information asymmetries between buyers and sellers, thereby greatly increasing market efficiency. More specifically, as early as 1997, Evans and Wurster (1997: 74) argued:

> The rapid emergence of universal technical standards for communication, allowing everybody to communicate with everybody else at essentially zero cost, is a sea change... Those emerging open standards and the explosion in the number of people and organizations connected by networks are freeing information from the channels that have been required to exchange it, making those channels unnecessary or uneconomical.

In other words, falling "transaction costs" (Williamson 1979) and the availability of information via the Internet are eroding the profit margins and the competitive advantages of businesses in many retail sectors.

On the other hand, the Internet provides new entrants, in numerous industries, with opportunities to alter the dynamics of competition. Many new ventures that did not exist prior to commercialization of the Internet have now become household names. They include firms such as eBay, Amazon.com, Yahoo, Google, RealNetworks, ETrade, and Expedia, to name a few. Interestingly, the same technology that was once perceived as a disruptive threat is now enabling existing brick-and-mortar retailers such as Barnes & Noble, Borders Books and Music, Best Buy, Circuit City, and Wal-Mart, amongst others, to become multi-channel players and compete in physical as well as online markets. In other words, over time brick-and-mortar retailers have found ways to leverage and complement their brick-and-mortar experience and skills to compete effectively online.

Early online retailers (for example, Amazon.com) had the task of "making the market" to ensure their own sustainability and profitability in the emerging online retail sectors. For a business, making a market involves the execution of a series of interrelated activities designed to get important stakeholders to buy into its "new" business model (Dedrick and Kraemer, Chapter 11 this volume). Therefore, market-making activities often have outcomes that not only benefit the firm initiating these activities, but extend to all incumbents and even future entrants in the particular industry. As discussed in detail later, these outcomes involve the transfer of market power to incumbents from other players in the particular retail sector's value chain.

The purpose of this chapter is (1) to illustrate how online goliaths such as Amazon.com and eBay have become market makers over a short time period (less than a decade) using new Internet technologies and the emerging online medium for interaction (that is, the cyber marketplace); and (2) to describe how online retailers continue to be market makers as Internet technologies evolve and change.

To address these issues, we first discuss the emergence of online retailing, using Amazon.com and eBay as prototypical online retailers, and highlight the pioneering role they have played in establishing online retail commerce. We chose to highlight these two firms, Amazon.com and eBay, because they are revelatory cases largely responsible for establishing business and revenue models for online retailing as we understand them today. From being mere start-ups a little over decade ago, they now rank amongst the top specialty retailers on the *Fortune* magazine list of retailers. Currently, they represent multi-billion dollar businesses that continue to influence and shape online retail commerce as this sector grows and draws sales away from some established brick-and-mortar retailers (see Table 5.1).

Amazon.com and eBay represent fundamentally different approaches to retailing. Amazon.com took the "traditional" direct-retailing format and adapted it online. The company uses Internet-based technologies to impact significantly on the traditional value chain of the book publishing industry,

Table 5.1. Online retailers vs top ten specialty retailers and general merchandisers

Company	*Fortune* rank (based on revenues)	2006 revenues ($ mn)	% change from 2005	2006 profits ($ mn)	% change from 2005	No. of employees (2006)
Online retailers						
Amazon.com	**237**	**10,711**	**26**	**190**	**−47**	**13,900**
eBay	**383**	**5,970**	**31**	**1,126**	**4**	**12,900**
Top ten specialty retailing firms						
1 Home Depot	17	90,837	11	5,761	−1	305,760
2 Costco	32	60,151	14	1,103	4	99,000
3 Lowe's	45	46,927	9	3,105	12	157,349
4 Best Buy	72	30,848	12	1,140	16	128,000
5 Staples	125	18,161	13	974	17	56,542
6 TJX	133	17,516	9	738	7	125,000
7 Gap	144	15,943	0	778	−30	154,000
8 Office Depot	156	15,011	5	516	89	38,000
9 Toy "R" Us	202	12,206	8	28	—	59,000
10 Circuit City	215	11,598	11	140	127	46,007
Top ten general merchandisers						
1 Wal-Mart	1	351,139	11	11,284	0	1,900,000
2 Target	33	59,490	13	2,787	16	352,000
3 Sears	38	53,012,	8	1,490	74	352,000
4 Federated	76	28,711	23	995	−29	188,000
5 J. C. Penney	116	19,903	5	1,153	6	155,000
6 Kohl's	152	15,544	16	1,109	32	68,500
7 Dollar General	273	9,170	7	138	−61	69,500
8 Nordstrom	286	8,561	11	678	23	52,900
9 Dillard's	307	7,849	2	246	102	52,056
10 Family Dollar Stores	359	6,395	10	195	−10	34,000

and has over time expanded beyond books. In less than a decade, it has become an important market maker in its own right by connecting thousands of smaller online and brick-and-mortar retailers to a vast group of online retail customers that it has managed to attract and retain on its website. In contrast, eBay.com brings together millions of buyers and sellers in an online marketplace daily, and has become a cultural phenomenon in its own right (*The Economist* 2005). eBay is a "pure" online intermediary that connects millions of buyer and sellers worldwide without taking control of or carrying inventory. In doing so, it has created a marketplace that spans many retail sectors and geographical locations around the world. Using the power of many, the company delivers the efficiency of a global market to buyers and sellers, irrespective of their size or location (*The Economist* 2005).

Using these two examples, we discuss how the presence of these online retailers has impacted incumbents or brick-and-mortar retailers such as Barnes & Noble, and others. Many established brick-and-mortar retailers have reacted to moves from online retailers such as Amazon.com and eBay by entering the online retailing sector themselves, and finding innovative ways to leverage their physical assets online. We conclude this chapter by highlighting some trends in online retailing and how online retailers are enabling further market-making activity as they continue to evolve and change.

Amazon.com as a Market Maker

Early history and growth

In 1994, Jeffrey Bezos, a senior vice-president in a Wall Street-based investment bank, D. E., Shaw noticed a statistic about the Internet: usage was growing at 2,300 percent a year. Bezos, a computer science and electrical engineering graduate by education, left his job and drew up a list of twenty possible products that could be sold on the Internet. He quickly narrowed the prospects to books, since there were far too many book titles for any single brick-and-mortar store to stock (*Wall Street Journal* 1996). He moved to Seattle and started Amazon.com in July 1995 and soon after attracted $8 million from Kleiner, Perkins, Caufield & Byers, a venture-capital firm based in the Silicon Valley.

In early 1997, Amazon.com had 250 employees. A significant majority of them developed software tools for operating on the Internet, signaling that Amazon.com was first and foremost a technology company and not another traditional book retailer. At this time, Amazon was advertising itself as "Earth's largest bookstore—with a selection of over 1.1 million titles." The company, however, differentiated itself from traditional bookstores with aggressive promotion and marketing (Kotha 1998). Amazon served its millionth customer in the autumn of 1997, after which its customer base quickly grew to ten million by the spring of 1999—less than four years since the company's inception. By 2006, the company's sales revenues reached over $10.7 billion (a figure that was higher than Nordstrom, another well-known Seattle-based retailer), and profits were $190 million.

Amazon.com as an information intermediary

As noted earlier, Bezos took the "traditional" direct-retailing format and adapted it online. Analysts refer to Amazon.com's approach as a "one-to-many" model of online retailing, where Amazon.com as the seller caters to millions of buyers. The company receives customer orders online and then ships products directly to them from company-operated warehouses (Kotha 1998). Its approach to maintaining and shipping merchandise to end customers does not differ significantly from other direct merchants such as L. L. Bean or Land's End. Moreover, the company offers a fixed-price format that is the prevalent pricing mode in most US retailing.

However, Amazon.com competes not just as another retailer, but as an "information broker." Over the years, it has found a way successfully to leverage the emerging electronic medium to offer services that a physical bookstore cannot match. For instance, the company offers a database of books in the millions, many times more than the selection the largest brick-and-mortar Barnes & Noble superstore might offer. It provides numerous technology-based services such as email services, online recommendations, online reviews, and the ability to pre-order a book online, amongst others. As discussed later, the company's technological platform can support other small retail businesses to operate on its website, an approach that is easier to accomplish online than in a traditional brick-and-mortar retail setting.

Amazon.com as a market maker

"Making" a retail market involves bringing together customers and suppliers and getting both these groups interested in transacting in a novel and unfamiliar way for products that they wish to buy and sell respectively. As noted, firms make markets by executing a series of interrelated activities designed to get these important stakeholders to buy into relatively new business models. For a new entrant, this might involve transforming an industry's value chain in a manner favorable to it. Therefore, market-making activities can often have outcomes that benefit all incumbents in the same stage of a value chain in an industry.

As noted, Amazon.com first used Internet-based technologies to alter the value chain of the book publishing industry, and then over time it expanded to other retailing sectors. To illustrate Amazon.com's impact on the book-retailing industry, we provide details about the functioning of this industry prior to Amazon.com's entry into online book retailing and then describe Amazon's role in transforming this industry before discussing Amazon.com's other market-making activities.

AMAZON.COM'S IMPACT ON THE BOOK RETAILING VALUE CHAIN

The US book-retailing industry, one of the oldest in the USA, has traditionally been fragmented, with over 2,500 publishers and thousands of bookstores (US Bureau of the Census 1992). The industry sells a variety of books that include trade, professional, mass market, elementary, high school and college text-books, and others. Each of these categories has varied in terms of sales, competition, profitability, and volatility.[1] At the time of Amazon.com's entry into books in 1995, retail book sales in the USA accounted for about $25.5 billion.

Figure 5.1 shows the structure of the US publishing and retailing industry prior to the entry of online retailers into this industry. As the figure indicates, there are thousands, if not millions, of aspiring writers (authors), who for the most part work with publishers to get their books published. If they are successful in attracting an interested publisher, they receive a small royalty (about 5–15 percent) for their work when books are published and marketed successfully. With regards to book retailing, books are distributed by whole-salers, who take orders from independent booksellers and chains and consoli-date them into lot-orders for publishers. Publishers supply wholesalers, who in

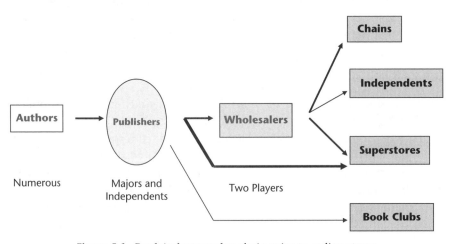

Figure 5.1. Book industry value chain prior to online stores

160

turn supply the hundreds of retail bookstores located throughout the country. According to industry estimates in 1996, wholesalers accounted for almost 30 percent of publishers' sales. In contrast to publishing and book retailing, wholesalers are highly concentrated, with firms such as Ingram Book Co. commanding the major share (50 percent in 1995) of the market. Competition in the wholesale sector revolves around the speed of delivery and the number of titles stocked. Ingram, for instance, receives more than 70 percent of its orders electronically and offers one-day delivery to about 82 percent of its US customers. In 1994, the average net profit for wholesalers was less than 1.5 percent. This figure was down from the traditional margins of about 2 percent a few years earlier (*Publishers Weekly* 1996a).

At the time of Amazon.com's entry into the industry in 1995, bookstore chains sold more books than independents for the first time (*Philadelphia Business Journal* 1996). Retail bookstores, independents, and general retailers accounted for 35–40 percent of industry revenues. From 1975 to 1995, the number of bookstores in the USA increased from 11,990 to 17,340, and these bookstores accounted for about 21 percent of the total retail book sales. The superstores, such as Barnes & Noble and Borders Books and Music, accounted for about 15 percent of all retail sales. Estimates suggest that from 1992 through 1995, superstore bookstore sales grew at a compounded rate of 71 percent while non-superstore sales grew at a rate of 4 percent.

During the mid-1990s, industry experts were cautioning that a shakeout was inevitable in smaller markets. Superstores, originally confined to big metropolitan areas, were increasingly entering markets with populations of 150,000 or less. Industry estimates indicated that superstores had to make around $200 a square foot to turn a profit. A typical Barnes & Noble superstore needed, for example, $3 million to $4 million in sales revenues to break even. Some industry observers questioned whether smaller cities could support one or more of these mammoth stores and whether superstores in these locations could sell enough books to turn a profit (*Publishers Weekly* 1996b). Mr Vlahos, a spokesperson for the American Booksellers' Association, noted (as quoted in *New York Times* 1996): "In the three years from 1993 to 1995, 150 to 200 independent-owned bookstores went out of business—50 to 60 in 1996 alone...By contrast in the same period, approximately 450 retail superstore outlets opened, led by Barnes & Noble and the Borders Group, with 348 openings." It was under these conditions, when Barnes & Noble (the industry leader in book retailing) was in the midst of one of its biggest rollouts, that Bezos launched Amazon.com as an online bookstore.

As Figure 5.2 illustrates, all of the participants in the book-retailing value chain could, in theory, directly reach end customers using Internet technologies. In 1997, the largest US distributor of books, Ingram, attempted to enter the "retailing" segment. It tested a service to create new online retailers to

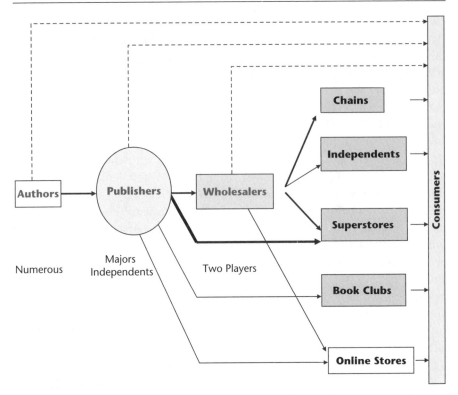

Figure 5.2. Book industry value chain after the entry of online book stores such as Amazon.com

mitigate the growing power of Amazon.com. All the would-be retailers had to do was lure the shoppers to their respective website. Ingram handled everything else, from maintaining the would-be-retailers' website to taking orders, processing credit-card billings, and shipping the books directly from Ingram's warehouses. In effect, the virtual bookshops became little more than a retail façade of Ingram. However, after six months of test marketing, it quietly pulled the plug (Bianco 1997). Ingram's experimental foray into online retailing failed in part because many of the new online entrants were unable to attract enough customers to their websites. Thus, the possibility that all the industry players could reach end-customers directly in book retailing failed to materialize.

With the emergence of online retailing, however, independent brick-and-mortar bookstores continue to go out of business. Additionally, as customers migrate to online bookstores, established book chains (for example, Dalton books) are finding it difficult to compete, and book clubs are no longer in a position to sustain themselves in their traditional form. Since Amazon.com's entry, Barnes & Noble and others (for example, Borders Books and Music) have tabled their expansion plans and are now focused on competing with Amazon.com and others to adapt and potentially to grow. In sum, with Amazon's entry into the book-retailing industry, "value" has migrated from increasingly outmoded business designs such as book clubs, chain stores, and independent bookstores to online retailers such as Amazon.com.[2] This, however, raises the question, how did Amazon.com become the most important beneficiary of this value migration?

To address this question, one has not only to examine how book retailing has been transformed but also look at Amazon.com's market-making actions. It would not be an exaggeration to note that Amazon.com single-handedly helped migrate value from the physical space to the online marketplace. In doing so, it has been largely responsible for creating online markets first for books and then later for other products.

ATTRACTING AND CONVERTING ONLINE CUSTOMERS

To persuade customers to visit its website, Amazon.com had to focus on "value" creation that traditional brick-and-mortar retailers could not. From its inception Amazon.com's value proposition focused on four related factors: convenience, a large selection, customer service, and lower prices. First, the Internet made it possible to order books (or other products) from the comfort and convenience of one's home or office, thus making time and location less relevant for online purchases. Customers, irrespective of their geographical location, were now able to order products at any time of the day. Second, by positioning Amazon.com as the "earth's biggest bookstore" (and later on as the "earth's biggest store"), Bezos made virtual size synonymous with physical size. From the continued growth and expansion of Barnes & Noble's superstores, during the early 1990s, it was apparent that customers enjoyed the larger selection offered by such large stores. He promptly highlighted in press releases and in the media that his company's database of 1.1 million books (in 1996) was many times larger than any Barnes & Noble superstore could carry (a typical Barnes & Noble superstore carried about 150,000 titles).

Third, as early as 1998, Bezos defined Amazon.com's mission as being the most "customer-centric organization in the world" (Amazon.com 1998). On the Internet, attracting users to websites is only part of the process of completing a sale. Converting web traffic into paying customers is a much more challenging task. It is perhaps here that offering superior online customer service plays a substantial role in influencing the ultimate sale (Kotha, Rajgopal, and Venkatachalam 2004). As part of its customer-service approach, Amazon.com used personalization techniques to leverage the advantages of the Internet technologies. Customers visiting the company's website could subscribe to email notification services and every registered customer could maintain his or her own personalized site. Providing these individualized personalized stores for each customer was the result of innovations spawned with the advent of the commercial Internet technologies, and Amazon.com was at the forefront of such innovations.

The Internet offered two natural advantages over physical retail: the relative ease of searching for products and storing information on users' activity. Amazon.com, to benefit from these advantages, began using collaborative-filtering techniques to generate recommendations for its customers. These recommendations were based on customers' past purchases, and what other customers of the same book or product purchased on its website. In addition to emphasizing customer service, Bezos spent a large percentage of the company's revenues on marketing and branding (Kotha 1998; Rindova, Petkova, and Kotha 2007). This was done in order to sustain the company's competitive advantage over rivals, many of whom were just beginning to imitate its market-making actions and benefiting from Bezos' pioneering efforts online. Finally, as a new entrant into book retailing, Amazon.com used lower prices (vis-à-vis brick-and-mortar stores) to increase the attractiveness of shopping online. The company routinely used (and still continues to use) price cuts as a strategy for gaining dominance in online retailing. Lowering prices and providing greater transparency attracted shoppers to try online purchasing, and at the same time pressured incumbents to find ways to respond to modify their business models in order to adapt to this new development.

As the company effectively exploited the advantages of the Internet, it also ensured that some of the perceived disadvantages of online retail were mitigated. One such "dissatisfier" for many early Internet users was the perceived complexity of transacting on the Internet, especially during its early days. Amazon.com's revolutionary 1-click technology set a new standard for ease of purchasing on the Internet and served to overcome much of this concern. Despite providing an enhanced shopping experience for shoppers on its website, the company recognized the importance of generating traffic. As an early initiative to direct more online users to its website, Amazon launched the "Associates" program in 1996. This program allowed associates to build links to Amazon's content and receive a fee on Amazon's products purchased via their websites. Within two years, the program had 30,000 members and has been evolving ever since. The strength of its "Associates" program has been recognized as one of the primary reasons for Amazon's durability as an online retailer and has been widely imitated by other retailers, but with limited success.

CREATING NEW CATEGORIES AND EXPANDING GEOGRAPHICALLY
Amazon realized that its online capabilities could be applied to make markets in retail sectors other than books. For example, in 1998, it launched an ambitious music store and a year later toys and electronics stores. By early 2000, Amazon's customers could buy drugs, tools and equipment, health and beauty products, and kitchen products from its website. Additionally, it expanded into new geographical markets as well. Toward the end of 1998, Amazon entered European markets such as the United Kingdom and Germany, with dedicated websites, and toward the end of 2000 Amazon.jp was launched to increase its Japanese market. Later that year, Amazon started a new French website. In 2007, Amazon operated in forty-one product categories and in six other countries besides the United States. Growth in new product categories and geographical markets has been largely responsible for continued growth in Amazon.com's revenues.

ATTRACTING EXISTING SUPPLIERS
As discussed above, Amazon.com was fast building capabilities of aggregating online traffic to its website and converting these online visits to actual purchases. Given its phenomenal growth, book publishers had no choice but to strike deals to have their books listed by the company so that they would benefit in turn from the firm's increasing online retail activity in book retailing. Moreover, publishers also benefited from the increased information available regarding customer search and purchase activity that they could use to plan future projects as well as publication volumes. For example, the extent of pre-ordering by Amazon's customers yielded better forecasts of a book's "latent" demand to publishers. For example, Amazon.com's customers pre-ordered over two million copies of *Deathly Hallows*, the last book in the Harry Potter book series when its publisher announced the forthcoming release of this book. The ability to track and fulfill personalized orders on such a massive scale is possible only through the use of computer- and Internet-based technologies.

AGGREGATING A COMMUNITY OF SMALL MERCHANTS
In another innovative move and to the chagrin of book publishers, Amazon introduced "The Marketplace" in 1999. Under this initiative, small merchants (mostly independent bookstores) could sell used books (and later other products) along with new books (and other products) on the company's website. Customers could potentially benefit by being able to view both new and used products simultaneously next to each other. Under this approach, product prices were made more transparent, and the purchasing options for customers increased dramatically. Ironically, the same technology that helped hasten the demise of the independent bookstores in the mid-1990s, when Amazon.com

entered book retailing, is now helping merchants once again compete on Amazon.com's technology platform and benefit from the millions of registered users the company has amassed.

In sum, Amazon.com first transformed book retailing and then followed this up by entering into other retail sectors of the economy both in the USA and abroad. The company, through its market-making actions, established itself as a dominant player in online retailing within a short time because of many of its market-making actions. Finally, once it had established itself, it then opened up its online technology platform to other small merchants to compete on its website, thus providing an opportunity for independent stores to become viable competitors once again.

eBay as a Market Maker

Early history

On the Friday before Labor Day, September 1995, Pierre Omidyar began building a computerized online-trading platform, which in its early stages was no more than software running on a web server. He named his online auction platform AuctionWeb. As buyers and sellers visited his website, the company began to benefit from word-of-mouth publicity that would drive its growth for years to come (Cohen 2002). As traffic grew, in 1996 Pierre re-named his venture *eBay* to reflect the company's business location in the California Bay Area.

When he first launched his website, Omidyar created product categories that occurred to him personally.[3] However, by the end of 1996, collectors of various categories were driving his company's growth. For example, in late 1996, antiques and collectibles listings on the website increased about 350 percent in just four months and the fastest-growing categories were collectibles such as coins, stamps, and baseball cards. As the site morphed into a haven for collectibles, it became a magnet for other collectors, because they could be connected to individuals with a similar passion. Collectors, on eBay, were individuals who bought and sold one-of-a-kind items that often came with a story and encouraged dialogs amongst the collectors (Bradley and Porter 2000). Unlike other Internet companies at that time, eBay was profitable immediately (Bradley and Porter 2000). As Omidyar reflected in 1998: "The biggest clue [that eBay was going to a phenomenal success] was that so many checks were piling up at my door, I had to hire part-time help to open them all" (Hansell 1998).

In 1997, after raising $5 million in venture-capital funding, Omidyar hired Meg Whitman, an experienced executive with "brand-building" experience, to run eBay. Whitman initiated several strategic actions that built the "eBay" brand. When it first opened, eBay offered 10 product categories, but by mid-1998 it was offering 846 categories organized into 12 major categories, with collectibles accounting for the majority of the listings. By 2002, automobiles had become the single largest category traded on eBay (based on global annualized gross merchandise sales), accounting for nearly four times the revenues generated by collectibles. At the end of 2006, eBay had 222 million registered users (more than the combined population of France, Spain, and Britain), of which 82 million were considered as active users (users who had bid for or listed items within the past year). At the time, the number of items listed on the company's website was 2.4 billion. eBay's net revenues for the year were $5.9 billion, and the net income was $1.12 billion.

eBay as a "pure" intermediary

eBay's approach differs from Amazon's in that it represents a many-to-many model, where millions of buyers interact with millions of sellers on the company's website. Using the power of many, the company delivers the efficiency of a global market to buyers and sellers, irrespective of their size (*The Economist* 2005). During the initial phase, eBay departed from the fixed-price format offered by brick-and-mortar retailers. The company chose to use the auction pricing mechanism to enable users to trade items on its website. It made money by charging customers listing and special fees, and final value fees. The beauty of this business model is that users do most of the work: photographing their products, composing their listing, communicating with potential buyers, packing, and then shipping their sales (*The Economist* 2005). eBay as the middleman earns a transaction fee for each trade, enjoying operating margins of 35 percent in the process. In other words, eBay is a classic "information" intermediary that enables buyers and sellers to transact business, without necessarily taking control of the products involved in the transactions consummated by the buyers and sellers on its website. By playing the role of the classic middleman, eBay has put to rest the argument that the Internet would kill *all* middlemen.

eBay's market-making activities

In many ways, eBay represents the quintessential online market marker. Through a series of actions, eBay has created, developed, and fostered online marketplaces in the USA and numerous other countries. These online communities that the company has been instrumental in creating are vibrant marketplaces that continue to grow at a rapid pace, especially in international markets such as China and India.

REINVENTING MARKET CATEGORIES

Although the academics debate whether eBay truly created an entirely new market or just reinvented existing market categories, it is fair to note that eBay invented the consumer-to-consumer online auction model, and this market, once a niche, has now expanded significantly to cover a variety of retail sectors including auctions, collectibles, flea markets, garage sales, and classified advertising. The company provides a technology platform (or multiple platforms) that enables a global community of buyers and sellers to interact and trade with each other. This technology platform is fully automated, and open twenty-four hours a day, seven days a week, enabling users to browse through listed items from any place in the world (eBay maintains localized websites in twenty-six locations). In its December 2006 annual report, eBay claims that, on any given day, there are more than 100 million items available through auction-style and fixed-price trading on its website (eBay 2006).

CREATING ONLINE MARKETS AROUND THE WORLD

Since eBay is a technology platform that supports online retailing, it has been able to scale up its online marketplaces rather rapidly. Its users (both buyers and sellers) in the USA now number in the millions. Additionally, the company has undertaken rapid international expansion. eBay began its international expansion in 1999 and has entered twenty-six locations around the world since 2000. In 2006, about 47 percent of the company's revenues resulted from its international operations. In contrast, Wal-Mart, the largest US physical retailer, operates in twelve nations, and it took Wal-Mart fifteen years to achieve this level of international penetration, having started international expansion in 1992. (Wal-Mart as a company started its operations in 1945 and was incorporated in 1969.) As a global platform, eBay enables cross-border trading, which accounted for over 15 percent of net revenues in 2005, a task that was complicated prior to online retailing, but made easier with the advent of the PayPal financial payment system (as discussed below).

The company focuses its effort on maintaining and expanding the functionality of this technology platform so that trading through its website continues to be safe and reliable. Its online community of users continues to grow, as product categories are constantly added and upgraded. To help foster continued growth, the company creates web tools (for example, feedback programs) and adds support services (for example, escrow, and insurance programs) to improve the reliability and safety of online trading. Many of these services have been instrumental in building eBay's ecosystem.

GROWING THE EBAY ECOSYSTEM

eBay's ecosystem consists of its trading platform, and the tools and services available on eBay's website that facilitate online trading. They also include a host of supporting businesses not directly operated by eBay, but businesses that assist eBay's buyers and sellers to ship their products to each other around the world. Two important efforts in building this ecosystem are worth highlighting.

The first involves an online payment system—PayPal—that eBay helped foster and grow to facilitate more efficient online trading on eBay and now on other retail websites throughout the Internet. Through PayPal, a company that it acquired in 2002, eBay offers a financial payment system that online shoppers employ to pay merchants *without* sharing sensitive financial information. This payment system emerged during the early days of the Internet, when established financial payment system providers (for example, Visa, MasterCard, and American Express) were reluctant to promote credit-card use online because of fraud and security concerns. To make payments, shoppers disclose only their email address to sellers. This system works on the existing financial infrastructure of bank accounts and credit cards, and offers online merchants a payment-processing solution that is less expensive than traditional credit-card transactions.[4]

As of December 2006, eBay noted that there were 133 million PayPal customer accounts in over 100 markets in over 190 countries and regions around the world. PayPal offered local services in fourteen countries and supported seven different foreign currencies. About 78 percent of marketplace transactions on eBay were completed using PayPal.[5]

The second involves the growth of a number of businesses that have been created to help eBay users trade more effectively. They include school districts that make money offering classes on how to trade on eBay, the "drop-off" stores for people who want their stuff sold for them on eBay (for example, iSold it), and many businesses that help people sell wares on eBay such as pink packing peanuts, and the emergence of commercial software designed to help buyers win auctions at the lowest possible price (CNBC 2005; *New York Times* 2006). Additionally, there are a number of book publishers who offer "how to" books describing trading approaches used on eBay's website. For instance, a search on Amazon.com's books section for eBay returned over 10,000 results in June 2007. In sum, eBay as market marker has enabled the emergence of a cottage industry to grow and support its online trading platform. The gross value of the merchandise traded on eBay was $52 billion in 2006, a number that does not account for the value of merchandise traded through eBay's ecosystem not directly controlled by it.

EMERGENCE OF MOM-AND-POP ONLINE STORES

Another aspect of eBay's market-making activity involves the cultivation of small merchants on eBay's website. eBay's technology platform hosts a large number of mom-and-pop stores. At the end of 2006, there were over 600,000 online store fronts established by eBay users in locations around the world (eBay 2006). Using customized pages, operators of eBay stores are able to showcase all their listings and describe their respective businesses.[6] Also, eBay provides a variety of tools to build such stores, manage operations, promote products, and track performance.

eBay and Amazon.com have, through their market-making activities, transformed retailing since 1995 and in doing so they have become household names. Despite entering different retail sectors in the mid-1990s, their marketing-making actions were more similar than different in many ways. First, both companies transformed the retail sectors they entered: eBay transformed the auctions market by moving such activity online, and Amazon.com transformed book retailing by transforming this sector's value chain before entering other retail sectors. Second, both companies through their market-making actions have come to dominate their respective retail sectors. Both Amazon.com and eBay pioneered many innovations (for example, 1-click ordering, personalized websites, escrow and insurance) that were directed at creating an "ecosystem" so that online retail could emerge, grow, and flourish. Third, both firms rapidly expanded their product categories, thus affecting many retail sectors of the economy. Further, they expanded their operations outside the USA and thereby extended their market-making activities beyond the US retail markets to help the emergence and growth of online markets in other parts of the world. They have empowered customers around the world through information, so that they can make better-informed retailing decisions.

Finally, both have enabled smaller players to compete successfully alongside large retailers by providing a technology platform out of which they could operate. This has prompted some like Bob Kagle of Benchmark capital, a well-known Silicon Valley venture-capital company, to note that "eBay is in a position to give back to America what Wal-Mart took away—the notion of the Main Street merchant. Mom and Pop running their little shop, doing business with other people, making a living at it, and feeling good about it" (quoted in Bradley and Porter 2000: 4). For these merchants, all or most of their income comes from selling on eBay's website (CNBC 2005). If eBay employed the people who operated mom-and-pop stores on its website, it would be the United States' second largest employer after Wal-Mart. Amazon.com too has made it possible for many small merchants to use its technology platform to reach end customers. The company now derives over 25 percent of its sales through the activity of such merchants. This emergence of such small operators is an interesting counter-development to the trend highlighted in Chapter 1, where it was argued that large retailers like Wal-Mart were capturing a lion's share of the retail sales globally, and thus consolidating the retail industry.

Evolving Dynamics of Online Retailing

We now turn to describe trends in online retailing and how retailers continue to be market makers, as Internet technologies and business models evolve in retailing. We begin by examining how the online retailing landscape has changed since 1995.

Online retailing: a changing landscape

In 1997, during the early days of online retailing, *The Economist,* using a two-dimensional framework, predicted that certain businesses are better suited than others for online commerce (see Figure 5.3). According to this framework, since shopping for a mortgage can be difficult and tedious, a website offering straight forward and easy-to-understand comparisons can prove to be successful. In contrast, because buying an audio CD is relatively straightforward and easy, online merchants who sell CDs need to offer far more than a physical music store to draw shoppers to their on-line stores. Based on this framework, the authors of this article speculated that online alternatives are more likely to attract customers if these alternatives are less tiresome than conducting business in the physical world.

As noted earlier, the categories initially popular on eBay were antiques and collectibles such as coins, stamps, and baseball cards. During the early days of eBay, such collectibles dominated the items listed and traded on the site. eBay's website was considered a haven for such items, and it was hard to envision other items dominating sales. However, by 2007 "Motors" ($16 billion) represented the largest single category of sales that were over a billion

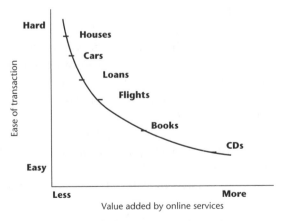

Figure 5.3. Value added by online services

Table 5.2. Categories of goods over $1 bn traded on eBay Inc., 2007

	Categories	GMV ($100,000) March 31, 2007[a]	First quarter 2007 vs first quarter 2006 (%)
1	Motors	16,508	11
2	Consumer Electronics	4,880	25
3	Clothing and Accessories	4,540	16
4	Computers	4,052	13
5	Home & Garden	3,584	24
6	Books/Movies/Music	3,124	4
7	Collectibles	2,684	6
8	Sports	2,584	11
9	Business and Industrial	2,232	19
10	Toys	2,136	10
11	Jewels & Watches	1,972	13
12	Cameras & Photo	1,524	6
13	Antiques & Art	1,352	12
14	Coins & Stamps	1,320	26

[a] Worldwide annualized gross market value (GMV) for the three months ended Mar. 31, 2007.
Source: eBay (2007).

on eBay, a fact that surprised even its own management. Of the fourteen categories that traded with over a $1 billion in gross market value, coin and stamps ranked last, with annualized sales reaching $1.3 billion (see Table 5.2). Collectibles and antiques had also fallen behind many other categories on eBay's website. However, in terms of change in growth from the previous year, coins and stamps were still robust.

Forecasts of US online retail

Although, eBay represents an important barometer for what sells online, it is also instructive to look at the overall US online retail market. According to Forrester, a management consultancy, US online retail sales accounted for about $155 billion in 2009, with the largest proportion of sales (over 50 percent) resulting from computer hardware and software, apparel, accessories, and footwear, and consumer electronics products. Forrester forecasts that US online retail sales will grow at a compounded growth rate of about 10 percent annually, and sales will reach $229 billion by 2013 (see Table 5.3 for forecasts). Of the categories listed in Table 5.3, apparel, accessories, and footwear; computer hardware, software, and peripherals; appliances and home improvement; and consumer electronics are expected to post the largest category sales in terms of revenues. As the table indicates, apparel, accessories, and footwear, followed by computer hardware, software, and peripherals, are expected to post the greatest online penetrations by 2013. It is clear from this list of items

Table 5.3. Forrester's forecast of US online retail sales, 2010–2013

	2010	2011	2012	2013
Total US online sales ($bn)	$176.9	$194.4	$211.7	$229.1
Growth (%)	13%	10%	9%	8%
Apparel, accessories, and footwear ($bn)	$30.9	$34.1	$37.2	$40.3
Appliances and home improvement ($bn)	$22.5	$25.2	$27.8	$30.3
Art and collectibles ($bn)	$2.2	$2.5	$2.9	$3.2
Auto parts ($bn)	$4.2	$4.7	$5.2	$5.8
Books ($bn)	$5.9	$6.3	$6.7	$7.1
Computer hardware, software, and peripherals ($bn)	$30.1	$32.4	$34.3	$36.0
Consumer electronics ($bn)	$14.6	$16.3	$17.8	$19.2
Event tickets ($bn)	$5.6	$6.0	$6.3	$6.7
Flowers ($bn)	$2.7	$2.9	$3.1	$3.3
Food and beverage ($bn)	$10.3	$11.9	$13.6	$15.4
Furniture ($bn)	$2.3	$2.7	$3.2	$3.7
Jewelry ($bn)	$4.0	$4.5	$5.0	$5.5
Movie tickets ($bn)	$1.2	$1.3	$1.4	$1.5
Music/video ($bn)	$7.1	$7.8	$8.4	$8.8
Office products ($bn)	$6.0	$6.5	$6.9	$7.4
Over-the-counter medicines and personal care ($bn)	$6.9	$7.8	$8.7	$9.6
Pets ($bn)	$2.1	$2.5	$2.9	$3.3
Sporting goods ($bn)	$3.2	$3.4	$3.6	$3.9
Toy and video games ($bn)	$7.6	$8.0	$8.9	$10.4
Other ($bn)	$7.5	$7.6	$7.7	$7.8

Source: Mulpuru (2009).

available online that many retail sectors have found the online space to be a viable marketplace for their products.

Impact of broadband connectivity

This continued growth in online retailing is being helped by an external development—the availability and diffusion of broadband connectivity into US households. As broadband connectivity becomes widely available, it is expected further to propel the growth of online retail sales around the world. From just 10 percent in 2002, the number of US households that had broadband connectons had grown to 25–30 percent by 2006 and had reached 65 percent by 2010 (Leichtman Research Group 2010). For retailers, broadband connectivity offers many interesting possibilities for further engaging retail customers through multimedia interactive content such as online video, community forums, price-comparison features, and click-to-call services. The availability of such capabilities, made possible by broadband connectivity, represents a continuation of retailers' efforts to influence what customers see and buy, thereby increasing their power over manufacturers and other players of the value chain.

The role of information

The success of the online retail sector depends largely on the effective provision of information to the consumer and the exploitation of information to meet consumers' changing needs. As more and more customers actively participate in online retail purchases, retailers have a greater ability to gather information on online customer shopping behavior. The information collected tends to be much more fine-tuned and much richer than what is possible through point-of-sales (POS) systems installed in traditional brick-and-mortar retail outlets. Since the early 2000s, the trend has been to find ways to exploit this vast trough of information, using advanced data-mining techniques, to serve customers better.

Exploiting such information is valuable, for it gives retailers added market power vis-à-vis manufacturers. By selectively making such customer information available to the manufacturers, retailers have a greater say over the products that they want to sell, quantities they want to stock, and prices they want to offer. In other words, this ability is a continuation of a power shift to retailers that enables them to make markets well into the future. However, there is a caveat: the availability of vast information available online, the price transparency that the Internet enables, and the ease with which comparison shopping can be done helps mitigate some of the power retailers have been able to gain. The availability of greater information to customers reduces the market power of any single retailer and increases the rivalry amongst retailers.

Small niche players

During the early days of online retailing, retailers typically sold products that were considered as the "long tail," products that were either early in their lifecycle and therefore not considered useful by mainstream customers, or past their useful life and therefore considered of vintage value. These products were often not easily available to potential customers through traditional brick-and-mortar channels. Pioneers such as eBay were instrumental in creating a market for such vintage products. However, with the growth of Internet-based commerce, larger retailers appear to be moving away from a "long-tail" model and toward providing one-stop shopping convenience to their customers. This, in turn, has created opportunities for many small mom-and-pop retail stores to offer niche products on the Internet.

Forrester estimates that 650,000 sole proprietors with eCommerce-functional websites operate on the Internet, and together this group sells roughly about $13 billion of merchandise (Mulpuru 2007). These firms focus on specific niches (for example, Hammocks.com, BocceBallsets.com, detroitcoffee.com) and together provide a vast selection of items not found in big retail stores, including Wal-Mart. For smaller players who target specific niche markets, ties with search engines or traffic aggregators, such as Google, provide visibility based on relevant online users' searches (Morgan Stanley Report 2006). Ties with aggregators, while helping aggregators diversify, also divert traffic from the aggregators' to the niche players' websites.

However, according to Forrester, the movement toward one-stop shopping convenience is also resulting in the consolidation of the industry, as larger online retail companies acquire smaller players that sell niche products with low-cost structures (*Forrester Research Inc.* 2007). However, it does not seem likely that such consolidation will result in fewer niche players in the future. This is because the relatively low level of barriers-to-entry is one of the most alluring features of the Internet and continues to draw thousands of entrepreneurs to set up businesses on the Internet.

An age of partnerships and cooperation

Since collective information is valuable in estimating future trends and gaining power over manufacturers, it appears that online retailers are not averse to sharing or making publicly available customer-related information. At the extreme end of the spectrum of partnerships and cooperation are large information intermediaries such as eBay and Amazon. Both these companies, as noted earlier, have prospered by creating a nexus of suppliers, small merchants, and customers, and by positioning themselves at the center of this vibrant network. Cooperation and partnerships with multiple players, small and large, continue to form the core of their business models.

Even amongst other retailers, there is a trend toward cooperative relationships where a retailer suggests a rival's website if it does not offer a particular product. For instance, such online retailers as Buy.com display a series of sponsored websites for products that they do not sell and direct customers to such sponsored websites. It appears that the potential loss of a customer to a rival is viewed as a minor inconvenience when compared to the overall benefits of providing an enriched shopping experience for customers. Through all these relationships, smaller players, such as Buy.com, seek increased traffic to their websites and then hope to convert this traffic into revenues.

Physical retailers in the age of the Internet

The emergence and growth of the Internet was initially perceived as a threat by many established brick-and-mortar retailers, and the media covering the rapid growth of firms such as Amazon.com, eBay, and Yahoo often proclaimed the demise of many established retail firms. However, since the mid-1990s, many established brick-and-mortar retailers have adapted by pursuing multi-channel strategies where online retail complements their physical presence (Grosso, McPherson, and Shi 2005). For instance, brick-and-mortar retailers are driving traffic to their physical stores by using techniques such as gift cards, rich-media advertisements, and e-mail notifications via the Internet. Their websites offer convenience, product information, and updates on pricing and promotions, whereas their physical stores offer customers the ability to touch and feel their goods before purchase. Some retailers, such as Best Buy, are also allowing customers to order online, and then pick up their product at their physical locations. Additionally, if a customer who ordered online is not satisfied with the purchase, he or she can return the merchandise at the closest brick-and-mortar location. In other words, companies are leveraging the complementary advantages of both the physical and virtual channels better to meet customer needs.[7]

The debate by the mid-2000s was no longer about whether "pure" online retailers or brick-and-mortar retailers would dominate the Internet; rather, since that time, the debate has centered more on how retailers in general are finding innovative ways to employ available Internet technology to create new, and to maintain existing, customer markets. In doing so, they continue to dominate other members of their respective value chains.

Concluding Thoughts

Despite the extensive media coverage accorded to the emergence and growth of online retailing, it still represents a small, although growing, sector of overall retailing. The future penetration of online retailing is still expected to be less than 10 percent of total US retail sales in the next few years. Although this number might seem small, the major impact of online retailers lies not in the displacement of physical incumbents but in transforming the ways that these incumbents operate. Online retailers such Amazon.com and eBay, through their market-making activities, have fundamentally altered the retail landscape. Most importantly, Amazon.com and eBay have forced "traditional" brick-and-mortar retailers in many retail sectors around the world to respond and adapt their business models to find innovative ways to compete effectively. Today, the issue is not whether brick-and-mortar retailers will survive vis-à-vis online players, but more about how retailers can continue to amass market power using Internet technologies.

According to *Forrester Research Inc.* (2010), online retail in both the USA and Western Europe remains "poised for a robust period of double-digit growth over the next five years. [...]. In the US, Web shopping will account for 8 percent of total retail sales by 2014," up from 6 percent in 2009. However, this trend in online shopping is not limited to the USA. As eBay and Amazon. com continue to diffuse Internet technologies around the world, many shoppers around the world will eventually begin to experience the wonders of online retailing. Moreover, as brick-and-mortar retailers co-opt Internet technology, they will also help the growth of online retailing. As global Internet users begin to exceed a billion, both brick-and-mortar retailer and online retailers as market makers are poised to transform retailing, as we currently understand it.

Part Three
Making Supplier Markets

6

The Asian Miracle and the Rise of Demand-Responsive Economies

Gary G. Hamilton and Cheng-shu Kao

Introduction

Since the 1970s, the world's most globally engaged economies have become increasingly demand-responsive economies. By demand-responsive economies, we mean that such economies are organized "backwards" from demand to production, instead of "forward" from production to demand. In making this claim, we are arguing that global retailers, generating intermediary demand in anticipation of final demand, have superseded manufacturers as the driving force that organizes, directly through supply chain contracts and indirectly through their vast market power, whole sectors of the global economy.

On the surface, this change may not seem all that significant. Ever since Adam Smith, economists have recognized that factors relating to demand are prominent features of all advanced market economies. Without demand, so the dictum goes, supply withers. The timelessness of this maxim, however, masks the changes that have occurred in how supply and demand are configured over time. Conceptualized in the abstract, supply and demand are merely aggregations, respectively, of all sellers and all buyers relative to a good. Far from being static, in reality, at different times and places, supply and demand represent very differently organized groups of sellers and buyers. Since the writing of Chamberlin (1962 [1933]) and Robinson (1969 [1933]) on "monopolistic competition," economists have recognized that the organization of sellers relative to buyers matters, but implications of monopolistic competition have seldom been applied to retailers, in large part because retailers have been seen as merely conduits between manufacturers and final consumers.[1]

More importantly, the implications of monopolistic competition have not been applied at the level of national economies. As we point out in this chapter, global retailers, or "big buyers" as Gary Gereffi (1994b) calls them, are not benign intermediaries. They are big enough to influence the internal organization of entire economies. Big buyers not only create demand; they also organize suppliers and develop supplier markets to fill that demand. Through using advanced consumer research, point-of-sales (POS) information, supply-line management, and sophisticated information technology, retailers and merchandisers have restructured the relationship between buyers and suppliers, making the latter a price-sensitive organizational extension of the former. These forged links between the market-focused big buyers, on the one hand, and globally dispersed and largely faceless manufacturers, on the other hand, have had direct repercussions on economies around the world. In general, the more globally involved the capitalist economy, the more demand responsive that economy has become.

How do economies become demand responsive, and what empirically and theoretically does that mean? This chapter gives a detailed answer to this question by showing how the Taiwanese economy developed in response to orders given by global retailers and brand-name merchandisers. In the first section, we use disaggregated trade data to demonstrate that the globalization of supplier markets for US-based retailers and brand-name merchandisers occurred first and most pervasively in East Asia, especially in Taiwan and South Korea, and to show the differential effects of these markets on structuring these Asian economies. The establishment of these suppliers in East Asia created what is known as "the Asian Miracle," the extraordinarily rapid and ongoing industrialization that occurred from 1965 through to the present day. A lot has been written about Asian economic development, but what is less known is that, in response to the retailers' orders, Asian economies developed in very different ways.[2]

In the main section of the chapter, drawing on hundreds of interviews done over a period of over twenty years, we show how these supplier markets in Taiwan actually developed and how many of these suppliers, in turn, responded to changing economic conditions by moving their businesses to Mainland China. These interviews allow us to specify how the Taiwan economy became organized "backwards" from the development of consumer markets in the USA to the development of suppliers markets for final and intermediate goods in East Asia.

The Globalization of Supplier Markets after the Second World War

Modern retailers are the "makers" of two types of markets, consumer markets and supplier markets.[3] In the last half of the twentieth century, both types of markets grew tremendously, and became increasingly global and increasingly rationalized over time. It is important to see these dynamics in a historical perspective, because the emergent qualities of these market dynamics create a momentum that is difficult to alter short of a global economic catastrophe (Feenstra and Hamilton 2006).

US supplier markets before 1965

Our point of departure is 1965. Before 1965, consumer goods suppliers for US retailers were almost entirely US firms. After 1965, these suppliers increasingly came from outside the USA. Before 1965, retailers had limited influence on large US-based manufacturers, but, after 1965, retailers increasingly began to create and organize supplier markets for the main consumer products they sold.

In 1965, the "retail revolution" that Bluestone and his colleagues (1981) identified was already well under way. At the end of the Second World War, US manufacturers had emerged as the most prestigious in the world, and the consumer products they offered represented the most extensive line-up of such products anywhere. The European and the Japanese economies were just in the process of recovering from the effects of the war, and some former manufacturing giants in those economies (for example, Daimler Benz, Mitsubishi) had re-established their prominence at home. In the previous decade, in the 1950s, imports of consumer goods into the USA had hovered around the levels they were at during the Great Depression. Most international trade from the USA was outbound. Exports of automobiles as well as a considerable range of consumer goods began to "Americanize" consumer desires in Europe (de Grazia 2005) and other parts of the world.

In the midst of this parade of consumer goods, US retailers, led by Sears, J. C. Penney's, and Macy's, began to expand their presence in US consumer markets. During the long years of the Great Depression, fair-trade laws made discount retailing illegal, and low demand had stymied the effort of retailers to expand throughout the USA. But, after the war, with economies improved and demand for consumer goods rising, department stores quickly began to expand their consumer markets.

Other events pushed this expansion forward. As described in Petrovic (Chapter 3 this volume), changes in the 1955 tax code reforms allowed rapid depreciation of capital construction, and a shopping center boom ensued as a direct consequence (Hanchett 1996). The Cold-War need for national defense prompted the US Congress, in 1956, to pass legislation creating the interstate highway system across the USA, linking all major US cities and creating ring roads around them. At the same time, the desire to own a family home led the parents of the baby-boom generation to move to newly created suburbs surrounding most large US cities. The number of shopping centers in the

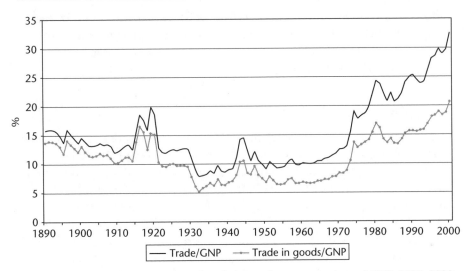

Figure 6.1. US total foreign trade and trade in goods as a percentage of GNP, 1890–2000

USA jumped from about 500 in 1955 to 7,600 in 1964, an expansion in shopping areas that accounted for about 30 percent of all retail sales in the USA in 1964. Only forty years later, in 2004, the number of shopping centers in the USA had reached nearly 50,000. As these new shopping centers developed, the same anchor stores and the same niche retailers began to appear in most places across the country, a development that led to the expansion and diversification of "chain stores."

Before 1965, the products fueling this rapid expansion in retailing came overwhelmingly from the US manufacturers. As seen in Figure 6.1, imports into the USA remained very low from the time of the Great Depression through the 1960s, with a brief upsurge during the Second World War, and, as stated above, most trade in manufactured goods after the Second World War until the late 1960s was as US exports. In 1965, the only Japanese import constituting over 10 percent of total US consumption for a single product was an intermediate good, steel, which was imported to compensate for a decline in US steel production brought on by a strike in the steel mills.

From 1965 onward, however, that picture of limited foreign imports would change rapidly and forever. As Figure 6.2 shows, starting in the late 1960s, imports of manufactured consumer goods began to rise rapidly and across all basic categories.

The rate of import growth as a percentage of total consumption is surprising, but even more surprising is the increase of diversification of the products being imported. As we will explain in more detail below, one of the initial factors causing the globalization of supplier markets is the use of store

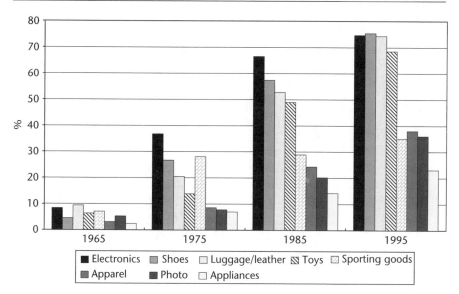

Figure 6.2. Import penetration as a percentage of total US consumption of selected consumer goods, 1965–1995

brands to get around fair-trade laws. As retailers expanded in the late 1950s and 1960s, large department stores, such as Macy's and Sears, began to use private labels more extensively. Kenmore washers and Craftsman tools are two examples of Sears's in-house brands, but the use of in-house brands for clothing and shoes also became commonplace. This expansion of garment and footwear production quickly exceeded the capacity (and willingness) of US manufacturers to provide these goods and led to the increasing use of Asian intermediaries (for example, Japanese trading companies) to fill the orders.

The growth of East Asian suppliers after 1965

Several aspects of these imports of consumer goods should be emphasized. First, most of the imports in every category came from newly industrializing countries (NICs) in East Asia. Even from the very first decade of growth, Taiwan, Hong Kong, South Korea, and Japan supplied most of the imported goods. Although the large enterprises in Japan and South Korea are well known throughout the world, Taiwan, with by far the smallest economy of the three, supplied an extraordinary number of products in large quantities for the US market. Figure 6.3 shows from which countries the consumer imports came. As is apparent, the Chinese areas (Taiwan and Hong Kong) supplied a large percentage of most types of consumer goods from the outset. Just comparing Taiwan and South Korea, Figure 6.4 displays the number of imported

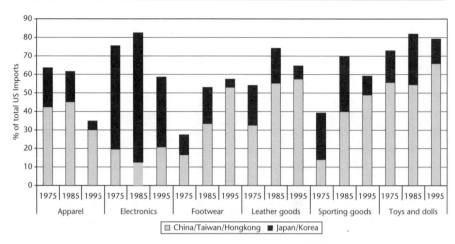

Figure 6.3. Imports from East Asia as a percentage of total US imports of consumer goods 1975–1995

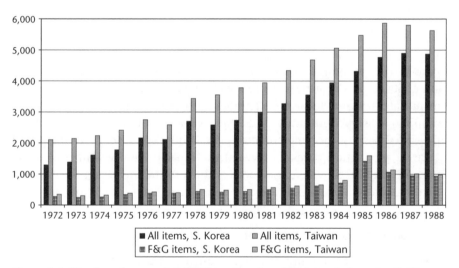

Figure 6.4. Number of seven-digit TSUSA categories of US imports from South Korea and Taiwan, total and footwear + garments (F&G) combined, 1972–1988
Note: F+G: footwear and garments combined.

items at the most disaggregated seven-digit Tariff Schedule of the United States Annotated (TSUSA) codes during the time (1972–88) that US customs agents used this product classification. Over the entire period, Taiwan manufactured more and a wider range of products for export than did South Korea. Not counting exports of automobiles, the Taiwanese and South Korean economies combined to send more exports to the USA than Japan from the 1970s on.

Most writers miss the significance of these US-bound exports. They typically emphasize the large volume and rapid growth of exports, which they explain through a "supply-side" narrative extolling the economic prowess of the exporting country. Using aggregated trade data, typically supplied by the exporting countries, they note the overall similarity in the exports, and as a consequence the overall similarity amongst the NICs. The similarity is indeed there—at the third digit TSUSA level. Feenstra and Hamilton (2006) show the "export landscape" for both South Korea and Taiwan using TSUSA data aggregated to three digits from 1972 to 1988. From these landscapes, it is apparent that most of the export value from these economies is primarily in just a handful of major categories and that, with a few exceptions, the export landscapes of the two countries look very similar. Moreover, the principal categories of exports from both South Korea and Taiwan are exactly those categories of consumer goods that fueled the retail revolution in the United States: garments, footwear, bicycles, toys, televisions, microwaves, computers, thousands of plastic household and office items, and a large array of electronic components that in turn became the building block of a vast and growing number of other products.

If we survey the main items of exports throughout the period from 1972 to 1985, it becomes clear that products secured through contract manufacturing form an extremely high percentage of the total exports. For instance, according to a report on the Korean garment industry, "until 1988, approximately 95 percent of garment exports were produced under contract to foreign firms, rather than under Korean-owned labels" (Lee and Song 1994: 148). According to Levy's analysis (1988: 46) of the footwear industry in South Korea and Taiwan, "in the initial phases of export expansion, export business in both nations was based overwhelmingly on the fulfillment of orders placed by Japanese trading companies, and designed for the US market." Japanese trading companies were soon supplanted as Western firms began to place their orders directly. In both countries, Western brand-name merchandisers, such as Nike and Reebok, controlled the export footwear industry (Levy 1988, 1991). Also, in his case study of the manufacture of personal computers in the two countries, Levy (1988) cites figures from the trade associations for electronic appliances showing that 84 percent of Korean-made personal computers and 72 percent of Taiwan-made computers were sold under non-local brand names. Taiwan was also the world's largest exporter of bicycles during the 1980s and early 1990s, and its export industry until the late 1980s was largely OEM manufacturing (Cheng and Sato 1998). At one point in the late 1970s, Schwinn placed an order of 100 million bicycles with Giant, "which was then only a small factory" (Cheng and Sato 1998: 7).

If we examine the lists of exported finished manufactured products in those early years of economic growth, it is difficult to find any major product category that was not dominated by contract manufacturing or any major retailers that were not involved in contract manufacturing in East Asia. Garments, household appliances, electronic products, toys, bicycles—the majority of all these finished exports were sold under foreign-owned brand names and product labels. Many manufactured exports from both countries, but especially from Taiwan, were component parts, and other types of intermediate goods, such as textiles. A sizable amount of other manufactured exports were inexpensive unbranded products, such as kitchen items and tools of various kinds, which were sold in a range of retail outlets, often in discount stores, such as Kmart and Wal-Mart. As long as they were purchased from South Korean and Taiwanese firms in contracted batches for assembly or sale elsewhere, however, even the simplest and least expensive items were driven by intermediary demand.

From the perspective of America's total imports in the late 1960s and 1970s, those imports from East Asia represented only a modest but steadily increasing percentage, especially in comparison with growing imports of oil from the Middle East. But from the perspective of Asia's industrial expansion, these US-bound exports accounted for a huge percentage of the total output of these Asian economies and drove these economies forward into capitalism.

The emergence of divergent economies

The apparent similarities between US imports from South Korea and Taiwan, however, mask the fundamental differences between these two Asian economies. As Feenstra and Hamilton (2006) have shown in some detail, these economies become progressively organized in response to big-buyer orders. These emergent differences are obvious from an examination of the disaggregated seven-digit trade data. In the very early years when US buyers were placing their first rounds of orders, buyers placed similar orders in different locations. For example, before 1975, garment exports were amongst the highest categories of exports from both countries, with garments providing about a third of the total value of Korea's exports to the United States and a quarter of Taiwan's. Amongst the 263 and 345 types of garments that South Korea and Taiwan, respectively, exported to the United States in 1972, the top five items provided 42 percent of the total value of garments from Korea and 39 percent from Taiwan. Three of the top five garment items are the same for both countries—namely, specific types of sweaters, knit shirts, and trousers, all for women and girls.

From about 1975 on, however, the buyers began to grow more sophisticated in terms of both the consumer markets for their products and the supplier markets for the relative capabilities of different manufacturers. Within the next decade, 1975–85, the South Korean and Taiwanese economies developed divergent specialties. The export segment of the Korean economy specialized in vertically integrated Fordist mass-production systems. Led by *chaebol,* such business groups as Hyundai and Samsung rapidly expanded in response to big-buyer orders for large volumes of the same type of finished product. At the time that the large South Korean firms grew larger, the export segment of the Taiwanese economy became more intensively oriented toward the goods that networks of small, medium, and modestly large firms could produce.

The trade data give evidence of this divergence. Footwear was a large export for both South Korean and Taiwanese economies, but, very early on, firms in the two economies specialized in a different system of shoe manufacturing that led big buyers to order different types of shoes from each country. Figure 6.5 shows these differences, and Brian Levy (1988: 47–8), who visited shoe factories in both locations in the early 1980s, describes the differences as follows:

> Neither Nike nor Reebok had the organizational capacity ... to meet ... surges in demand by subdividing ... enormous orders amongst dozens of small, efficient producers. Instead both companies turned to the giant Korean footwear factories, which had inhouse operations in excess of forty production lines. Firms met [these] orders by expanding their capacity even further. [A consequence of these orders was] continued dependence of Korean footwear industry on a single foot-wear item—non-rubber athletic shoes—which accounted in 1985 for an over-whelming 71.3 percent of Korean footwear exports ... By contrast to Korea, footwear exports from Taiwan have become increasingly diversified over time ... [The] small size [of Taiwanese firms] affords Taiwanese producers the flexibility necessary to fill rapidly shifting niches for small volume fashion items.

Divergence in the production between the two countries in rubber and plastic products is more dramatic. In 1972, when the data begin, both South Korea and Taiwan were exporting rubber and plastic raingear, but the large Korean firms quickly specialized in producing tires for vehicles, while small Taiwanese firms produced every manner of small plastic household products. The same is true for household appliances. Whereas Korean factories specialized in making microwave ovens, Taiwanese factories made small appliances, such as irons, toaster ovens, hair dryers, and so forth. (See Feenstra and Hamilton 2006: 246–9, for these data.)

In every industrial sector, the story is the same. Before 1985, Korean firms "mass produced," while Taiwanese firms "batch produced" goods, and both systems of production grew in response to orders. In effect, globalizing retail-ers and brand-name merchandisers patronized different supplier markets for different products. South Korean and Taiwanese manufacturers competed with each other in some of these supplier markets for specific goods, but, for the most part, they specialized in different products.

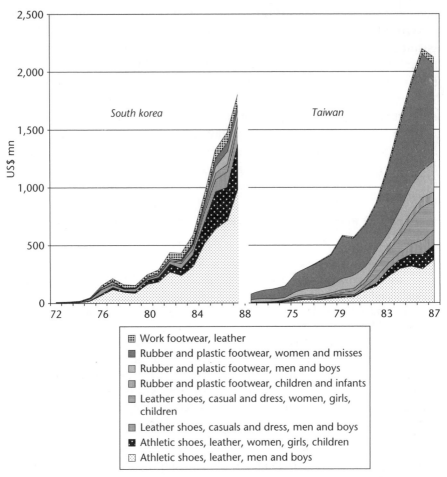

Figure 6.5. Categories of US imports of footwear from South Korea and Taiwan, 1972–1988

Now we will turn to the Taiwanese case in order to show the process by which these supplier markets emerged and by which the entire economy changed as a consequence.

The Rise of a Demand-Responsive Economy

It is hard to date the first moment when industrialization began, and perhaps it is useless to do so. But it is certain that the new economic trend in Taiwan began when the first big buyers arrived. We do not know who these buyers were, because no one sufficiently noticed them to record their arrival. It is also certain that the initial intermediaries were not the Taiwanese themselves. In those early years, as far as the Taiwanese were concerned, Taiwan was a closed island, and they and their resources were locked inside. Martial law was enforced. The government strictly controlled both people and money. The Taiwanese, therefore, simply did not know the foreign markets for which they would soon be making products. And, of course, very few locals spoke any English at all. The historical context makes it clear that the foreign buyers came to Taiwan before the Taiwanese went to the buyers in the USA, Europe, and Japan, as they would do with increasing frequency in the 1980s.

Japanese trading companies

It is very likely that the first buyers of Taiwan's products were Japanese trading companies. In our interviews from the late 1980s, factory owners across a wide range of industries recalled getting their opening working with Japanese firms in one way or another. In the late 1960s, as American retailers began to use Japanese trading companies to fill orders for garments and footwear, these trading companies encouraged a range of Japanese firms to relocate to areas outside Japan, where cheaper labor could be found.[4] Drawing on their expertise in marketing, financing, and information gathering, as Kojima and Ozawa (1984: 13) noted, the Japanese general trading companies "turned into overseas project organizers... and [played] a key role in helping Japanese manufacturers, and particularly small- and medium-sized enterprises, set up shop in labour-abundant developing countries to produce technologically mature, labour-intensive products by investing jointly and providing needed infrastructural services." Two former Japanese colonies, Taiwan and South Korea, were the two places Japanese firms placed sizable investments, first in Taiwan in the late 1960s and then in South Korea in the early 1970s (Feenstra and Hamilton 2006: 262–4).

Aside from our interviews and a few scattered references, however, it is difficult to find much on the role played by the Japanese trading companies in Taiwan's first period of rapid growth, from about 1965 to 1975. If they mention Japanese companies at all, most analysts (e.g., Gold 1986; Wade 1990) refer only to those notable cases of large Japanese manufacturing companies establishing joint ventures in the area of consumer electronics, such as Tatung's 1964 joint venture with Toshiba for producing television sets.[5] To most observers in the era, Japanese trading companies seem almost invisible, a presence about which little is known for sure. Our interviews, however, suggest that they served as the brokers that got Taiwan's industrialization underway, a crucial but unheralded role.

Several factors lead us to the conclusion. The first reason is the language. In the 1960s, many ethnic Taiwanese older than 35 or so could speak some

Japanese. They had learned Japanese during their compulsory primary-school education in the colonial period. Moreover, Japanese at this time was not only the language of instruction, but was also the language of international business, as well as the language of government. In the earliest years of growth, therefore, Japanese business people and ethnic Taiwanese could speak to one another with some level of understanding and cultural familiarity.[6]

Second, the Japanese trading companies in the 1960s began to expand their operations outside Japan. In the immediate post-war period, Japanese trading companies played an important role in rebuilding Japan's domestic economy. They coordinated and brokered exchanges amongst Japanese firms, especially firms in the same groups of firms that had constituted the pre-war *zaibatsu*. Having formed around family-owned holding companies, the zaibatsu were disbanded by the US occupation government on the grounds of being illegitimate monopolists. After the American occupation had ended, the firms constituting the former zaibatsu regrouped, but without the family-owned holding company at the top. In these reconstituted business groups, now called *keiretsu*, the general trading company, along with the main banks, served as one of the core firms that maintained the interrelatedness of group firms. By the 1960s, the general trading companies, called *sogoshosha*, served as the main import/export agents for firms in their respective business groups, and in addition began increasingly to serve as independent agents in establishing sources for goods for which they had received orders, but that were not supplied by member firms in the quantity, quality, or price desired by the ordering firm.

It was their role as independent agents that was especially important for Taiwan. In the early 1960s, after over a decade of rapid economic growth, Japanese labor costs began to climb. For the years 1964–6, the average monthly cost of labor in Japanese textile factories was three times higher than in Taiwan's, at $69 per month, as opposed to Taiwan's $23 per month (Duan 1992). In the same period, the average wage in US textile factories was $333 per month. The rising wages in Japan encouraged the general trading companies to begin to look at locations outside Japan as more profitable places to perform the tasks that they had perfected in Japan—skills at market making, infrastructure creation, and financial backing. In the same deal, the general trading companies would make money in multiple ways. They would receive orders from American and Japanese retailers, and then would arrange production for the orders. In the early years, they had to create competent suppliers: they would broker deals leading to joint ventures between a Japanese company and a local company and, if needed, would supply or otherwise arrange for financing. Then they would import and sell the machine tools needed to establish the factory, train the Taiwanese how to use the machinery, supply the intermediate goods needed to make a product, and then coordinate the delivery of the goods to retail markets in Japan or more frequently in the USA.

Third, during the late 1960s, Taiwan was the largest recipient of Japanese foreign investment (Economist Intelligence Unit 1983). Records on foreign direct investments in Taiwan show that the absolute total of US investments exceeded investments from Japan, but Japanese investments involved over three times as many individual investments than those from the USA (Duan 1992: 236). These figures point to a different investment strategy between the US and Japanese businesses. On the US side, a few large US multinationals (for example, RCA) set up stand-alone manufacturing plants in export-processing zones producing consumer electronics, and on average these investments were much larger than FDI (foreign direct investment) from Japan. In fact, in 1975, nine of the ten largest companies in Taiwan by revenues were all American companies; the other one, Philips Electronics Industries, was a Dutch company (Chu and Amsden 2003: 28). By contrast, guided by the general trading companies, Japanese companies usually established joint ventures with Taiwanese firms. Some of these Japanese companies themselves were modest-sized companies; others were subsidiaries of the large Japanese business groups. In both cases, however, the firms established with Japanese direct foreign investment were smaller and economically more diverse than American firms. Typically, the Japanese firm controlled the technology and supervised the manufacturing process, and a Japanese trading company secured the order and then marketed the final product. In the 1960s, Hitachi, Matsushita (Panasonic), Sanyo Electric, Ricoh, Mitsubishi Electric, Casio, amongst many other Japanese firms, started operations in Taiwan.

Fourth, although the figures seem more like rough estimates than firm assessments, a number of analysts (Olson 1970; Wade 1990; Fields 1995; Feenstra and Hamilton 2006) state that Japanese general trading companies served as the broker for over half of Taiwan's exports from the late 1960s through most of the 1970s. If this figure is accurate, then we must conclude that the general trading companies were not just mere merchants, but were rather active agents in financing, supervising, and supplying the Taiwanese manufacturers. In effect, the Japanese trading companies initiated Taiwan's supplier markets.

This seminal role, however, did not last long, for very soon Western buyers and Taiwanese trading companies began to play active roles in establishing Taiwanese suppliers of goods ordered by Western retailers and brand-name merchandisers. In the resulting mix, Japanese trading companies increasingly began to specialize in a narrow, but still important segment of the overall market economy—namely, in supplying Taiwanese manufacturers with capital goods and intermediate inputs required in the manufacturing process: machine tools, the gear boxes for bicycles, and specialty metals and chemicals needed in a wide range of products. Starting in the 1950s, Japanese exports to Taiwan increased almost every year until the late 1990s (*Taiwan Statistical Data Book* 1997: 194). If our interviews provide a sample of what was happening in the entire economy, it would seem that most of these Japanese exports were the result of orders placed by Taiwanese business people through Japanese trading companies. Through the 1990s, these trading companies continued to source and supply the intermediate goods needed to manufacture Taiwanese exports.

In those initial years of economic growth, however, Japanese trading companies played all the crucial roles that got the Taiwanese business people started. Moreover, they provided the Taiwanese with more than just access to distant markets, advanced technologies, and manufacturing know-how. Most importantly, they showed the Taiwanese how to make money from the global economy. They showed them how to participate as suppliers, and how to be reliable and trustworthy partners to firms that ordered goods from them, but about which they had little additional knowledge.

American buyers and local trading companies

Japanese trading companies probably served as the first global brokers for the Taiwanese. Their very success with sourcing goods in Asia, however, soon did them out of business. Soon after the Japanese trading companies had come to Taiwan, the American buyers arrived as well. They established buying offices in Taipei, Seoul, and Hong Kong. Sears opened its Taiwan buying office in 1967, Kmart and J. C. Penney's in 1971, and Associated Merchandising Corporation (buyers for Dayton Hudson, Federated Department Stores, and Target) and Mast Industries (buyers for The Limited) in 1973 (Gereffi and Pan 1994). By eliminating the middle man, American buyers could reduce their costs, but more importantly they could begin to work with the Taiwanese manufacturers. They could help them be better suppliers, and as they became better suppliers, the Western buyers began to order greater quantities of a much wider range of goods.

Here the US trade statistics are revealing. As shown above in Figure 6.4, in the very first year they were collected, 1972, the seven-digit US customs data show that Taiwan was already exporting products to the United States in over 2,100 categories. By 1985, the number had risen to over 8,400 categories. This increase represents an extraordinary growth in the variety of products Taiwan made for export to the USA.

Most of the value of these exports, however, was quite concentrated, with nearly 30 percent of the total value in only the top ten product categories and nearly 80 percent of the total value in the top hundred categories. The top twenty exports in 1972 were dominated by consumer electronics and items of clothing, most of which are probably the result of multinational manufacturing and joint ventures.[7] However, once outside the top twenty or so items, then one begins to find a wide variety of products that were almost certainly ordered by US retailers and made in Taiwanese-owned factories. Amongst the next twenty items of export are types of umbrellas, luggage, bicycles, toys, household utensils, handbags, Christmas tree lights, and curtains. Going further down the list, the array of products is dazzling: types of handbags, sewing machines, loudspeakers, religious articles made of plastic, inflatable rubber toys, guitars, belt buckles, gloves, clocks, headwear, badminton sets, baseballs, bicycle tires, tennis rackets—all these, along with many different kinds of garments and shoes.

The customs records show that, from 1972 to 1985, these second-tier products were shipped in greater and greater quantities and accounted for more and more of the total value. This shift occurred at the same time as Taiwanese manufacturers took increasing shares of the export production in consumer electronics made in Taiwan.[8] By the time our interviews start in 1987, Taiwanese businesses, rather than foreign-owned firms, dominated every sector of the Taiwan export economy.

As we interviewed factory owners from the late 1980s on, the question that we always had in the back of our minds was "How did this particular factory come to be making that particular product?" And, every time, the answer to that question was that they had had an order from a buyer. Without the order, they said, they would not have made whatever they were making. They explained that the capital invested in the factory and in the inputs used to make the goods had come out of their own pockets, or out of the pockets of a small group of family and friends who were the primary investors; therefore, they would not risk making something that had not already been ordered. When we probed where the order came from, they typically told us that American buyers had ordered the products, and, as proof, they would show us the US brand names on the products that they were shipping.

But at this point the obscurity would start. How were the orders actually arranged? Part of the obscurity was due to our failure to ask the crucial questions. In the 1980s and early 1990s, we, along with most other observers, focused more on how Taiwan business people put together their production networks than on how they obtained their orders. We knew they had the orders, we knew they depended on having the orders, and so we did not query them on the intricacies of how the ordering system worked. However, part of the obscurity also came from the fact that the orders had come from a variety of sources. Some came directly from the retailers or brand-name merchandisers, others were handled by Japanese trading companies, and yet others were arranged by local trading groups.

Knowing the importance of local trading companies, we interviewed several dozen different trading companies. We learned that, in the years of our interviews, mostly in the early 1990s, the owners of trading companies had to work hard to get orders. They would take their case of samples to the USA or Europe, and go from retailer to retailer looking for orders. These kinds of trading companies were colloquially referred to as "suitcase companies" (*pibao gongsi*). But suitcase companies became commonplace only after the Taiwanese were able to travel overseas freely and after the foreign-exchange markets were open, and this did not occur until the mid-1980s. The question that we did not ask was how the ordering system worked during the crucial decade between 1965 and 1975.

During that crucial decade, we also knew that the government did not provide much, if any, assistance. In the early 1990s, a lot of export manufacturers obtained contracts by showing their wares at trade fairs and in fixed stalls at the Taipei World Trade Center. But the Taipei World Trade Center did not open until 1988. Before that, the China External Trade Development Council handled most of the official matters involving trade. The Council was established in 1970, but was continually short staffed and underfunded. The government allowed only thirteen employees to be hired. The first general secretary of the Council, Wu Kuan-hsiung, recalled being so frustrated with the lack of government support that he quit after a few years and went to Singapore. As early as 1973, he had recommended the government build a trade center, but the plan was put off year after year. The government, he complained, liked industry, but not commerce or trade.

Putting together bits and pieces of information from our interviews and from other sources, we think it is likely that the American buyers and the local trading companies began to collaborate in the early 1970s and built a momentum that continued through the 1980s. One fact stands out for this period: local trading companies grew in number at a pace even faster than the Taiwanese economy in the same period. In 1973, official records show that there were 2,777 trading companies in operations in Taiwan,[9] but, by 1985, that number of trading companies had risen to 55,000. One out of every ten registered companies was a trading company. The trading companies were uniformly small, averaging less than ten employees each. Knowing the trading companies from our interviews in the early 1990s, we surmise that nearly every category of export products was represented by many local trading companies competing for orders. Although small, the local trading companies took on a multitude of roles, chief amongst which was to work both sides of the demand/supply equation. Their offices were usually in Taipei, near the buying offices established by American retailers. They worked to identify products that were salable to the big buyers and then worked to obtain orders for those products, thereby generating demand. Then the owners of the trading companies would help to arrange production networks to fill the order, thereby generating supply. They were more than simply matchmakers; rather they were instrumental in creating competent suppliers for American buyers. In fact, they helped to create a *market* of suppliers, a sellers' market, willing to bid on and to make nearly any product imaginable.

Another fact equally stands out about these local trading companies. Once a market of suppliers existed, once the trade fairs and the World Trade Center were in operation, there no longer existed the same role for the local trading companies. There basic role had been completed. From the late 1980s on, local trading companies began to diminish in number.

Imitation and Innovation

Although we did not ask many questions about the process of obtaining orders, we did ask again and again how factory owners were able to make the products for which they had the orders. Many of products were extraordinarily complex or required very complex manufacturing procedures. It always seemed remarkable to us that the Taiwanese manufacturers, often with very limited education, had been able to figure out how to make the products that they were, in fact, making. For instance, the Chairman of Thunder Tiger, a firm making airplanes for the hobbyist market, had only an elementary school education, and yet, amongst his many accomplishments, he had figured out how to manufacture miniature drone jet airplanes. Chairman Tseng, the manufacturer of plastic lawn chair furniture, who at the time of our interview had huge contracts from both Wal-Mart and Kmart, had only the equivalent of a junior high education, and yet he invented a one-step manufacturing process to change raw plastic into finished products. Their stories are not unusual. In fact, most factory owners in Taiwan's first wave of industrialization not only did not have advanced degrees, but also had no training in manufacturing in general or in making their specific product in particular.

The question that we asked repeatedly was how did they learn to make the products. The answer that we received was always some form of imitation and innovation based on an existing product. This process of imitation and innovation is usually a very difficult and complex process. The term often given to this process is "reverse engineering," which makes the process sound simple, but there is nothing easy or automatic about copying someone else's design. In the case of OEM production, the big buyers would often bring the samples, sometimes amounting to nothing more than just an idea designed on paper, with them to Taiwan, and ask the manufacturers, or more likely the owners of trading companies, "Can you make it for such and such a price?" Then, before they could obtain the order, they would have to deliver a prototype, just to show that they could do it. The turnaround time on such a query was often very short, because frequently the buyers would just sit in their hotels waiting for the prototype to appear. With a very short lead time, the Taiwanese manufacturers would have to produce their prototype.

This process of innovating based on an existing product design is a skill that Taiwan manufacturers learned to perfect. In the first decade of rapid growth, many of the OEM products were comparatively simple and were ordered in fairly small batches. Taiwanese manufacturers learned how to produce these products in a variety of ways, some from their experience in working in other factories, some from instructions provided by Japanese trading companies and suppliers of machine tools, and some from the big buyers themselves. However, once in business, they learned quickly from others in their production network. In this context, learning was both singular and collaborative.

It was singular in the sense that one firm typically took the lead to produce the prototype. The owner and key employees of this firm would design and make a prototype. At this stage, very few people might be involved, but those people would have to have a lot of knowledge about the product, and would have to go to some lengths to acquire this knowledge. Factory owners frequently told us that they would obtain this knowledge by going to trade shows, by finding samples of similar products and taking them apart, by closely reading trade journals where new developments were announced, and by pursuing others who had knowledge about the product or materials the products were made of. Wherever they obtained this knowledge, they would then actively try to innovate on the design to come up with something special that would give their goods a distinctive feel.

Learning was also collaborative in the sense that the process of production was a function of the network and not simply of the firm. Therefore, learning how to produce a given prototype required considerable cooperation amongst a group of independent manufacturers. These manufacturers would have to work together very closely on coordinating all aspects of production. In the course of this collaboration, the division of labor amongst manufacturers had to be cost effective, because any inefficiencies would cut into their collective profits. The network of producers, therefore, would constantly learn how to produce products with higher quality while achieving lower costs and how to work together seamlessly. This process of manufacturing also led to improvements in product design.

In another location, we show how this combination of individual imitative by, and cooperation amongst, business people is anchored in distinctively Chinese patterns of social organization (Kao and Hamilton 2009). We refer to these patterns as an adaptation of "round-table etiquette" applied to economic activity, with the result that Taiwanese business people could quickly take advantage of money-making opportunities that began to appear in the

1970s. The constant interaction between the product and the process of production, as well as between the firm and the networks of which the firms are a part, created in Taiwan's first wave of industrialization a particularly dynamic approach to manufacturing. Some examples from our interviews will illustrate these various levels of interaction.

Kai Hsiang: making jacks

The first time we interviewed Ling Wen-chuen, the general manager of Kai Hsiang, a hydraulic jack manufacturing firm in Chiayi, was in 1990. Although we would revisit him many times during the next fifteen years, that first visit left a lasting impression. At the time, he was a youthful 34 years old and was completely at ease with having us in his factory. A very jovial man, he kept us there for the better part of a day, which ended with a banquet that he hosted for the entire research team, for a total of twelve people. A close family friend of one of Kao's graduate students, Ling welcomed us warmly and answered all of our questions in detail.

In 1990, Kai Hsiang was the second largest of the six major jack factories in Chiayi. It employed about 200 people in the main factory and worked with a large network of subcontractors consisting of over 100 small firms. Kai Hsiang was one of a number of businesses owned by Ling Wen-chuen's parents, and his role as general manager was given added weight by the fact that it was a family business, technically owned by his father, but in reality collectively owned by the entire family.

The family businesses began with Ling Wen-chuen's grandfather, who owed a pharmacy in Chiayi. Having a taste for business, but not wanting to take over the family store, Ling's father, Ling Suen-yi, looked around for other opportunities. In the early 1960s, responding to the growing export markets in Japan for agricultural products (Feenstra and Hamilton 2006: 200–10), farmers in southern Taiwan had begun to invest heavily in rearing a range of animals commercially, including pigs, chickens, fish, and shrimp. Sensing an opening, Ling Suen-yi started a factory producing feed for chicken and fish. As a part of this business, he had to import the grains, such as corn, to make the feed, and he had to go around the island of Taiwan to market the animal meal to feed shops. Through his contacts in the feed business, Ling Suen-yi heard, in the early 1970s, about a Japanese luggage company that wanted to locate a contract manufacturer to make some low-end luggage. The Japanese were willing to invest some capital in such a company. Ling Suen-yi quickly took them up on the offer, and, investing some of his own money in the factory as well, he started making luggage. While Ling Suen-yi worked fulltime to establish his luggage factory, his wife took over the agribusiness. Through working with the Japanese company, he was able to upgrade the quality of his luggage and then to land some additional OEM contracts.

In 1980, while running a successful luggage export business, Ling Suen-yi was approached by a friend of a friend. This person owned a jack factory, which he wanted to sell. The factory was not doing well, and the person wanted to sell the factory to the Ling family at an attractive price. A few years earlier another jack factory had opened in Chiayi called Hsinfu. The owner of Hsinfu and Ling Suen-yi were friends, and, sensing an opportunity, Ling Suen-yi hoped to collaborate with Hsinfu to produce a wider range and larger quantity of hydraulic jacks. The year before they bought the jack factory, the person we interviewed, the son, Ling Wen-chuen, had just graduated from National Taiwan University in Taipei, with a BS degree in Forestry. In the year after his graduation, he had worked for his father in the luggage company, learning sales and marketing and making use of the English he had learned in college. When Ling Suen-yi bought the jack factory in 1981 for NT$20 million, his son, Ling Wen-chuen, immediately became the general manager.

In the late 1970s, in addition to Kai Hsiang and Hsinfu, four other jack assembly factories started operation in Chiayi. Although each one was independent and in competition with the other firms and although each had a network of dedicated subcontractors, they also shared some subcontractors who made specialized parts. As a function of being part of an extensive network of assembly factories and overlapping parts suppliers, the entire agglomeration of firms, although internally competitive, shared substantial knowledge about how to manufacture products with hydraulic components. As general manager of Kai Hsiang, Ling Wen-chuen made good use of this information to improve the production facilities in his factory.

The agglomeration of jack factories in Chiayi created a large demand for steel of a certain size and quality. Not far from Chiayi, near Kaohsiung, is the state-owned steel mill, China Steel, as well as several large privately owned steel mills. At first, the jack factories ordered steel from some of these factories, but they soon switched their orders to a newly established local steel mill. This firm had been established in the late 1970s by a local man who had worked as an apprentice in one of the Kaohsiung mills. As the jack factories began to receive substantial orders, this person was encouraged to open a mini-mill dedicated to serving the specific needs of the jack manufacturers in Chiayi.

In the first years of operation, Kai Hsiang was a subcontract manufacturer for Hsinfu, which was then on its way to becoming the world's largest producer of hydraulic jacks. Ling Wen-chuen told us that, in the first year of operation, they made NT$200 million in total revenues, with profit margins running at about 6 percent. After two years, they were able to turn a profit. As a subcontract assembly firm for Hsinfu, however, Kai Hsiang depended on

Hsinfu's ability to get OEM orders. Although the firm was quite successful, Ling Wen-chuen wanted to expand his business. Using his English language skills, he went to Taipei, and eventually to the USA, to meet American buyers. When we asked him how he knew what firms to go to, he said that that was no problem. What he had done was to go to the subcontracted firm in Chiayi that was making the brand-name-labeled cardboard boxes used to package the finished jacks and to see what American companies were ordering jacks. He then went to those companies, and, as a result, he was able get substantial OEM orders on his own behalf. These orders allowed him to expand his network of subcontractors. By 1987, within six years of buying the jack factory, Kai Hsiang became the second largest jack assembly firm in Chiayi.

Our first interview with Ling Wen-chuen was in 1990. Within five years of that first interview, most of the jack assembly firms in Chiayi, including Kai Hsiang, had moved operations to Mainland China. The Ling family luggage business continues in full operation, with one large factory in Mainland China and the small factory in Chiayi, where the high-end luggage continues to be made. The factory making animal feed ended operations at about the time that the farmers in southern Taiwan began to quit raising animals and seafood so extensively because of pollution among other causes. No longer running their agribusiness, Ling Suen-yi's wife opened a stock brokerage firm. The Ling family jokingly called their businesses "nomadic" (*youmu*), because they never stopped searching for new opportunities to make money.

Yeh-Bao: making bicycles

Located about 40 kilometers north and west of Taichung City, Ta Chia is one of many small villages lining the coast and skirting the river flood plains along Highway 1. Well removed from the main North–South freeways, Ta Chia before the 1970s was noted only for making small products woven from grass: hats, floor and bed mats, and grass slippers. Only eleven years later, by 1981, Ta Chia had become the center of Taiwan's export bicycle industry, and by that time Taiwan had become the world's largest bicycle exporter (Cheng and Sato 1998: 8). At the peak of the industry in Taiwan, in 1986, the number of bicycles exported reached more than ten million (Cheng and Sato 1998). Giant, Taiwan's best-known bicycle company, is located in Ta Chia. It is the largest of many bicycle assembly firms in the region. Yeh-Bao is another firm in Ta Chia, but its owner, Lin Shun-san, built his business by specializing only in the manufacture of bicycle frames.

Chairman Lin started his first business in 1975. At the time, he had recently graduated from a nearby technical school with a specialty in telecommunications and had received the equivalent of a high school degree. Not knowing what to do, he returned to his hometown, Ta Chia, to look for opportunities.

In the early 1970s, as Ta Chia was just becoming the center of Taiwan's bicycle production, there were many opportunities in this region to enter the industry in one capacity or another. With only very little capital and acting on the advice of a friend, Lin and his wife decided to start a company making plastic saddle bags that attach to the rear fender of low-end bicycles. They called their company Jun-ye (successful enterprise), and, depending on the workload, employed between ten and twenty people, all from the local village. Their orders for the saddle bags came from other firms in Ta Chia. These bags would be attached to the bicycles in the final stages of assembly, just before the bicycles were packaged and shipped to the OEM buyers.

Building on his personal connections within the local community of bicycle assemblers and part suppliers, Chairman Lin, in 1978, got an opportunity to establish a new firm to make one of the technologically most difficult parts to manufacture, the frame. He called his firm Yeh-Bao (wild treasure) in Chinese and A-PRO in English. At the beginning they used low-end metals, mainly aluminum and stainless steel, to construct the frame. The first couple of years, he recalled, were extremely difficult, because he had to work out the production technique for making the frame solid and unbreakable. To accomplish this task, precision welding is absolutely crucial, because so much pressure is placed on critical points on a bicycle, particularly the metal fork holding the front wheel. "Can you imagine," he said, "a 200 pound American guy riding on a ten pound bicycle at a speed of 30 miles an hour. Oh boy, the frame has to hold together. You know an automobile has four wheels, but a bicycle only has two."

Because competition at the low end was so tough, Chairman Lin decided he had to upgrade his position in the network of firms around Ta Chia. He borrowed money from his friends and bought new equipment in order to improve the quality of his frames. He also began to use new metals, such as carbon graphite, titanium, as well as higher grades of aluminum and steel. Then he hired the best welders he could find, paying then double and sometimes treble the going local wage for welders. When he first bought the specialty metals from a Japanese company, the Japanese company sent representatives to teach him and his welders the best techniques to cut and weld the frames. But Chairman Lin complained to us that Japanese companies never explain everything. They always keep some of the core technology to themselves. Therefore, as they began to work with the new metals, Lin and his employees had to work out many of the problems on their own, and they had to test and retest the durability of their frames. Chairman Lin, however, continued to buy the high-end materials from Japan (for example, titanium and carbon graphite) and to rely on Japanese manufacturers for key component parts, such as the Shimano gear boxes.

Once they had perfected the manufacturing process, Chairman Lin began to participate in international bicycle fairs, usually held in Cologne Germany and New York, and he started to obtain OEM orders, especially from Europe. His own business quickly improved. He had successfully upgraded his firm's position in the manufacturing network, just as the entire network had also upgraded itself as an OEM producer for major European and American retailers of bicycles. As Yeh-Bao grew in size, the firm was able to handle yet larger and more differentiated orders. Chairman Lin's strategy matched the strategy of the entire network of firms—namely, to make differentiated products of mass-produced low-end and middle-range bicycles and batch produced high-end models, this along with a lot of bicycle accessories.

By 1992, when we interviewed Chairman Lin the first time, he had established six independent factories in Taiwan, each making different component parts. The very first firm, Jun-ye, was still in operation, then managed by Lin's wife and making sophisticated bicycle accessories. Yeh-Bao was the largest of the six firms. Chairman Lin was the owner and boss (*laoban*) of each of these factories. We asked him, since he was making so many different bicycle parts, why not integrate vertically and make the entire bicycle himself, or at least become a downstream assembler. He answered decisively that that would not be a wise move. If you try to integrate vertically in Ta Chia, he said, "then everyone will be your competitor. If you keep your firms separate, then you will be everyone's supplier." He said there were other reasons not to integrate as well. If you make a small number of products, you do not have to make a huge capital investment in any one of them. Modest investments, he said, get better returns with lower risks. Finally, he noted that Taiwan's tax codes also favor having multiple companies rather than one big firm. Continually starting small firms means that you can deduct start-up costs, which would not be available if one began a new operation within an existing firm. Also, multiple firms create multiple lines of credit. One big company has only one credit line. And, finally, different sizes of firms are subject to different tax rates. Although all these reasons are important, he reflected, the main reason not to integrate vertically is the risk of going it alone, of trying to make money without help from others.

Chairman Lin thought it was much better for him to make himself indispensable within the overall network of firms. The bicycle industry is continually changing, he said; it is a "fashion industry." A network of firms is much more flexible in changing with the trends than is one big vertically integrated firm. "It used to be that the big firms in South Korean would make huge quantities of bicycles," but the Taiwanese producers were able to follow the trends so much faster that the "Koreans got out of the bicycle business."

Pou Chen: making shoes

Amongst Taiwanese firms, Pou Chen is a legend. In the late 1990s, Pou Chen, along with its subsidiary Yu Yuan, became the largest shoe manufacturer in the world, making nearly a quarter of all athletic shoes in the world. Also amongst private-sector Chinese firms, Pou Chen is one of the largest employers, with over 250,000 employees worldwide and with over 80,000 employees in one of its Mainland Chinese factories alone. Like other Taiwanese firms, however, Pou Chen started small.

When we first interviewed Pou Chen's owner, Tsai Chi-ray, in 1988, it was a considerably smaller firm of about 500 employees, operating 5 assembly lines producing shoes,[10] but, by Taiwan's standards of the day, even then it was relatively large. Our first interview with Pou Chen occurred just at the time when the company was beginning, surreptitiously, to move part of its operations to China. Secrecy was required because the Taiwan government absolutely forbade anyone from making investments in Mainland China, but after the 1985 Plaza Accord, which caused Taiwan's currency to appreciate, contract manufacturers in Taiwan had increasing difficulty in meeting the buyer's price points and still earn a profit. At our interview in 1988, we did not learn about their plans to move to China. Instead, we marveled at their operations in Taiwan.

In 1969, Tsai Chi-ray, along with his three younger brothers, started Pou Chen in their hometown of Yuanlin, in those years a modest-sized town in Changhwa County south of Changhwa City. Reasonably prosperous in the 1960s, Yuanlin was noted for its agricultural products, particularly mushrooms, asparagus, and preserved fruits, as well as its food-processing plants that canned and bottled and otherwise processed these food products for export as well as for domestic consumption. A graduate of a local teacher's college and then a teacher in the local junior high school, Tsai Chi-ray wanted to take advantage of the new economic opportunities that he saw appear in his hometown in the late 1960s. He borrowed NT\$ 500,000 (equivalent to US\$12,500) from close family members, so that he and his three younger brothers could start a factory.

With ten employees, in addition to the four brothers, Pou Chen began making the kind of plastic slippers known colloquially in the United States as "flip-flops." At the time the Tsai brothers opened their firm, a number of other factories in the area had also started making the same style of plastic shoes. Some of the Tsai family members had had previous experience making slippers out of woven grass, which they obtained from Ta Chia. Now they began to use that experience to make these new kinds of shoes. The flip-flop had been designed by an American firm in imitation of a style of Italian-made leather shoes for women. The flip-flops initially sold well in the American market, but the price per unit was very low. American buyers for the main retail outlets, especially Kmart, Sears, and Wal-Mart, then only a regional discounter, began to place orders in Taiwan. The raw plastic material used to make the flip-flops was readily available in Taiwan from Nanya Plastics, a subsidiary of Formosa Plastics. Working through a local trading company, the Tsai brothers were able to land a contract for a quantity of these plastic shoes. At the same time that this was occurring, the US demand for flip-flops surged, which led in turn to much bigger orders. The US buyers for the retail chains then began to come directly to the suppliers, Pou Chen included, and began to work closely with them to increase both the quantity and the quality of the products. Chairman Tsai recalled being especially impressed with the buyers from Wal-Mart, with whom he gradually developed a close relationship.

In the early 1970s, Pou Chen began to receive some direct orders from the main retail buyers. In response to these orders, Pou Chen increased the size of its factory and began to develop its own subcontracting network. At this time the market for non-leather shoes in the United States began to diversify. Pou Chen's breakthrough came when the company got some large orders for a new type of shoe, a canvas-covered plastic shoe, variously called a "sneaker" or "tennis shoe." The construction was fairly easy and the unit price was very low. Working with its production network, however, Pou Chen was able to keep its production costs low, produce these shoes in large quantities, and still make everyone a profit. At the same time that Pou Chen's orders for sneakers began to come in, two related developments pushed Taiwan shoe manufacturers in new directions. First, the technology used in making shoes changed dramatically when Mitsubishi's general trading company, CITC, transferred Japanese technologies for making shoes to Taiwanese suppliers. CITC was one of the primary intermediaries between a range of specialized retailers of sporting goods and Taiwanese shoe manufacturers. In Japan at the time, a new type of shoe was being developed, a highly functional and durable shoe that would become known as the "athletic shoe." These shoes required new machinery, advanced plastic materials, and high-quality sewing and lamination techniques. Making these shoes was also very labor intensive. Taking advantage of Taiwan's cheaper labor costs and batch production techniques, CITC taught Taiwanese suppliers the new shoe-making technologies and also sold them the machines and the materials to make the shoes.

The German shoe manufacturer Adidas had been trying to create a similar type of shoe with technologies similar to those developed by the Japanese. Keeping in step with its Japanese competitors, Adidas, in 1971, decided to try contract manufacturing in Taiwan as well, and signed an agreement with Hwagang, a shoe company located in northern Taiwan. In the following year, 1972, Reebok came to Taiwan, as did the Japanese company Mizuno. These companies signed contracts with a number of the shoe manufacturers, amongst them Chinglu, a firm located in the same county as Pou Chen. Although they had been in business for only about five years, all these contracts for athletic shoes made Taiwanese shoe manufacturers one of the main global suppliers for this new type of athletic shoe.

The extraordinarily rapid growth of the Taiwan's shoe manufacturers created huge demand for specialized inputs and for the machinery to make shoes, much of which were initially supplied by the Japanese trading companies. By the mid-1970s, local firms began to emerge that supplied both the inputs and the machinery. This follows the general rule in demand-responsive economies: orders for final products come first, markets for intermediate inputs for those products come later, which encourages niche suppliers for intermediate inputs to emerge.

The second important development in Taiwan's shoe industry was the arrival of Nike and a surging global demand for athletic shoes that was in part created by Nike. In the early 1970s, Kihachiro Onitsuka, the owner of Asics Tiger, cooperated with the American company called Blue Ribbon Sports, which later became Nike, to manufacture a shoe designed by Phillip Knight. Knight's story is well known. He saw that there was no shoe designed for running and other athletic endeavors. He designed the shoe and contracted with Asics Tiger to make it. In only a few years after their introduction, Nike captured a huge share of the newly developed market in athletic shoes in the USA. At first this market seemed to be a niche market that filled, as well as created, demand from the new popularity for jogging and aerobics. But the niche expanded, as more and more athletic-type shoes were worn for all occasions. At the beginning, Asics Tiger made Nike shoes, but, with competition from Adidas and Reebok, Knight decided to move his contract manufacturing out of Japan. He split his orders between footwear manufacturers in South Korea and Taiwan, with Korean companies making mass-produced shoes for low-end markets and Taiwanese companies making the batch-produced specialty shoes. In Taiwan, Nike's lead firm was Fung-Tai, also located in Taichung County, about 30 minutes north of Yuanlin.

From 1966 to 1985, the global export of sport shoes from Asia grew 1,200 times. Most of these shoes were produced in only two countries, Taiwan and South Korea. By 1985, Taiwan and South Korea produced 50 percent of all shoes imported into the USA. By this time, American shoe manufacturers had gone into a decline from which they would never recover. Because of the sudden demand in the USA, for these new types of shoes, the large retailers and trade-name merchandisers did a lot of research on how to put the shoes together to get maximum performance. In the early years, recalled Tsai Chi-ray, when Pou Chen made flip-flops and sneakers for the big-box retailers, price was the most important issue. Later, when Pou Chen began to cooperate with the brand-name merchandisers, the ability to use advanced technology was more important than price. What all these brand-name companies most needed were manufacturers who could transform these R&D models into a manufactured commodity that yielded a good profit for all concerned. The secret of the Taiwan manufacturers was the know-how to do this.

As Pou Chen continued to make sneakers for the big-box retailers, it started to invest heavily in the new equipment needed to produce athletic shoes, equipment sold to it by CITC. By 1977, it also set up its own internal research division (*Neibu Yanjiu Xiaozu*) to further develop materials to make shoes. It began to do some subcontracting work for other Taiwanese firms that had primary orders for athletic shoes. Then, in 1979, it received its first order from Adidas through a local trading company arm of Hwagang. At the time Hwagang handled all Adidas's local sales; the sales agent did a large portion of Adidas's contract manufacturing, and arranged for subcontracts to do the remainder. The arrangement was very successful for Pou Chen. Then, in 1982, Pou Chen became the primary OEM manufacturer for New Balance, and gained a good reputation for the quality of its shoes. The quality of its production attracted Reebok, which signed an agreement with Pou Chen in 1988. Then, in 1989, Nike signed on as well.[11]

By the time Pou Chen received its first big contract from Nike, Pou Chen was then transferring much of its manufacturing capacity to China. The golden period for Taiwan's shoe production was just ending, and the great rush to China was just starting. In retrospect, we can see that, in 1989, the golden period for Pou Chen was just about to begin.

Demand-Responsive Manufacturing

Between the late 1960s and 1985, Taiwanese manufacturers developed into sophisticated suppliers of consumer goods for global markets. In the beginning of the period, they had very little experience in any kind of manufacturing and very limited knowledge of the consumer goods that they would soon be making for overseas markets. At the end of the period, they had advanced expertise in the process of manufacturing for OEM buyers and equally advanced knowledge of the products that they were making. In slightly over fifteen years, Taiwanese manufacturers, the Taiwanese economy, and the global economy had become tightly interconnected and transformed.

After 1985, in the wake of the Plaza Accord that raised the value of Taiwan's currency about 40 percent relative to the US dollar, Taiwan manufacturers had increasing difficulty meeting the price points set by US retailers and brand-name merchandisers. In the next decade, from 1985 to 1995, waves of Taiwanese SMEs (small and medium-sized enterprises) began to move to Mainland China, and, once in China, the lead firms having the major contracts reorganized their production networks better to fit the needs of overseas buyers. These reorganizations by Taiwanese manufacturers greatly increased their capacity to make products on demand from overseas buyers. From this reorganization emerged a new set of Taiwanese-owned business groups that rank amongst the world's most successful enterprises. Three such enterprise groups—Pou Chen, the world's largest manufacturer of footwear; Hon Hai, the world's largest contract manufacturer for consumer electronics; and Quanta, the world's largest manufacturer of laptop computers—are barely known outside East Asia, but are amongst the largest exporting firms from Mainland China. In fact, of the top twenty exporters from China in 2008, ten were owned by Taiwanese.

The modular organization designed for flexible production grew out of the demand-responsive production systems that developed in Taiwan during the first fifteen years of rapid growth, from 1970 to 1985. Each of these case studies above illustrates this process of transformation.

- The manufacturing of each product came to rely on production networks that broke down the production process into distinct steps that standardized the product, the component parts, and the roles of the participants (Hamilton and Kao 2006).

- All varieties of contract manufacturing (for example, OEM, original design manufacturer (ODM), original brand manufacturer (OBM)) grew out of a progressively reorganizing economy in which individual firms were parts of larger economic units. As the orders for products increased, this form of manufacturing became highly sophisticated and highly responsive to buyer demand. This form of manufacturing is not a second class or substandard form of production, which some analysts make it out to be. The literature often describes the goal of OEM producers as needing to upgrade, but our interviews show that, even in this first wave of industrialization, demand-responsive manufacturing, as a definable process, began to take shape, and was progressively rationalized over time.

- Demand-responsive manufacturing was the result of self-conscious organizing on the part of Taiwanese manufacturers. It was done intentionally, in part because of the limited resources they possessed and because of the social organization that they were accustomed to.

- Our interviews show that, from the outset, Taiwanese manufacturers operated on three principles. The first principle of contract manufacturing is to make money for your buyer. If they do not make money, they will not be back. This understanding led Taiwanese manufacturers to organize by taking the buyer's perspective into account and, in fact, by making it their own perspective. The second principle of

OEM production is to work for the return contract. Meet the buyer's expectations in quality, quantity, and price point the first time. If the buyers come back, then they will have made money and will feel as though they could make more. The third principle of OEM is to make money for yourself. How you achieve these three principles is through taking calculated risks. However, if you do not make money for yourself, you will not be able to survive. Maybe you will not make money with the first few contracts, but if you make yourself indispensable to your buyers, you will make lots of money over the long haul.

- How do you organize to make money for your buyers? As we said, you do that by organizing from the perspective of the buyer. Organize backward from the product itself and from the order for that product. You have the specifications for the product, and you know how many they want. Do not try to develop a totally new product. Simply try to reproduce an existing product with high quality, at low cost, and in the desired quantity. The production unit you organize is in direct response to the product and the orders. Different ways to organize production evolve over time, but in the early years it was always a production network.

- How do you organize to make money for yourself? First, establish a foothold in the production networks, learn by doing, make incremental changes to improve what you are doing, cost down the production process, and accept low margins in the short run in the hopes of receiving larger margins going forward. Be a network player. And accept the network agreements about the profit margin. When the opportunity arises, fill the niches that appear in the production process or develop new niches that others will find useful.

- Second, try to get multiple orders for the same product from different sources. Multiple orders will allow you to develop a strategy of product differentiation, based on standardized parts for all models.

- Third, modularize the production across the producing units. Standardize each step in the production to make the manufacturing process transparent to all those engaged in making the product. Adopt external standards for the products, as specified by the buyer, and adopt internal standards for the process of production, as developed and specified by the network of independent manufacturers.

Conclusion

Taiwanese entrepreneurs developed and perfected a model of how to manufacture for foreign buyers. The model they developed contains a number of elements that led to a comprehensive reorganization of the Taiwanese economy, making the Taiwanese economy into a demand-responsive economy. This economy had the following features:

The economy was organized around products that big buyers ordered and services related to those products. For each product, sets of competing core firms emerged; these core firms assembled and sometimes made key parts and then subcontracted components to other firms. This production strategy led to the development of clusters of firms and to internal markets for intermediate goods and services. These flexible networks supplying final and intermediate goods and services would expand when demand was great and would contract when demand was low. Typically, the product concentration led to a geographical concentration as well, because the production system relied on a just-in-time delivery of parts to the assembly location. The Taiwanese learned these techniques from Japanese, but perfected them in Taiwan.

As overseas demand for products increased, product differentiation also increased. Product differentiation created concentric rings of manufacturing networks, networks that intersected across numbers of core manufacturers. These intersecting rings contained many niches for expansion and development of additional products and for supporting services. Buyer demand also led to rigid cost controls that fed back across all supporting sectors, which in turn created the continuing need to rationalize production and upgrade products relative to big-buyer orders. As Taiwan's entire economy became oriented to export production in response to buyer orders, it also became subject to economic trends in the USA. Economic downturns and rising retail concentration in the USA began to drive fluctuation in the Taiwanese economy, later prompting many Taiwanese business people to move all or a portion of their manufacturing to Mainland China. In Mainland China, they reorganized their businesses in response to rapid increases in retailer orders. Taiwanese, along with Hong Kong, business people, in turn, played a crucial role in creating export-oriented capitalism in China.

This brings us to our final point. It is our belief that the debates about the causes of East Asian industrialization need substantive revision. The current explanations are "supply-side narratives" that entirely ignore the role of intermediaries and the demand, as well as the demand responsiveness, they helped to produce. Global retailers and the reorganization of the global economy that retailers have helped to create have changed the way Asian economies fit into a global economic order. To miss these features of capitalist development is to miss some of the most important aspects of global capitalism today.[12]

7

Global Logistics, Global Labor

Edna Bonacich and Gary G. Hamilton

Introduction: The Meaning of Global Logistics

"Wal-Mart's business model does not work without us"—so said Professor John Liu, the Director of the CY Tung International Centre for Maritime Studies at Hong Kong Polytechnic University. The "us" to whom he referred are those people who specialize in logistics and maritime services. Liu was giving a tour of the state-of-the-art training center at his university, training that prepares technicians to deliver efficient, predictable, and low-cost service to global customers like Wal-Mart. The "basic tools of global retailing," he continued, "are containerized shipping and the Internet." He might have added a few items to his list of tools, but his point was well made. Global retailing and global logistics are so intimately and thoroughly interconnected that it is difficult to tell where one starts and the other stops.

Not so long ago, logistics meant simply the tasks of organizing and coordinating the transportation of goods.[1] Now practitioners have extended the term to cover the entire cycle of designing, ordering, placing into production, and transporting goods to final markets. The activity of integrating all aspects of this cycle is called "supply-chain management," and supply-chain management is at the heart of the market-making successes of Wal-Mart and all other large global retailers.

The market-making competence of these retailers can be seen in their ability to organize their suppliers and service providers, backwards from anticipated demand, so that even the smallest factory making components for a contract manufacturer will respond quickly to the decisions that retailers make. Relying on point-of-sale (POS) data collected electronically, retailers make decisions about the future production of goods, specific product mixes for specific locations, delivery schedules, inventory flows, and a large assortment of other issues. In effect, using electronic data interchange, or EDI, retailers determine what, when, where, and how manufacturers produce goods. This new system turns on its head the old ways of doing things, where manufacturers would produce in quantity and retailers would make selections and put in purchase orders in response to what the manufacturers were making. Nowadays, what is selling plays a big role in determining what actually gets produced. Production is geared to sales, rather than the other way around.

Logistics writ large, in the form of supply-chain management, is the essential ingredient that has allowed retailers to organize their suppliers and, thus, to gain an advantage over manufacturers. But this turnabout is only one aspect of what the transformation in logistics has produced. In this chapter, we focus on the new geography of the global economy, on expanding the boundaries of consumer markets while simultaneously shrinking the boundaries within which suppliers operate. This changing geography has created a new world of work, a world in which competition amongst retailers and their ability to set different price points for both consumers and suppliers directly influence the locations and organization of supply chains all the way down to the wages that distant manufacturers pay their workers.

With new logistical tools in hand, supply-chain managers constantly measure the efficiency and timeliness of all aspects of production, distribution, and sales. The concern over costs and time ultimately feeds back to the cost of labor in every link in the supply chain. One of the chief reasons retailers and merchandisers developed and made contracts with foreign suppliers in the first place was to escape the high cost of US and European labor. As time went on, however, a second and even more important reason to contract with foreign suppliers was for retailers and merchandisers to maximize control and flexibility over their supply chains. With such controls and flexibility in hand, retailers and merchandisers were free to expand their consumer markets around the world, testing one new location after another to see what consumer markets they could make.

As retailers grow larger and more global, they require ever more control and flexibility over their suppliers. The suppliers, in turn, are expected to turn out progressively larger orders of goods at decreasing costs per unit item. The retailers' expanding supply chains paradoxically have the effect of localizing manufacturing. Fewer places in the world serve as the primary locations for firms producing more and more of a particular kind of product. Supply-chain management identifies niches in the global economy in which competing firms can develop expertise and economies of scale, and, as this process occurs, manufacturing firms grow in size and in market power. As discussed in Chapters 8 and 9, huge contract manufacturers have emerged since 2000 to control sizable percentages of the global market in textiles (Nien Hsing for denim), garments (Li & Fung), consumer electronics (Hong Hai and Flextronics), and footwear (Pou Chen).[2] The same process happens in nearly every sector of production in which large retailers and merchandisers predominate, including the production of food, as Chapter 10 shows.

The next chapters in this part document this process. To achieve maximum efficiency in time and costs, retailers need large-scale manufacturers and service providers that flexibly and responsibly do most of the tasks required to get a product into the store. Global logistics allows those manufacturers to be located anywhere in the world, in any location that offers retailers and merchandisers the most advantages in time and cost.

In this chapter, we take the process one step further. The same process that concentrates manufacturing in specific locations also reshapes the markets for skilled and unskilled workers. It is, perhaps, inaccurate to call these new markets for labor global in scope, because labor is not as globally mobile as the goods that labor produces. Still, supply-chain management makes the conditions and cost of labor at each link of the chain an object of calculation in assessing the efficiency of the overall chain. The globalization of manufacturing and logistics, therefore, has the effect of separating the control of labor from the actual conditions and locations of work. Supply-chain managers view labor, like any other component of the supply chain, as a factor that needs to be assessed and controlled, and manufacturers, wherever they are located, need to view their workers from the point of view of supply-chain managers, no matter how distant.

Moreover, these supply-chain managers measure logistical services in the same way they do manufacturing costs. The transportation and warehousing sectors must also keep their costs at a minimum, including their labor costs. Not only production, but also distribution workers' wages and working conditions must be kept in line in order to keep global production profitable from the retailers' point of view.

Logistics and Intermediary Demand

Intermediary demand is the demand generated by what Gary Gereffi (1994b) calls "big buyers," who are mostly retailers and trade-name merchandisers. As a Wal-Mart executive once said, "We don't sell to our customers; we buy for them." The same can be said of all other retailers and merchandisers: they buy goods in anticipation of what their customers will later buy. Big-buyer purchases create intermediary demand.

This intermediary buying comes in two forms. For many items, especially for in-store brands, retailers take control of their ordered goods at the site of production and arrange for the shipment of these goods to their stores.[3] For other items, manufacturers and brand-name merchandisers control supply-chain logistics for the branded products that end up in the retailers' stores. A strong indicator of both types of buying is found in maritime statistics.

Focusing only on ocean transportation of containerized products (which accounts for over 80 percent of the value of total imports in the USA, the remainder entering by air or land transportation across the borders), and only on imports to the United States, we can see the importance of imports and maritime services in retailers' management of their supply chains.[4] In 2008, according to Leach (2010: 22), 17,121,000 TEUs (or 20-foot equivalent units, the standardized measure of container volume; one standardized container holds two TEUs) were imported into the United States, which in a recession year had declined slightly from the high point in 2006 (18,611,000 TEUs) to about the same volume of imports as in 2005. The *Journal* produces an annual list of the top 100 shippers (referring to importers, rather than shipowners, which are known as carriers) that import goods to the United States using ocean transportation. Of the total TEUs for 2008 (*Journal of Commerce* 2009: 22A), 720,000 TEUs, one out of every twenty-four imported containers, was brought in by Wal-Mart. The next biggest importer was Target, with 445,800 TEUs, and the third was Home Depot, with 300,400 TEUs. Thirty-six of the top 100 importers were retailers, as were six of the top seven, which in addition to the above included Sears, Lowe's, and Costco.

Amongst the top 100 importers were also foreign firms that manufacture electronic goods (for example, LG, Samsung, Panasonic, Cannon, Sony, and Hon Hai), brand-name merchandisers that contract firms to manufacture their products (for example, Nike, Jarden, Whirlpool, and Mattel), as well as a number of automotive companies, parts manufacturers, and food distributors (for example, Dole and Chiquita). All of these firms import goods for which they supervise the distribution. Giant retailers, however, stand out as the major maritime importers to the USA, with Wal-Mart being head and shoulders above the rest.

Wal-Mart's dominance of the importers' list is not new, and its lead has been widening, even in a time of recession. The giant retailer's growth as an importer can readily be traced during the first decade of the twentieth century. In 2001 the company brought in 260,000 TEUs. By 2003 the imports leaped to 471,600 TEUs, again in 2004 to 576,000 TEUs, to 695,000 TEUs in 2005. Although overall imports fell in 2008 from its high in 2007, Wal-Mart's total was 720,000 TEUs for both years. This rise in retailers' imports is not simply a Wal-Mart phenomenon, but rather reflects the tremendous growth of manufactured imports to the United States in recent years. Target's imports grew from 121,000 in 2001 to 445,800 TEUs in 2008, and Home Depot's rose from 80,000 to 300,400 TEUs over the same period.

To gain some perspective on these numbers, consider the last firm on the list of the top 100 importers, Dal-tile, a manufacturer of tiles that is owned by

Mohawk Industries. Dal-tile imported 10,900 TEUs in 2008, which is 5,450 full containers. That totals about fifteen containers every day of the year, each of which holds around 30 tons of goods. A lot of importers hover in this range. Now consider Wal-Mart, which receives and handles the distribution of nearly 1,000 containers, totaling about 30,000 tons of goods, every day of the year. The ability to manage these imports and get the products to the right store at the right time is truly the triumph of modern logistics and of Wal-Mart's mastery of its supply chains.

The retailer statistics tell only part of the story. These figures reflect only the containerized products that are imported by the retailers themselves. The retailers also receive imported goods from brand-name merchandisers that contract with other firms to make their goods. Nike appears on the list of the 100 importers as a manufacturer. The athletic shoe producer and retailer, however, does not own its factories, is well known for offshore contract manufacturing, and has become the target of several major anti-sweatshop campaigns. Bringing in 70,200 TEUs in 2008, Nike ranked eighteenth on the list of importers. Other brand-name merchandisers include Mattel Inc., a toy manufacturer, which sells the largest proportion of its toys through Wal-Mart, even though Mattel does its own importing. It is ranked thirty-eighth amongst the top 100 in the *Journal of Commerce* list, bringing in 35,900 TEUs in 2008. Another example is Jarden, a little known factory-less company ranked fifteenth on the list of importers (80,500 TEUs) that contracts and sells well-known branded products (for example, Mr Coffee, Sunbeam, Oster, Crock Pot, and Coleman, amongst others) to a large variety of retailers. And there is Whirlpool, a well-known manufacturer of home appliances, which is ranked twentieth on the list and which imports a large number of component parts and branded products, including KitchenAid, made elsewhere also in factories that it does not own. Wal-Mart and the other large retailers can be seen as "indirectly" importing goods like those produced by such brand-name merchandisers.

As these figures suggest, a very large percentage of all imports worldwide arrive by sea. Although airfreight is rapidly growing as well, container shipping remains the cheapest and often the most convenient mode of trans-porting goods, and, as John Liu noted in the opening paragraph of this chapter, containerized shipping is a "basic tool of global retailing." Indeed, they both grew up together.

In 1956, a year after the shopping center construction boom started, the first maritime shipment of containers occurred on a voyage between Newark and Houston. After that opening, the success of containerized shipping was rapid, although it was not until 1966 that competing carrier companies could agree on standardized containers (Levinson 2006). Once standardization had occurred, however, and the risk of competing systems vanished, investments began to pour into ships, ports, intermodal connections, railways, and trucking, so that, by the mid-1970s, the world's major ports were container ports capable of accommodating larger and larger container ships. And, in general, the size and importance of these ports followed the size and importance of international trade in those locations that followed supplier markets for global retailing.

In 1969, the list of the world's largest container ports listed only one Asian port, Yokohama, in seventh place, which had about four times less volume than first place New York (Levinson 2006: 209). By 1980, New York continued to top the list, but three of the top five were Asian ports: Hong Kong, Kaohsiung, and Singapore. Ten years later, in 1990, four out of the top five were Asian ports (Kobe, in addition to the three above), and New York had dropped to ninth place on the list. In 1998, the container port in Shanghai joined the top ten for the first time; the port in Hong Kong, listed amongst the top ten since the early 1970s, reverted to China with the retrocession in 1997. By 2000, New York had slipped to fourteenth place on the list, and five of the six largest ports were in Asia, including Hong Kong and Shanghai. By 2008, all the top five were Asian ports and New York had fallen to twentieth place on the list. Of these, three of the top five and seven of the top twenty ports were Chinese (in order: Shanghai, Hong Kong, Shenzhen, Ningbo, Guangzhou, Qingdao, and Tianjin).

The Rise of China

In 1980, the USA imported $1.1 billion worth of goods from China, far below Taiwan's US-bound exports valued at $6.7 billion. By 1990, despite a decade of rapid growth in US imports from Asia, China still exported only a little over $15 billion of goods to the USA, by which time Taiwan's exports to the USA had grown to about $22 billion. After 1990, however, China's exports to the USA (as well as to the rest of the world) leaped forward to over $45 billion in 1995, $100 billion in 2000, $243 billion in 2005, and $337.8 billion in 2008. In 2008, China's trading surplus with the entire world was $295.5 billion; in the same year, China's trading surplus with the USA was $266.3 billion—the largest trade deficit ever seen between two countries.[5]

The rise of China reflects a rapid consolidation of global manufacturing. In the decades preceding China's rise, Japan, Taiwan, Hong Kong, and South Korea became, increasingly, the primary locations where US retailers and brand-name manufacturers located suppliers for the consumer goods that they would, in turn, sell to their customers. As the previous chapter shows, US retailers and their buyers had taken an active role in creating suppliers that could competently provide the right goods at the right time at the right price.

East Asian manufacturers reacted rapidly to this opportunity to make money off the global economy by becoming better and better suppliers. In response to this intermediate buying, as Feenstra and Hamilton (2006) show, each of these East Asian economies began to diverge through supplying different products and through developing its own specialized production networks to make those products.

This divergence accelerated after 1985, when the Plaza Accord led to drastic upward re-evaluations in East Asian currencies, relative to the US dollar, which forced many Asian suppliers to shift the site of their low-end manufacturing to locations where labor costs were not so high. At first, in the late 1980s and early 1990s, Japanese and Korean manufacturers of labor-intensive products moved their production lines to South East Asia and Latin America. Japan's move to South East Asia was so extensive that Japan appeared to be building "a regional production alliance" (Hatch and Yamamura 1996). By 1985, facing higher property and labor costs, Hong Kong manufacturers had already begun to move their production facilities to the Pearl River Delta region in China. After hesitating for several years and experimenting with South East Asian sites, Taiwanese manufacturers followed suit. Starting in earnest in the early 1990s, waves of Taiwanese suppliers moved to China, often after having been encouraged, and some even required, to do so by US retailers and merchandisers.

In the 1990s, suppliers often split their production facilities. The labor-intensive production went to low-wage regions where the manufacturers could get the best deals: cheap land, low taxes on exports, no unionization for labor. The production of "up-market" products usually remained in the home country. The 1990s were also a time when production of high-technology products took off, and the production of high-technology components and products pushed Taiwan's and South Korea's economies to new heights. In large part, the success of Taiwanese and South Korean manufacturers resulted from their close collaboration with US retailers and came at the expense of Japanese manufacturers, who became their suppliers of technology-intensive component parts, such as flat-screen panels.

The Asian financial crisis in 1997 marked the beginning of the end of this growing Asian divergence in the products that East Asian countries produced for Western suppliers. As many economies in East and South East Asia collapsed, global retailers and East Asian suppliers began to consolidate, respectively, their sourcing and their manufacturing, in China. During this period, China had demonstrated not only financial stability, but also a willingness to join the World Trade Organization and to conform to WTO rules governing trade, which appeared to lessen the risk of investing in China. This conjuncture of events led to huge increases in foreign direct investment (FDI), which flowed into China from neighboring countries, led by Hong Kong and followed first by Taiwan, then Japan and South Korea. Japanese and South Korean investments poured into northeastern China, which could easily be reached by ship via the Yellow Sea. Hong Kong and Taiwan investment initially went into the Pearl River Delta, but later also flowed into the area around Shanghai. In the opening decade of the new millennium, China became the site of the world's leading manufacturers and exporters of consumer products.

In the ongoing debate in the USA and Europe about whether China's economic policies are unfairly taking advantage of the rest of the world, very few analysts discuss the role of global retailers and foreign manufacturers in China. Nonetheless, more than any other single factor, global retailers drive China's exports. More than 50 percent of China's exports come out of firms not owned by Chinese nationals (Blonigen and Ma 2010). To this total, we can add the exports of many other firms that local Chinese do own and operate. It is obvious that very few Chinese firms make any markets in any products outside China, and so it is equally obvious that global retailers, brand-name merchandisers, and a range of trading companies acting as intermediaries between retailers and manufacturers control most of the market making for Chinese exports.

Offshore Production and Logistics by Retailers

This realization leads us to the following question: what is the relationship between global retailers and their suppliers in China? Neither retailers nor brand-name merchandisers typically own production facilities. Instead, both arrange with contractors for the production of their goods. Brand-name merchandisers obviously need to maintain some control over the design and perhaps even over the manufacture of their branded goods. Retailers, however, would appear to have a different relationship to their suppliers. A common assumption is that the relationship is merely arm's length, that retailers merely purchase whatever they want to sell from suppliers of those products, with very little if any intervention into the process of design and manufacturing.

This may once have been the case, before extensive contract manufacturing began. But, in recent decades, this distinction between retailers and brand-name merchandisers has virtually disappeared. For one thing, most global retailers have successfully developed private-label (or store-label) programs, where they arrange with manufacturers or contractors to produce their own label. The result is not very different from the kind of arrangements used by merchandisers like Nike to get their goods produced.

To try to understand the degree to which retailers are involved in production in Asia, Bonacich interviewed an important executive of one of the giant retailers that imports products from Asia and that is fairly high on the list of top maritime shippers. This person was extremely helpful, but wished to remain anonymous. The person explained the approach of the giant retailers to offshore sourcing in Asia. Bonacich asked whether retailers are involved in Asian production only when they are producing their stores' private label. The executive disagreed:

> We are involved in all production in Asia, not just private label. We engage in the direct importing of both private label and branded goods. We work with the producers, oversee the production of our goods, and set up specifications for our products. It makes no difference whether the products are branded or private label. In neither case do we own any factories, so we are always dealing with someone else's factories.

This particular retailer has a private-label program that it began about a dozen years ago. The executive calculated that, if the retailer can get 20 percent better value in a private label than in a branded product, and better quality at the same time, it switches to private label. It then benchmarks the private label against the brand. Usually the retailer sells the brand right next to the private label. Essentially this tactic shows the brand-name merchandiser that its prices are too high. Pitting lower private-label prices against brand prices can play a role in driving down industry prices. It seems reasonable to assume that this has implications for labor standards in these industries as well.

When this retailer started outsourcing in Asia, it used a broker in the US that worked with a trading company in Asia. But now the retailer's policy is to try to get as close to the factory as possible and to limit the role of brokers and other middlemen. "We don't have our own offices in Asia, but some Asian companies are big enough that they serve as their own broker; so we can buy directly from them." In contrast, Wal-Mart has its own offices in Asia. In our informant's experience, it is the department stores that especially use buying agents. They form consortia for group purchasing. The big-box retailers are generally trying to get rid of all unnecessary middlemen.

How does this retailer use logistics effectively? First, the retailer uses POS data only for replenishment of items that are selling well. When it decides to try a new item, it uses its sales history elsewhere to determine the size of the order. The use of electronic data interchange (EDI) is still growing in Asia, according to our informant. One of the problems is a lack of a common standard. Thus, this retailer does not directly use EDI (or vendor-managed inventory (VMI)) for interacting with Asian suppliers. EDI is used extensively in the USA, noted the executive, and its use will soon be extensive in Asia too.

"Eventually the vendor and retailer community will develop a communications network to standardize ordering at an international level."

This retailer uses "just-in-time" practices for anything manufactured locally. It has daily and sometimes twice-daily deliveries. The company president has ordered that there should be only one day's worth of sales on the floor. This practice has allowed the company to reduce its number of stock-keeping units (SKUs) or specific items. Imports, by contrast, are planned inventories. They are rotated into the stores by SKU. They can be seasonal, like furniture, which is not replenished and involves a one-time buy, or they can be constant throughout the year, like men's shirts, which are restocked on a regular basis.

Bonacich asked Jon DeCesare, CEO and President of World Class Logistics Consulting, what he thought about the use of advanced logistics practices by the big box retailers in Asia.[6]

> The big-box retailers vary a great deal in their sophistication, so you can't generalize. They make general forecasts, and then fill in the details using POS data. In terms of sophistication, Wal-Mart wrote the book, and rewrites it every day. Target is trying to keep up, as is Best Buy and Home Depot. For example, Target will budget shelf space for a certain product, and they lose money if it isn't there on time. They reckon they save $100 million for every day they can take out of the transit time. So the supply chain is incredibly important to them. But what they mainly seek seems to be visibility, not replenishment orders. They want to make sure that goods are moving as planned. They want a glass pipeline. They want to be able to see where their SKUs are.

He thinks Asian manufacturers often do not have direct EDI connections, where POS data are transmitted electronically to the producer so that it can take charge of the retailer's replenishment needs, as is the case with many US suppliers. Rather, the retailers' inventory control departments get the POS data, make adjustments to orders, and then send them out. The producer then has to be flexible in supplying the goods to the retailers. Essentially, the retailer "outsources" inventory management to the producers.

An example is Huffy Bicycles, made in China, said DeCesare. Wal-Mart may order 50,000, which are then delivered to a Huffy warehouse in the USA. Wal-Mart then asks for them on a just-in-time basis—in smaller lots, like 5,000. But they also have the power and flexibility to tell them that they do not need any more after they have received 30,000. Then Huffy is stuck with 20,000 bicycles, which it has to figure out how to unload. "This is a common scenario," says De Cesare. Hamilton's interviews with bicycle manufacturers in Taiwan and China confirm this picture. In fact, one manufacturer complained bitterly about having to pay storage fees in the USA until Wal-Mart assumed ownership of the bicycles, which occurred only at the point of sale.

The Impact of Retailers on Labor in Production

The marriage between retailing and logistics has had substantial effects on labor markets around the world. Giant retailers use their considerable size and economic power, directly and indirectly, to pressure manufacturers and service providers to improve their efficiency and to lower their costs, including, importantly, their labor costs. They also exercise their influence on labor standards in both supplier and consumer markets to push for government and corporate policies that make labor a flexible component of supply-chain management. Retailers' influence has the effect of moving the site of control over labor from the place of work (for example, the shop floor, the factory) to the supply-chain managers, who make the crucial decisions about which firms supply goods and services and at what cost.

It is important to recognize that this shift in the locus of control over labor does not necessarily lower labor standards. Nor is it, necessarily, the intention of retailers to do so. In the effort to make supply chains more efficient and flexible in terms of quality and cost of goods and speed of delivery, retailers help to "modernize" the economies of developing countries. They force firms in both developed and developing countries to rationalize their production and distribution methods. Also, through codes of conducts, which they typically post on their websites, retailers and brand-name merchandisers may even improve the conditions and increase the wages of workers in those firms relative to what they are in other firms in the same location (see our discussion on this point below). However, whether they improve the conditions and wages for workers or not is an ancillary outcome of the retailers' most important task, which is efficiently and effectively to manage their supply chains. And, insofar as they do so, then the supply chains, as well as the economies in which they are embedded, become demand responsive— that is, they become effectively organized backward from demand to supply.

The extensive use of contract manufacturing, or outsourcing, is known as "flexible production." It is typically praised because it encourages production on an as-needed basis (limiting the costs of inventory accumulation), and avoids overproduction of unwanted goods that cannot be sold. Moreover, it allows for the production of small batches of specialized goods that can be targeted for specialized consumer groups and tastes. Flexible production is associated with product differentiation, with the multiplication of styles of products (and SKUs) of the same brand, such as the array of types and colors of IPods a customer can buy from Apple.

Flexibility, or contingent relationships, works well for retailers, but makes life difficult for the contract manufacturers and service providers. In turn, flexibility also makes life more difficult for the employees of these firms, employees who face increased contingency in the form of piece-rate, temporary and part-time positions, independent contracting, and so forth. These irregular forms of employment have grown enormously in the United States in recent years. Contingent workers often suffer from a host of ills, including not only irregular work, but also low pay and the absence of benefits. Big, stable companies lend themselves to unionization. Contingent relations make unionization much more difficult. With contingent connections, big buyers can effectively shut out unionization by shifting work to contractors in regions or countries where they will not have to deal with "labor problems."

The shift in the locus of control over labor to supply chain managers means that direct employers (the factory owners) cannot support worker organizations that would undermine their ability to meet the price and quality demands of big buyers, lest they lose their contracts. Contract manufacturers are, therefore, highly motivated to keep unions out of their factories by any methods whatsoever. Similarly, regions, export-processing zones, even entire countries face the same basic logic: if organized labor becomes a force that can improve wages, benefits, and working conditions, then contract manufacturers will become less competitive and will have to move to new locations to retain their contracts with retailers. In fact, as the next chapter shows, contract manufacturers often maintain factories in multiple locations, which allow them to shift production from one site to another, as conditions require.

Rural Migrant Labor in Southeastern China

The system of labor that has emerged in southeastern China is a good illustration of the indirect impact that retailers have on the conditions of workers engaged in manufacturing. Southeastern China, especially the large area in the hinterland of Hong Kong and Guangzhou in the Pearl River Delta, is the most important of China's three main export-producing areas. Many manufacturers from Hong Kong and Taiwan have located their factories in this region, and many Chinese firms have grown up in this area to supply services and component parts for these foreign-owned factories.

This area of Guangdong province has also been the site of a number of studies investigating worker conditions in these factories. Because these foreign-owned factories are responding to greatly expanded orders for goods, the factories have grown very large and the number of workers employed is huge when compared to the size and employment figures of these factories before they were relocated to China. For example, as described in Chapter 6, the footwear manufacturer Pou Chen was only a medium-sized firm in Taiwan before it began to move its manufacturing operations to China in the 1980s. As reported in Chapter 9, Pou Chen, whose Mainland name is Yue Yuen, now employs over 100,000 people in its Guangdong factories, around 80,000 of which are employed in one factory alone.

Because so many workers are required for these factories, in 2009, analysts, relying on Chinese government data, estimated that over 150 million rural migrant workers have moved from China's interior provinces to the coastal provinces where the export-oriented factories are located. The largest ratio of rural migrant workers to local residents is found in the Pearl River Delta, "where some 20 million rural migrant laborers live and work" in this relatively small area (K. W. Chan 2009: 11). These migrants, who make up most of the labor force for export industries, are denied the rights of urban residents and are forced to be temporary migrants moving back and forth between the countryside and the city.[7] According to Kam Wing Chan (2009: 10):

> The denial of local hukou (residency rights) to migrant workers, combined with their plentiful supply and lack of access to legal information and support, has created a large pool of super-exploitable, yet highly mobile or flexible industrial workforce for China's new economy, catering to global consumers . . . [The policy] has served very well China's economic growth strategy of being the world's "most efficient" (lowest cost) producer . . . China can continue to draw labor from rural to urban areas and export-processing zones without having to raise the wages much above the rural-subsistence level.

The "China price" is based on China's low labor costs, which result directly from China's policies to maintain this very large pool of temporary workers who are least able effectively to organize to secure their labor rights (A. Chan 2001).

Because most workers in China's export-processing factories are migrants, the factory owners typically provide large dormitories to house their employees with "anywhere from eight to twenty workers per room" and large cafeterias to feed them (Pun 2009: 158). These dormitories are close, and often even attached, to the factories themselves. The majority of those living in the dormitories are young, single women. These workers have little to no privacy, are closely supervised, and are required to follow the rules and regulations set forth by the owners. According to Smith and Pun (2006), the "dormitory labour regime" is unlike the dormitory system found in the paternalistic textiles factories in nineteenth-century Japan, which was set up to house single female workers fulfilling multi-year contracts. By contrast, in China, the dormitory system provides short-term facilities for temporary workers. These workers work seasonally and intensively, often preferring to work overtime to earn as much money in as short a time as possible. They provide the factory with a highly flexible labor force that offers, as a rule, little resistance to the demands of management. With this system of labor control, argues Pun (2009; see also Smith and Pun 2006), factory owners can lengthen the work day, suppress wage demands, access labor on a just-in-time basis, exert direct controls over the labor process, and rely on government policies and rural families' need for money to replenish the supply of temporary migrants.

Codes of Conduct and Monitoring

This system of labor control is closely connected to the purchasing system that retailers and brand-name merchandisers have developed over time. Retailers and merchandisers are reluctant to hold inventories of goods, and thus they push inventory management down into the factory, where just-in-time production becomes a necessary condition for getting contracts. Factories, as well as the Chinese government itself, have responded to this evolving system of export production by developing a just-in-time workforce that is capable of responding to big buyer demands.

Retailers do not want to be labeled as creators of "sweatshop-like" conditions in factories making products that they have ordered. Fearing the consequences of a bad reputation, most retailers and merchandisers have devised codes of conduct and systems of oversight that are supposed to ensure compliance from their contract manufacturers. These codes of conduct are typically posted on the website of these firms, so that all interested parties can see them. In addition, many of these companies have banded together to form, in the United States, the Fair Labor Association (FLA), which promotes the independent monitoring of the global supply chain to prevent labor abuses. Another group, which began in the United Kingdom but has a global orientation, is called the Ethical Trading Initiative (Birchall 2007).

Researchers, investigating the extent to which contract manufacturers in China have implemented these codes of conduct, have come up with counterintuitive results. Sum and Pun (2005) find three paradoxes that are outcomes of the adoption of codes of conduct. First, the competition in contract manufacturing to engage in "just-in-time, low-cost and fashion-conscious production," on the one hand, and the big buyers' requirement to implement extensive codes of conduct for labor, on the other hand, have led manufacturers to use "compliance with labor codes" as a marketing strategy to obtain more and larger contracts (Sum and Pun 2005: 197). The name of the contract manufacturing game is to obtain the contracts in the first place, and, for this task, adopting a code of conduct is useful, if not necessary.

Second, codes of conduct are doubly useful as a tool to "encourage workers to cooperate with management to avoid the loss of contracts and hence future employment opportunities" (Sum and Pun 2005: 197). Summaries of the codes of conduct are posted on the walls of the factories, where they are visible to inspectors. In relation to outsiders, such as big-buyer and third-party inspectors, managers encourage workers to enter into a "tactical alliance" that protects the factory from social auditing by outsiders. Workers are trained to answer questions in ways that comply with the code of conducts, even though the actual conditions of work are quite different.

Third, outwardly adopting a code of conduct requires contract manufacturers to develop "elaborate managerial and audit/documentation systems to defend the [contract manufacturer] against charges of infringing the Code ... [Hence] more effort goes into paperwork than into actual advancement of labour rights protection" (Sum and Pun 2005: 197).

The weakness of the codes-and-monitoring system goes beyond China, as is shown in an October 2006 revelation that Tesco (the giant British retailer that belongs to the Ethical Trading Initiative) was producing clothing in factories in Bangladesh that employed children. According to a *Financial Times* reporter (Birchall 2007), "the case illustrated the limits of systems established to monitor conditions in sectors such as clothing, footwear and toys. Wayward factories have become adept at covering up abuses, and even when monitors flag problems, little progress seems to be made in reducing them." A study (described in the same article) that investigated the effectiveness of the Ethical Trading Initiative found that monitoring has helped to eliminate child labor and improve factory safety, but has had little effect on the rights to form unions and to achieve any job security.

Neil Kearney, of the International Textiles, Garment and Leathers Workers Federation (ITGLWF)—a federation of trade unions in these industries from around the world—puts these efforts in perspective:

> These [multinational] companies adopt codes of conduct, some of them in very nice language, but then they negotiate deals which make it impossible for their contractors to honor the codes. The companies say to the contractor, "Please allow for freedom of association, pay a decent wage," but then they say, "We will pay you 87 cents to produce each shirt. This includes the wage, fabric, everything." (cited in Varley 1998: 95–8)

As a leader of an anti-sweatshop group put it: "If retailers are not willing to change the way they deal with their purchasing practices and be transparent about that, then codes will never be effective" (Birchall 2007).

US retailers can play a critical role in the reproduction of sweatshops, whether they intend to or not. The sheer size of their ordering power, coupled with huge competitive pressures amongst contractors and intermediaries to win the work, create a breeding pool for sweatshop proliferation. Most important, however, is the determination of retailers to cut costs to the bare bone, which leaves little room for contractors to maintain labor standards.

As an example, let us briefly consider Wal-Mart's relations with its suppliers in China, the country where most of its offshore production is located. The home office of Wal-Mart Global Procurement is in Shenzhen, China. By locating there, the company could exercise great oversight over its suppliers and over the factories they use (Useem 2004). Wal-Mart, however, is not just a passive recipient of Chinese-produced goods, but an active producer of those goods. The company is a major actor in China, not only as an expanding retailer, but, perhaps more importantly, as a shaper of production. Ex-store manager Lehman, interviewed for the television program *Is Wal-Mart Good for America?*,[8] reported that the company's pressure to cut production and shipping costs is just as intense in China as in the United States. The "natural" cheapness of Chinese production is not enough for Wal-Mart. The company puts pressure on already poor conditions to lower them still further.

Wal-Mart's procurement staff members are constantly making deals with hundreds of Chinese manufacturers on a daily basis in order to produce goods tailored to Wal-Mart's own stringent specifications; these include pricing, quality assurance, efficiency, and delivery. Wal-Mart is also known to demand that its suppliers change their bookkeeping systems and improve their logistics to meet rigid delivery schedules while maintaining the lowest price margins. In exchange for Wal-Mart contracts, Chinese companies are often required to open up their books to Wal-Mart, and cut prices where necessary, if Wal-Mart decides the supplier's profit margins are too large. Wal-Mart demands rock-bottom prices and forces its clients to cut costs in order to remain in contention for export orders.[9]

In a *Wall Street Journal* article of November 13, 2003, author Peter Wonacott tells the following story. Ching Hai is a contract manufacturer that produces juicers, fans, and toasters for some of the largest retailers, with Wal-Mart as its largest client. Over the previous decade, the average wholesale price for Ching Hai's products had almost halved, from $7 to $4, in order for it to continue doing business with the stringent cost demands of Wal-Mart. Wal-Mart's Chinese producers have had to find ways to lower their costs, which often leads to further demands on their labor force. Ching Hai was forced to cut its labor force in half, while maintaining the same level of orders. The company had a starting wage of $32 a month, which was lower than the local minimum wage, and a high rate of workplace accidents, and many employees had to work eighteen-hour days. In spite of all the cost-cutting efforts, the company was barely profitable. Pun and Yu (2008) also found a similar relationship between Wal-Mart's procurement practices and the codes of conduct that Wal-Mart wants its suppliers to follow.

In December 2006, a Hong Kong-based group, China Labor Watch, accused Wal-Mart of using suppliers that failed to pay legal wages or to provide proper working conditions.[10] The group surveyed 169 employees at 15 Wal-Mart suppliers in China and found that some of them paid workers as little as half the minimum wage, threatened to fire workers if they did not comply with mandatory overtime, and provided no required health insurance. One company had a single bathroom for 2,000 workers. Some of the firms fined employees as much as an hour's pay for arriving one minute late to work. And some were behind in paying wages.

Labor in Distribution

The process of importing requires various types of labor, including: the work of seafarers on the container vessels; the work of longshore and other dock workers; the work of railroad employees, who move the cargo inland; the work of truckers, who transport ocean containers to railheads and warehouses in the vicinity of the ports, where they are transloaded for trucking to inland destinations, and the work of warehouse and distribution center employees. These workers are the backbone of the logistics system. They are the people who enable the containerized freight to arrive safely, accurately, and in a timely manner at your local retail outlets.

Statistics show that US logistics costs have declined significantly since the early 1980s. They dropped from around 14.5 percent of GDP in 1982, to 8.5 percent in 2003 (Wilson 2004). The logistics industry prides itself that the reason for this shift lies in all the efficiency gains of supply-chain management. Inventory costs have been cut, and so have the costs connected with most of the modes of freight transportation. Yet we can ask, how much have these gains been made at the cost of workers? In their study of these questions, Bonacich and Wilson (2008) found that, in general, conditions have worsened for logistics workers.

US seafarers used to have strong unions, but their jobs have been almost entirely outsourced. Steamship companies, which transport containers across the ocean, often use what are called "flags of convenience." This involves registering ships in countries like Panama and Liberia, where there is little or no regulation of conditions on board the vessels. In addition, the steamship lines employ crewing companies to recruit seafarers, often from the poorest countries of the world. While container ships can be cleaner than some other types of ships, seafarers work for longer hours, as well as much longer tours of duty, than did US unionized workers. Of course, their pay is a fraction of the earlier system.

Longshore workers still have good jobs, at least on the Pacific Coast, where the International Longshore and Warehouse Union (ILWU) continues to have considerable clout. The steamship lines and terminal operators that employ the dock workers, organized as the Pacific Maritime Association (PMA), have made serious efforts to undermine the union. In 2002, during a contract dispute, they locked ILWU workers out, and brought the Pacific Coast ports to a halt for eleven days. The lockout failed to break the power of the union, though it did gain some technological concessions for the employers (Olney 2003). However, the union is always under threat, as some very powerful forces are arrayed against it.

As suggested above, trucking can be divided into a number of types. Here we focus on one particular area of trucking—namely, port drayage. These truckers haul containers from the ports to their first drop-off point. In Southern California this drop-off point is typically either a railhead, where the containers are loaded onto a train to be shipped to the Midwest or East, or a local warehouse or distribution center, where the container is unloaded and the goods are prepared for further shipping to their ultimate destinations.

The truckers engaged in port drayage, or port truckers, used to be members of the International Brotherhood of Teamsters (IBT), but their jobs have been deunionized. This occurred when trucking was deregulated in the late 1970s and 1980s by the federal government, and many drivers were converted from employees to independent "owner operators." In fact, port truckers still work for trucking companies, but as so-called independent contractors, which means that they have to own their own rigs and pay for upkeep and insurance. The switch to non-union truckers was accompanied by a shift from largely native-born to immigrant drivers. Having broken the union in this field, the employers switched to a lower-cost labor force.

The railroads have a long history of unionization, and unions are still prevalent in the industry. But railroad workers have been heavily impacted by efforts to cut the cost of freight train operations. The principal form that labor cost cutting has taken is the elimination of thousands of jobs. The consequence has been that railroad workers have to adapt to difficult work schedules and to increased danger of accidents.

In terms of warehousing, a major agglomeration of warehouses and distribution centers has been developed just east of Los Angeles County, in the Inland Empire counties of San Bernardino and Riverside. All the giant retailers, as well as many smaller ones, maintain import warehouses there. Wal-Mart, Target, Home Depot, Costco, Sears, Walgreen's, Staples, Kohl's, Toys "R" Us, Big Lots, and Ross Stores are amongst the retailers that run distribution centers in the area. One of the reasons for locating in this area was the availability of relatively low-cost land and abundant space for new construction. But another reason is the relatively low-wage, mainly non-union labor force that lives in the area. In addition, a huge temporary labor industry has now grown up around these distribution centers to provide them with contingent workers on an as-needed basis.

In examining the various groups of workers involved in the logistics system, Bonacich and Wilson (2008) came to the conclusion that there were four key features of the changes that had occurred for workers in the previous twenty-five or thirty years. First, labor has been made more contingent, even precarious. This precariousness is especially true for seafarers (crewing contract workers), port truckers (independent contractors), and warehouse workers (temporary employees). Second, workers have suffered from racialization; that is, they are more likely to be racial and ethnic minorities who are willing to work for less under more difficult conditions than whites. Third, unions have declined in most of the jobs, with the exception of dock and railroad workers. Finally, wages and working conditions have generally deteriorated, with, for example, much lower earnings for port truckers and seafarers, fewer and more dangerous jobs for railroad workers, unsteady work for seafarers and port truckers, and so on.

Role of Retailers in Lowering the Cost of Logistics Labor

It is difficult to trace the exact line of retailer pressure to reduce logistics costs, and the impact on workers. At one level, this pressure is compacted into a single transaction: the rates paid to the steamship lines for ocean shipping. Every year these rates are negotiated, and pressure is put on the steamship lines to push the rates down.

The steamship line rates are so important because they often encompass railroad and trucking costs. The steamships frequently offer door-to-door rates, where a single fee covers the entire cost of transportation from a Chinese port to the importer's warehouse in the United States. The lower the rate negotiated with the ocean carriers, the lower is likely to be the rates that are paid to the railroad and trucking companies, which in turn translates into pressure on wages and working conditions all along the line.

The big retailers are known for their ability to get special rates from the transportation community. They can leverage their huge volume to their advantage. Wal-Mart, for example, pays a significantly lower rate than the average-sized importer. The giant retailer "makes the market" on setting the price for the lowest ocean freight rate, and other importers bargain with the steamship companies relative to Wal-Mart's price.

The clearest evidence of retailer interference in logistics labor costs came with the 2002 West Coast ports lockout. In order to "reform" labor conditions at the ports, and reduce the power of the ILWU, a new group was formed called the West Coast Waterfront Coalition (WCWC). (The group persists as The Waterfront Coalition, or TWC.) This group, amongst which large retailers, including Wal-Mart, were prominent members, played an important role in helping to pressure the PMA (and the Bush administration) to take a firm stand against the ILWU in labor negotiations. Giant retailers, who have so much at stake in the cost of logistics, wanted to ensure that their interests were strongly pursued.

Conclusion

The continuing advances in global logistics have allowed global retailers to control their supply chains as if these supply chains encompassed a single, vertically integrated firm. The scope of these supply chains now spans the globe. All economies with any connections to global trade feel the effects of supply-chain management. To a lesser or greater extent, all these economies are reshaped organizationally through these supply chains.

It is, therefore, a fair question to ask at the conclusion of this chapter, to what extent can we describe global trade in a world so organized as "free trade"? In conventional terminology, free trade connotes trade that is unencumbered by government regulations, such as tariffs and tightly controlled financial systems that fix rates amongst currencies. If that is our definition of free trade, then, indeed, a trading world organized through retailers' supply chains is, by definition, free trade. But, if we add to this definition considerations of monopolistic and oligopolistic restraints on exchange opportunities, then we see that the huge market-making power of retailers channels the flow of goods and encumbers all those who, in some way, touch those goods. We should see this condition as the opposite, rather than the epitome, of free trade.

The global economy is increasingly an organized economy, organized backward from POS information of consumers around the world. Nations may argue over the conditions of trade between countries and try through multilateral and bilateral agreements to correct problems that may arise in the course of balancing national accounts. But most of these arguments evade the central point of how economies get organized and stay organized. We do not live in a world that David Ricardo would recognize when he developed the notion that nations each have their own comparative advantages and that, if trade were unencumbered by tariffs, trade would naturally move toward an equilibrium. Rather we live in a world of competitive advantage, where nations and firms create their own advantages and exploit them, if they are able, at the expense of other nations and other firms.

The market-making perspective developed in this book helps us see that market making is not a benign process. The creation of one set of opportunities for exchange has the potential to influence and even to shape other opportunities for exchange. As retailers have grown larger and have harnessed global logistics to their advantage, they increasingly structure the opportunities for exchange, not only for consumers, but also for manufacturers, service providers, and workers around the world. At present, retailers wear this cloak of responsibility very lightly.

8

Making the Global Supply Base

Timothy Sturgeon, John Humphrey, and Gary Gereffi

Introduction

As the preceding chapters have discussed at length, the structure of production and trade in the world economy has changed dramatically since the 1960s, when relatively self-contained national economies interacted through arm's-length trade in finished goods and raw materials. Retailers and branded merchandisers in the United States wrested power from manufacturers in consumer markets in the 1970s and 1980s, in part by establishing their own low-cost sources of supply in East Asia. Thus, a significant step was taken toward the creation of a more deeply integrated global economy, where the various stages of production and consumption are dispersed within increasingly elaborate and spatially extensive global value chains (GVCs). The GVC perspective directs our attention away from the opposing theoretical poles of production and consumption toward the integrated, meso-level analytics of market making; specifically, the making of supplier markets. Intermediate markets account for about two-thirds of all market transactions (Tininga 1992) and intermediate goods trade for about 60 percent of world trade (see Figure 8.2 below). Evidence for the rise of GVCs can be found in these statistics as well; developing countries increased their share of intermediate goods trade from less than 5 percent in 1988 to more than 30 percent in 2008 (Sturgeon and Memedovic forthcoming). Trade in intermediate goods is indicative of GVCs because fragmented production processes require that parts, components, and partially manufactured products pass across borders—sometimes more than once—before finished goods are shipped to final markets (Feenstra 1998).

In our view, the making of supplier markets in East Asia by retailers has been just one facet of GVC formation. The goal of this chapter is to broaden this story of global buying, global production, and economic development, and deepen it by grounding it in a series of company and industry case studies. Our main point is that the emergence of supplier markets in East Asia has been driven, not only by retailers and the consumer product manufacturers that supplied them, but also by manufacturers of brand, technology, and capital-intensive goods such as computers, communications equipment, white goods, and motor vehicles seeking new markets and low-cost sources of supply worldwide. In short, purchasing by global retailers has been part of a broader pattern of outsourcing and offshoring that has helped to "make" supplier markets in the East Asia region and elsewhere.

For traditional technology-intensive companies, including multinational corporations (MNCs) with offshore affiliates handling the chores of foreign production, domestic outsourcing was often a first step. However, in a very short time, the largest US-based suppliers had set up global operations and were producing shoulder to shoulder with local suppliers in developing countries. Through a process that mirrored the retail consolidation outlined in Chapter 3, the most successful US-based suppliers quickly became huge global players, with facilities in scores of locations around the world. A handful of elite East Asian suppliers also grew rapidly, in part by taking on more tasks for MNC affiliates, expanding production not only in China, but also in other Asian countries and, in a few cases, in Africa, East Europe, and Latin America as well. These two trends, by the end of the 1990s, dovetailed to create a single dynamic: the rise of a *global supply base* populated by large, international, highly capable suppliers, contract manufacturers, intermediaries, and service providers, something unique in the history of the world economy (Sturgeon and Lester 2004). Thus, our second main point is that the concept of market making in East Asia is not incompatible with industry concentration and consolidation. The geographic and organizational fragmentation that occurred in the 1980s was followed by concentration in specific places (for example, China) and industry consolidation as lead firms and suppliers scaled up in an attempt to meet the challenges of global production and competition.

As Gereffi (1994a, 1999) has argued, the role of "lead firm" in GVCs—the company that defines product characteristics and takes the financial risk of placing orders and putting products up for sale—has tended to vary significantly by industry. In the apparel, footwear, household goods, and agro-food industries, GVCs have traditionally been "buyer-driven." As they have acquired more power in the chain, retailers, in particular, have assumed this lead firm role (see Chapters 1, 3, 4, and 5). In the "producer-driven" chains in the electronics, white goods, and motor vehicle industries, retailers have accumulated less power and are more passive actors in GVCs. Because of product complexity and high-quality requirements, lead firms in producer-driven chains tend to exercise more control in GVCs even as they focus less on in-house production and more on design, marketing, and value-added services. Because goods in producer-driven chains are technology intensive and, early on, domestic suppliers lacked technical competence to make the required inputs, production in East Asia was largely accomplished by MNC affiliates—a fact examined in great detail in the literature on the MNC (Vernon 1971; Zanfei 2000; Yamin and Sinkovics 2009).

Although firms have been operating internationally since the days of the British East India Company, suppliers and supply bases tended to be domestic and beyond the reach of retailers and buyers without international operations. Foreign affiliates of MNCs, often motivated by local content rules, gradually increased their use of local suppliers, but were forced by these same rules to develop redundant supply relationships in each of the countries or regions where they produced. By the end of the 1990s, this situation had changed markedly. The most capable suppliers became more "global" by establishing new plants, acquiring customer facilities, and purchasing smaller local and regional producers. Suppliers and supply-chain intermediaries from East Asia also set up facilities to serve customers from a larger set of locations. With this new supply base in place, retailers, branded merchandisers, and manufacturers, whether they were selling globally or simply seeking to cut operating costs to compete at home, could quite easily tap into supplier capabilities in multiple locations without the cost, risk, or time required to set up their own factories and nurture local supply chains from scratch. The next step was to simplify these supply relationships by using the same set of global suppliers in each of the regions where production was carried out.

Thus, the rise of the global supply base is not simply a story of more and better producers coming on-stream in East Asia to supply MNC affiliates in producer-driven sectors, nor of retailers in buyer-driven sectors placing increasingly large orders with firms and intermediaries in East Asia. The two trends are connected. This chapter lays out how the new global supply base emerged. It is a complex story, one that has played out differently in various places and in diverse industries. Indeed, much of our understanding of the dynamics of GVCs comes from detailed research on how these production chains have evolved in specific industries. We rely on a series of sector- and firm-level examples, largely from three sectors that dominate manufactured goods trade—electronics, apparel, and motor vehicles—to highlight several different facets of the phenomenon.

In this chapter, we first present some evidence of how suppliers based in advanced economies, especially US-based suppliers to technology-intensive industries such as electronics and motor vehicle industries, began to establish global operations in the late 1980s, and then accelerated their global expansion the 1990s. Second, we describe how the sourcing strategies of transnational manufacturers, global retailers, and global brands spurred the emergence of a highly capable and responsive set of contract manufacturers and component suppliers from newly industrialized countries in East Asia. Third, we examine the related issues of modularity and consolidation in the global supply base, and discuss how they have helped to shape it and enable its growth. Finally, we take stock of the global supply base in light of the extreme volatility that has repeatedly wracked global markets during the past decade or so, especially the current global economic crisis.

The Globalization of Developed Country Suppliers

Lead firms did not only increase their reliance on suppliers through their global buyers and offshore affiliates in the 1990s. Outsourcing was a major strategy at home too, and as a result domestic suppliers won huge volumes of new business and grew spectacularly. As US-based companies embraced the main elements of "corporate re-engineering and restructuring" (Harrison 1994) with its focus on core competence, asset variability, and maximization of shareholder value, most outsourcing began domestically. In the 1990s, however, the largest suppliers and service providers in these industries and product categories developed global-scale operational footprints. In some instances, the motivation of suppliers was to expand their own market reach, but more often it was to provide integrated global supply capabilities for their largest customers.

Within the United States, the movement toward outsourcing began with non-manufacturing services, such as information technology, accounting, and call centers. By the 1980s, large companies were also outsourcing routine business functions such as accounting, legal services, advertising, billing, and payroll (Rabach and Kim 1994). Firms divested themselves of non-core activities such as provision of food, security, and janitorial services for their buildings. Despite recent alarm in the United States about "services offshoring" (see Sturgeon et al. 2006), most of these services remain difficult or impossible to source offshore—for both practical and regulatory reasons—and continue, in large part, to be provided by home-based suppliers (Batt, Doellgast, and Kwon 2006; Neilsen 2008). Nevertheless, there are some significant and very large-scale exceptions to this in industries where processes can be segmented, linkages between activities codified, and inputs and outputs transmitted electronically. Examples include call-center-based services, back-office business functions, IT services, enterprise computing, clinical trials, and contract medical research. In recent years, the economic geography of these services industries has begun to resemble the manufacturing industries—consumer goods (household goods, apparel, and footwear), electronics, and automotive and aircraft parts—that have been driving the growth of GVCs for decades.

The rise of global suppliers has been most pronounced in technology-intensive manufacturing industries, such as electronics and motor vehicles. In these industries, it has proved to be a powerful combination for suppliers to have facilities both at home, to work out the manufacturing details of new product designs in collaboration with their customers' design groups, and abroad, to perform high-volume production in locations with lower costs and proximity to promising new markets. In some cases, the offshore affiliates of these large domestic suppliers began to challenge developed country suppliers on their home turf. In other cases, a complementary pattern emerged where global suppliers rely on "second-tier" developing-country suppliers for components, services, and as subcontractors. A third pattern is for developed-country suppliers to specialize in products and services that require the initial co-location described above.

An example of this division of labor can be found in automotive parts. Suppliers making "original equipment" automotive parts for use in new vehicle final assembly have a requirement for initial co-location, while suppliers making "after-market" parts sold to repair shops do not. As a result, first-tier original equipment parts suppliers are generally global suppliers, while after-market parts suppliers operating mainly in Taiwan and China have been able to gain significant market share via exporting alone (Cunningham, Lynch, and Thun 2005).

Whatever the competitive battles and complementarities that have emerged amongst developed- and developing-country suppliers, the real news is that increasing supplier capability is allowing lead firms to implement global production strategies in ways that were undreamt of in the late 1980s. Lead firms outsourced to suppliers at home, and demanded that these firms set up operations offshore, both to serve and to substitute for their offshore affiliates. These sustained efforts to expand and consolidate their sourcing networks have helped to create a new class of huge global suppliers in a range of industries, and supplier consolidation has meant that there are larger, more capable suppliers to choose from. Global suppliers now have capabilities—accumulated through internal development and acquisition—to provide "one-stop shopping" for lead firms seeking regional and global supply solutions. This new class of suppliers has internalized many of the most difficult and costly aspects of cross-border integration such as logistics, inventory management, and the day-to-day management of factories, call centers, and engineering centers. To provide some detail, we briefly present several examples from the electronics and automotive industries.

Global suppliers in the electronics industry

In the electronics industry, a combination of globalization, outsourcing, and vertical bundling in the 1990s helped to push a small but elite set of supplier firms to move quickly beyond their traditional cluster- or national-scale footprint to become global in scope. Vertically integrated lead firms with global operations, including Lucent, Nortel, Alcatel, Ericsson, and Apple Computer, sold off most, if not all, of their in-house manufacturing capacity—both at home and abroad—to a cadre of large and highly capable US-based contract manufacturers, including Solectron, Flextronics, Jabil Circuit, Celestica, and Sanmina-SCI (Sturgeon 2002; Sturgeon and Lee 2005).[1]

Solectron (acquired by Flextronics in 2007) provides an example of how these contract manufacturers expanded. The company was concentrated in a single campus in Silicon Valley from its founding in 1979 through the 1980s. In 1991 Solectron's key customers in Silicon Valley, including Sun Microsystems, Hewlett Packard, and Cisco Systems, demanded that Solectron provide global manufacturing and process engineering support. The company went on an acquisition-fueled binge of global expansion and revenue growth; by 2001 the company's footprint had grown to more than 135 facilities worldwide, and annual revenues had increased from $265 million to $12 billion. In the process of this expansion the company gobbled up competitors, expanded customer facilities, and acquired an array of specialized firms with capabilities that allowed the company to offer a much broader package of services. In just a few short years, Solectron had morphed from a humble, if highly respected, regional contract manufacturer (the company won the Malcolm Baldridge Quality Award in both 1991 and 1997) to become the largest manufacturing firm that no one had ever heard of; a quintessential global supplier.

An example of a global electronics contract manufacturer that emerged as a lead firm spin-off is Celestica, an in-house manufacturing division of IBM that was spun off as an independent company in 1996. At the outset the firm had only two production locations, a large complex near Toronto, Canada, and a small facility in upstate New York, since closed. By 2001, after completing twenty-nine acquisitions of customer and competitor facilities, Celestica had accumulated nearly fifty facilities in North America, South America, Western and Eastern Europe, and Asia, and annual revenues had soared to more than $10 billion.

In the round of consolidation that followed the bursting of the technology bubble in 2001, Flextronics (listed in Singapore but managed from San Jose, California) emerged as the world's largest electronics contract manufacturer, a position that was further solidified through its acquisition of number-two-ranked Solectron in 2007. Flextronics' 2009 revenues were slightly less than $31 billion. Aside from dozens of stand-alone factories and technology centers around the world, Flextronics, with its strategy of "vertical integration," operates nine huge "industrial parks," where it has invited many of its most immediate suppliers of product-specific components (bare printed circuit boards and plastic enclosures) to co-locate with its final assembly plants for rapid response in regional markets.[2]

The sale and spin-off of in-house manufacturing and parts operations underline the structural shift that was occurring in these industries from in-house production to global outsourcing, and the accumulation of this off-loaded capacity within a relatively small number of huge suppliers shows the dramatic consolidation and increasing integration of the global supply base. But outsourcing, as such, does not tell the entire story. In the electronics industry, fast-growing lead firms with little if any in-house production capacity, such as EMC, Sun Microsystems, Cisco, and Silicon Graphics, also demanded that suppliers provide global support.

In some key locations, lead firms did not necessarily have plants to sell or spin-off, especially in newer locations such as China and Eastern Europe. Because of this, a great deal of the global expansion of suppliers in the 1990s was either "organic" in character, involving the enlargement of existing facilities and the establishment of new, "greenfield" plants,[3] or achieved through the acquisition of regional suppliers, in what some industry participants refer to as the "rolling-up" of regional supply bases into an (albeit imperfectly) integrated global supply base.

Global suppliers in the motor vehicle industry

In the motor vehicle industry, outsourcing and vertical bundling also exploded in the 1990s. Employment in final assembly and in parts had maintained a rough parity since 1929, but after 1985 employment began to shift dramatically into the parts sector. By 2000, parts employment stood at 61.4 percent of total sector employment, up from just 49.1 percent in 1985 (US Bureau of Labor Statistics, cited in Sturgeon and Florida 2004: 54). What is hidden by these statistics is the employment that supplier firms added by establishing and buying operations *outside* the United States.

Consider the example of Lear, which began the 1990s as a seat manufacturer for the American Big 3 automakers. By 2000, Lear had grown to 120,000 employees working at more than 200 locations in 33 countries, making a full range of automotive interior parts and systems that were used in vehicles bearing nameplates as diverse as Pontiac, Suzuki, Hyundai, Isuzu, Jaguar, Mazda, Opel, Ford, VW, Porsche, Mercedes, Chrysler, Saab, Subaru, Fiat, Daewoo, Renault, Toyota, Mitsubishi, Honda, Audi, BMW, Peugeot, Nissan, Volvo, and Rover. As a result, the company rose from the world's thirteenth largest automotive supplier in 1995 to the fifth largest in 2000, with record sales of $14.1 billion. Since then, Lear has suffered from the severe financial difficulties plaguing the automotive supply base, along with most other large suppliers. While 2008 revenues and employment are down from the peak in 2000, the company's geographic footprint has continued to expand.[4]

The spin-off of the internal parts divisions of General Motors and Ford in the late 1990s created the world's two largest and most diversified automotive parts suppliers almost overnight, Delphi and Visteon. Because they were spun out of huge parent firms with strong international operations, these "new" suppliers were born with a global footprint and the capability to supply complete automotive subsystems. For example, Visteon was born with broad capabilities in chassis, climate, electronics, glass and lighting, interior and exterior trim, and power trains. In 2000 the company operated 38 manufacturing plants in the USA and Canada; 23 in West Europe; 21 in Asia; 9 in Mexico; 6 in East Europe; and 4 in South America; system and module engineering work was carried out in 1 facility in Japan, 3 in Germany, 3 in England, and 4 in the United States. Like Lear and other large global suppliers with significant business with the American automakers, Visteon has experienced deep financial trouble in recent years. Nevertheless, the company, in 2010, still has a global footprint, with 21 manufacturing facilities and 2 technical centers in the United States and Canada, 8 manufacturing facilities and 2 technical centers in Mexico, 43 manufacturing facilities and 5 technical centers in Asia Pacific, 23 manufacturing plants and 10 technical centers in Western Europe, 8 manufacturing plants and 2 technical centers in Eastern Europe, and 6 manufacturing facilities in South America. The shift, in the main, has been from the United States and Western Europe to Asia.

The emergence of global suppliers was mostly, but not solely, a phenomenon of American firms. European and a few Japanese motor vehicle parts suppliers followed their customers into new markets and went on acquisition sprees to gain both a global footprint and the ability to supply larger subsystems of the car. Examples include Continental, Bosch, and Siemens (Germany), Valeo (France), and Yazaki and Denso (Japan).

By the late 1990s it had become a requirement for automotive suppliers, large electronics contract manufacturers, and suppliers in several other sectors to have a global footprint. In separate interviews conducted in 2000, Sturgeon and Lester (2004: 69–70) quote managers at two global automotive suppliers as saying:

> The industry began to change 5–10 years ago. If a supplier doesn't have a global strategy, it can't bid. New projects are no longer seen as an opportunity to expand globally—instead, a supplier must have a global base in place to even make a bid. This forces suppliers to have a global supply system in place.

Suppliers must support assemblers as a sole source for global product lines to support commonalization. We must supply the same part, with the same quality and price, in every location. If [the automaker] says to go to Argentina, we must go or lose existing, not just potential, business. Logistics are becoming a key competitive advantage; we must have the ability to move production to where customer's facilities are.

Here we see market making in action. Globalization and consolidation in the automotive supply base were driven by management strategy at lead firms, first to divest their companies of the high fixed costs and labor needs of business functions related to production and back-office work, and, second, to demand that their key suppliers support them on a global basis to increase scale, reduce transaction costs, decrease redundancy, and increase the commonality of products and processes worldwide.

The Rise of East Asian Transnational Suppliers

In the previous section, we argued that global buyers in "buyer-driven" GVCs were not the only actors responsible for the expansion of GVCs, and that domestic outsourcing in "producer-driven" GVCs soon morphed into global outsourcing, as domestic suppliers were driven by customers to set up global operations (Gereffi 2006). In this section, we examine the rise of an indigenous East Asian transnational supply base through a series of "best case studies" of successful local supplier development in East Asia.

Foreign affiliates of MNCs were set up in East Asia and elsewhere during the 1970s and 1980s to lower costs and gain access to local markets. Over time, offshore affiliates began to use local suppliers for a broader range of inputs, materials, and services. In some cases, locals employed at these foreign affiliates used what they had learned to establish firms to supply their former employers and others like them. As more functions were shifted out of the affiliates and supplier competence grew, the affiliate activities, gradually and unevenly, shifted to higher-value functions such as purchasing inputs, adapting products to local markets, working with suppliers on new product introduction, and coordinating regional activities.

In the 1990s, some of the leading developing country suppliers from places such as Taiwan, South Korea, and Singapore, in response to customer demands to lower costs and to produce within large emerging markets such as China, began to set up offshore facilities of their own. The combined demand from global buyers and transnational affiliates helped to create a new class of transnational supplier based in East Asia (Bonaglia, Goldstein, and Mathews 2007; Yeung 2009). In the apparel industry there was an additional motivation:

to tap the available quota for export to the United States under the Multi-Fiber Agreement (MFA). This triggered investment in countries that would not otherwise have large-scale apparel assembly, such as Sri Lanka and Bangladesh. In contrast to the pattern set in the 1970s and 1980s, control did not migrate to local suppliers in these new locations. Rather, customer service and network coordination functions stayed in the suppliers' headquarters in Taiwan, Hong Kong, Korea, and Singapore, while production was partially and sometime completely relocated to less-developed countries.

Gereffi (1994a) calls this pattern "triangle manufacturing," with developed-country buyers, Hong Kong and South Korean intermediaries, and developing-country factories creating a tripartite spatial division of labor. On top of this, regional production systems, in which American and European apparel man-ufacturers had been steadily moving production to nearby countries with lower costs, such as Turkey, Morocco, Mexico, and the Caribbean Basin, began to be penetrated by a few of the largest East Asian manufacturers and intermediaries. As more countries were added over time, more complex regional and even global-scale production systems emerged, with coordination functions handled by East Asian suppliers and intermediaries. In the following sections, we show the variety of paths to international production using a few case studies.

South Korean investment in the Indonesian apparel industry

The role of firms from South Korea in developing the Indonesian apparel industry shows clearly how foreign direct investment (FDI) within Asia cre-ated more elaborate production networks over time. Hong Kong, Taiwan, and South Korea dominated garment exports in the 1960s and 1970s. In South Korea, much of the export business was organized through intermediaries, especially large trading companies who "played a pivotal brokerage role, link-ing designers and buyers from the developed core nations to the small Korean businesses that are the direct producers of the clothing" (D. Smith 1996: 222). These same intermediaries linked garment producers to producers of textiles and other inputs located in South Korea. As a result of their control over the export quotas established under the MFA, firms wishing to export to the USA tended to work through these traders (Gereffi 1999).

In the 1980s, one of the responses of Korean manufacturers and traders to rising labor costs in South Korea was to move factories offshore—to China, Indonesia, Central America, and elsewhere. Korean manufacturing FDI in the ASEAN-4 countries increased dramatically at the end of the 1980s. The total for the three years 1987–9 was four times the total for the previous fourteen years, and 55 percent of this manufacturing investment went to Indonesia. Many foreign-owned clothing factories were set up, enabling Indonesia to move from thirteenth place to eighth place amongst global garment exporters between 1988 and 1992. About one-third of foreign-owned plants were set up by South Korean firms, and another third were established by firms from Hong Kong, Taiwan, and Singapore (Shin and Lee 1995: 187).

As with the contract garment assembly plants used by US companies in Mexico and Central America, the new Indonesian plants were inserted into a much broader division of labor. In many cases, they used materials and equipment supplied from South Korea. Two-thirds of their inputs were imported and two-thirds of output was exported (Dicken and Hassler 2000: 270). The plants were also linked with their parent company's marketing operations and through these to global buyers in the United States and Europe. A Taiwanese apparel manufacturer in Indonesia described how orders arrived at the plant:

> 90% of our orders for Indonesia are coming from our Taiwanese head office. The remaining 10% are orders from agents and representative offices in Jakarta. The Taipei office is working with the buying offices directly in America or their representative offices in Hong Kong or Singapore. Our main market is the US where we sell 80% of our products. (cited in Dicken and Hassler 2000: 275)

Similar processes were evident in China, where firms from Hong Kong and Taiwan created complex value chains with chain management and chain coordination functions at home and production operations in China. In many cases, firms from Taiwan and Hong Kong have relocated manufacturing plants to the Chinese mainland, but maintained ownership.

East Asian intermediaries: The case of Li & Fung

As we have seen in the case of South Korea, intermediaries (Spulber 1996, 1998) have played an important role in the rise of East Asian-based GVCs. Intermediaries help to create supplier markets by matching manufacturers with the right requirements to retailers and branded marketers seeking production in East Asia and beyond. The largest and best known of these companies is Li & Fung, a Hong Kong-based firm that specializes in sourcing for global buyers of apparel and household goods. Li & Fung coordinates production for many large American branded garment merchandisers and retailers, such as Donna Karan and the Gap. The company's website defines it as "one of the premier global consumer products export trading companies managing the supply chain for high-volume, time-sensitive consumer goods."[5]

Li & Fung offers a full service package for customers, taking responsibility for product development, the sourcing of inputs, management of all manufacturing processes—while owning only a handful of plants itself—and outbound logistics. The difference between this division of labor and value-chain configurations in which sourcing is done through specialist traders is that the retailer or branded marketer plays a role in product development. The extent of this role will depend upon the competitive strategy and market position of the buyer. Branded marketers and high-end retailers generally regard product development as an important part of their competitive advantage, while low-end retailers are often content to define broad concepts and to follow fashion trends, leaving the product-development process to intermediaries and manufacturers.

Global expansion began in earnest at Li & Fung in the mid-1990s, mainly through the acquisition of sourcing networks controlled by British-owned Hong Kong-based trading companies. The acquisition of one such competitor, Inchcape Buying Services, doubled the company's size and provided a customer base in Europe to complement its strength amongst American retailers. To support the new business from Europe, Li & Fung strengthened its sourcing relationships in India, the Caribbean, and the Mediterranean basin. In 1999 and 2000, Li & Fung further broadened its customer base in the United States and Europe through the acquisition of three more of its Hong Kong-based rivals, Swire & Maclaine Ltd, Camberley Enterprises Ltd, and Colby Group Holdings Ltd. The company also acquired Disney Sourcing, the consumer products sourcing arm of Disney International with responsibility for stocking Disney stores worldwide. By 2001, two-thirds of Li & Fung's revenues were being generated through its acquisitions. Revenues grew from $750 million in 1995 to more than $14 billion in 2008.

By the end of 2000, Li & Fung had acquired a global footprint, and in 2009 the company had approximately 14,000 direct employees working in 80 offices in 40 countries. About one-third of these offices are located in developed countries, mainly Europe and the United States (but also in South Korea, Taiwan, and Japan), to provide customer support services. Most of the remaining offices are located in developing countries, mainly in China (18), South Asia (12), and South East Asia (9), but also in Turkey, Egypt, Romania, Poland, South Africa, Mauritius, Mexico, Guatemala, Honduras, and Nicaragua. These offices provide supply-chain management services for the company's network of 12,000 suppliers, mainly contract garment and household goods manufacturers.

This strategy of intermediaries such as Li & Fung is to separate the service elements in the supply relationship from the production elements. This approach has advantages and disadvantages. It gives the intermediaries a free hand to find producers in various countries, and, in the case of the apparel industry, the MFA and preferential trade deals such as the African Growth and Opportunity Act (AGOA) have provided many opportunities for firms that can source production from multiple locations. The disadvantage lies in the lack of control over production and limited opportunities to introduce process innovations and cost controls. The danger, as always for the trader, is that the manufacturer and the buyer will deal directly with each other. In fact, this has happened again and again, as both manufacturers and buyers have gained competencies. Li & Fung has tried to shore up its position by offering turn-key solutions, including product design services, and by helping buyers assure their customer that their products meet labor and environment standards with its "responsible sourcing" program.[6]

The case of Singapore's Beyonics

To get a more finely tuned look at how outsourcing by MNC affiliates has helped to drive supplier upgrading in East Asia, let us now turn to the case of the Singapore-based firm Beyonics. The case reveals a common dynamic of affiliate outsourcing, local learning, entrepreneurship, supplier upgrading, regional expansion, and organizational consolidation. In 1981, two Singaporean engineers decided to start their own company after they had been laid off from the Singaporean subsidiary of the German camera manufacturer Rollei. Seeing that the local tool and die business in Singapore was underdeveloped— because most foreign firms tended to bring in their own tooling—the two set up their own tool and die shop on a chicken farm owned by one of the founder's parents. From their experience at Rollei they knew that advanced lathes for precision metal cutting spin very fast, but could be stopped quickly to make rapid set-up changes. The two retrofitted some inexpensive lathes with motorcycle brakes to achieve the desired effect. The company, which was originally called Uraco, generated $700,000 in revenues during its first year of operation, mostly by supplying precision metal parts to American disk-drive producers, which were investing heavily in manufacturing in Singapore and Malaysia at the time (*Business Times Online* 1995).

As Uraco grew, it began to supply a wider range of products to the disk-drive industry, including precision metal stampings and assembled electronic circuit boards. Most of the company's business was with Seagate, the leading American disk-drive manufacturer, but the company also exported precision parts to Hitachi's disk-drive operations in the Philippines. Because of the extreme volatility in disk-drive and PC markets, in 1987 managers began the first of many efforts to diversify Uraco's customer base by distributing electronic components, eventually winning distributorships from Motorola, Harris Semiconductor, and Siemens.[7]

In the mid-1990s, the company began to leverage its experience with electronic components, contract manufacturing, and warehouse management to manufacture and sell products of its own design, including connectors, crystals, automated warehouse vehicles, electronic ballasts for fluorescent lamps, light bulbs, and telecommunications products. Ultimately, these attempts were not successful, and the bulk of Uraco's business remained in providing contract manufacturing services and precision-engineered metal parts to foreign firms operating in the South East Asian region. As traditional distribution networks in the region matured, the need for the company's distribution services waned as well.

Nevertheless, in 1995 the company underwent a successful initial public offering on the Singaporean stock exchange. In 1996, as revenues were approaching $53 million, Uraco won an important contract to manufacture flatbed scanners for Hewlett Packard. In this year the company was operating 82,000 square feet of production space in three Singaporean factories, and 165,000 square feet of nearby production space in five factories in Johor and Selangor, Malaysia (*Business Times Online* 1996a). In 1997, the firm reorganized its business into three divisions: precision machining, contract manufacturing, and investment (*Business Times Online* 1996b, 1997). The company's troubles were not over, however, and flagging profitability led to a management reshuffle in 2000 and a name change, to Beyonics, in 2001. The company returned to profitability in 2001, when it generated nearly $300 million in revenues, with 62 percent coming from contract manufacturing services, 29 percent from precision engineering, and 9 percent from distribution (Geocities 2004).

The company's product and service offerings are electronics manufacturing services (that is, contract manufacturing), medical and consumer plastic injection molding and assembly, precision engineering services, precision metal stampings, and precision tooling design and fabrication services. This is a highly focused and complementary product portfolio, covering many of the processes and a few of the basic products required to produce a wide variety of electronics and closely related goods. The company has followed the rest of the electronics contract manufacturing industry toward the bundling of services to enable the production of complete products through its acquisitions of precision plastic moldings suppliers Techplas (in 2000) and Pacific Plastics (in 2002). In 2003 the company merged with a similar Singaporean contract manufacturer, Flairis Technology Corporation, to achieve additional economies of scale and scope. The company's distribution activities and attempts at selling its own branded products have been dropped entirely.

With this tighter focus the company has expanded dramatically. According to the market research newsletter *Manufacturing Market Insider*, Beyonics revenues of $1.57 billion (with a razor-thin net profit of 0.3 percent) ranked the company thirteenth on a list of the world's largest electronics contract manufacturers in 2008.[8] Through a combination of internal expansion and acquisition, Beyonics has developed a solid regional manufacturing footprint, most notably by establishing "vertically integrated" electronics contract manufacturing campuses in Kulai, Malaysia, in 2005; Suzhou, China, in 2006;

and Batam, Indonesia, in 2007. In 2010, the company operated 16 facilities: 3 in Singapore, 6 in Malaysia, 3 in China, 2 in Thailand, and 2 in Indonesia.[9]

While Beyonics may have grown much larger than most local firms in East Asia that started as suppliers to MNCs, there are several lessons to be drawn from this "best" case. First, Beyonics' managers demonstrated the use of dynamic capabilities (Teece 2009) for sensing opportunities, seizing them, and transforming the company as needed. Second, they stumbled by trying to diversify and develop their own products, which required end-user marketing competences they had not yet developed, but recovered when they refocused on providing producer services to MNCs in the region. Third, like most large electronics contract manufacturers, Beyonics has struggled to remain profitable, even as the company has grown rapidly. Fourth, as the company expanded, it chose a variety of lower-cost locations within East Asia, balancing its investments in China with locations in Malaysia, Thailand, and Indonesia.

What the Beyonics case illustrates most dramatically, however, is how with enough time (a twenty-eight-year span in this case), local firms with extremely humble roots have been able to grow, master advanced technologies, and set up multiple locations in East Asia, largely by serving American MNC affiliates in the region. Here, we see market making in East Asia, not via arm's-length buying by retailers and branded manufacturers in the United States, but by the combination of local sourcing (import substitution) by MNCs operating in the region with sustained efforts by local entrepreneurs who rely, at least in part, on local capital markets to raise the funds needed for regional expansion.

Taiwan's electronics contract manufacturers

While there are significant PC components, subsystems, and peripheral devices in which Taiwan-based firms are not active—namely, software, printers, hard disk drives, and higher-value semiconductors such as microprocessors and memory—the sum of the capabilities that have emerged in Taiwan comprise a powerful, agile supply base for the design, manufacture, and delivery of PCs and related products, especially notebook computers.[10] Working in close geographic proximity, mostly along the Taipei–Hsinchu corridor in Taiwan, this supply base grew to constitute an extremely efficient system that could respond very rapidly to orders from lead firms (Dedrick and Kraemer 1998). Notebook computers, which generally have a high enough value-to-weight ratio to make air shipment viable, can be shipped to customers within two to three days of incoming orders.

This powerful productive engine has developed, almost in its entirety, in response to orders from lead firms based in the United States, and more recently Japan. At the same time, the development of contract manufacturing in Taiwan and elsewhere has provided lead firms with an increasing range of sourcing options. This process of co-evolution has meant that Taiwan's electronics industry has been able to develop without a significant cadre of local lead firms. From the late 1970s to the present day, sourcing from Taiwan has expanded from computer monitors, to various components and subsystems, to complete desktop and notebook PC systems.

Firms from the American PC industry have played an especially important role in the development of Taiwan's electronics contract manufacturing sector. In the early 1980s, IBM began sourcing PC monitors from television and television tube producers in Taiwan, including Tatung and Chung Hua. As the demand for PCs expanded rapidly and the open architecture of IBM-compatible PCs became firmly established in 1984 with the IBM model AT, some entrepreneurial firms in Taiwan, such as Acer and Mitac, recognized the opportunities and moved aggressively to develop the capability to design PCs and peripheral devices based on the emerging standard. IBM's modular system architecture relied on a central processing unit supplied by Intel and on an operating system from Microsoft, and, because the contracts famously did not block Intel and Microsoft from selling to IBM's competitors, a bevy of new entrants, intense price competition, and a series of boom and bust cycles soon followed. These conditions caused contract manufacturing to become a popular strategy for lead firms in the United States seeking to cut costs and limit investments in fixed capital.

The surging demand for contract manufacturing services encouraged existing Taiwan-based contract manufacturers producing consumer electronics and electronic components, such as Hon Hai, to develop capabilities to assemble PCs. Then, in the late 1980s, a set of firms that had been focused on the design and manufacture of hand-held calculators entered the field. These firms, which included Quanta, Compal, and Inventec, eventually became the dominant notebook computer producers, in part because the design and assembly competencies that drove miniaturization in calculators were well suited to notebook computers, where small size, low weight, and efficient power consumption are key factors for success. Although much simpler, calculators are similar to PCs in that they are built around a central processing unit that determines system architecture and most of the product's functionality.

The modular system architecture of PCs, and the dominant role of the central processing unit (CPU) and operating system software in setting system architecture, along with intense competition and short product life cycles, created the conditions for the emergence of a set of firms that specialized in the iterative, post-architectural portions of product design. This includes, for example, the board-level input/output system (BIOS) of the PC, which determines how the machine handles the input and output from its main board to the other elements of the system, such as storage and displays; and industrial design, which determines the physical appearance of the product. However, because most functionality resides in chips sets and software—system elements that computer producers do not design—control over the innovative trajectory of the industry has continued to reside in "platform leaders" such as Intel and Microsoft (Gower and Cusumano 2002), which have traditionally worked closely with branded PC firms on future requirements. However, as the notebook format has come to dominate consumer PC sales, and branded PC firms have either left the business (IBM) or changed their business focus to bundling services with PCs (Hewlett Packard), Intel has begun to work more closely with Taiwanese firms on the requirements for next generation CPU design (Kawakami 2008).

The story of lead firm, supplier, and platform leader co-evolution that we have outlined here reveals a powerful dynamic of outsourcing, upgrading, and subsequent outsourcing; the enabling role of open standards and modular product architecture in PCs; the intense competition and rapid product life cycles that drove lead firms to seek to spread risk and lower costs through outsourcing; and the entrepreneurial agility that many firms in Taiwan displayed in shifting to export production by recognizing and seizing new opportunities to specialize in narrow segments of the value chain. But there were two other important factors that have not yet been discussed. The first is the Taiwanese government, which helped by licensing, refining, and disseminating foreign technology and encouraging, and in some cases underwriting, the entry of local firms into promising market areas, especially for IT-related products. The second is the role of Japanese technology partners, which provided critical technologies and components, such as disk drives, but with little support and with restrictions, such that Taiwanese firms were inhibited from building on the technology to develop independent product development strategies. Licensing agreements of this kind have continued to be important in Taiwan's flat panel display industry (see Akinwande, Fuller, and Sodini 2005).

The migration of Taiwan's electronics production to Mainland China began in the mid-1990s, following Compaq's demand for a sub-$500 desktop PC. The migration started with components and peripherals, and then spread to the assembly of desktop PCs and motherboards, with the latest stage being notebook computers. As sales of notebook PCs expanded rapidly, surpassing desktop units in the early 2000s, production in Taiwan soared from 2.3 million units in 1995 to a peak of 14.3 million in 2002. After 2002, notebook PC production in Taiwan dropped just as rapidly, even as Taiwanese firms produced a larger share of the world's output, reaching 92 percent in 2008. At the same time, production by the largest five Taiwanese notebook PC producers—Quanta, Compal, Wistron, Inventec, and Asustek—grew to more than 70 million units in 2006.

Under the tight control of headquarters in Taiwan, manufacturing subsidiaries co-located with their component suppliers to respond to the time-to-market, ramp-up, and cost-reduction requirements set by lead firms. This migration contributed to the dramatic expansion of two industry clusters for electronics manufacturing, one in the Pearl River Delta near Hong Kong and the second in the Yangze River Delta region near Shanghai. Smaller Taiwanese contract manufacturers and component suppliers were not able to make this move, leading to a dramatic consolidation amongst firms specializing in notebook PC production: the number of Taiwanese notebook PC producers fell from forty-five in 1993 to only twenty-one in 2006, with market share shifting dramatically in favor of the largest five producers (Kawakami 2008).

Modularity, Consolidation, and Crisis in the Global Supply Base

The making of the global supply base was enabled by the deployment of information technologies, which, along with better standards for sharing information, enabled companies to achieve more precise forms of coordination, even with highly complex and technologically sophisticated products and processes, a mode of governance that we have referred to elsewhere to as *value-chain modularity* (Sturgeon 2002; Gereffi, Humphrey, and Sturgeon 2005). By the end of the 1990s, the depth and breadth of the global supply base, along with new Internet-based tools for buyer–supplier matchmaking, quotation, and operational coordination, was opening a new chapter in the development of the global supply base, in which the barriers to global sourcing could fall far enough to encourage smaller and less technologically adept retailers and start-ups to engage in global sourcing.

On the supply side, new requirements to respond rapidly to buyers and make timely deliveries of complex products from multiple locations around the world put a premium on size and technological competence, and raised barriers for new entrants. Smaller local suppliers in developing countries were often relegated to the margins of the value chain, if they were included at all. The result was a process of consolidation, where the largest suppliers gained at the expense of smaller, regional producers. Today, in the midst of an unprecedented global economic slowdown, the survival of this system has come into question on several fronts. Even prior to the current crisis, supplier profitability in some sectors, such as automotive and electronics, had been low to negative for many years (Sturgeon, Van Biesebroeck, and Gereffi 2008). Repeated severe economic cycles, previously contained within specific regions and industries, and now being experienced across the board, have exacerbated this persistent low profitability in the global supply base, triggering a wave of plant closures and driving some of the largest and most capable firms to financial ruin. Nevertheless, prior experience reveals that outsourcing and offshoring have not reversed following economic crises.

Value-chain modularity

The making of the global supply base has been enabled by rapid advances in computerized design, automated production planning and inventory control, logistics and production planning software, and robotic manufacturing equipment. Tighter integration between lead firms and suppliers has been facilitated by the development of global industry standards (both open and de facto), not only in the electronics industry, where standards at the component level have created modularity in system design, but in all global industries. For example, even when components are unique to specific products and design architecture is integral and proprietary, as they are in the motor vehicle industry, information technology can help firms coordinate cross-border activities; exchange complex design files; track incoming, in-process, and finished inventories; and direct the shipment of finished goods directly from factories to lead firms. In services, information technology and low-cost, high-bandwidth communications systems installed during the late 1990s facilitate the expansion of remote call centers for after-sales service and the real-time provision of a host of other business services. Because these are not capabilities that can be acquired cheaply or maintained easily, and because they allow suppliers to handle larger and more diverse orders, increasing value-chain modularity has helped to drive consolidation in the global supply base.

Consolidation in the global supply base

After decades of expansion and fragmentation in the global supply base, driven by the needs of multinational firms to develop unique supply bases in each of the countries where they operated, a cycle of expansion, shakeout, and consolidation has played out repeatedly since the late 1990s. It is important to point out that GVCs were not distributed equally across the globe. More production locations were added to the system, but large-scale agglomeration economies, focused around historic production centers with new, world-class port facilities, favored specific cities and regions. This triggered unprecedented booms in some places, such as the region around Shanghai and the Pearl River Delta region of southern China, while other regions continued to struggle or remain entirely severed from GVC-related economic development.

Within this system of uneven development, consolidation has been especially acute in some of the most geographically extensive and dynamic global value chains, such as motor vehicles, electronics, apparel, consumer goods, and horticulture, reversing the trend toward organizational fragmentation and geographical dispersion outlined earlier. It is hard to overstate the rapidity of this consolidation and the enormity of the changes that it has wrought in key industries. Substantial segments of important industries such as autos and electronics were utterly transformed. Value chains that had been increasingly fragmented and dispersed were rationalized, beginning in earnest during the latter half of the 1990s, creating more tightly integrated global systems comprised of far fewer, much larger players. The fragmentation and dispersion that had marked the 1970s and 1980s, it seems, had reached their limits.

For MNCs, the rationalization of in-company operations has involved the concentration of production in fewer, larger plants, often placed to serve regional markets. The division of labor between these plants has also been rationalized. Even when companies expand internationally to meet the needs of new markets, new subsidiaries are designed to function within a larger international division of labor. Lead firms have moved aggressively to source from fewer suppliers with larger operations in a smaller number of low-cost locations, even as they redouble their efforts to sell globally. As China becomes a more important location for many global suppliers, some investment has been either shifted or diverted there from competing existing low-cost locations in South East Asia, Eastern Europe, and Mexico, although rising wages in China's coastal region are driving some new investment inland and to countries with lower wages, such as Vietnam.

Consolidation in the global supply base is primarily driven by a desire on the part of lead firms to simplify and streamline supply-chain management. As the complexity of inter-firm transactions has risen along with outsourcing, so too has the impulse to simplify the supply chain. Using fewer, larger, more capable suppliers has meant a smaller number of relationships to manage, and the ability to collaborate with the same set of suppliers worldwide. Since design work tends to be carried out in advanced-country locations and high-volume manufacturing in developing-country locations, this approach requires suppliers to establish a tightly integrated global network of subsidiary operations, and, most recently, to rationalize those operations by concentrating activities in a few key locations to build up scale economies and simplify logistics.

The impact on suppliers has been clear. The largest and most capable global suppliers, such as the San Jose-based electronics contract manufacturer Flextronics and the Detroit-based automotive seat supplier Lear mentioned earlier, stepped up to internalize many of the truly difficult and risky aspects of global production, such as FDI, global purchasing and inventory control, capacity planning, fixed asset management, and logistics. In apparel, intermediaries such as Hong Kong-based Li & Fung and manufacturers such as Taiwan's Nien Hsing and Pou Chen and China's Yue Yuen, also moved to set up global operations and offer a broader package of services. In fresh fruits and vegetables, the large supermarkets in the UK, such as Tesco and Asda (owned by Wal-Mart), rationalized the supply systems that they had developed in the1980s and 1990s. They have begun to outsource functions such as planning year-round supply, customer research, and benchmarking (product variety, space allocated to different products, and so on) to "category managers." According to one leading UK importer, the goal is to reduce the number of direct suppliers for the complete fruit and vegetable product offering from dozens to perhaps three or five. These first-tier suppliers will be responsible for organizing the rest of the chain (Dolan and Humphrey 2004).

This overarching trend, from vertically integrated lead firms with "captive" supply bases dedicated to them, to outsourcing into a series of national and regional supply bases, to consolidation and the rise of global suppliers, is depicted in Figure 8.1. The role of modularity in facilitating this transition is depicted in the character of inter-firm linkages, shifting from idiosyncratic to

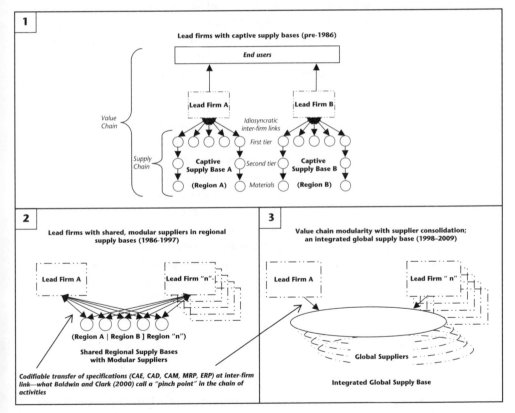

Figure 8.1. The evolution of supply-base modularity, consolidation, and global integration

codifiable, standardized, and modular in later periods. Note that we define the "value chain" as the full range of value-added activities, from component and material production to end use, and the "supply chain" as the specific set of companies that serve a specific lead firm in the context of producing a specific product or service.

Unmaking the global supply base?

At the time of writing (January 2010), the consolidation of the global supply base appears to be accelerating further as the global economy undergoes a severe contraction. For suppliers with the ability to form modular value-chain linkages, business depends not on the success or failure of any single customer or narrow industry but on the ability to switch to growing customers or industry segments when hard times arrive. The difference in the recession of 2007–9 is that there has been a very steep drop in orders across the board, not to mention difficulties in obtaining the credit needed to keep the wheels of global production and trade turning. In a broad downturn, there are very few if any sectors or customers where new business can be won. In a period where business grinds to a halt, global suppliers suffer more than most, given their huge investments in factories, equipment, and large-scale employment. What we can predict is that some will fail, or become easy takeover targets, with further consolidation the result.

While there is no way to predict the future course of offshoring, outsourcing, and the nascent global supply base with any certainty, past experience is instructive. The long-term trend in intermediate goods trade from 1962 to 2006, with a variety of bubbles and crises, as noted in Figure 8.2, suggests that outsourcing and offshoring tend to accelerate both in boom times, when companies are scrambling quickly to add new capacity, and directly following downturns as well, when cost cutting comes to the fore and companies are reluctant to expand internally in the face of uncertainty.

While history has shown that that volatility does not spell a retreat from outsourcing, the bigger question is supplier survival, both in the near and the long term. Supplier markets may be dramatically remade through consolidation, but it seems unlikely that they will be entirely unmade.

Conclusions

This chapter has outlined how the new global supply base has come about, how it has begun to remake the global economy, and what its prospects are going forward. Retailers have been only one of several driving forces in the development of this supply base. While the global supply base is concentrated

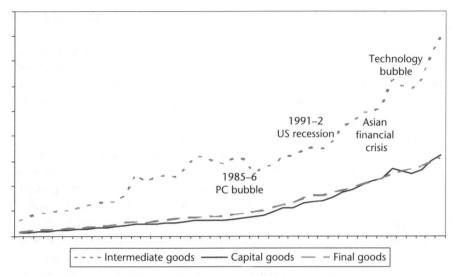

Figure 8.2. World imports of intermediate, capital, and final goods, 1962–2006

in East Asia, it now extends far beyond that region, creating a more-or-less integrated network of plants, service facilities, distribution and collection points, and logistics hubs in key locations across the globe.

Suppliers from developed countries, especially the United States, expanded their roles and set up global operations through the 1990s. Beginning in the late 1990s, decisions by lead firms (retailers and technology-intensive producers alike) sought to simplify and consolidate their sourcing networks and in the process created a new class of *global suppliers*. As global suppliers added capabilities and scale, they began to offer their customers *turn-key* access to a *full package* of manufacturing processes, finished products, complete product lines, and even complementary bundles of services, including product design, component purchasing, final packaging, global logistics, and after-sales repair. To establish their global footprints and provide full-package capabilities, global suppliers invested in new plants, acquired regional competitors and facilities previously owned by MNC affiliates, and in some cases "vertically integrated" by entering the business of upstream and downstream component suppliers and service providers.

While global suppliers have lowered the bar for lead firms to participate in global value chains, they have at the same time raised the bar for local manufacturing firms that want to enter GVCs as suppliers. As global suppliers expanded their operational footprint to new locations, such as Southern Asia, Central America and the Caribbean, Eastern and Central Europe, parts Of sub-Saharan Africa, and the Middle East, it became harder for new entrants to compete. Firms and countries that try to enter global value chains today must meet standards and performance requirements that are much higher than firms entering one or two decades ago.

Within these broad patterns, there is plenty of room for variation in company strategy, even in what might appear to be the same market niches. Thus, The Limited and Gap, Nike and Reebok, Ford and Toyota, Coca Cola and Pepsi, Hewlett Packard and Fujitsu, and so on, might follow different specific strategies related to outsourcing and offshoring based on managerial choices (Berger 2005) or the institutional norms of the company's home country (Lane and Bachmann 1997; Sturgeon 2007). A major theme in this chapter is that market making in global supply chains is not just about offshoring, fragmentation, and specialization. By highlighting that there is consolidation, concentration, and rebundling going on in particular locations and within MNCs around the globe, we reinforce the core idea that market making takes place through the exercise of "power" by big firms and large countries. These issues are captured by the GVC perspective, and introduce critical elements of agency and institutional variation into the story that would be lost in a straightforward "market-forces" account of global integration.

This chapter has emphasized the self-reinforcing, co-evolutionary character of the market-making process. In earlier chapters in this volume, we have seen how experiments with global sourcing in the 1970s and 1980s by a handful of pioneering retailers and multinational manufacturing firms created the initial markets for export-oriented economies in East Asia. Retailers and branded manufacturers in rich countries became more experienced with international outsourcing; developing countries acquired the infrastructure and capabilities needed to sustain more complex operations; and suppliers upgraded their capabilities in response to larger orders for more complex goods. As these resources improve over time, more lead firms gain the confidence to embrace the twin (and often entwined) strategies of outsourcing and offshoring. The global supply base has been made in a self-reinforcing cycle of outsourcing and supply-base upgrading that connects firms across developed and developing countries; its frontiers and capabilities continue to evolve.

9

Transnational Contractors in East Asia

Richard P. Appelbaum

Introduction: The Changing Dynamics of Global Production

The explosive globalization in the labor-intensive production of consumer goods is by now a well-known and well-documented phenomenon. Small firms as well as large ones have been able to access factories around the world. The global networks through which this international production is coordinated are typical buyer-driven global commodity chains "in which large retailers, marketers and branded manufacturers play the pivotal roles in setting up decentralized production networks in a variety of exporting countries," typically located in the developing world (Gereffi and Memedovic 2003: 3). While some of these factories have historically been large (for example, in the footwear industry), most contractors have been relatively small. Their size has reinforced their vulnerability to the big buyers: many factories have historically been part of "captive networks," limited to simple, low value-added assembly operations that follow detailed instructions from their clients (Gereffi, Humphrey, and Sturgeon 2005).

We are now entering an era in which a qualitatively higher degree of integration between production and distribution has begun to reshape the entire buyer-driven global commodity chain (Abernathy et al. 1999; Bonacich 2005; Bonacich and Wilson 2005). Two trends have emerged in the past decade, particularly in the Pacific Rim region, that are erasing the boundary between "manufacturer," on the one hand, and "retail buyer," on the other: the emergence of giant retailers, and the emergence of commensurately large factory contractors who serve them. The first trend constitutes the central focus of this volume, and will not be treated in this chapter. The second trend, however, remains understudied and as a result largely untheorized.

In the following discussion I will argue that the emergence of giant transnational contractors may alter the dynamic of global supply chains, including the current seemingly unstoppable dominance of giant US- and EU-based retailers as market makers. At the very least, I will argue, the rise of China as an economic power will probably impact on the current dynamic in several ways. At a minimum, giant contractors—"Big Suppliers"—are themselves market makers for their own suppliers, exerting increasing control over key aspects of the production supply chain. More speculatively, if the current trends continue, the giant contractors may come to challenge the power of all but the biggest "Big Buyers" they serve. This could alter the governance structure of some global supply chains, raising the possibility that Taiwanese- and Chinese-based multinational "Big Suppliers" may themselves someday morph into "Big Buyers," challenging the firms they now serve. In other words, the current shift in the governance structure of global market dynamics—from manufacturer to retailer—may turn out to have been merely a stage, associated in part with the ready availability of low-cost labor in the rising East Asian economies during the past three decades. But, as these economies mature, moving from export-oriented industrialization to producing for their own internal markets, the dynamics that once favored the growing power of US- and EU-based "Big Buyers" may also shift, eroding the market-making ability of the latter relative to multinationals based in the East Asian economies.

The Emergence of Giant Transnational Contractors

The appearance of giant factories as global suppliers for Wal-Mart and other large retailers is a largely unexpected development, since so many business and management theorists, emphasizing "flexible specialization," the "virtual corporation," and other forms of decentralized production and distribution, have argued that the era of the gigantic production facility was over (see, e.g., Piore and Sabel 1986; Kapinsky 1993; Pine and Davis 1999). No longer would entrepreneurs assemble tens of thousands of workers at capital-intensive factory complexes like River Rouge or Cannon Mills. But since the late 1990s, giant transnational corporations have emerged, mainly from Hong Kong, Taiwan, South Korea, and China, that operate massive factories under contract with consumer goods buyers—retailers and branded merchandisers—a trend that may well portend a dramatic twenty-first-century shift of organizational power within global supply chains. The emergence of these giant transnational contractors has yet to be examined.

In the textile and apparel industries, for example, the consolidation of production, both at the factory and the country level, is highly pronounced, and will greatly accelerate now that the thirty-year-old Multi-Fiber Agreement

(MFA), whose quota system resulted in the dispersal of clothing production to some 140 countries, expired on January 1, 2005. The end of the MFA is predicted to lead to a consolidation of production into larger companies and a smaller number of supplying countries because of the economies of scale that can be achieved (Speer 2002). Industry sources claim that large retailers and manufacturers such as the Gap, J. C. Penney, Liz Claiborne, and Wal-Mart—which once sourced from fifty or more countries—will source from between ten and fifteen when quotas no longer constrain their sourcing decisions (Malone 2002, Just-style.com 2003; McGrath 2003). A large body of research projects that, with the end of the MFA, China alone may eventually claim as much as half of all export-oriented apparel production (Nordås 2004), with potentially devastating effects on those developing countries in South Asia, Central America and the Caribbean, and Africa that have become highly dependent on textile and apparel exports. (For a detailed treatment, see UNCTAD 2004, 2005.)[1]

Examples of giant East Asia-based contractors abound. In the textile and apparel industries, the Taiwanese multinational Nien Hsing Textile Co. Ltd, "the largest specialized denim fabric and garment in-one-stream manufacturer in the world," boasts a "customer base from designer brands such as Calvin Klein, DKNY, Tommy Hilfiger, Nautica, Mudd Jeans, GAP, Levis Japan to retail private labels or importers such as J. C. Penney, Wal-Mart, Target, VF Jeanswear (Lee, Wrangler), Sears, No Excuses etc."[2] Nien Hsing has factories in Taiwan, Mexico, Nicaragua, and Lesotho. Yupoong Inc., a Korean multinational that has become the world's second largest cap manufacturer, has factories in the Dominican Republic, Vietnam, and Bangladesh. Yupoong's "flexfit" hats (motto: "worn by the world") are exported to some sixty countries (see Yupoong 2003). In consumer electronics, large contract factories also provide integrated production and final assembly of circuit boards, personal computers, cell phones, handheld digital devices, game consoles, and other IT devices for brand names such as Dell, Hewlett-Packard, Ericsson, and Siemens. South East Asia, and China in particular, have become the center of the most advanced consumer electronics fabrication (UNCTAD 2002; Lüthje 2005). The world's largest electronics contract manufacturer, the US-based Flextronics, employs nearly 100,000 workers worldwide, half of whom are in Asia, mainly southern Malaysia (close to its Asian headquarters in Singapore) and southern Guangdong Province in China (Flextronics 2003; Lüthje 2005).

A number of these large firms, particularly those from Taiwan, have set up operations in Latin America and Africa. By 2003, for example, Taiwanese firms had invested an estimated $2.1 billion in South Africa, Swaziland, and Lesotho, employing more than 110,000 workers, representing a fifth of the workforce in the latter country (Du Ling 2003).

Supply-chain management in China's apparel and textile industries

China's textile and apparel production remains concentrated in small and medium-sized firms in the coastal areas, although this is changing, both as firms move inland in search of cheaper labor, and as larger firms—with advanced forms of supply-chain management—become more central. Cao Ning identifies three kinds of supply-chain management that are found in China (Cao 2005): vertical integration, traditional purchasing, and third-party coordinated.

In *vertically integrated supply chains*, retailers have internalized the supply chain, at the least owning their own assembly plants, and sometimes achieving additional backwards integration through ownership of yarn and textile factories and even cotton farms. Hong Kong's Esquel Group, "one of the world's leading producers of premium cotton shirts," is an example.[3] Esquel produces its own brand (the "Pye" label), although it produces primarily for other clients.[4] Overall, the firm's 47,000 employees manufacture 60 million garments annually, with 17 factories in 9 countries, including garment-manufacturing facilities in China, Malaysia, Vietnam, Mauritius, and Sri Lanka, as well as cotton farms and yarn factories. Esquel's retail outlets in Beijing in 2000, which carry its "Pye" series clothing, provide an example of vertical integration: "From the cotton field to the retail outlet, Esquel is the absolute coordinator" (Cao 2005). According to its website:

> Esquel's vertically integrated operations ensure the highest quality in every step of the apparel manufacturing process. Production begins in Xinjiang province in northwestern China, where the Group grows its own Extra Long Staple (ELS) Cotton and Organic Cotton, continues through spinning, weaving, dyeing, manufacturing, packaging and retailing.[5] Esquel's textile and apparel production is complemented by strong product development capabilities. The Group's design and merchandising team work closely with its research and development center to create unique finishings such as wrinkle-free and nanotechnology performance qualities that consistently give Esquel the cutting edge in the apparel industry.

The degree to which such vertical integration signals a move from manufacturing to retailing is open to debate, however. While Esquel's high degree of vertical integration can be seen as a form of market making in terms of control over suppliers, the company remains primarily a manufacturer for others. Its high-end Pye brand represents a small percentage of the company's total revenues.

The second kind of supply-chain management, according to Cao (2005), is the familiar *traditional purchasing supply chain*, in which the retailer contracts with independent manufacturers to produce garments according to specification (OEM). Either the retailer or the manufacturer can assume responsibility for supply-chain coordination. Manufacturer-coordinated supply chains are of special interest, because they signal a possible shift in supply-chain control from retailer to manufacturer. One form of manufacturer coordination— "vendor managed inventory"[6]—is illustrated by the Hong Kong-based TAL Group.[7] TAL, founded in 1947 as a single textile spinning mill in Hong Kong,[8] has grown into one of the major apparel manufacturers, incorporating design, logistics, and fabrication. Its global workforce of 23,000 employees, producing annual sales of $600 million, is found in factories in Hong Kong, Thailand, Malaysia, Taiwan, China, Indonesia, Vietnam, Mexico, and the United States. TAL's clients include Brooks Brothers, L. L. Bean, J. C. Penney, Giordano, Land's End, Liz Claiborne, Nautica, and Tommy Hilfiger, with the majority of its sales to retailers. TAL accounts for one out of every eight dress shirts sold in the USA. Its success is attributed to its ability to manage its supply chain efficiently:

> Today, TAL boasts that it is one of the few Asian suppliers capable of handling a variety of EDI documents, such as purchase order (PO), advance ship notice (ASN), invoice, point-of-sales (POS) data, order status, etc. . . . From the late 1990s to today, the hurdle has once again been raised: firms are now being asked to synchronize their supply and demand activities far more effectively and this means ensuring that far-flung product development, marketing/sales, and supply chains are in close coordination. TAL responded by enabling vendor managed inventory with customers such as J. C. Penney. In doing so, TAL was able to link its designers and its factory floors half a world away to the points of sale in the US, resulting in ever greater efficiencies for its customers and expanded business opportunities for TAL . . . Now as an integrated synchronization services provider with manufacturing capabilities, TAL not only has visibility into demand at the retailer's point of sale, i.e. to demand from the final consumer, but can link this information back directly to production operations on the factory floor as well as to product development and R&D activities. (Koudal and Long 2005)

By relying on TAL as its principal supplier, J. C. Penney is able virtually to eliminate inventory of its private-label dress shirts. TAL runs POS data from Penney's North American stores through its proprietary software to determine the quantity of different styles, colors, and sizes of shirts to make—all without the need to consult with J. C. Penney itself. TAL even designs and market tests J. C. Penney's new shirts.

> The new process is one from which Penney is conspicuously absent. The entire program is designed and operated by TAL Apparel Ltd. . . . TAL collects point-of-sale data for Penney's shirts directly from its stores in North America, then runs the numbers through a computer model it designed. The Hong Kong company then decides how many shirts to make, and in what styles, colors and sizes. The manufacturer sends the shirts directly to each Penney store, bypassing the retailer's warehouses—and corporate decision makers. (Kahn 2003)

TAL provides similar services to Brooks Brothers and Land's End. Vendor-managed inventory gives the manufacturer increased market-making power over its suppliers, thereby signaling some shift in power from retailer to contractor: it is now the contractor, rather than the retailer, who manages the supply chain (Kahn 2003). TAL's New York City-based design team develops the style, TAL analyzes sales data to determine the quantity to produce for J. C. Penney stores, and TAL's Asian factories turn out the product. According to one management consultant who has studied the industry: "You are giving away a pretty important function when you outsource your inventory management. That's something that not a lot of retailers want to part with" (cited in Kahn 2003).

The third kind of supply-chain management, according to Cao (2005), is the *third-party coordinated supply chain*, in which garment trading companies provide the coordination, oversee quality control, and sometimes provide fashion design. The prime example of this form of supplier market making is the Li & Fung Group, the giant multinational trading company is based in Hong Kong, with a staff of 25,000 distributed across more than 70 offices in 40 countries and territories, with 2006 revenues of $10.4 billion (Li & Fung 2007). As discussed in the Chapter 8, trading companies such as Li & Fung have become more powerful, taking the lead in supply-chain management (Kahn 2004b; Pun 2005). Li & Fung is organized into three core businesses: exporting services, value-chain logistics, and retailing.

- Li & Fung Ltd manages the export supply chain for a variety of consumer goods,[9] "work[ing] together to find the best source for different components or processes, and drawing on a global network of some 10,000 factories." Activities span the supply chain, including initial product development and design, raw material sourcing, production planning, factory sourcing, manufacturing control, quality assurance, export documentation, and shipping consolidation. Its venture capital fund invests in consumer products companies in Europe and the United States. By way of example (this from an interview with Li & Fung CEO Victor Fung in the *Harvard Business Review*), the company might fill a large order by sourcing its yarn from Korea, doing the dyeing in Taiwan, purchasing buttons and zippers in China, and assembling the final product in Thailand (Magretta 2002).

- Integrated Distribution Services (IDS) Group provides "value-chain logistics" throughout Asia in "three core business areas": marketing (sales, billing, and collection), logistics (shipping, warehousing, and delivery), and manufacturing (fabrication, testing, and packaging).

- Li & Fung Retailing Ltd operates more than 950 retail outlets, with 11,500 employees, in Greater China, Singapore, Malaysia, Thailand, Indonesia, the Philippines, and South Korea for Toys "R" Us, Circle K, and Branded Lifestyle. Toys "R" Us is a joint venture with the US-based parent company (in 1999, Li & Fung acquired 100 percent ownership of the business in Hong Kong, Taiwan, Singapore and Malaysia). Branded Lifestyle represents major European and US brands in Asia, seeking to establish a consciousness of "brand values" for its clients (these include Salvatore Ferragamo and Calvin Klein, amongst others).

Retailers move closer to their suppliers

The emergence of large contract factory suppliers alters the power dynamics of global manufacturing, as lean retailing, with its associated cost cutting and quick response, compels retailers to shift such critical functions as inventory management and sales forecasting to giant contract suppliers (Kahn 2003). The example of TAL, discussed above, provides one illustration of this trend. In some cases, this shifting of key functions has even meant the migration of many pre- and post-production functions, including design, warehousing, and control over logistics, to Asia—as is seen with Luen Thai in China (Kahn 2004b).

Luen Thai Holdings Ltd is a leading apparel supplier, with more than 25,000 employees, 12 manufacturing facilities, and 14 offices in 9 countries, and with 2006 revenues of $662 million (Luen Thai 2006, 2007). The company produces more than eighty million pieces of garments annually, including sleepwear, pants and shorts, sports and active wear, ladies' fashion, intimate wear, and children's wear (Luen Thai 2006). Luen Thai is rapidly expanding, having recently acquired GJM from Warnaco, Tomwell Ltd from the Jones Apparel group, and a 50 percent stake in On Time, and a 50–50 joint venture with Guangzhou Huasheng Garment Company. Additionally, it has formed a joint venture with Yue Yuen for its sports and active wear.[10] The company, pursuing a "design to store" ("D2S") business model, has created a "supply-chain city" in Dongguan—a two-million-square-foot factory, a 300-room hotel, a dormitory for the factory's 4,000 workers, and product-development centers.[11] The factory permits apparel manufacturer Liz Claiborne and other Luen Thai customers[12] to work in a single location, their designers meeting directly with technicians from the factory and fabric mills to plan production far more efficiently. The consolidated supply chain is projected to reduce Liz Claiborne and Luen Thai staff by 40 percent, cutting costs and improving turnaround by providing tight coordination over logistics. Liz Claiborne, which currently sources from some 250 suppliers in 35 countries, plans to consolidate sourcing in a handful of places, utilizing facilities such as the Luen Thai complex; it has already begun to relocate staff from its Hong Kong and New York City offices. This process of consolidation has been reinforced by the ending of the MFA, which, as noted elsewhere, has encouraged major apparel companies to concentrate production in a smaller number of much larger facilities in a relative handful of countries. In addition to the labor cost savings that would result from concentrating production in China, Liz Claiborne and Luen Thai executives believe that "the real gains would come by reorganizing their entire production process so as to be able to cut down on turnaround times for new clothes and coordinate logistics" (Kahn 2004a). Having everyone in a single location—designers, fabric and raw-material suppliers, sewing—is viewed as significantly cutting costs and improving turnaround time, "getting new styles into stores faster."

> Instead of having 100 people spread between New York and Asia doing the same job, the new supply-chain city will enable the two companies to reduce staff to 60 people in China, concentrating all functions closer to the factory floor…By moving all but the most critical designers and trend spotters to Asia, the company can dispense with the tedious back and forth, slashing precious weeks off production times and getting up-to-minute fashions into stores sooner…In the new supply-chain city, everyone from the fabric mill to the store will use the same scan-and-track inventory system. Goods can roll off the factory floor and go straight to a store…(Khan 2004a)

The world's largest footwear suppler: A counterweight to Nike?

Yue Yuen/Pou Chen Industrial Holdings Ltd,[13] based in Hong Kong, is the world's largest maker of branded athletic and casual footwear, with $3.7 billion in revenues in the FY 2006 (Yue Yuen 2007b).[14] The company produced nearly 200 million pairs of branded athletic shoes for export in 2006, an increase of nearly three-quarters over the previous five years, representing 17 percent of the world total (Merk 2006; Yue Yuen 2007a). The company is Nike's biggest supplier, providing 15–30 percent of its shoes (estimates vary widely), with one Indonesian factory reportedly turning out a million shoes a month for Nike; other major footwear clients include Reebok, Adidas, Asics, New Balance, Puma, Timberland, and Rockport (owned by Reebok). While most of its shoes are made in factories throughout southern China (four out of six are in Dongguan Province), the company also has factories in Vietnam and Indonesia.[15] Overall, it operated 373 production lines as of 2006 (Yue Yuen 2007a). Yue Yuen is also expanding its sports apparel production, having acquired Pro Kingtex, invested in Eagle Nice, and formed a joint manufacturing venture with Luen Thai, amongst other activities, although this segment contributes less than 2 percent of the company's total revenues (Yue Yuen 2006, 2007b).

Yue Yuen's global workforce of 280,000 people in 2006 had grown by half since the turn of the century, primarily as a result of its steady growth as the leading manufacturer of athletic shoes, but also because of the growth of its Greater China (China, Taiwan, and Hong Kong) wholesale and retail operations. In terms of its manufacturing capabilities, Yue Yuen manages what are probably the world's largest footwear manufacturing plants in Dongguan, China (with over 15 million square feet of manufacturing floor space) and Ho Chi Minh City, Vietnam (1.3 million square meters) (Yue Yuen 2007a). Its sprawling factory complex in Dongguan alone reportedly employs some 110,000 workers, including 21,000 for Nike and 13,000 for Adidas. The Nike production sector includes recently renovated dormitories for its workers (eight women to a spartan room, in two rows of bunk beds), cafeteria, and a recently constructed "activities center" that includes a library and reading room, karaoke and dancing facility, a chess room, and meeting rooms and classrooms. Nike reportedly invested some $4.5 million in these renovations; it uses the new facilities to offer workers courses in personal finances, computers, and counselling.[16]

As of September 2006 Yue Yuen expansion into wholesale and retail sales boasted a network of more than 2,100 wholesale distributors in the greater China region, operating 640 retail outlets, distributing products from the major brands made in its factories (Merk 2003; Yue Yuen 2007b).[17] Revenues from the company's wholesale and retail operations in Greater China grew by four-fifths over the previous year—although they still represented only a small percentage (5.4 percent) of total revenues. As of FY 2006, Asian markets accounted for 30 percent of Yue Yuen's total turnover—second only to the United States (38 percent) (Yue Yuen 2007b). The company remains bullish about its wholesale and retail operations. The company, however, did not meet its goal of opening 1,000 additional stores or counters by 2008, a goal based in part on its belief, in 2007, that the Beijng Olympics would serve as a catalyst for increased sporting goods sales in China (Yue Yuen 2007b).[18]

Yue Yuen is also engaged in the upstream production of raw materials, shoe components, and even production tools—affording a high degree of vertical integration over its supply chain. In 2002, for example, it acquired Pou Chen's interest in sixty-seven upstream footwear material providers, including raw materials, equipment, and shoe components (Yue Yuen 2006). It is also seeking downstream integration, in terms of exerting tighter control over its logistics. As the company reported

> To accelerate its downstream vertical integration, SupplyLINE Ltd, a joint venture between Yue Yuen and Logistics Information Network Enterprise ("LINE"), a wholly-owned subsidiary of Hutchison Port Holdings, was formed to act as a Lead Logistics Provider, offering fully integrated supply chain and logistics solutions that shorten lead times for inbound materials and outbound products. (Yue Yuen 2006)

The company is clearly emerging as a market maker with regard to its own suppliers, as well as its Asian consumers. Yet, when dealing with major brands such as Nike or Reebok, how much of a market maker is Yue Yuen in the retail sector? When Yue Yuen's costs rose sharply in 2004,[19] it was able to pass on less than a third of the cost increase to its customers, forcing the company to post a 1.6 percent year-to-year decline in profits, the first such decline in twelve years. While some analysts regard this decline as indicative of the relatively weak bargaining power of even the largest contractors vis-à-vis the brands that rely on them (Fong 2005), others disagree (Hermanson 2005). Moreover, the company reported that, in 2006, "the average selling price continued its upward trend, reflecting the product mix change and the increase in underlying material costs" (Yue Yuen 2007b), suggesting that it was in fact able to pass on some of its cost increases to its buyers.

Whereas Wal-Mart's relationship with its suppliers is famously fleeting, determined purely by price considerations, the athletic footwear industry requires close cooperation between buyer and supplier, achieved through stable, ongoing relationships. Yue Yuen, for example, began as a supplier for Wal-Mart in the 1970s, but eventually developed the know-how, technological capacity, and size to move up to high-end brands such as Nike. Because the major brands require a highly diversified product mix and flexible production systems, Yue Yuen's high degree of vertical integration (including control over inputs and logistics) enables it to work with customers that require rapid market response. These same requirements afford the company a fair amount of bargaining power with even its largest customers.

Yue Yuen is already engaged in a limited way in original brand manufacturing; is it likely to "learn through doing," and eventually replace Nike and its other clients as a leading designer and retailer of athletic shoes? Nike and Yue Yuen are highly dependent on one another, reducing the probability that Nike will cut production if Yue Yuen begins to market its own low-cost brands in China (Ho 2005). On the other hand, Yue Yuen is a highly profitable business, thanks to its broad and loyal client base; it is unlikely to threaten those relationships by creating potentially competing brands (K. W. Chan 2005; Pun 2005).

At the present time, it is clear that, while Yue Yuen is a powerful market maker with regard to its own suppliers, it remains subordinate to its buyers, particularly the largest ones such as Nike. Beginning with design, and throughout the complex process of manufacturing athletic footwear (which involves as many as 200 different steps), Nike's hand is felt—as is evidenced by the thousand production specialists Nike employs to work closely with its suppliers (Merk 2006: 6–8). Yue Yuen is more dependent on Nike than the reverse;[20] moreover, it has carved out a highly profitable niche as the world's leading supplier, a niche it would not want to jeopardize.[21] Jeroen Merk, who has conducted a detailed study of Nike's relationship with Yue Yuen, concludes:

> Even though Yue Yuen has enough skills and cash to launch their own brand, they deliberately decided not to do so because that would make them a direct competitor of many of their customers. In fact, Yue Yuen is very concerned with protecting brand secrets. The company makes sure that its R&D centre never puts competing brands in the same place. This also implies that Yue Yuen cannot break into end-markets directly. (Merk 2006: 17)

Although Yue Yuen viewed the 2008 Beijing Olympics as a significant opportunity for expansion into retailing, the company did not plan to develop and market its own brands for the occasion. According to one newspaper account:

> The company will make the most of the 2008 Beijing Olympics to gain market share in the mainland . . . Pou Chen executives emphasized that their company would never develop own-branded shoes to rival its customers including Nike. Yue Yuen has long promoted Nike, Adidas and Reebok sport shoes at its stores. (Taiwan 2007)

China's Rapid Growth and the Prospects for Upgrading

China's rapid economic growth has averaged around 9 percent annually since 1990. Even allowing for exaggerated claims and poor governmental statistics, China's growth is explosive by any standards. Bear in mind that this is an average; the growth poles of China—South China in Guangdong Province around the Pearl River Delta, Shanghai, and the Yangtze River Delta—are growing at much greater rates. The lion's share of this growth is concentrated in South China, which accounts for nearly half of all the country's exports. The region boasts the highest concentrations of manufacturing, the largest factories, the greatest influx of labor from rural areas, the world's third and fourth busiest ports (in Hong Kong and Shenzhen), and the world's largest freight facility (*IAM Journal* 2005: 17).

A wide range of consumer goods industries have contributed to this growth. As noted previously, China is predicted to account for as much as half of the world's textile exports once the full effect of the end of the MFA is realized. In 2004, China accounted for 45.1 million computers, an increase of 39 percent from just one year earlier; 70.5 million air-conditioning units (an increase of 43 percent), 30.3 million refrigerators (30 percent), and 23.5 million washing machines (19 percent). Similar yearly increases were posted in metal-cutting machinery (36 percent), cement equipment (63 percent), metal rolling equipment (60 percent), and tractors (84 percent). "Morgan Stanley . . . says that China now absorbs half of the world's cement production, a fourth of its copper, and a fifth of its aluminium" (*IAM Journal* 2005: 15). This accelerated growth has created enormous energy needs; the International Energy Agency reports that China accounted for a third of the increase in global demand for oil between 2002 and 2004 (*IAM Journal* 2005: 13–14).

Government policy in China has fostered the creation of vibrant industrial districts comprised of clusters of suppliers, manufacturers, and contractors that specialize in a single product, fostering economies of scale, lowering transaction costs, and cutting prices. It has opened land for the development of industrial parks, given tax benefits to businesses, built transportation networks and other infrastructure, and subsidized utilities. Private companies, with government support, build factory complexes that include dormitories and hospitals. The resulting clusters create synergies that foster technological development (Barboza 2004). According to Ruizhe Sun, president of the China Textile Information Center: "In terms of vertical supply chain, China has no competition. We have button makers, fabric makers, thread makers, zipper makers, you name it" (cited in Barboza 2004).

At the high end of the technology spectrum, the Shenzhen campus of Huawei Technologies—manufacturer of globally competitive telecommunication equipment—boasts a research center, football fields, swimming pools, and housing for 3,000 families. Baosteel, based in Shanghai, is in 2010 the third largest producer of steel in the world. The Lenovo Group, amidst much fanfare, bought IBM's ailing PC business in December 2004. The Haier Group, China's leading maker of home appliances, has offices in 100 countries. And TCL Electronics, China's most profitable maker of televisions, acquired the TV business of France's Thomson in 2004; its website claims TCL-Thomson Electronics to be "the largest color television enterprise in the world." More than a dozen Chinese companies number amongst the *Fortune Global 500* (see Table 9.1). And China is investing heavily in the next

Table 9.1. A sample of Chinese "global champions," 2004 ($bn)

Company	Sector	Revenue ($bn)	Net income ($bn)
Sinopec	Oil/gas	71.45	3.90
PetroChina	Oil/gas	48.18	12.45
Hai'er	White goods	12.29	0.19
Baosteel	Steel	7.09	1.14
CNOOC	Oil/gas	6.68	1.96
Chalco	Aluminium	3.91	0.80
Huawei	Telecoms	3.83	0.62
TCL	Electronics	3.29	0.04
Lenovo	PCs	2.90	0.14
Galanz	White goods	1.60	0.70
Tsingtao	Brewery	1.04	0.03

Source: The Economist (2005).

generation of technologies: it plans to train 50,000 engineers in advanced chip design over the next few years, by creating design training centers in universities in seven cities, and is investing heavily in nanotechnology. All of this suggests a strong future counterweight to the power of Wal-Mart and other big buyers, as China moves rapidly from being an export platform to becoming an industrial power in its own right. This transformation will probably depend less on expertise in production, and more on expertise in selling—that is, in making consumer markets. Still, it is reasonable to expect that some of the emerging Chinese firms will become major brand managers in their own right, and that there will also be a slew of Chinese retailers poised to compete with global retailers for the share of the China's consumer market.

The economic power of giant retailers remains limited in China, which initially regulated the expansion of foreign retailers (for example, requiring substantial local partnerships). Wal-Mart may account for some 3 percent of China's total exports,[22] but, in terms of retail presence, by the end of 2004 the company had only forty-three stores in China, accounting for less than $1 billion in revenue, barely 2 percent of its international sales. Since joining the World Trade Organization, China has eased its restrictions on foreign retailers, and Wal-Mart continues to open new stores, including supercenters in Beijing and Shanghai, the first in those cities,[23] with talk of increasing its floor space in China by as much as half in the near future (C. Chandler 2005). Wal-Mart CEO David Glass views China as one place where continued expansion is possible (Gilman 2004).[24]

> If you look at Europe, it's difficult to green-field or grow a company of much size. But you can build an enormous-sized company in China if you make some fairly aggressive assumptions about what's going to happen to it. It's the one place in the world where you could replicate Wal-Mart's success in the US.

Yet even Wal-Mart may face an uphill battle in China. China's state-run Shanghai Brilliance group, China's largest retailer, claims sales of $8.1 billion in 3,300 stores. And Wal-Mart is also competing with France's Carrefour, which has 60 "hypermarkets" with sales of $2 billion (C. Chandler 2005). Yet the biggest challenge to retail expansion in China may be cultural: with small apartments and limited space for consumer items, the growing number of middle-class Chinese shoppers are accustomed to shopping on foot, making frequent trips for small volume purchases.

Directions for Future Research

There is growing evidence that consolidation in consumer goods industries, with increasingly integrated production and distribution systems between giant retailers and equally giant contractors, may be replicating the vertical integration characteristic of the earlier "Fordist" organization of production. These dynamics remain poorly understood. What is needed is long-term research to chart the impact of changes in retailing and contracting. In particular, I would suggest a number of interrelated questions that could guide systematic, long-term investigations, focusing principally on China, but also on East Asia generally—bearing in mind that the present moment is but a snapshot with the changing dynamics of the world economy:

- How does the trend toward concentration of production in large transnational contractors impact the relative power of contractors vis-à-vis retailers in supply-chain networks—for example, the ability of contractors to negotiate production costs, or "move up" into such higher value-added activities as designing and marketing their own labels?

- How do recent innovations in supply-chain management influence the relationship between big buyers and their suppliers—for example, when the largest suppliers take over many of the functions of supply-chain management from retailers? What is the role of giant trading companies, such as Li & Fung, which appear to be becoming increasingly central in supply-chain management?

- What will be the impact if a growing number of retailers move geographically closer to their principal suppliers—for example, in the form of Luen Thai's "supply-chain city" (a move that also undoubtedly signals a desire to be closer to China's rapidly emerging markets)?

- How does the rise of China as an industrial power change the dynamics of the global supply chains in which Chinese firms are involved? Will China's largest suppliers move increasingly into retailing, first locally, then regionally? How will this affect the dominance of the world's current retail giants? And how will China's growth in capital-intensive industries (such as shipbuilding, automotive, aircraft, construction, and so on) affect the relative power of retail-controlled supply chains?

- To what extent will the emergence of large contractors generate linkages with other firms and sectors that contribute to industrial upgrading and more broadly based economic development? Does their vertical integration restrict the formation of local economic linkages that might stimulate more broad-based economic growth?

- Finally, what will be the impact of China's move into advanced technologies, on the dynamics of global supply chains?

Part Four
Industries and Market Making

10

The Global Spread of Modern Food Retailing

Benjamin Senauer and Thomas Reardon

Introduction

Today you could walk into supermarkets or a supercenter (selling food and general merchandise) in Mexico City or Shanghai or hundreds of other cities around the world and think you had just entered an upscale store in an American or European suburb. Of course, once you looked at the customers and employees or at some of the different food products, you would realize you were not in the USA or Europe. However, the general appearance and operation of the supermarket would appear very familiar. In the late 1980s, modern food retailing was pretty much exclusive to the United States, Western Europe, and a few other economically advanced countries such as Australia and Canada. In a phenomenally short period (since the middle 1990s), modern food retailing has spread around the world to countries in Latin America, Asia, Eastern Europe, and even parts of Africa. The global expansion of modern food retailing is an excellent example of the concept of market making. Food retailers are remaking their consumer and supplier markets.

On the consumer side, supermarkets and other formats such as supercenters have transformed the food shopping experience for hundreds of millions of consumers around the world. People in Brazil, China, South Africa, and dozens of other countries who used to shop only at open-air public markets, street vendors, and small family-operated stores are going to modern supermarkets and supercenters as well as other modern retail formats (such as chains of hard discounts, neighborhood stores, and convenience stores). They are no longer waited on personally by the shopkeeper or vendor, but, like Americans and Western Europeans, they are walking up and down the aisle making their own selections before checking out. The selection of products is many times greater typically than in the traditional markets and stores and the overall quality, variety, and safety of the food much better. In addition, in many cases the prices are lower than in the traditional markets and small shops, especially at first in processed foods, and with a lag, in fresh foods.

At the same time, modern food retailing has so dramatically altered the consumer market that it has also reshaped the supply chain. Most aspects of the traditional agro-food systems, including production, transportation, and marketing, in developing countries have been markedly inefficient. They have been characterized by low productivity levels, high post-harvest losses because of factors such as spoilage, and poor quality and food safety standards.

Modern Food Retailing

Although there are many additional variations, we will cover only the basic store formats of modern food retailing. Supermarkets are departmentalized, self-service stores that carry a wide selection of food and household goods that are consumed regularly. Most supermarkets are now part of a chain of stores. They are substantially larger and have a much broader selection than traditional grocery stores. Customers move along aisles stocked with products with a cart or basket to fill. The items are paid for at cash registers in the front of the store. Many of these features, which we take for granted, were remarkable innovations when they first appeared. The first self-service grocery store was opened in 1916. Before that clerks had to wait on each customer and get the items wanted from behind counters. Many products were kept in bulk form and were measured out and packaged for customers. The New York-based King Cullen (1930) and Big Bear (1932) stores are typically considered the first real supermarkets. By 1937, there were 3,000 supermarkets in operation in forty-seven states (Zimmerman 1955).

Supermarkets spread rapidly in the 1950s and 1960s, along with the growth of suburbs. Supermarkets and the food manufacturing industry grew together in a symbiotic relationship. Supermarket chains developed their price advantage over traditional retailers by buying in bulk and thus exploiting economies of scale. The natural partner from whom to buy in bulk was a large-scale food manufacturer. In the same way, to establish mass brand presence, be priced competitively, and develop economies of scope with a diversity of products, large food manufacturers found supermarket chains to be natural partners, with clear advantages over mom-and-pop shops in all but the manufacturer's degree of bargaining power with the client. This symbiosis was as true of large food manufacturers and supermarkets in the USA in the 1940s as it is in developing countries today.[1] Jointly, supermarkets and large food manufacturers transformed the consumer food market. While this is true in general, some of the largest early supermarket chains, such as A&P, the largest retailer in the world in the mid-twentieth century, had quite a strained relation with many big manufacturers, and relied to a large extent on private labels. In the case of A&P, this strategy eventually contributed to its downfall, mostly at the hand of the antitrust authorities.

Supercenters, such as those operated by Wal-Mart, began to appear in the USA in the 1990s; they combined a supermarket and mass merchandise retailing in a single, very large store. A similar combination format actually appeared in France first, where it was referred to as a hypermarket. The so-called combination stores were common in the USA before they appeared in France. In fact, French managers went to the USA to study the principles of modern retailing, and came up with the hypermarket format.

Wholesale clubs, such as Sam's Club and Costco, also carry both food and general merchandise. They require a membership to shop, and lean toward large sizes and bulk sales. Limited-assortment stores, such as Aldi and Sav-A-Lot, are small, "bare-bones", "hard-discount" food stores. They typically carry fewer than 2,000 items and few, if any, perishables. Convenience stores, such as 7-Eleven, offer a very limited selection of food and non-food items (Food Institute 2007).

The Universal Product Code (UPC) providing bar codes on individual packages was adopted in the 1970s. Scanners came into use to expedite checkout and eliminate the necessity of stamping a price on each item. However, unlike in other retail sectors where scanners were adopted, few advances in the overall supply chain occurred. There was an imbalance of bargaining power between the food retailers and the major food manufactures, which favored the latter in the USA, as large food manufacturers had innovated with national brands in the late 1800s and early 1900s when supermarkets were in their infancy. Therefore, well-established food manufacturers had considerable bargaining power until well into the late twentieth century, when the pendulum of market power swung toward the retailers. In contrast, the market power balance has clearly been on the side of the large retailers in the UK from the mid-twentieth century (Wrigley and Lowe 2002).

Manufacturers had adopted the practice of periodically running large batches of a product and then pushing it through the system with special discounts. The distribution system had become bloated with inventories sitting in warehouses. The inventory cost hurt retailers' competitiveness. Hence, food retailers instituted a version of "lean inventory management" in the early 1990s under the banner Efficient Consumer Response, widely referred to as ECR. The development of ECR was in large part a response to Wal-Mart, with its highly efficient distribution system and "every day low pricing" (EDLP) strategy. Wal-Mart had already affected supermarket sales in household merchandise and was beginning to open supercenters, which directly competed with supermarkets (King and Phumpiu 1996; Coggins and Senauer 1999). ECR was designed to "drive costs" from the distribution system, a phrase frequently used. ECR used the advances in information technology to link retailers, distributors, and suppliers electronically, so that they could coordinate more closely. Timely, accurate, paperless information on sales, inventory replenishment needs, and payments were to flow one way, with a smooth, continual product flow matched to consumption in the other direction. Warehouses became distribution centers with the goal of speeding the flow of goods rather than storing inventory. Direct store delivery, in which a truckload was sent directly from the supplier to retail stores without ever going through a distribution center, was adopted for some products. The most innovative and best-managed food retailers were most successful at achieving the goals of ECR and thus achieving a competitive advantage with lower costs (King and Phumpiu 1996; Coggins and Senauer 1999).

By the end of the 1990s the major food retailers had largely remade the supply chain in the USA and Western Europe. With their control of the flow of information, they now had the upper hand in their relationship with food manufacturers and other suppliers. The shift in power from food manufacturers to retailers in the USA (following a trend that had occurred a decade or more before in the UK) was also affected by the waves of consolidation that occurred in US food retailing and the growth of "private-label" or "store-brand" products, which competed directly with the national brands. (Both the consolidation and the private-label trends started later in the USA than in the UK, as discussed in Wrigley and Lowe (2002).) For example, stores began to sell cereals that were similar to General Mills's Cheerios and Kellogg's Cornflakes, but that sold at a much lower price. The new supply-chain practices allowed food retailers efficiently to expand geographically. These practices also helped in chains' internationalization.

By 2005, many of the major food retailers in Europe and some of the major chains in the United States were operating internationally, as shown in Table 10.1 (*Supermarket News* 2007). The two largest global general-merchandise retailers, Wal-Mart and Carrefour, are also the world's two leading food retailers. This is because food accounts for at least a third of the sales revenue of their most important store formats, Wal-Mart Supercenters and Carrefour Hypermarkets. Wal-Mart is, in fact, the largest US food retailer, as is Carrefour in France, its home country. As they have entered the markets of developing countries like Mexico and transition countries like Poland, food has been an even more important component of their strategy. This is because people with lower incomes spend a higher proportion of their household budgets on food.

Deloitte, the accounting and consulting firm, publishes an annual *Global Powers of Retailing* study. The 2007 report makes clear that the fastest sales

Table 10.1. The ten largest global food retailers, 2007

Company	Headquarters	Sales ($bn)[a]	No. of stores	No. of countries
1. Wal-Mart[b]	United States	$312.40	6,380	16
2. Carrefour[b]	France	$92.6	12,179	38
3. Tesco	England	$69.6	2,365	14
4. Metro Group	Germany	$69.3	2,458	27
5. Kroger	United States	$60.6	3,726	1
6. Ahold	Netherlands	$55.3	6,422	11
7. Costco[b]	United States	$52.9	460	8
8. Rewe	Germany	$51.8	11,242	14
9. Schwarz Group	Germany	$45.8	7,299	22
10. Aldi	Germany	$45.0	7,788	14

[a] Total sales, including non-food, for most recent financial year, usually 2006.
[b] Food accounts for at least one-third of the total sales of these companies.
Source: Supermarket News (2007).

growth for the world's 250 largest retailers is occurring outside the developed countries. Their average sales growth was only 2.4 percent in France in FY 2005 and 2.1 percent in the UK, whereas it was 20.3 percent in Latin America. The majority of the top 250 global retailers are involved in food retailing. Some 54 percent operated supermarkets, superstores, or other formats in which food products constituted a major proportion of retail sales (Deloitte 2007).

Wal-Mart de Mexico provides a good example of international business operations of a major global retailer. Wal-Mart's expansion outside the United States began in 1991 in Mexico. In a joint venture with the Mexican retailer Cifra, the country's largest and strongest retailer at the time, a Sam's Club was opened in Mexico City. Wal-Mart acquired majority ownership of Cifra in 1997, and the name was changed to Wal-Mart de Mexico. After Wal-Mart had bought Cifra, it kept the experienced local managers, but introduced its efficient US purchasing and distribution system, while investing in expansion. Just as in the United States, Wal-Mart's core strategy was focused on low prices (Malkin 2004). Today Wal-Mart is the largest general-merchandise and food retailer in Mexico. However, the acquisition by Soriana of Gigante in December 2007 means that there is now a large domestic rival. Wal-Mart operated several formats in Mexico, with a total of 783 stores in 103 cities throughout the country and 140,000 employees. Wal-Mart de Mexico sales were equivalent to $18.3 billion in 2006. Total sales grew by 15.3 percent in 2006 in real terms (corrected for inflation)—more than three times the rate of GDP/capita growth—with comparable store (for stores open more than a year) real sales growth of 6.9 percent. With sales growth that is much more robust than it has been in the United States for Wal-Mart in recent years, it should not be surprising that Wal-Mart de Mexico expanded rapidly, investing $1.1 billion and opening 120 new stores since 2004 (Wal-Mart 2007).

Interestingly, Wal-Mart operates a more diverse range of store formats in Mexico than in the United States, and food constitutes a much larger share of total sales. As of January 2007, Wal-Mart Mexico operated 118 supercenters, 77 Sam's Clubs, 218 Bodega Aurrera, which offer a limited assortment of food, housewares, and staple goods, 60 Superama supermarkets, 311 VIPS restaurants, and 62 Sububia apparel stores, plus smaller numbers of some other formats. Food accounted for 45 percent of supercenter sales, 49 percent for Sam's Clubs, 48 percent for Bodegas, and 70 percent for Superama supermarkets (Wal-Mart 2007). These figures are a good example of the greater importance of food in most large retailers in developing and transition countries, as already discussed. The competition between Wal-Mart and the main domestic chains has encouraged domestic chain mergers and acquisitions, such as the one noted above, as well as competitive investments in procurement system modernization, such as in distribution centers (see Reardon et al. 2007).

The Spread of Modern Food Retailing into Developing Countries

It is useful to distinguish several distinct phases or "waves" in the geographic spread of modern food retailing beyond the countries with advanced market economies. From earliest to latest adopters of supermarkets in emerging market areas, there have been three waves of diffusion, and an emerging fourth.

First Wave. Experiencing supermarket-sector "take-off" in the early to mid-1990s, the first-wave countries include much of South America and East Asia outside China (and Japan), Northern-Central Europe, and South Africa—a set of areas where the average share of supermarkets in food retail went from roughly only 10–20 percent circa 1990 to 50–60 percent on average by the early 2000s (Reardon and Berdegué 2002; Reardon et al. 2003). Compare that to the 70–80 percent share that supermarkets had in food retail in 2005 in the USA, UK, or France, and one sees a process of convergence. Examples include front-runners where the supermarket take-off started in the early 1990s, such as Argentina with a 60 percent supermarket share in food retail in 2002 (Gutman 2002), Brazil with 75 percent (Farina 2002), Taiwan with 55 percent in 2003 (Chang 2005), and the Czech Republic with 55 percent (Dries, Reardon, and Swinnen 2004). While a small number of supermarkets existed in most countries during and before the 1980s, they were primarily local firms using domestic capital,[2] and tended to exist in major cities and wealthier neighborhoods. That is, they were essentially a niche retail market serving 5–10 percent of national food retail sales in 1990 (for at-home consumption: not bought at restaurant/retail for consumption away from home). However, by 2000, supermarkets had risen to occupy 50–60 percent of national food retail amongst these front-runners, almost approaching the 70–80 percent share for the United States or France. South America and parts of developing East Asia and transition Europe had thus seen in a single decade the same development of supermarkets that the United States experienced in five decades.

There is a second set of countries perched at the tail end of the first wave and near the start of the second wave, which we class with the first wave, with their supermarket "take-off" in the mid-1990s, such as Costa Rica and Chile, with close to 50 percent market share by 2002 (Reardon and Berdegué 2002), and, in 2003, South Korea with 50 percent (Lee and Reardon 2005), the Philippines and Thailand with approximately 50 percent each (Thailand Development Research Institute 2002; Manalili 2005), and South Africa with 55 percent (Weatherspoon and Reardon 2003).

Second Wave. The second-wave countries include parts of South East Asia and Central America and Mexico, and Southern-Central Europe, where the share went from around 5–10 percent in 1990 to 30–50 percent by the early 2000s, with the take-off occurring in the mid- to late 1990s; examples of rapid growth by 2003 include Mexico with a 40 percent share of supermarkets in total food retail (see Reardon, Berdegué, and Timmer 2005), Colombia with a 47 percent share (see Hernandez 2004), Guatemala with 36 percent in 2002 (see Orellana and Vasquez 2004) Indonesia with 30 percent (Rangkuti, 2003), and Bulgaria with 25 percent (Dries, Reardon, and Swinnen 2004).

Third Wave. The third wave includes countries where the supermarket revolution take-off started only in the late 1990s or early 2000s, reaching about 10–20 percent of national food retail by circa 2003; they include some of Africa (see below), some countries in Central and South America (such as Nicaragua (see Balsevich 2005), Peru, and Bolivia), and some countries in South East Asia (such as Vietnam (see Tam 2004)), China, India, and Russia. The latter three countries were the foremost destinations for retail foreign direct investment (FDI) in the world in 2004 (T. Burt 2004) and remain so in 2010.

China had no supermarkets in 1989, and food retail was nearly completely controlled by the government; the sector began in 1990, and by 2003 had climbed meteorically to a 13 percent share in national food retail, with $71 billion of sales, 30 percent of urban food retail, and growing the fastest in the world, at 30–40 percent per year (Hu et al. 2004). Many of the driving forces for supermarketization were in place (rising incomes, urbanization), and it merely took a progressive privatization of the retail market and, even more importantly, a progressive liberalization of retail FDI, which started in 1992 and culminated in 2004, to drive immense competition, even a full-out race, in investment amongst foreign chains and between foreign chains and domestic chains. This expansion and competition greatly accelerated in 2005 with the full liberalization of FDI that occurred as a condition to accession to WTO by China. Russia is a similar case, with a late start because of policy factors holding back the take-off despite propitious socioeconomic conditions, and then a very rapid take-off spurred on by an immense competition in investments underway in the early and mid-2000s (Dries and Reardon 2005).

India is an interesting case, with its substantial middle class acting as a "springboard" for the spread of supermarkets; the country is amongst the top three retail FDI candidates in the world and is poised at the edge of a supermarketization take-off, although the share in food retail is still only, at most, 5 percent. In 2010, FDI is still far from fully liberalized, and regulations concerning joint ventures in retail still block what observers think is an imminent flood of foreign investment. Yet already a massive wave of domestic capital investment, which should rise to $20 billion sometime before 2015, is rushing into the Indian retail sector and already beginning to transform it, fueled by rapid economic growth. Even though retail FDI by 2008 was not yet liberalized, Metro and other global chains have already entered and operate cash and carry stores (wholesale to small shops and food service and hotels), and joint ventures have started, such as Bharti with Wal-Mart, with the latter assuring the "back end" operations while Bharti assures the "front end" of retailing, opening stores in March 2008 (Reardon and Gulati 2008).

Sub-Saharan Africa presents a very diverse picture, with only one country (South Africa) firmly in the first wave of supermarket penetration (Weatherspoon and Reardon 2003), and the rest either in the early phase of the "third wave" take-off of diffusion or in what may be a pending—but not yet started—take-off of supermarket diffusion. Kenya (Neven and Reardon 2004) and Zambia (Neven et al. 2006) are in the early phase of the "third wave," and have substantial numbers of supermarkets, initiated by both domestic investment and FDI from South Africa. This investment was attracted by a middle-class base and high urbanization rates, but supermarket penetration is still approximately where South America was in the early 1980s. The share of supermarkets in urban food retail is about 10–20 percent in the large/medium cities, and the share of produce hovers around 5 percent (see Neven and Reardon 2004 for Kenya). Even with mainly domestic investment and some South African retail capital and technology, there is still considerable uncertainty about the rate at which the supermarket sector in these countries will grow. The great majority of Africa, however, can be classified as not yet entering a substantial "take-off" of supermarket diffusion. At the upper end of this group are a score or so of supermarkets in countries like Mozambique and Tanzania, Uganda, and Angola, places where South African retail FDI is just starting (see Weatherspoon and Reardon 2003 for evidence on investments by the South African chain Shoprite) and may by 2020 be recognizable as a "fourth wave." Supermarkets in these countries show signs of early growth and are surrounded by a more general trend of the growth of self-service in large semi-traditional stores in urban areas as in the first third of the twentieth century in the USA.

In addition to these somewhat distinct phases of expansion, there are also certain trends that are common to the global spread of modern food retailing. Supermarkets gain market share most quickly in groceries, and in processed and packaged goods, because of advantages in both scale and the efficiency of their supply logistics compared to mom-and-pop stores. Their growth in fresh foods is usually slower (just as it was in the USA in the twentieth century, not becoming important in produce, for example, before the 1960s–1970s), because traditional markets and vendors are nestled in the neighborhoods and thus provide easy access, and in the early stages are more attuned to local consumer habits and have better connections to local suppliers. Over time supermarkets begin to adapt to and shape their customers' preferences and also establish a supply network that is more efficient, as well as imposing higher standards of food quality and safety for fresh products than previously existed (Reardon, Timmer, and Berdegué 2004). The increased importance of fresh produce retail is very recent, even in first- and second-wave countries. For example, produce became important in Mexican supermarkets only since 2000 (Reardon et al. 2007); produce was minor in Hong Kong hypermarkets and supermarkets until they launched in-store wet markets in the early 2000s and quickly gained share from traditional wet markets (Reardon and Gulati 2008).

Another common trend is for supermarkets to open first in the largest urban areas, then to spread to smaller cities, and in some countries the expansion has reached towns in rural areas. The modern food retailing sector has become typified by both a greater presence by multinational, foreign-owned companies and by consolidation and more concentration. The multinational operators, such as Carrefour, have advantages in their access to investment capital and their procurement and logistics efficiency.

Figure 10.1 shows clearly just how rapid the recent expansion of modern retailing has been compared to the much slower historical spread in countries like the United States and France. Some of the countries in which modern food retailing appeared most recently have seen even faster growth in the sector than those emerging economies where the expansion began earlier, such as Brazil and Korea. The rate of expansion in China has been nothing short of phenomenal.

The customer base of modern food retailers has spread well beyond just the expatriate and higher-income segments of the population in developing countries. Few rigorous empirical studies have been conducted of who shops at these supermarkets and what they are buying. In general, however, the emerging evidence indicates: (1) that, controlling for wave or stage,

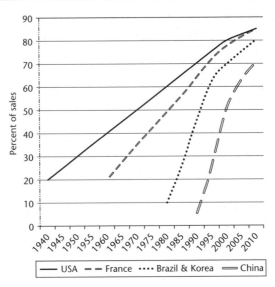

Figure 10.1. Supermarket share of the retail food market, 1940–2010

supermarkets penetrate first the upper-income, then the middle, and later the poorer consumer segments; (2) supermarkets have already penetrated well beyond the middle class into the food markets of the poor in the first-wave countries and some of the second-wave countries (as can be seen in comparing the supermarkets' share in food retail versus the share of the middle and upper classes in overall population in these countries); (3) while upper and middle consumer segments are increasingly buying fresh produce from supermarkets, the poor still mainly buy processed staples (rice, wheat and maize flour, edible oil, bread, noodles, snacks, beverages, and condiments, as well as dairy) from supermarkets.

An example is a household survey carried out in Nairobi, Kenya, in 2003 that interviewed a sample of 445 food shoppers, which covered all income groups. The survey found that a surprising 80 percent of the households shopped at a supermarket at least once a month and that the figure was 60 percent for even the poorest families in Nairobi. However, higher- and upper-middle-income households, which essentially constitute what will be referred to as the emerging global middle class in developing countries in a later section of this chapter, were crucial in terms of sales. Although they made up only 15 percent of Nairobi's population, they accounted for 44 percent of supermarkets' sales. The study revealed a clear pattern in what was purchased at supermarkets, which were mostly processed foods. Only 15 percent of those sampled bought fresh fruits and vegetables there. Poorer households bought mostly easy-to-store bulk items like sugar and soap and purchased less than

1 percent of their fresh produce at supermarkets. The most frequently given reason for shopping at a supermarket was "low prices", followed by "large assortment." On the one hand, the most common reasons for buying from traditional retailers, such as kiosks and over-the-counter shops, were that they were "easy to get to" and the "availability of credit." The research found that prices for processed foods, such as sugar, cooking oil, flour, and bread, were some 3–4 percent lower at supermarkets than traditional retail outlets. On the other hand, fresh fruits and vegetables were less expensive at traditional retailers, almost 90 percent lower at open-air markets, although the quality might not be as good. In other countries with healthier economies than Kenya, the growing middle class could be expected to be doing more of its food shopping predominantly at supermarkets, including purchasing fresh fruits and vegetables there (Neven et al. 2005).

Factors Driving the Spread of Modern Food Retailing

The global expansion of modern food retailing is being driven by factors that can be placed in three categories. As shown in Table 10.2, one can distinguish between push or supply-side, pull or demand-side, and external enabling factors. Food retailers in the advanced economies are increasingly faced with domestic markets that are saturated, particularly in Western Europe, which has pushed them to go abroad. Profits in many cases are under pressure from intense competition. In these highly developed countries, expenditures on food are still growing, but very slowly, especially for groceries as opposed to restaurant and other food service meals.

In addition, food retailers are more capable of operating over far broader geographic areas because of the innovations in information technology, which allow them to monitor closely inventories and track the movement of goods through the supply chain. They have been able to improve greatly

Table 10.2. Factors driving the spread of modern food retailing

Push/supply factors	Pull/demand factors	Enabling/external factors
Domestic market saturation	Per capita income growth in other countries	Political stability
Reduced growth in food spending	Urbanization	Trade liberalization
Competitive pressure on profits	Entry of women into the work force	Globalization of other industries (i.e., finance)
Supply-chain technology	Emergence of middle class	Communication and transportation technology
Fear of being left behind	Size of market potential	Cultural globalization
	Importance of scale	End of the Cold War
	Inefficiency of traditional food systems	

the efficiency of their supply chains. The companies with the highest efficiency have a competitive advantage that they have tried to transfer to their operations in other countries. Another push/supply-side factor is that large retailers must be concerned if they let major international competitors get well established in a particular foreign market first (Reardon, Timmer, and Berdegué 2004; Senauer and Venturini 2005).

At the same time there are demand-side forces that can be thought of as pulling major food retailers to expand into other countries, especially those with emerging market economies. Many of these countries, especially some of the largest, such as Brazil, China, and India, have been experiencing robust economics growth. China's economy has grown at 10 percent or more annually for over a decade. Expenditures on food are growing rapidly in these countries. According to Engel's Law, the lower the initial per capita income level of the population the greater will be the expansion in food demand for a given rise in income. With additional income, many of the people in these developing countries want to add more animal protein and greater variety and improved quality to their diets, which have been dominated by one or two staples, such as corn, rice, or wheat (Senauer and Venturini 2005).

The emerging middle class in seventeen developing and three transition countries was estimated to contain over one billion people in 2000. These consumers lived in households with at least $2,500 in income per person (Myers and Kent 2003). Foreign currencies were compared to US dollars using purchasing power parity (PPP) to correct for distortions in foreign currency exchange rates. In another analysis that focused on food expenditures, the emerging middle class was identified as persons living in households with annual total consumer expenditures per capita of $2,695 per capita or more in 2000, a very similar level to the other study. Based on data for Lima, Peru, the emerging middle class corresponded to the top quintile in terms of per capita expenditures. The households in the top quintile spent over three times more on fresh vegetables, fresh fruit, and red meat than the average purchases of people in the lower four quintiles. They spent over four times more on yogurt, butter, and cheese; and over six times more on prepared foods consumed at home (Senauer and Goetz 2004). This makes clear why this middle class is so attractive to food retailers. The size of the emerging middle class in China in 2003 was estimated to be 352 million, in India 105 million, in Russia 89 million, in Brazil 57 million, all of which continue to grow rapidly (Senauer 2005).

In addition, the increasing urbanization and growing participation of women in jobs outside the home have created opportunities for modern food retailers. Also, the ownership of a refrigerator allows a family to shift its food shopping patterns. With a refrigerator, people do not need to shop as frequently, even daily in many cases for fresh foods, or as close to home, as they would without a refrigerator. They can stock up on less frequent trips to a more distant supermarket (Reardon, Timmer, and Berdegué 2004).

With rapid economic growth and large populations, the size of not just the present, but especially the future potential, market for retail food in countries such as China and India makes them extremely attractive opportunities. Beyond that, the larger scale that can be achieved with expansion in a country or a region, or even globally, allows for increased efficiency. There are scale economies in a distribution system that serves more stores. The investments in information technology and logistics can afford to be greater and the costs of distribution centers and transport are spread over more retail outlets.

Traditional food production and marketing systems are burdened by inefficiencies and marked by low levels of capital, labor, and land productivity. Post-harvest crop losses during storage, transportation, and marketing are frequently in the order of 30 percent. Losses may be even higher for perishable products, such as fresh fruits and vegetables, since they were not kept chilled during distribution, which also affects quality.

Although trade liberalization has dominated the globalization debate, retail (and processing) FDI liberalization is a far larger force in affecting the "remaking of markets" in developing countries. In fact, the liberalization of retail FDI in many developing countries in the early 1990s was the main "sufficient" factor (beyond the necessary factors of the propitious demand-side situation of rising incomes and urbanization) to initiate the supermarket revolution in the 1990s in developing countries (Reardon and Timmer 2007).

Moreover, the global expansion of food retailers, as with other industries, has been facilitated by the globalization of other services, including the financial industry, as well as by improvements in communication with the Internet and transportation, with convenient jet travel to most places in the world. The movement of information and key personnel is crucial to a global business. Food preferences still vary significantly between countries, and even within regions of many nations. However, cultural globalization has brought preferences closer together, which makes it easier for food retailers to expand internationally.

Transformation of the Supply Chain

The rapid growth of supermarkets is profoundly transforming the marketing channels and the agro-food markets in many developing countries. Supermarkets initially gained a large share of the market for packaged groceries, but more recently have been making rapid gains in fresh products, such as dairy and fruits and vegetables. Modern food retailers, such as Carrefour and Wal-Mart, as well as many competing domestic chains, need large product volumes and operate centralized procurement operations. They want to deal with only a small number of large, reliable suppliers and not a multitude of small fragmented producers. The retailers are imposing stringent quality standards, and are beginning to impose safety standards. Procurement contracts and "preferred" suppliers are replacing traditional wholesale markets already in an advanced way for processed products, and in initial phases for fresh products. Sourcing is becoming regional or even global. The use of modern logistics practices is driving costs from the system, as was done in the United States and Europe.

These supply-chain changes are leading to a consolidation of the procurement system—in particular for processed products. Examples include a Chinese medium-sized supermarket chain cutting back sharply on its processed food suppliers (Hu et al. 2004) and Russian supermarket chains doing the same for their dairy suppliers (Dries and Reardon 2005). This sort of "exclusion" is still far less common in fresh produce for several reasons. Supermarkets in developing countries have only very recently introduced fresh produce. (We noted above the example of Mexico, which is typical amongst second-wave countries, where supermarkets started to have a substantial retailing effort in fresh produce only in the 2000s). Moreover, supermarket chains still mainly rely on traditional sourcing from wholesale markets. Where they have begun to modernize fresh produce procurement, such as via specialized wholesalers or via direct sourcing, the general tendency is toward use of the "upper tier" (in terms of land or non-land assets) of horticultural producers (Reardon and Berdegué 2007). Thus, for example, even the specialized wholesaler working for Carrefour in Indonesia sources from small tomato farmers, but these tend to be the "elite" of the small farmers in terms of assets like irrigation, access to infrastructure, and education (Natawidjaja et al. 2007). Moreover, the nationwide network and even regional and global networks of supermarkets in developing countries mean that local farmers become more exposed to competition.

The modern food retailers' procurement contracts set quality and consistency requirements that most small producers cannot meet, in particular in the case of processed plus semi-processed foods (constituting some 80–90 percent of the food sales of supermarkets, the rest being fresh produce and fish). As noted above, to the extent that supermarkets are moving away from sourcing from the traditional wholesale markets, these higher private standards are beginning to affect produce growers and form a challenge, especially for small farmers. These private standards are becoming more important in agro-food systems than the public grades and food safety standards established by governments and international agreements (Reardon et al. 1999). Meeting a retailer's requirements for fresh produce may necessitate major investments in packing and cooling facilities, cold storage and shipment, and trucking capacity. Carrefour applies the same quality certification to some 200 items globally, and other international retailers are also applying similar quality standards across countries (Reardon and Berdegué 2002).

Considerable attention has been given to the effects of the World Trade Organization (WTO) accords and CODEX Alimentarius (an international food code) protocols on agro-food quality and safety standards. In reality, the private standards established by global food retailers have a greater impact in many cases, except for the international trade of basic agricultural commodities. Likewise, there has been a focus on the potential for exporting fruits and vegetables and other agricultural products from developing countries to the industrial ones. However, the domestic market opportunity may be greater. For example, supermarkets in Latin America buy 2.5 times more produce to sell to local consumers than these countries export to the rest of the world (Reardon and Berdegué 2002).

Why are modern retailers in developing countries moving toward procurement system modernization? In many countries, modern food retailers have found the traditional wholesale markets and distribution systems challenging. Javier Gallegos (2003), who was the head of marketing for Hortifruti, the dedicated produce wholesaler for the CARHCO chain of supermarkets in Central America (bought by Wal-Mart in 2006), clearly outlined the shortcoming of the traditional supply chain:

> The market is fragmented, unformatted, and lacks standards. The growers produce low quality products, use bad harvest techniques; there is a lack of equipment and transportation, there is no post-harvest control and infrastructure; there is no market information. There are high import barriers and corruption. The informal market does not have: research, statistics, market information, standardized products, quality control, technical assistance, infrastructure. (Gallegos 2003)

Modern food retailers operating in developing regions have both qualitative and quantitative goals in re-engineering the supply chain, with the first increasing product quality and food safety and with the second reducing costs and increasing volume. Traditional procurement systems have relied on wholesalers and wholesale markets. The new procurement systems have four key elements or "pillars": (1) centralized procurement systems, (2) specialized/dedicated wholesalers, (3) preferred suppliers, and (4) high-quality and improved safety standards (Reardon, Timmer, and Berdegué 2004; Reardon and Timmer 2007).

As food retailers expand the number of stores in their chain in a country or region, they shift from a system of each store handling its own procurement to the centralization of procurement operations utilizing regional distribution (wholesale) centers. This organizational change in procurement occurs earliest in processed products, then in semi-processed, and very recently has started in fresh produce. For example, Ahold, a Dutch supermarket chain, and Tesco, a British chain, both operate central distribution centers (DCs) to serve their stores in the Czech Republic, Hungary, and Poland. Carrefour, the French hypermarket chain, distributes to fifty stores in southeastern Brazil from a DC in Sao Paulo. Procurement of perishable products such as fresh fruits and vegetables and dairy products, which used to be largely local, has become regional and even, in some cases, global. Centralization increases scale economies and efficiency, although transportation costs typically increase (Reardon and Timmer 2007; Reardon, Timmer, and Berdegué 2004).

The second pillar is moving from relying on spot markets, such as traditional wholesale markets and brokers, to wholesalers and logistics firms, which are specialized for product categories and dedicated to meeting the needs of modern food retailers. Hortifruti was established to procure the fresh produce for the major supermarket chain in Central America. Freshmark serves a similar function for Shoprite, the largest supermarket chain in Africa. At the same time, the retailers require these dedicated wholesalers and their suppliers to adopt best-practices distribution and logistics processes. These practices include electronic interchanges replacing paper transactions. Physical improvements in how, especially fresh, products are harvested, shipped, and stored are required, with a continuous cold (refrigerated) chain from the grower/shipper to the retail store. These changes have improved both efficiency and product quality (Reardon, Timmer, and Berdegué 2004; Reardon and Timmer 2007).

The third pillar involves establishing longer-term contractual relations with "preferred suppliers," usually via the dedicated wholesalers. This practice is an example of "vertical coordination," which brings many of the benefits of vertical integration via acquisition and merger without the costs and management problems. A food processor or producer is "listed" as a preferred supplier. The contract usually contains incentives for the supplier to stay with the buyer and to make the investments in equipment and processes to meet the particular requirements of the retailer. If a supplier does not meet the retailer's expectation, they can be "delisted," losing a major customer. Xincheng Foods acts as the primary produce wholesaler for the two largest food retail chains in China. Xincheng leased some 1,000 hectares (about 2,500 acres) of prime farm land, hired farm workers, invested in tractors, drip irrigation, and greenhouses to supply high-quality produce to the supermarkets and to the export market, Xincheng also contracted with some 4,500 small farmers for additional production (Hu et al. 2004; Reardon and Timmer 2007).

The final element of modernizing the supply chain is the implementation of private quality and food safety standards by the retailers that its suppliers must meet. The regulation of food safety and quality has not been a primary concern for the governments in developing countries. Even if rules and regulations are in place, the monitoring and enforcement are usually missing. The private standards substitute for the absence of government regulation and also serve several other important purposes. The safety of the food supply should be a government responsibility, but in its absence large food retailers need to consider both their liability and public reputation.

Private standards also harmonize the product and delivery attributes amongst partners in the supply chain, which improves efficiency and reduces transaction costs. The food retailers can also use their private quality and safety standards as a means of differentiating themselves from the competition. Global food retailers can lower costs by applying the same standards across countries. Carrefour started to apply the same quality certification to numerous items globally, for example (Reardon and Berdegué 2002). Finally, though, the food retailers need sufficient market power to impose their standards and suppliers capable of actually meeting them (Reardon and Timmer 2007).

Implications for Farmers and Agricultural Development

The global spread of modern food retailing is bringing more change to the agricultural sector in many developing countries than decades of government programs, projects by non-governmental organizations (NGOs), and international development assistance. The procurement requirements of modern food retailers offer both opportunities and challenges for agricultural producers. Becoming a supplier to a supermarket chain can open the door to a market that is growing in terms of volume, value added, and diversity. Producers can move from supplying a local market to one that is regional, national, and even international.

To supply a large domestic food retail chain increasingly requires producers to meet the same standards of efficiency, quality, reliability, and food safety necessary to export to international markets. To fulfill these requirements, though, requires improvements in production techniques and substantial investments in everything from information technology to modern packing houses with cooling units. Food retailing is a low-margin business typified in general by a high level of price competition. These pressures mean retailers are pushing their suppliers to lower product and transaction costs. Not surprisingly, supermarket procurement becomes increasingly dominated by the most capable farmers and firms, which are normally the larger operations (Reardon and Timmer 2007).

Small farmers with limited assets are largely being excluded from the supermarket supply chain because they lack the knowledge or capital to make the necessary changes and investments. To understand the reasons more fully, we must simply review supermarket procurement strategy and requirements. Above all, supermarkets require consistent, reliable supplies of a standardized quality. In comparison to traditional markets, supermarkets demand: (1) a higher, consistent quality that satisfies food safety standards, (2) a reliable supply of large volumes, (3) modernized logistics practices, such as truck transportation and chilled storage, (4) strict delivery conditions in terms of grading, packaging, labeling, timing, and so on, (5) a high level of efficiency resulting in low prices and transaction costs, and (6) advanced management and information technology systems (Neven and Reardon 2003).

Suppliers typically do not receive payment from supermarkets immediately upon delivery, which is what small farmers are used to in traditional marketing channels. As supermarkets become established in a country, they shift from store-level delivery to centralized distribution centers, from traditional brokers and wholesalers to dedicated wholesalers and a system of preferred suppliers, and impose their own private quality and safety standards, rather than rely on government ones (Weatherspoon and Katjiuongua 2003). Economists would argue that an essential reason that small producers are being excluded is the high transaction costs and transaction risk (Dorward et al. 2004). It is costly to deal with many small suppliers rather than a few large consolidated ones. Moreover, there is greater risk they will not deliver products with the reliability and consistency required.

The institutional innovations required to link small producers into the supermarket supply chain are likely to be the most essential element for their participation. These institutions must be arranged to reduce substantially the high transaction costs and risks associated with sourcing products from small farmers. Contract farming, also referred to as out-grower schemes, and cooperatives, farmer associations, and other forms of farmer-controlled enterprises have been increasingly seen as a potential way to improve the inputs and technical support available to small farmers, as well as expanding their marketing opportunities (Coulter et al. 1999). They might also serve to lower transaction costs and risks, particularly if the contracting is with a farmer cooperative or association.

In contract farming, private agribusiness companies establish a contractual arrangement with individual farmers for a specific quantity and quality of product at specified terms. The contract frequently includes the provision of inputs, such as seed and fertilizer, as well as technical and even financial support. There are some clear benefits and also some problems with contract farming and out-grower arrangements. Farmers may fail to make delivery or default on the credit repayment, and supervisory and transaction costs with many small producers can be very high (Coulter et al. 1999). The greater risks and costs have led to the exclusion of small farmers.

Current farmer-owned enterprises are different from the state-controlled cooperatives of the past. The latter were usually unresponsive to farmer needs and generally performed poorly. The new cooperatives perform best with small, cohesive groups of farmers and when directly linked with an agribusiness enterprise buying their production. They are more likely to succeed when the functions are kept relatively simple and focused and when they concentrate on higher-value products rather than low-value staples. The successful ones are also more likely to have been built upon already existing farmer organizations and have a clear member-driven agenda. The link with agribusiness and other private-sector market intermediaries is critical to ensuring there is a viable market (Coulter et al. 1999). These characteristics suggest such cooperatives deserve careful consideration as an institutional structure for integrating small farmers into the supermarket supply chain.

Farmer cooperatives can work well in combination with contract farming. Group liability for credit repayment reduces the risk of default, and transaction costs are reduced by the scale economies. The governments of developing countries and donors can provide an enabling setting for successful outgrower schemes and farmer-owned enterprises, particularly in terms of the appropriate laws and regulations. Government agencies and NGOs can promote farmer cooperatives, especially those that develop contractual links to a supermarket procurement channel and other expanded market opportunities. This promotional role requires that the government agencies and NGOs develop good working relations with both the farmer groups and agribusinesses. A high priority needs to be placed on improving the business and technical skills of the groups (Coulter et al. 1999). The most viable institutional structure will depend on the particular situation and participants involved. As Haggblade, Hazell, and Reardon (2002) stressed, flexibility is important to be able to adjust to changing circumstances.

The history of agriculture in the developed economies of countries such as the United States offers an important lesson. Increasing labor productivity in the agricultural sector is essential to improving the incomes of farmers. However, as productivity rises, fewer farmers and agricultural workers are needed. In 1900, 40 percent of the US population lived and worked on farms; now only 2 percent do, and somewhat over 100,000 large farms account for the majority of agricultural output (Offutt and Gunderson 2005; USDA NASS 2007). US agricultural policy has tried to ease the effects of this transformation with limited success.

In the final analysis, as the number of farms shrinks in developing countries, in no small part because of the spread of modern food retailing, hundreds of millions of people will transition to employment in other sectors of the economy over time. It is fortunate that modern food retailing is expanding most rapidly in countries that have been experiencing robust economic growth, such as China. Therefore, their economies are in a better position to handle the large migration out of agriculture and rural areas. However, strong government policies and programs are necessary to help provide these people with the education and skills to find jobs in other sectors. Efforts are also needed to encourage private businesses to help create more off-farm job opportunities in rural areas.

11

Market Making in the Personal Computer Industry

Jason Dedrick and Kenneth L. Kraemer

Introduction

Since the mid-1980s, personal computer makers have been steadily changing from manufacturers to market makers. Leading PC makers once designed and built their own PCs and sold them through a mix of direct and mostly indirect distribution channels.[1] PCs were built to forecast, and fluctuating demand led to alternating periods of costly inventory build-up and product shortages. Given the rapid depreciation and obsolescence of PCs and their components, and the common practice of price protection given to retailers, this production and distribution model was very costly to PC manufacturers.

This model was severely disrupted in the 1990s by the rise of direct sales specialists Dell and Gateway. By selling directly to the customer and building only products to order, these companies were able to reduce inventory and introduce new products without needing months to clear out old inventory in the channel. Dell's rapid growth and superior financial performance, in particular, put enormous pressure on the rest of the industry, eventually driving some competitors out of the market and forcing others to revamp their distribution channels and supply chains. While different models were applied over the years, PC makers moved to selling directly to the customer or to working closely with retailers to match supply and demand through sophisticated marketing, forecasting and supply-chain management. A key element has been the use of the Internet as a distribution channel and information technology more generally to streamline processes within the firm and across the supply chain.

The impacts are greatest in the USA, where direct sales increased from less than a quarter to over one half of the market between 1995 and 2005. The direct channel is especially important in serving the commercial market,[2] where PC makers offer a variety of services together with hardware to support IT departments in organizations. In the indirect channel, aimed at the consumer market, sales shifted from dealers and specialist stores to larger consumer electronics and office retailers, such as Best Buy and Office Depot, who work closely with PC makers to shape and efficiently fulfill market demand.

The US pattern contrasts with other markets. Worldwide the indirect channel accounts for two-thirds of sales, and the dealer/reseller segment is larger than retail. Retail exhibits many different local patterns as a result of local consumer preferences, government regulations, and differences in historical evolution. This local complexity makes it difficult for branded PC makers to become global market makers. Instead, branded PC makers such as Dell, HP, Acer, Sony, and Toshiba are forced to adjust their distribution models to fit local markets. Internet sales, in particular, are constrained by consumer preferences and by the quality of IT and delivery infrastructure (Kraemer et al. 2006).

In some country markets, domestic competitors maintain extensive dealer networks (for example, NEC, Toshiba and Fujitsu in Japan, Samsung in Korea, and Lenovo in China). Elsewhere, local retailers developed their own store brand PCs, or collaborated with local companies to act as market makers (for example, Germany, Brazil). In many markets, "white-box"[3] PCs make up a large share of the market. In these markets, small local shops build PCs for individual customers or small businesses. However, while there is a great deal of variation, the global trend is also toward more direct sales and toward large electronics retailers taking market share away from specialist dealers and resellers.

Although PC makers have become market makers, retailing PCs to commercial customers and consumers, the PC industry offers a different and interesting twist on the "market-makers" theme. In other industries, retailers used their relationship with the final customer to gain leverage over brand-name manufacturers. They also developed store brands, essentially coordinating the manufacturing process, even though they did not own any factories themselves. In the PC industry, major branded manufacturers became market makers in their own right, primarily by selling directly to the final customer, and also in collaboration with major retailers. PC makers perform market-making activities such as targeting markets, defining products, capturing customers, organizing efficient supply chains, and integrating hardware, software, services, and content to deliver new user experiences. Meanwhile, some retailers have developed "store" brands, but most have either lacked the ability to compete directly with brand-name vendors, or decided it is not profitable to try to do so.

Evolution of the PC Industry

Historically, computer companies were vertically integrated, handling all aspects of manufacturing and distribution. The introduction of the PC, which was a modular product whose architecture was open, changed the industry into horizontal industry segments, each of which specialized in different aspects from microprocessors to components and peripherals to PC systems to operating systems and applications to distribution (see Figure 11.1). PC companies designed and assembled modular systems from components and software developed by outside suppliers. These systems were distributed through a variety of channels, including wholesalers, corporate resellers, department stores, electronics superstores, specialty retailers, and the vendors' own direct sales force. The connection between the PC maker and the final customer was often weak (via advertising and marketing) or non-existent. This market diversity made it difficult to match supply and demand, leading to a build-up of inventory that was costly, given the rapid depreciation of the product.

In the mid-1990s, a major shift began in the US market toward direct sales of PCs, led by Dell and Gateway. By selling directly to the end customer, the PC maker was able to respond to demand and also to shape the demand to match available supply (for example, by using telesales staff to promote or offer discounts on products in stock). The direct model also cut out the distributor and retailer, thereby eliminating two layers of inventory, avoiding costly price protection guarantees to retailers, and allowing new products to be brought to market without clearing old inventory out of the channel (see Figure 11.2). The direct model put the PC maker in the role of "market maker," with control over pricing and branding and the ability to bundle a variety of products and services to the customer.

In the US market, the direct model came to dominate the corporate market, as a result of the success of Dell and the shift to greater use of direct sales by Compaq, HP, and IBM. The direct model was augmented by e-commerce, as

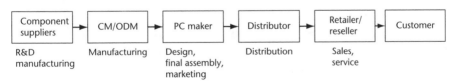

Figure 11.1. Indirect distribution

Note: CM = contract manufacturer; ODM = original design manufacturer. (ODMs are mostly Taiwanese firms that provide manufacturing and design services. Over 80% of notebook PCs are now manufactured by ODMs. CMs provide manufacturing services to a broad array of electronics firms.)

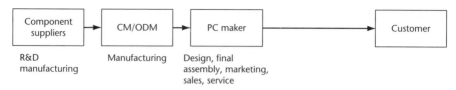

Figure 11.2. Direct distribution

customers could easily compare, configure, and buy PCs online from the PC vendor, or place the order by phone. In the consumer market, while many customers began to buy direct, many still preferred shopping in a physical store. However, the retail market for PCs changed. Whereas the indirect channel dominated with 76 percent of PC shipments in 1995, direct sales accounted for nearly 55 percent of all PC shipments by 2005 (see Table 11.1).

Market-Making Models in the US PC Market

Many variations of market making are used in the direct and indirect models, with different companies choosing different mixes of the two. Four such variations in the US PC market are shown in Table 11.2 and are described here.

1. In the *traditional channel* third-party intermediaries supply branded PCs to business and consumer end users. These intermediaries may be distributors, value-added resellers (VARs), systems integrators (SI), or large merchandisers (for example, department stores, large electronic stores, or large discount stores). In addition, distributors supply branded PCs to the many specialty

Table 11.1. US PC shipment share by channel, 1995–2005 (% of total units)

Channel	1995	2000	2005
Direct[a]	23.79	41.70	54.46
Direct inbound	16.02	22.31	17.31
Direct outbound	7.77	12.67	24.76
Internet direct	0.00	6.72	12.39
Indirect[b]	76.21	58.30	45.54
Retail	29.76	24.05	21.36
Dealer/VAR/SI	37.32	29.77	19.85
Other	9.13	4.48	4.33

[a] *Direct sales include*: (1) sales by customer-initiated inbound calls, (2) sales by a feet-on-the-street sales force, and sales by vendor-initiated outbound calls, (3) sales made strictly online directly by the end user with no human interaction from the vendor.

[b] *Indirect sales* are those sold through a distributor, aggregator, system integrator, value-added reseller, mass merchant, or retailer, including vendor-owned retail stores.

Source: IDC (2006).

Table 11.2. Comparison of market-making models in US PC market

Characteristics	Indirect traditional channel	Retail collaboration	Direct PC maker as retailer	Retailer as PC maker
Channel roles	Channel as intermediary between manufacturer and the market	Re-intermediation: PC maker and retailer collaborate in going to market	PC maker disintermediates the traditional channel and goes direct to the market	Retailer employs ODMs to make own-brand PC and go to market
Channel members	Channels include large distributors, VARs, SIs, and electronics/discount stores	Channels include large retailers	Channels include vendor sales force, inbound and outbound phone sales, online sales, vendor-owned stores	Retailer is the channel
Examples	HP and Apple: IngramMicro, TechData, Fry's, Costco, Best Buy, CompUSA	Gateway/eMachines, and HP with Best Buy, Costco, Office Depot	Dell: Web, telesales, experimenting with own stores Apple: Web, telesales, Apple Stores	Wal-Mart, CompUSA, white-box dealers, with ODMs/component suppliers
Market strength	Commercial and consumer markets	Consumer market	Commercial market	SME, consumer markets

retailers, especially smaller ones. Hewlett-Packard is the iconic illustration of this variation, but also involves retail collaboration (as described below). The traditional channel is the dominant variation used by vendors for many other related products (for example, components, peripherals, supplies) whose manufacturers are too small to deal directly with retailers.

2. *Retail collaboration* was created by eMachines, whose CEO was a former Best Buy executive. It is incorporated by Gateway, which bought eMachines and continues to sell both brands. It involves

- close collaboration between the PC maker and a few major retailers, using very sophisticated demand forecasting models to match supply and demand, and
- three-month product cycles with sell-out at the end of each cycle to avoid inventory build-up (Ralston, Kraemer, and Dedrick 2004).

The market-making mechanism is shared by the branded PC maker and the retailer, who cooperate in determining target markets, product design, and advertising programs. The number one consumer PC vendor, HP, reportedly developed a similar approach in the retail channel for consumer and SME (small and medium enterprise) markets.

3. The *PC maker as retailer* is the classic illustration of the pure direct-sales model that employs the vendor's own direct-sales force in the field, its own and third-party telesales, and Internet sales to reach customers. It proved especially attractive to the commercial market, but also caught on with consumers in the USA.

The direct model is associated mostly with Dell for the commercial market (Kraemer, Dedrick, and Yamashiro 2000) and originally with Gateway for the consumer market (Dedrick, Kraemer, and MacQuarie 2001). It also is used by other PC makers such as Apple and HP. In this case, the PC maker acts as retailer and market maker and disintermediates the channel. Direct sales have been expanded by Dell and Apple to include other electronics products such as big-screen TVs, printers, and portable music players. The most familiar forms of direct sales are telesales and online sales, but both Dell and HP have feet-on-the-street sales forces that deal with large corporate and multinational customers.

The vendor-owned store is a variation of PC maker as retailer. Although abandoned by Gateway (Dedrick, Kraemer, and MacQuarrie 2001), it is highly successful for Apple. Dell is currently experimenting with its own stores. Apple's success is partly due to the design and location of its stores, which are generally in high-end retail malls and districts and do not compete directly with electronics retailers who also sell its products. Also, retailers cannot obtain Macs or iPods elsewhere, unlike the Wintel standard PCs, and so they lack leverage with Apple.

4. *Retailer as PC maker*, the private-label brand was experimented with by WalMart, CompUSA, and other retailers (Tzeng and Shen 2005). It is also used by small local makers who long held a strong position in the small business market. Although declining, private labels still supply about 20 percent of the total PC market in the USA and more in developing countries. Retailers can easily source PCs from contract manufacturers and original design manufacturers, as well as from distributors who provide final assembly. There is no real barrier to selling private-label brands, yet, as of 2007, large retailers in the USA have not done much to develop their own PC or electronics brands, unlike retailers in clothing, tools, furniture, and other products.

Evolutionary patterns of PC makers as market makers

When these models are applied to the branded PC firms in the industry, it is clear that no single firm fits the direct and indirect models perfectly, although Dell and Gateway were closest to the direct model and HP and Compaq were closest to the indirect model in 2000. Since then, the companies have chosen

Table 11.3. US branded PC makers as market makers, percentage of shipments by channel, 1995–2005 (%)

Vendor	Indirect				Direct			
	Retail		Value-added reseller/system integrator		Vendor-direct sales force and telesales		Pure Internet and third-party Internet	
	1995	2005	1995	2005	1995	2005	2000[a]	2005
Apple	36	39	53	13	11	43	7	4
Dell	0	0	0	6	100	67	15	27
Gateway	0	67	1	3	99	25	8	5
HP	20	51	80	21	0	24	2	5
Compaq[b]	34	-	58	—	8	—	2	—
IBM	30	0	57	51	14	36	6	13

[a] Note that this column contains values for 2000 rather than 1995. The 1995 values for each vendor add to 100. Internet sales were 0% in 1995, the year that the Internet was opened for commerce.
[b] Compaq was acquired by HP in 2002. Its 2005 data are included in HP's results.
Source: IDC (2007).

different mixes of the two models, with their distinct patterns apparent when changes in channel use from 1995 to 2005 are compared (see Table 11.3).

The table shows the following:

- All PC makers listed moved to greater use of direct sales, but indirect sales still dominate for most companies.

- Although all PC makers moved to greater Internet sales by 2005, they comprise only 5 percent for Apple, Gateway, and HP with a greater share for IBM (13 percent) and Dell (27 percent). Gateway actually went down in its Internet share between 2000 and 2005.

- Dell, which was 100 percent direct in 1995, has remained largely direct, with 27 percent of sales from the Internet. Dell has begun to use value-added resellers and system integrators (6 percent), mainly for the SME market, where its own direct sales force is too expensive and which retail is not equipped to serve.

- Hewlett-Packard, which was 100 percent indirect in 1995, had become nearly 30 percent direct in 2005, partly by acquiring Compaq, which had established a direct sales business. The ratio of retail to VAR/SI shifted from 2:8 to 5:2.

- Apple moved the farthest toward engaging in its own market-making activity. Whereas only 18 percent of shipments were direct in 1995, 47 percent were direct by 2005. This change was largely through its own retail stores and telesales rather than the Internet.

297

- Gateway migrated from nearly 100 percent direct to mainly retail collaboration (67 percent), after its acquisition of eMachines and introduction of Gateway brand products into large retail outlets. In between 1995 and 2005, it opened and then closed over 200 of its own Gateway Country Stores in an unsuccessful market-making strategy. In 2007, Acer, Taiwan's largest PC maker, acquired Gateway, and made it a wholly owned subsidiary. In 2009, Acer relaunched Gateway-branded computers in online and retailer markets in and outside the USA.

These individual patterns illustrate that the industry remains dynamic, with each firm seeking relative advantage through different combinations of direct and indirect approaches to market making.

Market-Making Activities by PC Makers

Two fundamentally different market-making approaches to customer and supplier markets underlie the direct and indirect channels: supply–push in the indirect channel and demand–pull in the direct channel (see Table 11.4). Individual firm innovations also resulted in variations of these approaches.

Market making through the indirect channel historically followed a supply–push approach to both customer and supplier markets (see Table 11.4, column 2). For customer markets, vendors decided what products to offer to customers, developed sales targets for regions, supplied the products to distribution, and provided high margins to retailers and value-added resellers to push the product through their own advertising and sales campaigns. The vendor also provided umbrella advertising for its brand and products, and protected the channel through price protection to retailers who had to discount to move inventory.

For supplier markets, vendors developed quarterly sales forecasts, placed orders for systems/components to suppliers and required them to keep a 45–60 day inventory in the vendor's regional distribution centers to reduce the risk of stock-outs. Both vendor and supplier bore substantial inventory risk if the sales forecasts were high, because another 45–60 day inventory was already in the supply chain. In recent years, vendors have made significant improvements in supply-chain management, with techniques such as vendor-managed components inventory, supply hubs close to the assembly site, and interorganizational IT systems to coordinate with suppliers. As a result, indirect vendors have seen significant improvements in inventory turnover and other measures of supply-chain efficiency. Today, the indirect model continues to be an important way to reach markets, particularly consumer and

Table 11.4. Market-making activities in PC industry

Market-making activities	Indirect (Supply–push)	Direct (Demand–pull)
Customer markets		
Market and product definition	Hardware and software, e.g., HP/Compaq	Hardware, software, and a "relationship", e.g., Dell
Capture customers	Vendor provides the box; retailers and resellers offer "value beyond the box": touch & feel, additional software, services	Vendor offers custom box and relationship through vendor direct sales force, inbound and outbound call centers
	Vendor develops brand; retailers do advertising	Vendor develops brand, makes sales calls to capture customers
		Develops customized website, offers PC services to lock in customers
Incentives and risk	Incentives for channel partners, but vendor takes inventory risk	Vendor and suppliers bear risk; no retail
	Collaborative variation involves shared risk by retailer and vendor	
Demand management	Only what is in inventory. Retailers can push products with advertising and sales	Can match demand and supply; can shape demand
Supplier markets		
Product management	Vendor designs product, procures key components, manages supply chain	Vendor designs product, procures key components, does final assembly, manages logistics and distribution centers
Outsourcing	Development, manufacturing, assembly, logistics, distribution, support	Development, manufacturing, support
IT-based supply-chain management	Vendor supply–push; IT critical for supply-chain management	Customer demand–pull; IT critical for demand signals & supply chain mgt.

SME markets, and in developing countries without adequate information and transportation infrastructure to support direct sales.

The collaborative variation on indirect market making emerged as a response to problems with the indirect channel in managing demand and controlling inventory between the PC maker and end customer. By making quarterly commitments to sell predefined quantities, the retailer takes the market risk. In turn, the PC maker is able to incorporate the latest components into new designs each quarter in order to have a fresh supply of new products. The quarterly commitments enable the PC maker to provide accurate forecasts of demand so there is no inventory in the supply chain. These commitments also enable better forecasting of long-term demand by the PC maker, which in turn gives them greater price leverage with the original design manufacturers (ODMs) and suppliers who can see the potential volume of business.

In addition, the PC maker is able to provide umbrella marketing for its retail partners and to mount joint advertising campaigns to promote sell-through of all products with the retailers. For example, eMachine's collaborative model, which focused on market making with large electronics retailers, was also adopted by Gateway when it acquired the firm. A similar approach has been taken by HP for its HP and Compaq brand PCs, which are the biggest sellers by far in the US retail market. As will be seen below, the collaborative model was emulated outside the USA by the German PC maker Medion, which collaborated with the very large supermarket chains and mass retailers in Europe.

In contrast to the supply–push approach, the direct model involves a demand–pull approach to market making (see Table 11.4). For customer markets, vendors promote customization (build to order), standardization (download of corporate standard software to all PCs), and low cost, especially to commercial customers (business, government, education) to attract their business. Vendors take orders through their own direct sales force, call centers, or the Internet, giving vendors direct understanding of customer demand and the ability to detect new market trends early. The direct relationship also enables the vendor to up-sell customers by offering related products at low cost (computer plus printer, monitor, training and service), sell components that are in inventory by offering discounts, and shape demand by offering newer technologies at the same price as current ones. Vendors develop advertising to build brand image, promote specific products, and drive customers to their websites and call centers. A substantial direct sales force and "executive centers" are also used to promote large commercial contracts. For example, Dell has executive centers located at manufacturing plants whose purpose is to sell customers on the Dell model and Dell's execution of it through briefings, an in-plant tour, and an informal lunch or reception with Dell executives and staff (Dell interview 2000).

Commercial contracts usually involve thousands and frequently tens of thousands of PCs to be delivered over several years, which have major implications for supplier markets. Vendors are able to forecast demand better, plan production, and negotiate prices with suppliers based on known demand. Because the PCs are built to the customer's order and delivered direct as a complete package, there is no inventory in distribution. Inventory in the supply chain can be reduced through IT, supply-chain management, and factory systems. And, because the vendor controls final assembly and logistics, it can better ensure product quality and timely delivery, even when parts of a complete system (for example, monitors or peripherals) are shipped direct to the customer from suppliers' factories.

The result is a brand image of low cost, customization, and advanced technology, a package that helped propel Dell to be the industry leader for commercial markets, and, for a while, Gateway to be a leader for direct sales to consumer markets. Dell's success forced other major PC makers to emulate its market-making strategy by developing direct capabilities. Although Dell retains the lead on most performance measures, emulation and process innovation by other vendors have resulted in the performance gap being closed.

Market making by others

A special feature of the PC industry is that technical standards are set by key component and software suppliers, who engage in market-making activities to promote their own brand and products, and who both cooperate with and compete with the PC makers.

Intel develops reference designs for PCs based on each new processor and chip set that it introduces. These standard designs reduce the ability of branded firms to differentiate based on technical architecture, while also making it easier for non-brand firms (white-box makers) to compete with the branded firms by simply following the standard. Intel also provides technical assistance (engineering, training, testing services) to the white-box makers, which are mostly small and medium-sized firms without engineering staffs (Tzeng and Lang 2003; R. Chan 2005; Yeo 2006). Intel cooperates with the branded PC firms by providing funds for its "Intel Inside" co-branded labeling, marketing, and advertising, but also has its own marketing and advertising programs to promote the Intel brand. These activities are designed to increase Intel's market power and to keep the branded PC makers in line, while cooperating with them in joint marketing efforts.

Intel is not alone. Microsoft also funds co-branded marketing and advertising for PC makers as well as manufacturers of non-PC devices that run on its operating systems (for example, phones and PDAs). Its own advertising for Windows products promotes retail sales of its operating systems, but also helps drive sales of new PCs to take advantage of the capabilities of its software.

These activities are a double edged sword from a market-making perspective. The Wintel standard helped to make the PC market through standardization of hardware and software interfaces and greater interoperability of PCs, which is increasingly important in a globally interconnected world. Branding and advertising programs also increased the overall demand for computing through greater public awareness and stimulation of demand. However, these programs also reinforced the monopoly power of Intel and Microsoft, enabling them to keep prices high and to punish PC makers who strayed from the standard (for example, using AMD (advanced micro devices) chips or promoting open source software) by supporting their competitors (retailers, white-box makers). We would argue that Intel and Microsoft could have a greater effect on demand simply by cutting their prices, enabling vendors to reach more customers, particularly in big emerging markets such as China, India, Brazil, and Mexico.[4]

Impacts of Market Making on Customers and Suppliers

The impacts of market making by PC makers and others have been largely positive for customers while quite mixed for suppliers.

Customers

Consumers are offered a richer variety of purchasing options thanks to the innovation in market making by the PC industry. They can shop and buy online, or window shop online and buy in a vendor's retail store, or choose from a number of physical retail outlets. The ability of PC makers and retailers to eliminate excess inventory also means lower prices and fresher products with the most recent technologies. Consumers also benefit from more product information and the ability to compare prices online, even if they shop in person. However, consumers now have fewer choices of retail PC brands, as a result of mergers (HP–Compaq, Gateway–eMachines, Lenovo–IBM), and the exit of brands from the US market, such as AST, Packard Bell, and Acer (which is just returning to the US market with their purchase of Gateway, as well as their own branded products). HP (including its Compaq brand) controls over half of the in-store retail PC market, with only Gateway, Sony, and Toshiba as major competitors in the USA. Yet, given the rapid introduction of new products and ever lower prices, it is hard to argue that consumers are suffering from this consolidation.

Commercial customers reap all these consumer advantages and more. With build-to-order procurement and systems that download corporate approved software and system images and the ability to migrate to newer technologies that come along for the platform, large firms can more easily manage PC resources from procurement to disposition. Furthermore, they achieve greater standardization of platforms. Small and midsize businesses (SMBs) can acquire installation and maintenance services through channel partners (VARs and SIs) or through white-box makers as well as from their vendors.

Suppliers

The PC makers' market-making activities that led to industry consolidation also increased their market power over their ODM/CM contractors and the entire supply chain. It impacted on the industry structure, the way firms must do business, the roles they perform, and their prices and profits.

INDUSTRY STRUCTURE

The branded PC makers reduced the number of suppliers they do business with, resulting in a two-tier supplier structure of very large and midsize-to-small firms. Although they use fewer contractors and engage in long-term relationships with them, the PC makers still shift contracts for specific products amongst suppliers based on cost, quality, or unique capabilities (Dedrick and Kraemer 2006).

DOING BUSINESS

PC makers have adopted just-in-time supply hubs and vendor-owned inventory to reduce inventory costs. Contract manufacturers are pushed to provide direct shipment services. In some cases, the PC maker never takes physical possession of the product, which is built by outside suppliers and shipped directly to the end customer or retailer. The exception is build-to-order assembly, which Dell and others keep inside their own factories (Kraemer, Dedrick, and Yamashiro 2000). However, IBM–Lenovo outsourced build-to-order production in the USA and Europe, and Apple did the same in the USA, so there appears to be no real barrier to complete outsourcing of manufacturing.

SUPPLIER ROLES

As PC makers have shifted their focus from manufacturing to retailing/market making, their suppliers have taken on new roles. ODMs, mostly Taiwanese companies who design and manufacture PCs for all of the major PC vendors, now:

- do new product development, especially for notebook PCs;
- provide warranty and repair services in some cases.

As these suppliers gained capabilities, the PC makers were able to concentrate on marketing, branding, product management, and supply-chain coordination.

The production model pioneered by the PC industry has been adopted to varying degrees in other parts of the electronics industry as well. Contract manufacturers and ODMs have taken over more manufacturing and parts of the design process, especially for lower-end and more mature products. Typically, contract manufacturers have specialized in efficient production, logistics, and related services for a wide range of products such as printers, network equipment, iPods, and video games. But for some products, such as cell phones, joint development with ODMs is becoming more common. However, the outsourced manufacturing and development approach is little used by Japanese and Korean firms, who are still much more vertically integrated than US firms.

PRICES AND PROFITS

The biggest impact of market making on suppliers, for both the direct and the indirect model, is the constant pressure from PC makers to cut costs to meet industry competition. Dell's efficient direct model enabled it to lower prices. Other vendors had to match prices by greater use of outsourcing and continual pressure on suppliers to cut costs. Vendors force the ODMs to compete with one another for business and expect quarterly cost reductions of 5–7 percent.[5] Suppliers go along with these practices in the hopes that lower prices will grow the market and enable them to gain economies of scale. Low profits, on the order of 1–2 percent, led some ODMs to integrate forward and to develop their own brand products, while others moved upstream to produce components and subassemblies. The result for the PC industry is a continual increase in the number of units sold, but only a modest increase in sales revenue, and a continual decline in profits for both PC makers and suppliers. The exceptions are Microsoft and Intel, who continue to enjoy rich margins, leading PC makers and suppliers to complain that they are killing themselves to make money for Microsoft and Intel.

The Global Picture

Outside the USA, the market-making picture is quite different. The direct sales model for PCs has been successful only in some markets. For example, Dell's market share is 35 percent in the USA, but only 18 percent worldwide (IDC 2006). Comparison of the US and worldwide trends shows that there is growing use of the direct model generally, but that the indirect model still dominates outside the USA (Table 11.5).[6] Moreover, the rest of the world tends

Table 11.5. Worldwide PC shipment share by channel, 1995–2005 (% of total units)

Channel	1995	2000	2005
Direct[a]	21.70	27.90	33.70
Direct inbound	9.58	11.65	9.50
Direct outbound	12.12	12.80	18.86
Internet direct	0.00	3.45	5.34
Indirect[b]	78.30	72.10	66.30
Retail	24.11	29.80	28.60
Dealer/VAR/SI	49.22	39.68	35.39
Other	4.97	2.62	2.31

[a] Direct sales include: (1) sales by customer-initiated inbound calls, (2) sales by a feet-on-the-street sales force, and sales by vendor-initiated outbound calls, (3) sales made strictly online directly by the end user with no human interaction from the vendor.
[b] Indirect sales are those sold through a distributor, aggregator, system integrator, value-added reseller, mass merchant, or retailer, including vendor-owned retail stores.
Source: IDC (2006).

Table 11.6. Non-US PC makers as retailers, percentage of shipments by model, 1995–2005 (%)

Vendor	Indirect model				Direct model			
	Retail		Value-added reseller/System integrator		Vendor-direct sales force and telesales		Pure Internet and third-party Internet	
	1995	2005	1995	2005	1995	2005	2000	2005
Lenovo	—	1	—	56	—	37	—	6
Acer	31	3	67	96	3	0	10	0
Fujitsu	—	10	—	64	—	23	5	3
Sony	—	49	—	33	—	5	10	13
Toshiba	56	—	44	-	0	—	2	—

Source: IDC (2007).

to use dealers, VARs, or system integrators more than retailers, regardless of region (see Appendix).

This broad pattern for the leading non-US PC makers is also illustrated in the evolution of individual firms from 1995 to 2005 (see Table 11.6). Four of the five leading Asian brands (Acer, Fujitsu, Lenovo, and Toshiba) use VAR/SI over retail. Sony uses retail, including its own Sony Style stores, over VAR/SI and shows increasing use of the Internet. As with US firms, the leading non-US vendors use different mixes of direct and indirect strategies for their markets, though still mainly indirect.

The VAR/system integrator channel dominates outside the United States because most countries do not have the large nationwide retailers, as in the USA (as illustrated in earlier chapters), or national distribution networks. Moreover, neither commercial customers nor consumers are accustomed to buying by phone or over the Internet (Kraemer et al. 2006). As a result, local retail models differ amongst countries. We label this difference generally "retailer as PC maker." Some countries, such as Japan, use traditional two-tier channels, with local retailers dominating, as illustrated by the "electronics district" in major Japanese cities (for example, Akihabara in Tokyo). Others with strong domestic PC brands (such as NEC and Fujitsu in Japan, Samsung in Korea, and Lenovo in China) are marked by vendor-dominated nationwide networks of dealers who carry only those brands. In Brazil, local brands are sold in supermarkets and other non-traditional retail outlets. In Europe, the German company Medion decided to leverage the already established but unexploited mass-market retailer chains, such as food retailers, supermarkets, and discounters (for example, Aldi, Carrefour, and Metro) to sell PCs to consumers—a model similar to eMachines (Ordanini, Kraemer and Dedrick 2006). In many developing countries, small white-box makers have up to half the market. They buy assembled notebooks from the ODMs, assemble desktops themselves, and install PCs for consumers and small businesses.

These differences suggest multiple models in different places rather than an emerging global model for PC or consumer electronics retailing. Market making for PCs is almost always local and must be done through local distribution networks. The need for localization is also a reason why many vendors or their contract manufacturers must keep some local final assembly capabilities, and/or very sophisticated supply-chain and logistics systems. Because other markets are much less PC-centric than the USA and more focused on wireless technologies and games (for example, Japan, Korea, China), the power of mobile service providers and interactive game services is greater. In their case, the focus is on the service rather than the sale of the hardware *per se*.

Under these circumstances, the branded PC and consumer electronics makers or retailers in the USA face significant hurdles if they are to become truly global market makers. Moreover, it is in the interest of the core technology standard setters such as Intel to limit the market power of any would-be global market maker. Standards issues become even thornier on a global level. Governments and local actors become involved, and often different standards prevail in different countries. While the Wintel standard became a *de facto* global standard, there are, and will be, multiple standards for 3G cell phones, DVDs, wireless networking, and many other technologies. As we move into the next phase of the PC and consumer electronics industries, we may see more fragmentation of market making rather than more standardization, with the fragmentation aided by governments and technology alliances amongst competing groups of companies.

Future Trends in Market Making

Systems integration

The trend that is most likely to redefine significantly the PC and consumer electronics industries, and the nature of market making in those industries, is the proliferation of technologies with the potential to be interconnected in the "digital home." Consumers no longer buy PCs, TVs, cameras, or audio systems as separate items with separate functions. Instead, they store digital photos on PCs, download music from PCs to iPods, save TV shows on PCs, and play movies on portable DVD players. And now they are listening to music and playing games on cell phones. The challenge is getting these technologies to work together, which has proved to be a big hurdle for consumers, retailers, and technology companies.

Convergence

Partly because of the systems integration hurdle and also because of competing visions, the PC-centric orientation of the PC industry is being challenged by network-centric and PC-independent visions. The network-centric idea is that user applications and content will be stored on the Internet and accessible from anywhere with a variety of devices such as an MP3 player, PDA, phone, or PC—but the PC will no longer be central. The PC-independent vision is that the functionality of a PC will be built into some consumer electronic devices such as TVs, set-top boxes, and DVRs (for example, Tivo) and consumers will no longer require a media center PC. It is unclear which of these visions (or some other) will hold sway in the future, but it is likely that the PC will play a significant role in convergence.

Apple's music service illustrates such convergence. What is being sold is an entertainment ecosystem rather than just an MP3 product. Apple integrated an independent device (the iPod) with the PC (Mac or Wintel). The iTunes software provides the capability to download songs stored on the network (the Internet-based iTMS), to manage a music library, to play songs, and to transfer them to the iPod. Apple needed to keep tight control over the hardware, software, and electronic commerce components in order to make a market for digital music. HP tried to do the same with digital photos, but it had to be more open in allowing interconnection with competing camera, PC, and printer brands. Apple is trying to extend the iPod success with the iPhone, which adds communication capabilities and phone carriers to the ecosystem.

Technology integration and new services

For retailers, the issue is providing customers with the help they need to get the technologies to work together. The integration challenge creates new opportunities in market making. Firms that can make the disparate technologies work for consumers will have a new role as market makers. Attempts to do so include Best Buy's Geek Squads (Krazit 2006) or Circuit City's Firedog service, which make house calls to get balky systems to work, and Apple's in-store experts, who will show customers how to use the products they sell. Given that the digital home incorporates products from multiple computer and electronics companies, retailers are in a good position to be market makers if they can develop the needed expertise. Sensing this situation as an opportunity, the distributor Ingram Micro is developing a new business based on providing support to these emerging digital home integrators.

Standards

At the technology end, the big issue is standards. Here the problem is that companies need to establish standards for products to work together, but some hope to capture monopoly profits by having their own standards adopted. Also, no one wants to cede power and profits to a future Microsoft or Intel. The result is often years of delay in introducing technologies, or a profusion of standards that do not work together in the home. In the PC industry, Microsoft and Intel set the standards, and everyone else (except Apple) went along. In the digital home era, everyone from Microsoft and Intel to Sony, Toshiba, Nokia, Cisco, and even Yahoo! and Google are all trying to set standards. PC makers who do not create technologies are left in the position of lining up on one standard or another, or supporting multiple standards, and hoping to be right. Retailers are in the same position, as no retailer has the market power to determine standards by its own choice of what to carry.

The choice of vision

It is likely, therefore, that future market making will include PC-centric, network-centric, and PC-independent visions, perhaps with a mix of these visions for individual firms. While market making in the PC industry was historically focused on the commercial market, which led the consumer market in adopting new technologies, now it is the consumer market that leads. This dramatically changes the nature of market making, as individual consumers can have very different motivations from corporate IT departments. Consumers care about style, ease of use, convenience, and service and do not get enjoyment or job security from getting technologies to work together. Thus, the future of market making will be driven more by those who understand the customer and less by those who create the technology.[7]

APPENDIX

Channel shares of PC shipments
by world regions

Table 11.A1. Asia Pacific PC shipment share by channel, 1995–2005
(% of total units)

Channel	1995	2000	2005
Direct	25.77	16.40	16.60
Direct inbound	0.56	1.32	2.33
Direct outbound	25.21	13.19	12.89
Internet direct	0.00	1.89	1.38
Indirect	74.23	83.60	83.40
Retail	13.64	30.18	32.61
Dealer/VAR/SI	60.16	52.43	49.97
Other	0.43	0.99	0.82

Source: IDC (2006).

Table 11.A2. Latin America PC shipment share by channel, 1995–2005
(% of total units)

Channel	1995	2000	2005
Direct	20.85	28.32	40.43
Direct inbound	3.39	4.57	5.95
Direct outbound	17.46	22.21	32.93
Internet direct	0.00	1.54	1.55
Indirect	79.15	71.68	59.57
Retail	8.01	23.59	18.95
Dealer/VAR/SI	65.60	45.11	38.64
Other	5.54	2.98	1.98

Source: IDC (2006).

Table 11.A3. Western Europe PC shipment share by channel, 1995–2005 (% of total units)

Channel	1995	2000	2005
Direct	17.12	16.74	22.48
Direct inbound	10.27	9.00	10.03
Direct outbound	6.85	6.66	10.36
Internet direct	0.00	1.08	2.09
Indirect	82.88	83.26	77.52
Retail	22.80	32.60	34.47
Dealer/VAR/SI	58.39	48.45	40.38
Other	1.69	2.21	2.67

Source: IDC (2006).

Table 11.A4. Central/Eastern Europe PC shipment share by channel, 1995–2005 (% of total units)

Channel	1995	2000	2005
Direct	20.61	23.60	21.21
Direct inbound	0.37	0.41	0.40
Direct outbound	20.24	22.99	19.64
Internet direct	0.00	0.20	1.17
Indirect	79.39	76.40	78.79
Retail	12.29	31.25	33.69
Dealer/VAR/SI	67.05	45.08	45.07
Other	0.05	0.07	0.03

Source: IDC (2006).

Table 11.A5. Middle East/Africa PC shipment share by channel, 1995–2005 (% of total units)

Channel	1995	2000	2005
Direct	26.23	25.61	29.05
Direct inbound	1.04	1.69	0.42
Direct outbound	25.19	23.06	28.16
Internet direct	0.00	0.86	0.47
Indirect	73.77	74.39	70.95
Retail	6.27	8.50	21.01
Dealer/VAR/SI	67.50	63.41	49.82
Other	0.00	2.48	0.12

Source: IDC (2006).

Notes

Introduction

1. The latest information about the global spread of shopping centers can be found at the website of the International Council of Shopping Centers: www.icsc.org/index.php.
2. The monumental works by the late Alfred D. Chandler, Jr (1962, 1977, 1990) bear vivid testimony to the accuracy of this statement that large manufacturers were driving the US and European economies.
3. Recently Nelson Lichtenstein also titled his book on Wal-Mart *The Retail Revolution: How Wal-Mart Created a Brave New World of Business* (2009). Though the book is certainly one of the best studies on Wal-Mart, it is also narrowly focused on a single firm, and so misses most of what we describe here as the main characteristics of the retail revolution.
4. Since we have not dedicated a distinct chapter to the issues of consumption, we address it here in rather more detail than the first four trends, which are each dealt with extensively in various chapters of this volume. A major part of this section is drawn from Hamilton and Fels (2010).
5. Sears and Kmart merged in 2004 into Sears Holding Corporation. Federated and May Department Stores merged in 2005.
6. For a good review of these arguments, see Ailawadi (2001).
7. Morris Tabaksblat, the CEO of Unilever, describes this fundamental change in marketing in the following way: "The maker can no longer make the consumer do what he decides...The era of 'push selling' is definitely over. We are now well and truly in the era of 'pull marketing.'...The question is no longer, 'What can we sell the consumer?' but 'What learning can we draw from the consumer in terms of his or her needs and then how can we help satisfy those needs?'" (G. E. Morris 1997).
8. Cortada (2004) emphasizes that "No segment of the American economy has changed so much because of information technology than [*sic*] retail, with the possible exception of the Trucking Industry" (p. 258). Also: "Other factors also played a part—such as globalization and national economic conditions, to mention two obvious ones—but other than in banking, one would be hard pressed to find an industry influenced so profoundly by one family of technologies" (p. 272).
9. The US figure is an estimate, because the official figures for the retail industry do not include non-employer firms. The number of non-employer firms engaged in retailing is reported separately, but the number of persons working in such firms is only an estimate. At the same time, this number certainly does not represent more than

15% of all retailing employment in the USA, while it is as high as 45% in Spain and over 60% in Italy.

10. This analysis suggests that occupational categories should no longer be thought of in national terms, but rather as global divisions of labor. If we use commodity-chain or value-chain analysis, we should see that product creation, manufacture, distribution, and sale are truly global in character. For instance, Harvey Molotch's book *Where Stuff Comes From* (2003) allows us see how product design has become a highly professionalized occupation that is quite distinct from other occupations relating to manufacturing, marketing, and sales—all of which in one form or another can be outsourced.

Chapter 1

1. The main reason that the productionist bias is less recognized is that it squares better with the common-sense view of the economy. The equilibrium bias is often criticized as being too "artificial," an accusation that has little theoretical merit, but is easy to accept intuitively. The productionist perspective, on the other hand, seems a natural way to define the economy as being about satisfying human "material" needs or increasing wealth. When criticized at all, this is typically done from the "consumerist" perspective, which misses yet again the crucial importance of market making for the organization of the economy.

2. Theories that suffer from equilibrium bias typically see the firm as a "production function." This creates theoretical problems (see, e.g., Mirowski 1989) for the discussion of how the marginalist theorists of the first half of the twentieth century struggled with the notion of production. But, in principle, production becomes a problem only insofar as it is externally determined.

3. Indeed, a typical reaction of so many theories suffering from the productionist bias is to see "distribution" as a realm that can be organized, just like production, on the engineering principles of efficiency.

4. We will spend more time discussing the productionist than the equilibrium bias, because we see this volume as primarily countering the productionist viewpoint. Throughout the volume, we attempt to establish the importance of market making by retailers—i.e., by the type of economic actor that, not being involved in pro-duction in any major sense, was also the most ignored and misunderstood by productionist theories. These theories have been developed mostly in fields of "applied economics," from industrial organization and development (industriali-zation) policy, to organization studies and business history. If we are successful in completing this task, we believe that we will have set a firm foundation from which to counter the equilibrium bias of mainstream economics. This later task would include putting market-making activities and their institutional outcomes squarely in the center of economic theory, and is clearly beyond the scope of our current discussion.

5. Throughout this chapter we use generic terms buying and selling to denote market activities in general, instead of more specific terms such as retailing and marketing.

Market making, then, refers to creating institutions—i.e., markets—in which the activities of buying and selling take place.

6. In the years following the Napoleonic Wars, the chartered companies of European powers (e.g., the British East Indian Company) lost their hold of international trade to aggressive and rapidly expanding merchant enterprises that organized far-flung networks of firms and that linked into other networks of firms organized by ethnic and local traders. For nineteenth-century British trading companies, see Chapman (1992) and Jones (1996, 2000); for their links with Chinese business networks in China, see Hao (1986), in South East Asia, see Suehiro (1989); for their links to Indian merchant networks, see Markovits (2000, 2008); for their links with local merchants in Latin America, see Orlove (1997).

7. There are several reasons for the increasing popularity of the productionist perspective, including: the religious, and especially Puritan distrust of consumption, selling, and profit; the fascination with the technological sophistication and transformative effects of the new industrial enterprise; the role that manufacturers and infrastructure (transportation, communication networks, power supply, etc.) developers played in the rise of the modern state, its administrative and military capacities; the degree to which engineers, scientists, and industrialists developed into influential interest groups; general misunderstanding of markets and the market economy; and so on. We cannot address fully this powerful and pervasive current of thought in this volume, but are hoping to demonstrate its detrimental effect on the understanding of market making and market makers.

8. Some early examples of this work have been collected by Chandler and Daems (1980). For Chandler's legacy and the influence of his work on later scholarship, see the special issue of *Business History Review* (82/2 (Summer 2008)) devoted to this topic.

9. Spulber (1998) assumes a static economy that can be divided into roles. Our conception views intermediation as leading to dramatic shifts in the overall organization of economies.

10. Clower and Howitt (1996: 24) also provide a more formal definition of market making as: "The organization by income-seeking agents of specialized trading arrangements that offer (for an implicit or explicit price) other potential agent-traders convenient facilities for acquiring desired commodities in exchange for other commodities on terms that are specified by the organizer of the market facility."

11. The idea of market making, as defined here, is obviously broader than a narrow notion of product marketing, yet it is more precise than many broad definitions of marketing that refer to a firm's generalized orientation toward the market and its trading partners. Above all, however, the notion of market *making* emphasizes the activities of making and shaping the market, not just operating in the externally defined markets.

12. In most lists of the largest companies (e.g., Forbes) factory-less brand-name merchandisers are typically listed among the manufacturers and not among the retailers. They are, in fact, a type of modern market maker that specializes in designing, promoting, and creating a market for brand-named products, without actually making those products themselves.

13. The misunderstanding of the retailer's role, or even of the market-making activity in general, is pervasive in the productionist literature. At best, retailers are seen as efficient distributors of goods and services, but their expenses on advertising, their pricing and promotional strategies, and other market-making activities are seen as unnecessary and wasteful from the perspective of the society. The identification of the true price with the manufacturer-suggested price has been the basis of the retail (resale) price-maintenance policies, ubiquitous in the developed economies of the mid-twentieth century. Interestingly, one of the main objections in the post-Depression era was not that retailers inflate prices so much as that they sell below the recommended price, thus undermining the manufacturer's goodwill and reputation of its products, and leading to harmful competition.

14. The exceptions to this, as shown in Petrovic (Chapter 3 this volume), were a few very large retail department stores, mail-order operators, and early chain stores, such as A&P and Woolworth's. Most of them, however, grew large by integrating wholesaling and retailing functions, and sometimes operating as wholesalers for other retailers, too.

15. These two well-known strategies of consumer markets pricing are distinguished by the intensity and frequency of price promotions. The "hi–low" strategy offers frequent and deep price promotions (markdowns, rebates, coupons) over a substantial part of merchandise assortment, while maintaining high prices on non-sale items; the everyday low price strategy is the opposite.

16. Store brands (private brands/labels, own brands) refer to goods that are either directly manufactured or, more commonly, branded by the retailer. Such brands have been on the rise, in terms of both the proportion of sales and brand recognition and status, across many categories of products, especially non-durables. A single mass retailer, such as Wal-Mart, Tesco, or Carrefour, can easily manage thousands of products under several dozen store brands. Other mass retailers, such as Ikea, offer only store brand merchandise.

Chapter 2

1. It is bad enough that automobile lights come in a bewildering array of sizes and bases that make it necessary to shop for new auto lamps with the car's owners' manual in hand.

2. Public safety in an elevator remains a cause of concern to many, but such fears have been dramatically reduced by yearly safety inspections required by local building codes. The inspection report is normally dated and posted in each elevator, near the phone for calls to help if the elevator should stall.

3. National BankAmericard, Inc. (NBI) was spun out of the Bank of America in 1970 to run the BankAmericard Program. This provided issuing banks with a share of ownership of the network.

4. See Cardweb.com, Inc.

5. If a manufacturer refused to provide a different code format desired by a second retailer, the manufacturer feared that it might be forced to comply by the Federal

Trade Commission under the doctrine of equal treatment. Manufacturers would not want to have separate product inventories for two retailers, each carrying special codes.

6. Chicago population figures from http://condor.depaul.edu/history/chicago/population.html (accessed June 19, 2008).

7. The service was originally called Parcels Post, implying parcels by post. Now it is called simply Parcel Post.

8. While most containers are 40 feet long, 8 feet wide, and 8.5 feet high, container ship capacity is always reported in TEUs: a single 40-foot container is counted as 2 TEUs. Reflecting McLean's background in trucking, the container is sized for highway trucking and is wide and high enough for loading with standard forklifts.

9. Information about the ship can be found on the Maersk website, and a picture and specification of the fully loaded ship at a container terminal is available at www.kgomez.com/mystery/maersk.php (accessed June 19, 2008).

10. Mass merchants faced an immediate question of where cost savings were going to come from if they were to adopt bar codes and scanning, and who would put the bar codes on all the items. There was also the problem of scanning large and heavy objects that would not easily pass the scanner at the checkout. There were only simple hand-held scanners in the mid-1980s, and their operation was not as simple as the wands used today in most retail stores to supplement the laser scanners at the checkouts. The pen-like scanning laser diode devices similar to hand-held laser pointers required the clerk to sweep the pen across the bar codes to get a reading. But in 1987, patent number 4,694,182, called *Hand held bar code reader with modulated laser diode and detector*, was issued to P. Guy Howard of Spectra–Physics, Inc. of San Jose, CA, which would lead, in time, to the ubiquitous hand-held scanners in every department store and home center today. With these new scanners, clerks need only aim the red laser light onto the code for it to be read. Generally a beep equals a successful read. The eventual availability of hand-held scanners allowed each electronic register in a department store to use the bar-code systems easily to check out customer purchases, and helped drive the adoption of bar codes and scanners in all retail stores.

11. Wikipedia has a brief but comprehensive discussion of EDI and a listing of the most common formats ("Electronic Data Interchange," http://en.wikipedia.org/wiki/Electronic_Data_Interchange#Standards (accessed June 19, 2008)).

Chapter 3

1. Hypermarkets, and hard discounters, which have often been hailed as specifically European contributions to modern retail formats, are, in fact, not only adaptations of the US formats, but were, in most cases, a result of direct emulation of the latter by European entrepreneurs who traveled to the USA after the war (Colla 2003; Schröter 2004).

2. While nominally many European retailers have a much higher international presence, this presence is almost always regional. For instance, out of the twenty-five

non-US-based firms on the top forty list, only six have operations in the USA, and only eight, including the two leading Japanese firms, Seven and I, and Aeon, have operations in Japan.

3. This means that several other retail globalization issues, such as the retailers' role in making "supplier markets," the organizational structure and evolution of retail firms, as well as the influence of the retail evolution on overall economic development, will have to be ignored or addressed only in passing.

4. Department stores were the core form of organizing the new world of goods of industrial capitalism, compared not only to smaller specialty stores, but also to often grand, yet temporary formats such as world fairs and universal expositions (Greenhalgh 1988; Rydell 1989). For their relation with the broader culture of collecting, displaying, and organizing objects in the nineteenth century, see Harris (1990) and Bennett (1995).

5. Parisian Bon Marché, the most famous department store of the nineteenth century, distributed 1.5 million catalogs for the winter season of 1894, 260,000 of these abroad (Crossick and Jaumain 1999). A few years later, US mail-order giants Sears and Montgomery Ward, which served as "department stores" for rural America, would distribute between three million and four million catalogs several times a year, each containing more than a thousand pages (Hoge 1988).

6. At the same time, the smaller size of German department stores and the availability of financing led to the early development of department store chains, an issue that US department stores faced only in the 1930s (Coles 1999).

7. As Nystrom (1930) points out, there were a number of wholesale–retail partnerships in the mid-nineteenth century that could be qualified as chain-store organizations. A. T. Stewart had a controlling interest in several stores outside New York, and in the early 1860s opened fully owned branches in Boston, Philadelphia, and Chicago. A&P, however, was probably the first retailer to open several stores of similar design and manage them in a centralized manner.

8. Other notable chains that started before 1910 included Kroger (1882) and National Tea Company (1899) grocery stores, Kress (1896), Kresge (1897), and W. T. Grant's (1906) variety stores, United Cigar Stores (1900), and J. C. Penney stores (1902).

9. Those numbers, impressive as they are, do not fully capture the extent of the chain revolution, since many firms that legally figured as independents in the 1929 Census, were in fact linked to chain-type organizations through franchising and other agreements. The number should perhaps be increased by at least 20,000–30,000 franchised car dealerships and by up to 40,000 franchised gasoline stations, which do not count as chain stores according to the Census definition. At the same time, the Census number obviously includes a large proportion of very small chains that consisted of only two or three stores, and thus does not give us a very good indicator of the extent of market integration through replication.

10. See, for instance, the survey reported by Beckman and Nolan (1938), in which "sanitary and clean" and "good store appearance" were not only low on the list of reasons for buying from chain stores, but were also cited with the same frequency as the reasons to buy from independents.

11. In 1920, there were two car makers and two oil companies among the biggest ten US companies, and in 1930 the number of oil companies on the list increased to four (Collins and Preston 1961). Today, the same two car makers, Ford and General Motors, are still on the list, and the number of oil companies decreased to three, but only because another two major gas station operators, BP and Royal Dutch/Shell, are not domestic companies. Out of the current top twenty largest global companies (by revenues), eleven are either car makers or oil refiners, and an additional two, Wal-Mart and Carrefour, are chain-store operators.

12. Early DuPont company studies of supermarket shopping, conducted between 1945 and 1959, attracted a lot of attention by showing that up to two-thirds of actual purchases are unplanned, and that this percentage increased over time (Clover 1950; Shaffer 1960). Of course, the more the supermarket's merchandise assortment got standardized, the more customers could shop without a specific purchase plan in mind. Trying to account for this fact, Stern (1962) distinguished between four different types of impulse buying, from "reminder buying" to "pure impulse buying."

13. There were more than 3,000 such stores in 1929, exhibiting a standardized and patented layout of a single U-shaped path through the store, which exposed customers to the entire merchandise assortment arranged on wall shelves and in cases. However, Piggly Wiggly stores were small and stocked with a very basic line of grocery merchandise; hence they could not benefit from the effect of self-service either on consumers' shopping behavior or on operating costs.

14. The only exception to this could be the development of e-retailing in the late 1990s. However important this new format might become in the future, the focus on the globalization of established American retail formats in this chapter means that online retailing will be mentioned only in passing. For a more detailed discussion within this volume, see Chapter 5 by Kotha and Basu. The rest of this section builds on Petrovic and Hamilton (2006).

15. This famous phrase appears in George Marshall's speech at Harvard, on June 5, 1947, which signaled the beginning of the ERP (see, e.g., http://en.wikipedia.org/wiki/Marshall_Plan).

16. Early operators of European hypermarkets, as well as of somewhat similar Japanese "general superstores," consciously emulated operations of American supermarkets.

17. The same period witnessed a rapid international expansion of US automotive services, hotel/motel chains, car rentals, and other similar franchises that are not being covered in this survey. Individual companies' data in this section are derived from companies' annual reports and websites, unless indicated otherwise.

18. Several lists of the largest shopping centers are available, including the ones provided by Emil Pocock (2009) at Eastern Connecticut University, by Tom Van Riper (2007) for Forbes.com, and on Wikipedia. The claim here is based on Pocock's list; according to other lists, the number of Asian malls in the top ten would be seven or nine. The tenant composition was assessed from the shopping centers' websites.

Chapter 4

1. A report of the European Productivity Agency wrote in 1954: "When Europe is taken as a whole the tendency for self-service seems to be more an experiment than a development" (cited by Schröter 2005: 79).
2. Generally land-use policies in the UK are much more restrictive than in most other European countries, but this was typically not directed toward the discrimination of certain retail formats.
3. Thus hypermarkets are very similar to the supercenters of Wal-Mart in the United States (see below).
4. Looming in the background at that time were the successes of the extreme right-wing party the NPD at several state-level elections in 1966–7.
5. General exemptions existed for certain assortments, especially for furniture and DIY (do-it-yourself) products such as household repair suppliers.
6. Fears among the political establishment of petit bourgeoisie radicalism among dissatisfied small retailers might have been a reason for the introduction of social protectionist regulation in France, as a contemporary UK report (Hall 1971: 53) points out, referring explicitly to the Poujadist movement in France.
7. Retail price maintenance had already been abolished in 1945, subject to the possibility of ministerial exceptions. These exceptions were also abolished in 1973.
8. These analyses are to a large extent based on materials published by the companies in print or on the Internet. In addition, various press reports have been used.
9. On the history of Carrefour, see Lhermie (2003); see also Burt (1986), Dupuis, Choi, and Larke (2006), and Durand and Wrigley (2009).
10. The hypermarket has nearly the size of Wal-Mart's biggest supercenter at Crossgates Commons in Albany, which opened in May 2008. Its 259,650 square feet (24,100 square meters) are spread over two floors, while most European hypermarkets are completely at ground level.
11. Cora later became part of the Belgian Group Louis Delhaize.
12. Delhaize le Lion is not to be confused with its Belgian competitor Louis Delhaize.
13. Some of these stores were later converted to Gateway Superstores, which were later taken over by Asda, and thus are part of Wal-Mart today.
14. President Group was already in a partnership with Southland Inc. to manage over 800 7-Eleven stores in Taiwan.
15. The handover of another four hypermarkets in Slovakia to Tesco was barred by local authorities for monopoly reasons.
16. Because of a huge acquisition by Wal-Mart, it has now lost this position in China.
17. On the history of Aldi, see Brandes (2004); see also Wortmann (2004).
18. This description of the origins of the Aldi discount strategy is based on one of the very few public statements of Karl Albrecht in 1953, cited in Brandes (2004: 20–2).
19. Netto also acquired Carrefour's unsuccessful Danish Ed stores in 1995.
20. The concept is described on the US home page of Aldi (www.aldifoods.com), even though some of the features described here as typical for the Aldi discount concept can be found in all German—and many European—supermarkets: here customers

have to pay for shopping bags, there is no assistant to bag groceries, and there is a coin system for shopping carts, which have to be returned to the store by customers.

21. Aldi stores and supermarkets had frequently existed in a kind of symbiosis: consumers would combine the extremely low prices for basic foods at an Aldi store with the variety found in a nearby supermarket. Aldi and Edeka had several times engaged in joint property development.

22. Because two other department-store chains also merged the same year, when Karstadt acquired Hertie, the whole German department-store sector became consolidated into two groups.

23. A brief overview of the national varieties of different retail formats can be found in Zentes, Morschett, and Schramm-Klein (2007: 13–18).

24. www.metro.com.cn/kitchen_1.htm (accessed May 5, 2008).

25. Including Greece and Turkey.

26. On the history of Tesco, see especially Dawson, Larke, and Choi (2006).

27. In 2005, Tesco started operations of a store format (Homeplus) that sells only non-food products, mostly the same items available at Extra hypermarkets.

28. Metro's partner SHV also held a small share in these operations.

29. The large stores of the Spar group were taken over by Wal-Mart.

30. The store count underestimates the size of supermarket operations in the United States, since these stores are usually much larger—similar to British superstores—than those in other countries.

31. See n. 12 above.

32. The dimensions of retailers' embeddedness are further explored by Wrigley, Coe, and Currah (2005) and Tacconelli and Wrigley (2009).

33. On the rationalization of local grocery supply chains and their impact on local suppliers, see Senauer and Reardon, Chapter 10 this volume.

34. www.telegraph.co.uk (accessed Nov. 13, 2009).

35. Discount companies like Aldi do all their global sourcing of private-label non-food items via specialized import companies. Since discounters offer most non-food items only once or twice a year, they do not build up the know-how and organizational structures needed for direct sourcing.

36. At the same time, there is no cross-penetration between the three large European countries of modern retailing, the UK, France, and Germany—despite several attempts starting in the late 1960s and continuing to the mid-1990s. In these countries it has been impossible for foreign hypermarket chains to gain the size needed to achieve competitive buying power. Foreign hypermarket entries by the United States failed, too. Thus the success of Wal-Mart in the UK, where it bought Asda, one of the leading grocery retailers (with sufficient buying power of its own), has remained an exception, while its failure in Germany rather proves the rule.

37. It is difficult to make a general statement about cash and carry, another format not restricted by German retail regulations. The fact that Metro is concentrated in Europe is at least partially due to the fact that it was SHV, its former ally, that expanded into the emerging markets of Latin America and Asia.

Chapter 5

1. A survey commissioned by the American Booksellers' Association found that some 106 million adults purchased about 456.9 million books in any given quarter. The survey, which looked at book-buying habits of consumers during the calendar year 1994, revealed that six in ten American adults (60%) say they purchased at least one book in the last three months. Annually that corresponds to 1.8 billion books sold, an average of 17 books per book-buying consumer a year. The average amount paid for the three most recent books purchased by consumers in the previous thirty days was about $15.

2. With the growing popularity of Amazon.com, the issue is not whether companies in the traditional value chain will be dis-intermediated, but more about how incumbents such as Barnes & Noble and others could effectively leverage their physical assets and compete against Amazon.com.

3. These included computer hardware and software, consumer electronics, antiques and collectibles, books and comics, automotive, and miscellaneous (Cohen 2002).

4. According to eBay: "A merchant can open a PayPal account and begin accepting credit card payment within a few minutes. Merchants are approved instantly for a PayPal account, and do not need to provide a personal guaranty, acquire any specialized hardware, prepare an application, contact a payment gateway or encrypt customer data. Furthermore, PayPal charges lower transaction fees than most merchant accounts, and charges no setup fees and no recurring monthly fees" (eBay 2006: 5).

5. Although "off-eBay" penetration of PayPal represented only about 2% of retail ecommerce opportunity worldwide in 2005, the company was making concerted efforts in getting online retailers to accept payment through PayPal. For example, eBay signed up Apple's iTunes store (the largest legal music retail website in the world) to accept PayPal.

6. The benefit of using a store format is that it enables sellers to list their items for sale at lower insertion and final value fees than regular auction and fixed-price listing.

7. It should be noted that direct retailers with physical stores (e.g., L. L. Bean, Eddie Bauer) captured 52% of the Internet sales as early as 2003, and those without stores (e.g., Amazon) garnered 31%. This should not be a surprise, because the Internet represents an evolutionary technology (as opposed to a disruptive one) that helps direct retailers further to improve their efficiencies in reaching and interacting with customers, rather than just through mailing them catalogs.

Chapter 6

1. For an exception, see Spulber (1996, 1998).

2. For a related discussion of this literature, as well as an analysis of the rise of capitalism in East Asia, see Hamilton (2006).

3. For a more complete discussion of the transformation of US retailing after the Second World War, see Feenstra and Hamilton (2006) and Hamilton, Petrovic, and Feenstra (2006).

4. During the decades after the American occupation of Japan had ended, Japanese business groups grew at a pace much faster than Japan's rapidly growing economy. In addition to selling finished products, the general trading companies for the main business groups imported intermediate goods needed by firms within the group. However, in the 1960s, as the main *keiretsu* firms grew more proficient in securing their own inputs and marketing their own products, many in Japan began to worry that the trading companies would lose their central role. This decline in local business "led to a belief that the trading companies would gradually become less and less useful and would eventually die out, a belief popularized in the so-called 'demise theory'" (Kojima and Ozawa 1984: 13). This belief prompted most trading companies to internationalize their operations.

5. Constance Lever-Tracy (2000) argues that Japanese trading companies had only a limited role in the development of East Asian economies outside Japan. However, her argument misses the important contribution that the Japanese trading companies made to create competent suppliers in Taiwan and South Korea.

6. The Kuomintang government, however, did not help in this matter. The government banned the speaking of Japanese in public, a law that was in force after 1947. The mainland migrants to Taiwan, of course, viewed the Japanese with dislike and distrust. After all, they had fought a war against the Japan. Taiwanese residents, however, did not experience the Second World War in the same way. Although they were not without hard feelings toward the former colonizers, local Taiwanese could deal with the Japanese without animosity.

7. Among the top ten exports were two types of TVs, one type of radio, one type of integrated circuit for an unspecified final product, one type of Christmas tree lights and one type of mahogany plywood, as well as three types of clothing (acrylic sweaters, knit shirts, and trousers made from synthetic material) and one category of footwear (vinyl shoes), all for women and girls. The consumer electronic products were likely made in factories wholly or partially owned by Americans or Japanese, but the other products likely came from factories owned by Taiwanese.

8. It was not until 1990, however, that most multinational manufacturers withdrew from Taiwan (Chu and Amsden 2003: 37).

9. This number is, of course, sizable in its own right, especially as compared to Korea in the same period (Feenstra and Hamilton 2006: 268–72).

10. It is almost certain that the Tsai brothers owned other shoe companies in the region. At the time, the general pattern was to own multiple companies and thereby to be a part of multiple networks, instead of creating one big firm to integrate the operations vertically.

11. Nike's agreement with Pou Chen came after Nike had made a near disastrous attempt to contract production from Chinese firms in China. In the 1980s, Nike located a manufacturer in China to make a large portion of their shoes, but the effort failed because of poor-quality manufacturing and the lack of supporting suppliers. Then Nike returned its operation to Taiwan, and started to work with Pou Chen.

12. This chapter is drawn from a book on which we are currently working, entitled *Making Money: How the Asian Economy Works from an Asian Point of View*. We would like to thank the Rockefeller Foundation for supporting a portion of the research reported here. Also, an early version of this chapter appeared in Y. W. Chu (2010).

Chapter 7

1. For a full analysis of the changing nature of logistics, see Bonacich and Wilson (2008). This chapter draws on that analysis.
2. As explained in Chapter 9, Li & Fung is a Hong Kong-based trading company that arranges apparel manufacturing with a large number of retailers and brand-name merchandisers, including Wal-Mart, and with hundreds of apparel manufacturers. The *Wall Street Journal* reported on January 29, 2010 that Wal-Mart had signed a sourcing deal with the giant merchandise provider Li & Fung with the expectation that it would buy $2 billion worth of goods through Li & Fung in the first year of the deal.
3. Even though retailers order and arrange for transportation of goods, the retailer may not assume actual ownership of these goods until the final sell occurs. A number of suppliers in Taiwan explained to Hamilton that Wal-Mart required them to pay for storage of their goods until the actual sale took place, at which time Wal-Mart owned the product—i.e., at the moment of sale.
4. Ocean shipping also includes bulk shipping—not just containers. This includes things like lumber and big machinery, as well as automobiles, some of which are now containerized.
5. For statistics relating to US and China trade, see www.uschina.org/statistics/tradetable.html.
6. This was a phone conversation on July 1, 2004.
7. All Chinese citizens are classified, according to a household registration system, called the *hukou* system, as "rural" or "urban" permanent residents and are assigned rights and privileges accordingly. Rural migrants moving to a urban location are necessarily temporary migrants and cannot receive the "minimum protection" (*dibao*) in the form of social services that is available to people classified as urban residents (Chan 2009).
8. www.pbs.org.
9. http://moneycentral.msn.com/content/P82353.asp.
10. "Wal-Mart Suppliers Face Abuse Accusations," *Los Angeles Times*, Dec. 9, 2006, p. C4.

Chapter 8

1. A *Wall Street Journal* article focusing on Oracle, GM, Pepsi, and other US big firms suggests that the pendulum may now be swinging back to vertical integration (Worthen, Tuna, and Scheck 2009).
2. Countries with Flextronics industrial parks are Poland, Hungary (2), Mexico (2), Brazil, India, and China (2). See www.flextronics.com/about/pages/industrialparks.aspx.
3. At Celestica, for example, 40% of global capacity expansion was "organic" in nature.

4. According to the company's website, in 2008 Lear's net sales were $13.6 billion, employment was 71,000, the number of facilities was 210, and the number of countries was 36 (www.lear.com/jsp/common.jsp?page=al_co_companyoverview, accessed Jan. 15, 2010).

5. See www.lifung.com/eng/global/home.php (accessed Dec. 2, 2009).

6. See www.lifung.com/eng/business/responsible.php for more information (accessed Dec. 12, 2009).

7. The opportunity for electronic component distribution in Singapore and Malaysia stemmed from the lack of an adequate conduit to connect local chip assembly and test operations with the growing subassembly and product-level manufacturing that foreign firms were doing in the region. Offshore affiliates of both semiconductor and product-level firms had increased their Asian operations, and Uraco's new distribution arm helped to connect the dots.

8. www.mfgmkt.com (accessed Aug. 12, 2009).

9. In addition to computer-aided design (CAD) tools, capital equipment in these facilities included 86 electronic circuit board assembly lines using surface-mount technology (SMT), 250 plastic molding machines, 85 metal die-casting machines, 1,000 computer numerically controlled (CNC) drill and tap machines, and 30 multi-spindle high-speed coil winding machines.

10. This section is adapted from Sturgeon and Lee (2005).

Chapter 9

1. See also Malone (2002); Speer (2002); Just-style.com (2003); Kearney (2003); McGrath (2003); Nordås (2004).

2. www.nht.com.tw/en/about-2.htm.

3. The following information comes from Esquel's website, www.esquel.com/en/index.html.

4. Esquel's client list includes Banana Republic, Brooks Brothers, Hugo Boss, J. Crew, J. C. Penney, Marks and Spencer, Nike, Nordstom, Polo Ralph Lauren, and some fifteen other leading brands (www.esquel.com/en/index6.html).

5. Esquel's Gaoming factory complex (Guangdong Province) does the weaving, dyeing, and assembly. The firm's recently opened weaving mill occupies 29 acres, and is described as "China's most advanced woven fabric manufacturing facility," an environmentally friendly facility featuring "the textile industry's most advanced machinery and advanced computer control systems to reduce operational errors, ensure quality and shorten production time" (www.esquel.com/en/index7.html).

6. See www.vendormanagedinventory.com.

7. The following information comes from TAL's website, www.talgroup.com/eng/home.html.

8. The company was originally called South China, then—through a collaboration with Jardine Matheson—became the textile Alliance Group (TAL).

9. In addition to garments and footwear, Li & Fung export management includes furnishings, toys, stationery, home products, sporting goods, and travel goods.

10. Yue Yuen, the world's leading manufacturer of footwear, became a "strategic shareholder" in Luen Thai when it acquired a 9.9% stake in 2004; this firm is discussed below.

11. A second supply-chain city is being developed in Qing Yuan, also in Guangdong Province; in addition, Luen Thai maintains supply-chain centers in the USA and the Philippines (Luen Thai 2006).

12. Luen Thai's principal customers also include Polo Ralph Lauren, Limited Brands, Adidas, Dillard's, Nike, and Fast Retailing (Luen Thai 2006).

13. Yue Yuen Industrial Holdings is the principal source of Pou Chen's shoe production; as of June 2004, Pou Chen held 50.1% of the stock in Yue Yuen (www.yueyuen.com).

14. Yue Yuen's fiscal year ends on September 30.

15. China, Indonesia, and Vietnam together account for 90% of all athletic footwear production (Merk 2006).

16. I visited the Nike/Yue Yuen factory in Dongguan in September 2005, as a guest of Nike. The immaculate and ultra-modern activities center, newly opened, showed no signs of having yet been used; even the polished glass tables had no smudges or fingerprints.

17. Other clients include Polo Ralph Lauren, Kenneth Cole, Calvin Klein, and NBA Properties. Yue Yuen is the exclusive China licensee for Converse, Wolverine, and Hush Puppies (Xinhua 2007). About 60% of Yue Yuen's footwear production is for Nike, Reebok, and Adidas-Salomon (Merk 2003).

18. Based on its Interim Report for the first six months of FY 2007 (ending March 31), the company's growth trajectory appears to be continuing, despite rising wage pressures and the continuing cost of the petroleum-based imports that constitute a major part of the company's costs. Yue Yuen added 14 additional production lines, bringing its total to 387; its year-to-year production of shoes increased 15% (111 million pairs for the six-month period); and wholesale/retail sales grew by 37%, accounting for 8.0% of total revenues (in comparison with 5.4% for FY 2006) (Yue Yuen 2007c). On the other hand, on July 26, 2007, Credit Suisse initiated coverage on Yue Yuen with an "underperform" call because of what it regarded as the company's "decreasing exposure to the retail business sector," claiming that "Yue Yuen is actively considering spinning off its retail business arm in China" (Xinhua 2007).

19. The cost of the petrochemicals that comprise a significant portion of the raw materials used in making shoes increased 50–60% (Fong 2005).

20. In 2002, 28% of Yue Yuen's athletic shoe production was for Nike, yet it supplied only 15% of Nike's total demand (Merk 2006: 16).

21. Yue Yuen's net profit rate in 2002 (11.9%) was higher than Nike's (6.2%), Reebok's (2.9%), or Adidas's (3.4%) (Merk 2006: 17). The company has continued to post near double-digit profits (10.02% in 2006) (http://finance.google.com/finance?q=HKG:0551).

22. According to one frequently cited statistic, "if Wal-Mart were a country, it would be China's sixth-largest export market." Wal-Mart executives talk of doubling their purchases from Chinese suppliers (C. Chandler 2005).

23. Wal-Mart already has a supercenter in Shenzhen.
24. With the exception of Mexico and a few other developing economies, Wal-Mart has generally not fared well in securing significant market share; see C. Chandler (2005).

Chapter 10

1. See, e.g., Farina et al. (2005), for the case of dairy processing and retail in Argentina and Brazil.
2. The existence of these early supermarket chains serving a tiny niche market in some developing areas, e.g., in Puerto Rico, was noted as early as 1953 by Holden (1953) in the Holden–Galbraith study.

Chapter 11

1. Direct channels include telephone and Internet sales made directly by the manufacturer. Indirect sales involve sales to distributors and/or retailers.
2. The commercial market refers to enterprise, SMEs, governments, education, and other organizational segments, whereas the consumer market refers to households and individuals.
3. "White box" refers to generic PCs that carry the brand of the retailer or distributor rather than the manufacturer.
4. Although admittedly, many customers in those countries already pay close to zero for Windows, and for application software, given high piracy rates.
5. Numbers based on field interviews with ODMs and suppliers by the authors.
6. Indirect sales worldwide are over 66% of total sales; excluding the USA would make the figure much higher.
7. This research is supported by a grant from the Alfred P. Sloan Foundation to the Personal Computing Industry Center at The Paul Merage School of Business, University of California, Irvine. We gratefully acknowledge the International Data Corporation (IDC) for providing data for the study and Paul Gray for comments on the chapter.

References

Abaza, M. (2001). "Shopping Malls, Consumer Culture and the Reshaping of Public Space in Egypt," *Theory, Culture, and Society*, 18/5: 97–122.

Abernathy, F. H., Dunlop, J. T., Hammond, J. H., and Weil, D. (1999). *A Stitch in Time: Lean Retailing and the Transformation of Manufacturing: Lessons from the Apparel and Textile Industries*. New York: Oxford University Press.

Abolafia, M. Y. (1996). *Making Markets: Opportunism and Restraint on Wall Street*. Cambridge, MA: Harvard University Press.

Adams, H. (1973 [1918]). *The Education of Henry Adams*. Boston: Houghton Mifflin.

Adelman, M. A. (1966). *A & P: A Study in Price-Cost Behavior and Public Policy*. Cambridge, MA: Harvard University Press.

Ailawadi, K. (2001). "The Retail Power-Performance Conundrum: What Have We Learned?" *Journal of Retailing*, 77/3: 299–318.

Akinwande, A., Fuller, D., and Sodini, C. (2005). "Leading, Following or Cooked Goose: Explaining Innovation Successes and Failures in Taiwan's Electronics Industry," in S. Berger and R. Lester (eds), *Global Taiwan: Building Competitive Strengths in a New International Economy*. Armonk, NY: M. E. Sharpe.

Alexander, A., Shaw, G., and Curth, L. (2005). "Promoting Retail Innovation: Knowledge Flows during the Emergence of Self-Service and Supermarket Retailing in Britain," *Environment and Planning*, 37/5: 805–21.

Amazon.com (1998). *Annual Report*. http://phx.corporate-ir.net/phoenix.zhtml?c=97664&p=irol-reportsannual.

Armstrong, A., and Hagel, J. (1996). "The Real Value of On-line Communities," *Harvard Business Review* (May–June), 134–41.

Asian Food Marketing Association (2004). "Workshop Proposal: The Rise of Supermarkets—Improving Performance and Competitiveness in Agro-Food Systems," mimeo.

Bair, J. (2009) (ed.). *Frontiers of Commodity Chain Research*. Palo Alto, CA: Stanford University Press.

Baldwin, C. Y., and Clark, K. B. (2000). *Design Rules: The Power of Modularity*. Cambridge, MA: MIT Press.

Balsevich, F. (2005). "Essays on Producers' Participation, Access and Response to the Changing Nature of Dynamic Markets in Nicaragua and Costa Rica," unpublished doctoral dissertation, Michigan State University, East Lansing.

Balsevich, F., Berdegué, J. A., Flores, L., Mainville, D., and Reardon T. (2003). "Supermarkets and Produce Quality and Safety Standards in Latin America," *America Journal of Agricultural Economics*, 85/5: 1147–54.

Barboza, D. (2004). "In Roaring China, Sweaters Are West of Socks City," *New York Times*, Dec. 24.

Barger, H. (1955). *Distribution's Place in the American Economy since 1869*. Princeton: Princeton University Press.

Barth, G. (1980). *City People: The Rise of Modern City Culture in Nineteenth-Century America*. Oxford: Oxford University Press.

Batt, R., Doellgast, V., and Kwon, H. (2006). "Service Management and Employment Systems in US and Indian Call Centers," in S. Collins and L. Brainard (eds), *Brookings Trade Forum 2005: Offshoring White-collar Work—The Issues and Implications*. Washington: Brookings Institution.

Beckman, T., and Nolan, H. (1938). *The Chain Store Problem*. Columbus, OH: McGraw-Hill.

Bell, D. E., Lai, R., and Salmon, W. J. (2004). "Globalization of Retailing," in J. Quelch and R. Deshpande (eds), *The Global Market: Developing a Strategy to Manage across Borders*. San Francisco: Jossey-Bass, 288–312.

Bennett, T. (1995). *The Birth of the Museum*. London: Routledge.

Berekoven, L. (1986). *Geschichte des deutschen Einzelhandels*. Frankfurt am Main: Deutscher Fachverlag.

Berger, S. (2005). *How We Compete*. New York: Doubleday.

Bianco, A. (1997). "Virtual Bookstores Start to Get Real," *Business Week*, Oct. 27, pp. 146–7.

Bianco, A. (2006). *The Bully of Bentonville: How the High Cost of Wal-Mart's Everyday Low Prices is Hurting America*. New York: Currency/Doubleday.

Birchall, J. (2007). "An Onus on Retailers to Keep Hands Clean," *Financial Times*, Jan 15.

Bliss, P. (1960). "Schumpeter, the 'Big' Disturbance and Retailing," *Social Forces*, 39/1: 72–6.

Blonigen, B. A., and Ma, A. C. (2010). "Please Pass the Catch-up: The Relative Performance of Chinese and Foreign Firms in Chinese Exports," in R. C. Feenstra and S. J. Wei (eds), *China's Growing Role in World Trade*. Chicago: Chicago University Press.

Bluestone, B., Hanna, P., Kuhn, S., and Moore, L. (1981). *The Retail Revolution: Market Transformation, Investment, and Labor in the Modern Department Store*. Boston: Auburn House Publishing Company.

Bonacich, E. (2005). "Labor and the Global Logistics Revolution," in R. P. Appelbaum and W. I. Robinson (eds), *Critical Globalization Studies*. New York: Routledge, 359–68.

Bonacich, E., with Hardie, K. (2006). "Wal-Mart and the Logistics Revolution," in Nelson Lichtenstein (ed.), *Wal-Mart: The Face of Twenty-First Century Capitalism*. New York: New Press, 163–87.

Bonacich, E., and Luce, S. (2006). "China and the US Labor Movement," paper presented at the Annual Meeting of the American Sociological Association in Montreal.

Bonacich, E., and Wilson, J. B. (2005). "Hoisted by its own Petard: Organizing Wal-Mart's Logistics Workers," *New Labor Forum*, 14/2: 67–75.

Bonacich, E., and Wilson, J. B. (2006). "Global Production and Distribution: Wal-Mart's Global Logistics Empire with Special Reference to the China/Southern California Connection," in S. Brunn (ed.), *Wal-Mart World*. New York: Routledge, 227–41.

Bonacich, E., and Wilson, J. B. (2008). *Getting the Goods: Ports, Labor and the Logistics Revolution*. Ithaca, NY: Cornell University Press.

Bonaglia, F., Goldstein, A., and Mathews, J. (2007). "Accelerated Internationalization by Emerging Multinationals: The Case of the White Goods Sector," *Journal of World Business*, 42: 369–83.

Bowles, Samuel (1986). "The Production Process in a Competitive Economy: Walrasian, neo-Hobbesian, and Marxian Models," in L. Putterman (ed.), *The Economic Nature of the Firm: A Reader*. Cambridge: Cambridge University Press, 329–55.

Bradley, S. P., and Porter, K. A. (2000). "eBay, Inc. Case Study," *Journal of Interactive Marketing* (Autumn), 73–97.

Brandes, D. (2004). *Bare Essentials: The Aldi Way to Retail Success*. Frankfurt am Main: Campus.

Brinkley, J. (1992). "On Tape: A President Intrigued by a Scanner," *New York Times*, Feb. 13, sect. A.

Broehl, W. G., Jr (1968). *The International Basic Economy Corporation*. Washington: National Planning Association.

Brown, S. A. (1997). *Revolution at the Checkout Counter: The Explosion of the Bar Code*. Wertheim Publications in Industrial Relations. Cambridge, MA.: Harvard University Wertheim Publications Committee, distributed by Harvard University Press.

Bucklin, L. P. (1967). *Shopping Patterns in an Urban Area*. Berkeley and Los Angeles: University of California, Institute of Business and Economic Research.

Bucklin, L. P. (1972). *Competition and Evolution in the Distributive Trades*. Englewood Cliffs, NJ: Prentice Hall.

Burt, S. (1984). "Hypermarkets in France: Has the Loi Royer had any Effect?" *International Journal of Retail & Distribution Management*, 12/1: 16–19.

Burt, S. (1986). "The Carrefour Group: The First 25 Years," *International Journal of Retailing*, 1/3: 54–78.

Burt, S. (1994). "Carrefour: Internationalising Innovation," in P. J. McGoldrick (ed.), *Cases in Retail Management*. London: Pitman, 154–64.

Burt, S., Dawson, J., and Larke, R. (2006). "Royal Ahold," in J. Dawson, R. Larke, and M. Mukoyama (eds), *Strategic Issues in International Retailing: Concepts and Cases*. London: Routledge, 140–69.

Burt, S., Dawson, J., and Sparks L. (2004). "The International Divestment Activities of European Grocery Retailers," *European Management Journal*, 22/5: 483–92.

Burt, T. (2004). "Global Retailers Expand Markets," *Financial Times*, June 22, p. 15.

Business History Review (2008). "Special Issue on Alfred D. Chandler, Jr," 82/2: 203–319.

Business Times Online (1995). "Precision Engineering Group Uraco Plans Expansion in Jahor," July 14, p. 3, www.businesstimes.com.sg.

Business Times Online (1996a). "Uraco Aims to Boost Revenue to US$400m," Apr. 22, www.businesstimes.com.sg.

Business Times Online (1996b). "Uraco Tops Actives with 16.7m Shares Traded," Dec. 12, www.businesstimes.com.sg.

Business Times Online (1997). "Uraco Managing Director Quits: 3 Executives Replace Him," Jan. 23, www.businesstimes.com.sg.

Calder, L. G. (1999). *Financing the American Dream: A Cultural History of Consumer Credit*. Princeton: Princeton University Press.

Cao, N. (2005). "Different Structures in the Textile Industry's Supply Chain," *Peking University Luen Thai Center for Supply Chain System R&D Bulletin*, Apr. 30, trans., www.pkultc.com/englishindex.asp.

Chamberlin, E. H. (1962 [1933]). *The Theory of Monopolistic Competition: A Reorientation of the Theory of Value*. 8th edn. Cambridge, MA: Harvard University Press.

Chan, A. (2001). *China's Workers under Assault: The Exploitation of Labor in a Globalizing Economy*. Armonk, NY: M. E. Sharpe.

Chan, K. W. (2005). Associate Director, Hong Kong Christian Industrial Committee, interview, Sept. 15.

Chan, K. W. (2009). "From Made-in-USA to Made-in-China: Global Financial Crisis and Migrant Workers in China," unpublished manuscript.

Chan, R. (2005). "Intel in New Push for the Clone Notebook Market," *DigiTimes.com*. Dec. 9.

Chandler, A. D., Jr (1962). *Strategy and Structure: Chapters in the History of the American Industrial Enterprise*. Cambridge, MA: Harvard University Press.

Chandler, A. D., Jr (1977). *The Visible Hand*. Cambridge, MA: Harvard University Press.

Chandler, A. D., Jr (1990). *Scale and Scope: The Dynamics of Industrial Capitalism*. Cambridge, MA: Harvard University Press.

Chandler, A. D., Jr, and Daems, H. (1980). *Managerial Hierarchies: Comparative Perspectives on the Rise of the Modern Industrial Enterprise*. Cambridge, MA: Harvard University Press.

Chandler, C. (2005). "The Great Wal-Mart of China," *Fortune Magazine*, 151/15, July 25, www.fortune.com/fortune/print/0,15935,1081806,00.html.

Chang, C. C. (2005). "The Role of Retail Sector in Agro-food System," Chinese Taipei. Presentation at the Pacific Economic Cooperation Council's Pacific Food System Outlook 2005–6 Annual Meeting in Kun Ming, China, May 11–13.

Chapman, S. (1992). *Merchant Enterprise in Britain from the Industrial Revolution to World War I*. Cambridge: Cambridge University Press.

Cheng, L. L., and Sato Y. (1998). "The Bicycle Industries in Taiwan and Japan: A Preliminary Study toward Comparison between Taiwanese and Japanese Industrial Development," *Joint Research Program Series*, No. 124. Tokyo: Institute of Developing Economies.

Chessel, M.-E. (1999). "Training Sales Personnel in France between the Wars," in S. Jaumain and G. Crossick (eds), *Cathedrals of Consumption: The European Department Store 1850–1939*. Aldershot: Ashgate, 279–98.

Chu, W. W., and Amsden, A. (2003). *Chao yue hou jin fa zhan: Taiwan de chan ye sheng ji ce lue*. Taipei: Lian Jing.

Chu, Y. W. (2010) (ed.). *Chinese Capitalism: Historical Emergence and Political Implications*. London: Palgrave, Macmillan.

Chua, B. H. (2003). *Life Is Not Complete without Shopping: Consumption Culture in Singapore*. Singapore: Singapore University Press.

Clover, V. T. (1950). "Relative Importance of Impulse-Buying in Retail Stores," *Journal of Marketing*, 15/1: 66–70.

Clower, R., and Howitt, P. (1996). "Taking Markets Seriously: Groundwork for a Post Walrasian Macroeconomics," in David Colander (ed.), *Beyond Microfoundations: Post Walrasian Macroeconomics*. Cambridge: Cambridge University Press.

CNBC (2005). *The eBay Effect: Inside a World-Wide Obsession*, documentary, June 29.

Coase, R. (1937). "The Nature of the Firm," *Economica*, 4 (Nov.), 386–405.

Coggins, J., and Senauer, B. (1999). "Grocery Industry," in D. C. Mowery (ed.), *US Industry in 2000: Studies in Competitive Performance*. Washington: National Academy Press, 155–78.

Cohen, A. (2002). "Is this any Place to Run a Business?" *Fortune Small Business* (Nov.), 55–65.

Coles, T. (1999). "Department Stores as Retail Innovation in Germany: A Historical–Geographical Perspective on the Period 1870–1914," in S. Jaumain and G. Crossick (eds), *Cathedrals of Consumption: The European Department Store 1850–1939*. Aldershot: Ashgate, 72–96.

Colla, E. (2003). "France," in S. Howe (ed.), *Retailing in the European Union: Structures, Competition and Performance*. New York: Routledge, 23–55.

Collins, N., and Preston, L. E. (1961). "The Size Structure of the Largest Industrial Firms, 1909–1958," *American Economic Review*, 51/5: 986–1011.

Cortada, J. (2004). *The Digital Hand: How Computers Changed the Work of American Manufacturing, Transportation, and Retail Industries*. New York: Oxford University Press.

Coulter, J., Goodland, A., Tallontire, A., and Stringfellow, R. (1999). "Marrying Farmer Cooperation and Contract Farming Service Provision in Liberalizing Sub-Saharan Africa," *Natural Resources Perspectives*, No. 48, Overseas Development Institute (ODI), United Kingdom.

Crossick, G., and Jaumain, S. (1999). "The World of the Department Store: Distribution, Culture and Social Change," in S. Jaumain and G. Crossick (eds), *Cathedrals of Consumption: The European Department Store 1850–1939*. Aldershot: Ashgate, 1–45.

Cuesta, V. (2004). "Treinta años de hipermercados en España ¿Saturación o renovación?" *Distribución y Consumo* (Mar.–Apr.), 46–56.

Cunningham, E., Lynch, T., and Thun, E. (2005). "A Tale of Two Sectors: Diverging Paths in Taiwan's Automotive Industry," in S. Berger and R. Lester (eds), *Global Taiwan: Building Competitive Strengths in a New International Economy*. Armonk, NY: M. E. Sharpe.

Davis, H. B. O. (1985). *Electrical and Electronic Technologies: A Chronology of Events and Inventors from 1940 to 1980*. Metuchen, NJ: Scarecrow Press.

Davis, R. T. (1959). *The Changing Pattern of Europe's Grocery Trade: A Comparison of Seven Markets with the United States*. Palo Alto, CA: Stanford University Press.

Dawson, J. A. (1981). "Innovation Adoption in Food Retailing: The Example of Self-Service Methods," *Service Industries Review*, 1/2: 22–35.

Dawson, J., Larke, R., and Choi S. C. (2006). "Tesco: Transferring Marketing Success Factors Internationally," in: J. Dawson, R. Larke, and M. Mukoyama (eds), *Strategic Issues in International Retailing: Concepts and Cases*. London: Routledge, 170–95.

de Grazia, V. (2005). *Irresistible Empire: America's Advance through Twentieth-Century Europe*. Cambridge, MA: Harvard University Press.

Dedrick, J., and Kraemer, K. L. (1998). *Asia's Computer Challenge: Threat or Opportunity for the United States and the World?* New York: Oxford University Press.

Dedrick, J., and. Kraemer K. L. (2006). "Is Production Pulling Knowledge Work to China: A Study of the Notebook PC Industry," *IEEE Computer*, 39/7: 36–42.

Dedrick, J., Kraemer K. L., and MacQuarrie, B. (2001). "Gateway Computer: Using E-Commerce to Move beyond the Box and to Move More Boxes," working paper, Personal Computing Industry Center, The Paul Merage School of Business, Irvine, CA.

Delgado, C. L., Hopkins, J., and Kelly, V. A. (1998). "Agricultural Growth Linkages in Sub-Saharan Africa," research report no. 107, Washington: International Food Policy Research Institute.

Deloitte (2007). *2007 Global Powers of Retailing: The Search for Sustainable Growth.* New York: Deloitte, Touche, and Tohmatsu.

Deloitte (2009). *Feeling the Squeeze: Global Powers of Retailing 2009.* New York: Deloitte Development LLC.

Denis, C., McMorrow, K., and Röger, W. (2004). "An Analysis of EU and US Productivity Developments," *European Economy, Economic Papers*, 208 (July).

Dicke, T. S. (1992). *Franchising in America: The Development of a Business Method, 1840–1980.* Chapel Hill, NC: University of North Carolina Press.

Dicken, P., and Hassler, M. (2000). "Organizing the Indonesian Clothing Industry in the Global Economy: The Role of Business Networks," *Environment and Planning A*, 32/2: 263–80.

Dirven, M., and Faiguenbaum, S. (2003). "Dynamics of Santiago's Wholesale Market of Lo Valledor and its Forward and Backward Linkages," paper presented at the FAO technical workshop on "Globalization of the Food System: Impacts on Food Security and Nutrition," Oct. 8–10, Rome.

Dolan, C. and Humphrey, J. (2004). "Changing Governance Patterns in the Trade in Fresh Vegetables between Africa and the United Kingdom," *Environment and Planning A*, 36/3: 491–509.

Dorward, A., Kydd, J., Morrison, J., and Urey, I. (2004). "A Policy Agenda for Pro-Poor Agriculture Growth," *World Development*, 32/1: 73–89.

Dries, L., and Reardon, T. (2005). "Central and Eastern Europe: Impact of Food Retail Investments on the Food Chain," London: FAO Investment Center – EBRD Cooperation Program, Report Series No. 6, Feb.

Dries, L., Reardon T., and Swinnen J. (2004). "The Rapid Rise of Supermarkets in Central and Eastern Europe: Implications for the Agrifood Sector and Rural Development," *Development Policy Review*, 22/9: 525–56.

Dries, L. and Swinnen, J. F. M. (2003). "The Impact of Globalization and Vertical Integration in Agri-Food Processing On Local Suppliers: Evidence from the Polish Dairy Sector," paper presented at the FAO technical workshop on "Globalization of the Food System: Impacts on Food Security and Nutrition," Oct. 8–10, Rome.

DSN Retailing Today (2002). "40th Anniversary: Forty People and Events that have Shaped Mass Market Retailing," 41/15.

Du Ling (2003). "Taiwanese Investment in South Africa, Swaziland, and Lesotho: A Case Study by Ambassador Du Ling," statement by Representative Du Ling, Taipei

Liaison Office in the Republic of South Africa at the African–Asian Society, Balalaika Hotel, Sandton, June 12, www.roc-taiwan.org.za/press/20030909/2003090901.html.

Duan, C. P. (1992). *Taiwan zhan hou jing ji*. Taipei: Ren jian chu ban she.

Dunlop, J. T., and Rivkin, J. W. (1997). "Introduction," in S. A. Brown, *Revolution at the Checkout Counter*. Cambridge, MA: Harvard University Press, 1–38.

Dunn, W. S. (1962). "French Retailing and the Common Market," *Journal of Marketing*, 26/1: 19–22.

Dunning, J. H. (1979). "Explaining Changing Patterns of International Production: In Defense of the Eclectic Theory," *Oxford Bulletin of Economics and Statistics*, 41/4: 269–95.

Dunning, J. H. (2000). "The Eclectic Paradigm as an Envelope for Economic and Business Theories of MNE Activity," *International Business Review*, 9 (Spring), 163–90.

Dupuis, M., Choi, S. C., and Larke, R. (2006). "Carrefour Being Aware of the Domestic Market," in J. Dawson, R. Larke, and M. Mukoyama (eds), *Strategic Issues in International Retailing*, London: Routledge, 91–113.

Durand, C. and Wrigley, N. (2009). "Institutional and Economic Determinants of Transnational Retailer Expansion and Performance: A Comparative Analysis of Wal-Mart and Carrefour," *Environment and Planning A*, 41: 1534–55.

eBay (2006). *Annual Report*, http://investor.ebay.com/secfiling.cfm?filingid=950134-07-4291.

eBay (2007). *Quarterly Report, April 25, 2007*, http://files.shareholder.com/downloads/ebay/118201758x0x91268/649ccffe-1298-4bd0-ab53-1b33e9f9abd2/eBayInc-Q12007EarningsRelease.pdf.

The Economist (1997). "A Survey of Electronic Commerce," May 10, pp. 1–18.

The Economist (2005). "Meg and the Power of Many," June 9.

Economist Intelligence Unit (1983). *Japanese Overseas Investment*. London: Economist Intelligence Unit.

EHI Retail Institute (2007). *Handel aktuell. Ausgabe 2007/08. Struktur, Kennzahlen und Profile aus dem deutschen und internationalen Handel*. Cologne: EHI Retail Institute.

EHI Retail Institute (2008). *Retail Fact Book: Structures, Key Figures, and Profiles of the International Retail Trade Sector*. Cologne: EHI Retail Institute.

Emmet, B., and Jeuck, J. (1950). *Catalogues and Counters: A History of Sears, Roebuck and Company*. Chicago: University of Chicago Press.

Euromonitor (2002). *Retail Trade International*. London: Euromonitor plc.

European Comission (2009). *Europe's Digital Competitiveness Report: Main Achievements of the 2010 strategy, 2005–2009*. Brussels, Aug. 4, http://ec.europa.eu/information_society/eeurope/i2010/docs/annual_report/2009/com_2009_390_en.pdf (accessed Aug. 8, 2009).

Evans, D. S., and Schmalensee, R. (2005). *Paying with Plastic: The Digital Revolution in Buying and Borrowing*. 2nd edn. Cambridge, MA: MIT Press.

Evans, P. B., and Wurster, T. S. (1997). "Strategy and the New Economics of Information," *Harvard Business Review* (Sept.–Oct.), 70–83.

Farina, E. (2002). "Consolidation, Multinationalization and Competition in Brazil: Impacts on Horticulture and Dairy Products Systems," *Development Policy Review*, 20/4: 441–57.

Farina, E. M. M. Q., Gutman G. E., Lavarello, P. J., Nunes, R., and Reardon T. (2005). "Private and Public Milk Standards in Argentina and Brazil," *Food Policy*, 30/3: 302–15.

Feenstra, R. C. (1998). "Integration of Trade and Disintegration of Production in the Global Economy," *Journal of Economic Perspectives*, 12/4: 31–50.

Feenstra, R. C., and Hamilton G. G. (2006). *Emergent Economies, Divergent Paths: Economic Organization and International Trade in South Korea and Taiwan.* Cambridge: Cambridge University Press.

Feenstra, R. C., and Wei, S. J. (2010) (eds). *China's Growing Role in World Trade.* Chicago: Chicago University Press.

Fields, K. J. (1995). *Enterprise and the State in Korea and Taiwan.* Ithaca, NY: Cornell University Press.

Fishman, C. (2006). *The Wal-Mart Effect: How the World's Most Powerful Company Really Works—and how it's Transforming the American Economy.* New York: Penguin Press.

Flextronics (2003). *Corporate Fact Sheet Asia.* CD-ROM files. Singapore.

Fong, M. (2005). "Why Yuan Revaluation May Not Be a Cure-All," *Wall Streeet Journal.* Feb. 1, p. A11.

Food Institute (2007). *Food Industry Review, 2005 Edition,* Elmwood Park, NJ: Food Institute.

Forrester Research Inc. (2007). "US Retail eCommerce Forecast, 2006 to 2011," May 4.

Forrester Research Inc. (2010). "Forrester Forecast: Double-Digit Growth for Online Retail in the US and Western Europe," Business Wire Mar. 8; ProQuest Newsstand, ProQuest Web, Sept. 3.

Fukami, G. (1953). "Japanese Department Stores," *Journal of Marketing*, 18/1: 41–9.

Gallegos, J. (2003). "CSU: Corporacion Supermercados Unidos: Excelencia sin Barreras," PowerPoint presentation, Hortifruti, San Jose, Costa Rica.

Gates, B. (1995). *The Road Ahead.* New York: Penguin.

Geocities (2004). "Beyonics Technology," company profile, www.geocities.com/fa_book/Benyonics_181201.html (accessed Jan. 23, 2004).

Gereffi, G. (1994a). "The International Economy and Economic Development," in N. Smelser and R. Swedberg (eds), *The Handbook of Economic Sociology.* Princeton: Princeton University Press, 206–33.

Gereffi, G. (1994b). "The Organization of Buyer-Driven Global Commodity Chains: How US Retailers Shape Overseas Production Networks," in G. Gereffi and M. Korzeniewicz (eds), *Commodity Chains and Global Capitalism.* Westport, CT: Praeger, 95–122.

Gereffi, G. (1999). "International Trade and Industrial Upgrading in the Apparel Commodity Chain," *Journal of International Economics*, 48/1: 37–70.

Gereffi, G. (2006). *The New Offshoring of Jobs and Global Development.* Geneva: International Labour Organization, International Institute for Labour Studies.

Gereffi, G., Humphrey J., and Sturgeon T. (2005). "The Governance of Global Value Chains," *Review of International Political Economy*, 12/1: 78–104.

Gereffi, G., and Memedovic O. (2003). *The Global Apparel Value Chain: What Prospects for Upgrading by Developing Countries.* Vienna: United Nations Industrial Development

Organization, Sectoral Studies Series, www.unido.org/file-storage/download/?file% 5fid=11900.

Gereffi, G., and Pan, M. L. (1994). "The Globalization of Taiwan's Garment Industry," in E. Bonacich, L. Cheng, N. Chinchilla, N. Hamilton, and P. Ong (eds), *Global Production: The Apparel Industry in the Pacific Rim*. Philadelphia: Temple University Press, 126–46.

Gibbons, H. A. (1926). *John Wanamaker*. New York, London: Harper & Brothers.

Gilman, H. (2004). "The Most Underrated CEO Ever," *Fortune Magazine*, Mar. 21, www.fortune.com/fortune/subs/print/0,15935,602843,00.html.

Giridharadas, A. (2006). "In India, Mom and Pop Get Shoved Aside," *International Herald Tribune*, Oct. 20, pp. 1, 13.

Godley, A., and Fletcher, S. R. (2001). "International Retailing in Britain, 1850–1994," *Service Industries Journal*, 21/2: 31–46.

Gold, T. B. (1986). *State and Society in the Taiwan Miracle*. Armonk, NY: M. E. Sharpe.

Goldman, A. (1981). "Transfer of a Retailing Technology into the Less Developed Countries: The Supermarket Case," *Journal of Retailing*, 57/2: 5–29.

Goldman, A., Ramaswami, S., and Krider, R. E. (2002). "Barriers to the Advancement of Modern Food Retail Formats: Theory and Measurement," *Journal of Retailing*, 78: 281–95.

Goldman, M. I. (1960). "Retailing in the Soviet Union," *Journal of Marketing*, 24/4: 9–15.

Goletti, F. (1999). "Agricultural Diversification and Rural Industrialization as a Strategy for Rural Income Growth and Poverty Reduction in Indochina and Myanmar," Markets and Structural Studies Division, Discussion Paper MSS No. 30, International Food Policy Research Institute, Washington.

Gower, A. and Cusumano, M. (2002). *Platform Leadership: How Intel, Microsoft, and Cisco Drive Industry Innovation*. Cambridge, MA: Harvard Business School Press.

Greenhalgh, P. (1988). *Ephemeral Vistas: The Expositions Universelles, Great Exhibitions and World Fairs, 1851–1939*. Manchester: Manchester University Press.

Greif, A. (2007). *Institutions and the Path to the Modern Economy: Lessons from Medieval Trade*. Cambridge: Cambridge University Press.

Grosso, C., McPherson, J., and Shi, C. (2005). "What's Working Online," *McKinsey Quarterly* (July–Sept.), 18–20.

Grove, A. (1996). *Only the Paranoid Survive*. New York: Doubleday.

Gurdjian, P., Kerschbaumer, G., Kliger, M., and Waterous, J. (2000). "Bagging Europe's Groceries," *McKinsey Quarterly*, 2: 68–75.

Gutman, G. (2002). "Impact of the Rapid Rise of Supermarkets on Dairy Products System in Argentina," *Development Policy Review*, 20/4: 409–27.

Guy, C. M. (2007). *Planning for Retail Development: A Critical View of the British Experience*. London: Routledge.

Haberman, A. L. (2001) (ed.). *Twenty-Five Years behind Bars: The Proceedings of the Twenty-Fifth Anniversary of the UPC at the Smithsonian Institution, September 30, 1999*. Wertheim Publications in Industrial Relations. Cambridge, MA.: Harvard University Wertheim Publications Committee, distributed by Harvard University Press.

Haggblade, S., Hazell, P. and Reardon, T. (2002). "Strategies for Stimulating Poverty-Alleviating Growth in the Rural Nonfarm in Developing Countries," Environment and Production Technology Division (EPTD), Discussion Paper No. 92, International Food Policy Research Institute, Washington.

Hall, M. (1971). "The Small Unit in the Distributive Trades: Committee of Inquiry on Small Firms," Research Report No. 8. London: Her Majesty's Stationery Office.

Hamilton, Gary G. (2006) (ed.). *Commerce and Capitalism in Chinese Societies*. London: Routledge.

Hamilton, G. G., and Fels, D. (2010). "Consumerism and Self-Representation in an Era of Global Capitalism," in J. Hall, L. Grindstaff, and M.-C. Lo (eds), *Handbook of Cultural Sociology*. London: Routledge.

Hamilton, G. G., and Kao, C. S. (2006). "Reflexive Manufacturing: Taiwan's Integration in the Global Economy," in G. G. Hamilton, *Commerce and Capitalism in Chinese Societies*. London: Routledge, 184–200.

Hamilton, G. G., and Kao, C.-S. (2009). "The Round Table: A Reconsideration of Chinese Business Networks," in Wong Siu-lun (ed.), *Paradigms and Perspectives on Hong Kong Studies*. Hong Kong: University of Hong Kong Press, 175–200.

Hamilton, G. G., and Kao, C.-S. (forthcoming). *Making Money: How the Global Economy Works from an Asian Point of View*.

Hamilton, G. G., Petrovic, M., and Feenstra R. C. (2006). "Remaking the Global Economy: US Retailers and Asian Manufacturers," in G. G. Hamilton (ed.), *Commerce and Capitalism in Chinese Societies*. London: Routledge, 146–84.

Hanchett, T. W. (1996). "US Tax Policy and the Shopping-Center Boom of the 1950s and 1960s," *American Historical Review*, 101/4: 1082–110.

Hanchett, T. W. (2000). "Financing Suburbia, Prudential Insurance and the Post-World War II: Transformation of the American City," *Journal of Urban History*, 26/3: 312–28.

Hansell, S. (1998). "Private Sector: Creator of the On-Line Swap Meet," *New York Times*, Nov. 15.

Hantuba, H., and de Graaf, J. (2003). "Linkages between Smallholder Farm Producers and Supermarkets in Zambia," paper presented at the FAO technical workshop on "Globalization of the Food System: Impacts on Food Security and Nutrition," Oct. 8–10, Rome.

Hao, Y.-P. (1986). *The Commercial Revolution in Nineteenth Century China: The Rise of Sino-Western Mercantile Capitalism*. Berkeley and Los Angeles: University of California Press.

Hardwick, M. J. (2004). *Mall Maker: Victor Gruen, Architect of an American Dream*. Philadelphia: University of Pennsylvania Press.

Harris, N. (1990). *Cultural Excursions: Marketing Appetites and Cultural Tastes in Modern America*. Chicago: University of Chicago Press.

Harrison, B. (1994). *Lean and Mean: The Changing Landscape of Corporate Power in the Age of Flexibility*. Cambridge, MA: Harvard University Press.

Hatch, W., and Yamamura, K. (1996). *Asia in Japan's Embrace: Building a Regional Production Alliance*. Cambridge: Cambridge University Press.

Henksmeier, K. (1960). *The Economic Performance of Self-Service in Europe: A Report*. Paris: OEEC.

Henksmeier, K. (1988). "50 Jahre Selbstbedienung: ein Rückblick," *Dynamik im Handel. Sonderausgabe, 50 Jahre Selbstbedienung* (Oct.), 10–37.

Hermanson, J. (2005). Personal email communication, American Center for International Labor Solidarity, Feb. 7.

Hernandez, L. (2004). "Colombia Retail Food Sector Annual, 2004," GAIN Report Number CO4011, Washington: USDA Foreign Agricultural Service.

Hilton, M. L. (2004). "Retailing the Revolution: The State Department Store (Gum) and Soviet Society in the 1920s," *Journal of Social History*, 37/4: 939–65.

Ho, T. M. C. (2005). Personal email communication, Apr. 25.

Hoge, C. C., Sr (1988). *The First Hundred Years Are the Toughest: What Can We Learn from the Century of Competition between Sears and Montgomery Ward*. Berkeley, CA: Ten Speed Press.

Holden, R. H. (1953). "Marketing Structure and Economic Development," *Quarterly Journal of Economics*, 67 (Aug.), 344–61.

Hollander, S. C. (1960). "The Wheel of Retailing," *Journal of Marketing*, 25/3: 37–42.

Hollander, S. C. (1964). "Who Does the Work of Retailing?" *Journal of Marketing*, 28/3: 18–22.

Hollander, S. C. (1970). *Multinational Retailing*. East Lansing, MI: Michigan State University.

Holt, D. B. (1997). "Poststructuralist Lifestyle Analysis: Conceptualizing the Social Patterning of Consumption in Postmodernity," *Journal of Consumer Research*, 23/4 (Mar.), 326–50.

Honeycombe, G. (1984). *Selfridges, Seventy-Five Years: The Story of a Store*. London: Park Lane Press.

Hower, R. M. (1943). *History of Macy's of New York, 1858–1914: Evolution of the Department Store*. Cambridge, MA: Harvard University Press http://articles.techrepublic. com.com/2100-10877_11-6044445.html.

Hu, D., Reardon, T., Rozelle, S., Timmer, P., and Wang, H. (2004). "The Emergence of Supermarkets with Chinese Characteristics: Challenges and Opportunities for China's Agricultural Development," *Development Policy Review*, 22/4: 557–86.

Hughes, G. B. (1958). "Europe's First Department Store?" *Country Life*, 123 (May 15), 1058–9.

Humphrey, J., and Memodovic, O. (2003). "The Global Automotive Industry Value Chain: What Prospects for Upgrading by Developing Countries?" Sectoral Studies Series. Vienna: United Nations Industrial Development Organization.

IAM Journal (2005). "China Dolls," International Association of Machinists and Aerospace Workers, AFL-CIO, Spring.

IDC (2004). "Can Anyone Disrupt Dell's Direct Model?" *IDC Opinion*. Framingham, MA: IDC.

IDC (2005). Data compiled on request from *IDC Worldwide PC Channel Market*. Framingham, MA: IDC, Apr.

IDC (2006). Data compiled on request by Christina Richmond, Research Manager, Hardware Channels and Alliances, IDC, from *IDC Worldwide Quarterly PC Tracker*. Framingham, MA: IDC, Jan. 23.

IDC (2007). Data compiled on request by Kathy Nagamine, Research Manager, Hardware Channels and Alliances, from *IDC Worldwide Quarterly PC Tracker*. Framingham, MA: IDC Jan. 25.

Internet World Stats (2008). "Usage and Population Statistics," http://internetworld-stats.com (accessed June 19, 2008).

Jakle, J. A., and Sculle K. A. (1999). *Fast Food: Roadside Restaurants in the Automobile Age*. Baltimore: Johns Hopkins University Press.

Jakle, J. A., Sculle, K. A., and. Rogers, J. S. (1996). *The Motel in America*. Baltimore: Johns Hopkins University Press.

Jefferys, J. B. (1954). *Retail Trading in Britain, 1850–1950*. Cambridge: Cambridge University Press.

Jones, G. (1996). *The Evolution of International Business*. London: Routledge.

Jones, G. (2000). *Merchants to Multinationals: British Trading Companies in the Nineteenth and Twentieth Centuries*. Oxford: Oxford University Press.

Journal of Commerce (2009). "Top Importers in 2008," May 25, pp. 21A–26A.

Just-style.com (2003). "Garment Industries in Bangladesh and Mexico Face an Uncertain Future," AROQ: just-style.com, Oct. 20. www.sweatshopwatch.org/global/articles/jsmexbang_oct03.html.

Kahn, G. (2003). "Made to Measure: Invisible Supplier Has Penney's Shirts All Buttoned Up," *Wall Street Journal*. Sept. 11, p. A1.

Kahn, G. (2004a). "Making Labels for Less: Supply-Chain City Transforms Far-Flung Apparel Industry," *Wall Street Journal*, Aug. 13, B1.

Kahn, G. (2004b). Personal email communication to Edna Bonacich, Sept. 1.

Kambil, A. (1997). "Doing Business in the Wired World," *IEEE* (May), 56–61.

Kao, C.-S., and Hamilton, G. G. (2000). "Reflexive Manufacturing: Taiwan's Integration in the Global Economy," *International Studies Review*, 3/1: 1–19.

Kapinsky, R. (1993). *From Mass Production to Flexible Specialization: Micro-Level Restructuring in a British Engineering Firm*. London: Institute of Development Studies.

Kawakami, M. (2008). "Exploiting the Modularity of Value Chains: Inter-Firm Dynamics of the Taiwanese Notebook PC Industry," Institute of Developing Economies (IDE) Discussion Paper 146, Apr.

Kawakami, M. (2010). "Inter-Firm Dynamics of Notebook PC Value Chains and the Rise of Taiwanese Original Design Manufacturing Firms," in M. Kawakami and T. J. Sturgeon (eds), *The Dynamics of Local Learning in Global Value Chains: Experiences from East Asia*. London: Palgrave Macmillan.

Kearney, N. (2003). "Trade in Textiles and Clothing after 2005," General Secretary, International Textile, Garment, and Leatherworkers' Federation (TGLWF), presentation to the EU Directorate General on Trade, Conference on "The Future of Textiles and Clothing Trade After 2005," Brussels, May 5–6, http://trade-info.cec.eu.int/textiles/documents/153.doc.

King, R., and Phumpiu P. F. (1996). "Reengineering the Food Supply Chain: The ECR Initiative in the Grocery Industry," *American Journal of Agricultural Economics*, 78/5: 1181–6.

Kao, C. S., and Hamilton, G. G. (2009). "The Round Table: A Reconsideration of Chinese Business Networks," in S. L. Wong (ed.), *Paradigms and Perspectives on Hong Kong Studies*. Hong Kong: University of Hong Kong Press, 175–200.

Kojima, K., and Ozawa T. (1984). *Japan's General Trading Companies: Merchants of Economic Development*. Paris: Organisation for Economic Cooperation and Development.

Kotha, S. B. (1998). "Competing on the Internet: How Amazon.com Is Rewriting the Rules of Competition in the Book Retailing Industry," *Advances in Strategic Management*, 15: 239–65.

Kotha, S. B., Rajgopal, S., and Venkatachalam, M. (2004). "The Role of Online Buying Experience as a Competitive Advantage: Evidence from Third-Party Ratings for e-Commerce Firms," *Journal of Business* (Apr.–June), S100–S134.

Koudal, P., and Long, V. W.-T. (2005). "The Power of Synchronization: The Case of TAL Apparel Group," A Deloitte Research Case Study. May, www.deloitte.com/dtt/cda/doc/content/DTT_DR_TAL_May2005Web.pdf.

Kraemer, K. L., Dedrick, J., and Yamashiro, S. (2000). "Dell Computer: Refining and Extending the Business Model with IT," *Information Society*, 16: 5–21.

Kraemer, K. L., Dedrick, J., Melville, N., and Zhu K. (2006). *Global E-Commerce: Impacts of National Environment and Policy*, Cambridge: Cambridge University Press.

Krazit, T. (2006). "Need your PC Fixed? Get Ready to Pay Up," CNET News.com, Mar. 1.

Lane, C., and Bachmann, R. (1997). "Cooperation in Inter-Firm Relations in Britain and Germany: The Role of Social Institutions," *British Journal of Sociology*, 48/2: 226–54.

Latham, F. B. (1972). *1872–1972: A Century of Serving Consumers: The Story of Montgomery Ward*. 2nd edn. Chicago: Montgomery Ward.

Leach, W. R. (1993). *Land of Desire: Merchants, Power, and the Rise of a New American Culture*. New York: Vintage Books.

Leach, P. T. (2010). "Locked in for Growth," *Journal of Commerce*, Feb. 1, pp. 16–23.

Lebhar, G. M. (1963). *Chain Stores in America, 1859–1962*. New York: Chain Store Publishing Corporation.

Lebow, V. (1948). "Our Changing Channels of Distribution," *Journal of Marketing*, 13/1: 12–22.

Lee, J.-H., and Reardon, T. (2005). "Forward Integration of an Agricultural Cooperative into the Supermarket Sector: The Case of Hanaro Club in Korea," Joint Working Paper, Department of Industrial Economics, Chung-Ang University, Seoul, Korea, and Department of Agricultural Economics, Michigan State University, East Lansing, Michigan, March.

Lee, S. H., and Song, H. K. (1994). "The Korean Garment Industry: From Authoritarian Patriarchism to Industrial Paternalism," in E. Bonacich, L. Cheng, N. Chinchilla, N. Hamilton, and P. Ong (eds), *Global Production: The Apparel Industry in the Pacific Rim*. Philadelphia: Temple University Press, 147–61.

Leichtman Research Group (2010). "Broadband Internet Access & Services in the Home 2010," www.leichtmanresearch.com/research/bband_home_toc.pdf.

Lever-Tracy, C. (2000). "The Irrelevance of Japan," in D. Ip, C. Lever-Tracy, and N. Tracy (eds), *Chinese Business and the Asian Crisis*. Hampshire: Gower Publishing, 183–204.

Levinson, M. (2006). *The Box: How the Shipping Container Made the World Smaller and the World Economy Bigger*. Princeton: Princeton University Press.

Levy, B. (1988). "Korean and Taiwanese Firms as International Competitors: The Challenges Ahead," *Columbia Journal of World Business* (Spring), 43–51.

Levy, B. (1991). "Transactions Costs, the Size of Firms, and Industrial Policy: Lessons from a Comparative Case Study of the Footwear Industry in Korea and Taiwan," *Journal of Development Economics*, 34: 151–78.

Lewis, W. W. (2004). *The Power of Productivity: Wealth, Poverty, and the Threat to Global Stability*. Chicago: Chicago University Press.

Lhermie C. (2003). *Carrefour ou l'invention de l'hypermarché*. 2nd edn. Paris: Vuibert.

Li & Fung (2007). Li & Fung Group website, www.lifunggroup.com/front.html (accessed Aug. 30 2007).

Lichtenstein, N. (2006) (ed.). *Wal-Mart: The Face of Twenty-First-Century Capitalism*. New York: New Press.

Lichtenstein, N. (2009). *The Retail Revolution: How Wal-Mart Created a Brave New World of Business*. New York: Metropolitan Books.

Lohr, S. (1997). "Digital Commerce," *New York Times*. May 19, p. C5.

Longstreth, R. (1999). *The Drive-In, the Supermarket, and the Transformation of Commercial Space in Los Angeles, 1914–1941*. Cambridge, MA: MIT Press.

Lowe, M., and Wrigley, N. (2009). "Innovation in Retail: Internationalisation: Tesco in the USA," *International Review of Retail, Distribution and Consumer Research*, 19/4: 331–47.

Luen Thai (2006). "Investor Relations: About Us," http://luenthai.quamnet.com/luenthai/IR-index.htm.

Luen Thai (2007). Luenthai Holdings Limited, *Annual Report 2006*, Apr. 20, www2.luenthai.com/files/LTN20070419219.pdf.

Lüthje, B. (2005). "Global Production, Industrial Development, and New Labor Regimes in China: The Case of Electronics Contract Manufacturing," in M. Gallagher, C. K. Lee, and A. Park (eds), *China: The Labor of Reform*. London: Routledge.

MacDonald, S. B., and Gastmann, A. L. (2001). *A History of Credit and Power in the Western World*. New Brunswick, NJ: Transaction Publishers.

McGrath, P. (2003). Chairman of the Board of United States Association of Importers of Textile and Apparel (USA ITA), testimony before the United States International Trade Commission, Investigation 332-448, "Competitiveness of the Textile and Apparel Industries Investigation," Jan. 22, http://usaita.com.

McNair, M. P., and May, E. G. (1976). *The Evolution of Retail Institutions in the United States*. Cambridge, MA: Marketing Science Institute.

McNair, M. P., Gragg, C. I., Jr, and Teele, S. F. (1937). *Problems in Retailing*. 1st edn. New York and London: McGraw-Hill.

McNichol, D. (2006). *The Roads that Built America: The Incredible Story of the US Interstate System*. New York: Sterling Publishing Company.

MacPherson K. L. (1998) (ed.). *Asian Department Stores*. Honolulu, HI: University of Hawaii Press.

Magretta, J. (2002). "Fast, Global, and Entrepreneurial: Supply Chain Management, Hong Kong Style," *Harvard Business Review*, enhanced edn, Oct., original article published in *Harvard Business Review* (Sept.–Oct. 1998: 103–14).

Mahoney, T., and Sloane, L. (1966). *The Great Merchants, America's Foremost Retail Institutions and the People Who Made Them Great*. NY: Harper and Row.

Malkin, E. (2004). "Mexican Retailers Unite Against Wal-Mart," *New York Times*, July 9.

Malone, S. (2002). "Who Loses to China?" *Women's Wear Daily*, Nov. 26.

Manalili, N. M. (2005). "The Changing Map of the Philippine Retail Food Sector: The Impact on Trade and the Structure of Agriculture and the Policy Response,"

Presentation at the Pacific Economic Cooperation Council's Pacific Food System Outlook 2005–6 Annual Meeting in Kun Ming, China, May 11–13.

Mandell, L. (1990). *The Credit Card Industry: A History*. Boston: Twayne Publishers.

Markovits, C. (2000). *The Global World of Indian Merchants, 1750–1947: Traders of Sind from Bukhara to Panama*. Cambridge, Cambridge University Press.

Markovits, C. (2008). *Merchants, Traders, Entrepreneurs: Indian Business in the Colonial Era*. Houndmills: Palgrave Macmillan.

Marx, K. (1967 [1887]). *Capital*. Volume One. New York: International Publishers. German edn, 1867.

Marx, K. and Engels F. (1967 [1849]). *The Communist Manifesto*. London: Penguin Books.

Marx, T. G. (1985). "The Development of the Franchise Distribution System in the US Automobile Industry," *Business History Review*, 59/3: 465–74.

Mathews, G., and Lui, T. L. (2001). *Consuming Hong Kong*. Hong Kong: Hong Kong University Press.

Maxwell, S. and Slater, R. (2003). "Food Policy Old and New", *Development Policy Review* 21/5–6: 531–53.

Merk, J. (2003). "The International Production of Branded Athletic Footwear," unpublished paper written for the International Conference on Global Regulation, Centre for Global Political Economy, University of Sussex, Brighton.

Merk, J. (2006). "Nike's Mirror Image: Yue Yuen and the Implementation of Labour Codes," paper presented at the International Studies Association annual conference, San Diego, CA, Mar. 22–5.

Meyer-Ohle, H. (2003). *Innovation and Dynamics in Japanese Retailing: From Techniques to Formats to Systems*. New York: Palgrave Macmillan.

Miller, D., and Merrilees B. (2004). "Fashion and Commerce: A Historical Perspective on Australian Fashion Retailing 1880–1920," *International Journal of Retail & Distribution Management*, 32/8–9: 394–407.

Miller, M. B. (1981). *The Bon Marché: Bourgeois Culture and the Department Store, 1869–1920*. Princeton: Princeton University Press.

Mirowski, P. (1989). *More Heat than Light: Economics as Social Physics, Physics as Nature's Economics*. Cambridge: Cambridge University Press.

Moeran, B. (1998). "The Birth of the Japanese Department Store," in K. L. MacPherson (ed.), *Asian Department Stores*. Honolulu, HI: University of Hawaii Press, 141–75.

Molotch, H. (2003). *Where Stuff Comes From: How Toasters, Toilets, Cars, Computers and Many Other Things Come To Be As They Are*. London: Routledge.

Morgan Stanley Report (2006). "The State of the Internet," Nov. 8.

Morris, G. E. (1997). "The End of Push Marketing," *Advertising and Marketing Review*, www.ad-mkt-review.com/public_html/air/ai034.html.

Morris, J. (1999). "Contesting Retail Space in Italy: Competition and Corporatism 1915–1960," *International Review of Retail Distribution and Consumer Research*, 9/3: 291–305.

Mulpuru, S. (2007). "Trends 2007: eCommerce and Online Retail," *Forrester Research Inc.*, Feb. 20.

Mulpuru, S. (2009). "US Ecommerce Forecast, 2008 to 2013," *Forrester Research Inc.*, Feb. 2.

Myers, N., and Kent, J. (2003). "New Consumers: The Influence of Affluence on the Environment," *Proceedings of the National Academy of Science*, 100/8: 4963–8.

Natawidjaja, R., Reardon, T., and Shetty, S., with Noor, T. I., Perdana, T., Rasmikayati, E., Bachri, S., and Hernandez, R. (2007). *Horticultural Producers and Supermarket Development in Indonesia*. UNPAD/MSU/World Bank. World Bank Report No. 38543, published by the World Bank/Indonesia, July.

National Postal Museum (2008). "Precious Packages—America's Parcel Post Service," www.postalmuseum.si.edu/exhibits/2b2f_parcel.html (accessed June 19, 2008).

Nelson, R. R., and Winter S. G. (1982). *An Evolutionary Theory of Economic Change*. Cambridge, MA: Harvard University Press.

Neven, D., and Reardon, T. (2003). "The Rapid Rise of Kenyan Supermarkets: Impacts on the Fruits and Vegetables System," paper presented at the FAO technical workshop on "Globalization of the Food System: Impacts on Food Security and Nutrition," Rome, Oct. 8–10.

Neven, D., and Reardon, T. (2004). "The Rise of Kenyan Supermarkets and Evolution of their Horticulture Product Procurement Systems," *Development Policy Review*, 22/6 (Nov.), 669–99.

Neven, D., Reardon, T., Chege, J., and Wang, H.-L. (2005). "Supermarkets and Consumers in Africa: The Case of Nairobi, Kenya," Staff Paper 2005-04, Dept. of Agricultural Economics, Michigan State University, East Lansing, MI.

Neven, D., Katjiuongua, H., Adjosoediro, I., Reardon, T., Chuzu, P., Tembo, G., and Ndiyoi, M. (2006). "Food Sector Transformation and Standards in Zambia: Smallholder Farmer Participation and Growth in the Dairy Sector," Staff Paper 2006–18, May, Michigan State University, East Lansing.

New York Times (1996). "A Nonchain Bookstore Bucks the Tide," Sept. 8, p. 4.

New York Times (2006). "Demystifying the eBay Selling Experience," Jan. 21, p. 5.

New York Times (2007). "Wal-Mart's Welcome to India Includes Demonstrations," Feb. 23, p. C3.

Nielsen, P. B. (2008) (ed.). 'International Sourcing: Moving Business Functions Abroad', Statistics Denmark, www.dst.dk/publ/InterSourcing.

Nielsen Company (2007). "Trends in Online Shopping: A Global Nielsen Consumer Report," http://th.nielsen.com/site/documents/GlobalOnlineShoppingReportFeb08.pdf.

Nordås, H. K. (2004). *The Global Textile and Clothing Industry Post the Agreement on Textiles and Clothing*. Geneva: World Trade Organization.

Nystrom, P. H. (1917). *Retail Store Management*. Chicago: LaSalle Extension University.

Nystrom, P. H. (1930). *Economics of Retailing*. New York: Ronald Press Company.

O'Hara, M. (1995). *Market Microstructure Theory*. Oxford: Blackwell Publishing.

Offutt, S., and Gunderson, C. (2005). "Farm Poverty," *Amber Waves of Grain*, Sept., www.ers.usda.gov/AmberWaves/September05/Features/Farm Poverty.htm (accessed Apr. 7, 2007).

Olney, P. (2003). "On the Waterfront: Analysis of ILWU Lockout," *New Labor Forum*, 12/1: 28–37.

Olson, L. (1970). *Japan in Postwar Asia*. New York: Praeger Publisher.

Ordanini, A., Kraemer, K., and Dedrick, J. (2006). "Medion: The 'Orchestrator' Business Model," IT in Business, Center for Research on Information Technology and Organizations, UC Irvine, Nov.

Orellana, D., and Vasquez, E. (2004). "Guatemala Retail Food Sector Annual, 2004," GAIN Report Number GT4018, Washington: USDA Foreign Agricultural Service.

Orlove, B. (1997) (ed.). *The Allure of the Foreign: Imported Goods in Postcolonial Latin America.* Ann Arbor: University of Michigan Press.

Palmer, M. (2005). "Retail Multinational Learning: A Case Study of Tesco," *International Journal of Retail and Distribution Management*, 3/1: 23–48.

Pasdermadjian, H. (1954). *The Department Store: Its Origins, Evolution, and Economics.* London: Newman Books.

Pellegrini, L. (1996). *La distribuzione commerciale in Italia.* Bologna: Il Mulino.

Petrovic, M., and Hamilton G. G. (2006). "Making Global Markets: Wal-Mart and its Suppliers," in N. Lichtenstein (ed.), *Wal-Mart: The Face of Twenty-First-Century Capitalism.* New York: New Press, 107–42.

Philadelphia Business Journal (1996). Sept. 27.

Pine, J. B., and Davis, S. (1999). *Mass Customization: The New Frontier in Business Competition.* Boston: Harvard Business School Press.

Piore, M. and Sabel C. (1986). *The Second Industrial Divide: Possibilities for Prosperity.* New York: Basic Books.

Pocock, E. (2009). "Largest Shopping Malls," www.easternct.edu/~pocock/MallsWorld.htm (accessed Oct. 2, 2009).

Porter, M. (1986). *Competition in Global Industries.* Boston: Harvard Business School Press.

Potz, P. (2002). "Die Regulierung des Einzelhandels in Italien: Grundlagen und Einfluss auf die Handelsstruktur," WZB Discussion Paper FS I 02-104, Berlin.

Prahalad, C. K., and Hamel, G. (1990). "The Core Competence of the Corporation," *Harvard Business Review*, 68/3: 79–91.

Prime, N. (1999). "IKEA: International Development." in M. Dupuis and J. Dawson (eds), *European Cases in Retailing.* Malden, MA: Blackwell Publishers, 33–48.

Publishers Weekly (1996a). Jan. 1.

Publishers Weekly (1996b). Mar 11.

Pun, N. (2005). Director, China Working Women's Network, interview, Sept. 15.

Pun, N. (2009). "The Making of a Global Dormitory Labour Regime: Labour Protection and Labour Organizing of Migrant Women in South China," in Rachel Murphy (ed.), *Labour Migration and Social Development in Contemporary China* (London: Routledge).

Pun. N., and Yu, X. M. (2008). "When Wal-Mart and the Chinese Dormitory Labour Regime Meet: A Study of Three Toy Factories in China. *China Journal of Social Work*, 1/2: 110–29.

Rabach, E., and Kim, E. M. (1994). "Where is the Chain in Commodity Chains? The Service Sector Nexus," in G. Gereffi and M. Korzeniewicz (eds), *Commodity Chains and Global Capitalism.* Westport, CT: Praeger, 123–41.

Ralston, B., Kraemer, K. L., and Dedrick J. (2004). "The Retail Model in the Computer Industry: eMachines," working paper, Personal Computing Industry Center, The Paul Merage School of Business, Irvine, CA, June.

Rangkuti, F. (2003). "Indonesia Food Retail Sector Report 2003," USDA GAIN Report. ID3028, Nov. 12.

Rappaport, E. D. (1995). "A New Era of Shopping: The Promotion of Women's Pleasure in London's West End, 1909–1914," in L. Charney and V. R. Schwartz (eds), *Cinema and the Invention of Modern Life*. Berkeley and Los Angeles: University of California Press, 130–55.

Rappaport, E. D. (2000). *Shopping for Pleasure: Women in the Making of London's West End*. Princeton: Princeton University Press.

Raucher, A. R. (1991). "Dime Store Chains: The Making of Organization Men, 1880–1940," *Business History Review*, 65/1: 130–63.

Reardon, T. (2003). "The Rapid Rise of Supermarkets in Latin America and Asia: Fundamental Effects on Domestic Agri-food Systems and Trade," paper presented at the Global Market for High-Value Food Workshop, Economic Research Service, US Department of Agriculture, Washington, Feb.14, www.farmfoundation.org (accessed Aug. 27, 2003).

Reardon, T. (2005). "Emerging Market Opportunities and Challenges from the Rise of Supermarkets," Power Point presentation, USDA's 2005 Agricultural Outlook Forum, US Department of Agriculture, Washington.

Reardon, T., and Berdegué, J. A. (2002). "The Rapid Rise of Supermarkets in Latin America: Challenges and Opportunities for Development," *Development Policy Review*, 20/4: 371–88.

Reardon, T., and Berdegué, J. A. (2007). "The Retail-Led Transformation of Agrifood Systems and its Implications for Development Policies: A Background Paper Prepared for the World Bank's World Development Report 2008: Agriculture for Development," Rimisp and MSU, Jan.

Reardon, T., Berdegué, J. A., and Timmer, C. P. (2005). "Supermarketization of the Emerging Markets of the Pacific Rim: Development and Trade Implications." *Journal of Food Distribution Research*, 36 (Mar.): 3–12.

Reardon, T., and Gulati, A. (2008). "The Rise of Supermarkets and their Development Implications: International Experience Relevant for India," IFPRI Discussion Papers 752, International Food Policy Research Institute (IFPRI).

Reardon, T., and Timmer, C. P. (2007). "Transformation of Markets for Agricultural Output in Developing Countries since 1950: How Has Thinking Changed," in R. Evenson and P. Pingali (eds), *Handbook of Agricultural Economics, Volume III*, New York: Elsevier, 2807–55.

Reardon, T., Timmer, P., and Berdegué, J. A. (2004). "The Rapid Rise of Supermarkets in Developing Countries: Induced Organizational, Institutional, and Technological Change in Agrifood Systems," *eJADE, Electronic Journal of Agricultural and Development Economics*, 1/2: 168–83.

Reardon, T., Timmer, C. P., Barrett, C. B., and Berdegué, J. A. (2003). "The Rise of Supermarkets in Africa, Asia and Latin America," *American Journal of Agricultural Economics*, 85/5: 1140–6.

Reardon, T., Codron, J.-M., Busch, L., Bingen, J., and Harris, C. (1999). "Strategic Roles of Food and Agricultural Standards for Agrifood Industries," contributed paper selected for presentation at the IAMA World Food and Agribusiness Forum, Florence, Italy.

Reardon, T., Berdegué, J. A., Echánove F., Cook, R., Tucker, N., Martínez, A., Medina, R., Aguirre, M., Hernández, R., and Balsevich, F. (2007). "Supermarkets and Horticultural Development in Mexico: Synthesis of Findings and Recommendations to USAID and GOM," report submitted by MSU to USAID/Mexico and USDA/Washington, Aug.

Regan, W. J. (1963). "The Service Revolution," *Journal of Marketing*, 27/3: 57–62.

Resseguie, H. E. (1965). "Alexander Turney Stewart and the Development of the Department Store, 1823–1876," *Business History Review*, 39/3: 301–22.

Reuters (2006). "Circuit City chases service with new Firedog brand," CNET News.com 11/1/06. Also, http://en.wikipedia.org/wiki/Firedog.

Rezabakhsh, B., Bornemann, D., Hansen, U., and Schrader, U. (2006). "Consumer Power: A Comparison of the Old Economy and the Internet Economy," *Journal of Consumer Policy*, 29: 3–36.

Rindova, V. P., Petkova, A. P., and Kotha, S. B. (2007). "Standing Out: How New Firms in Emerging Markets Build Reputation," *Strategic Organization* (Jan.–Mar.), 31–70.

Robinson, J. (1969 [1933]). *The Economics of Imperfect Competition*. 2nd edn. London: Macmillan.

Ross, A. (2004). *Low Pay, High Profile: The Global Push for Fair Labor*. New York: New Press.

Ross, R. J. S. (2004). *Slaves to Fashion: Poverty and Abuse in the New Sweatshops*. Ann Arbor: University of Michigan Press.

Rouibah, K., Khalil, O., and Hassanien, A. E. (2009) (eds). *Emerging Markets and E-Commerce in Developing Economies*. Hershey, PA: Information Science Reference.

Runsten, D. (2003). "Globalization, NAFTA, and the Restructuring of Mexican Food Processing: Consequences for Small Producers," paper presented at the FAO technical workshop on "Globalization of the Food System: Impacts on Food Security and Nutrition," Oct. 8–10, Rome.

Rydell, R. (1989). "The Culture of Imperial Abundance: World's Fairs in the Making of American Culture," in S. Bronner (ed.), *Consuming Visions, Accumulation and Display of Goods in America, 1880–1920*. New York: W. W. Norton, 191–216.

Salmon, W. J., and Tordjman, A. (1989). "The Internationalisation of Retailing," *International Journal of Retailing*, 4/2: 3–16.

Scheybani, A. (1996). *Handwerk und Kleinhandel in der Bundesrepublik Deutschland: Sozialökonomishcer Wandel und Mittelstandspolitik 1949–1961*. Munich: Oldenbourg.

Schröter, H. G. (2004). "'Revolution in Trade': The Americanization of Distribution in Germany during the Boom Years, 1949–75," in A. Kudo, M. Kipping, and H. G. Schröter (eds), *German and Japanese Business in the Boom Years: Transforming American Management and Technology Models*. New York: Routledge, 246–67.

Schröter, H. G. (2005). *Americanization of the European Economy: A Compact Survey of American Economic Influence in Europe since the 1880s*. Dordrecht: Springer.

Schumpeter, J. A. (1950). *Capitalism, Socialism, and Democracy*. New York: Harper.

Scranton, P. (1994). "Manufacturing Diversity: Production Systems, Markets, and an American Consumer Society, 1870–1930," *Technology and Culture*, 35/3 (July), 476–505.

Scranton, P. (1999). "Multiple Industrializations: Urban Manufacturing Development in the American Midwest, 1880–1925," *Journal of Design History*, 12/1: 45–63.

Senauer, B. (2005). "The Growing Market for High-Value Food Products in Developing and Transition Countries," *Journal of Food Distribution Research*, 32/1: 22–7.

Senauer, B., and Goetz, L. (2004). "The Growing Middle Class in Developing Countries and the Market for High Value Food Products," *ICFAI Journal of Agricultural Economics*, 1/2: 7–12.

Senauer, B., and Venturini, L. (2005). "The Globalization of Food Systems: A Conceptual Framework and Empirical Patterns," in E. DeFrancesco, L. Galletto, and M. Thiene (eds), *Food, Agriculture, and the Environment*. Milan: Franco Angeli Press.

Shaffer, J. D. (1960). "The Influence of 'Impulse Buying' or In-the-Store Decisions on Consumers' Food Purchases," *Journal of Farm Economics*, 42/2: 317–24.

Shaw, G., and Alexander, A. (2006). "Interlocking Directorates and the Knowledge Transfer of Supermarket Retail Techniques from North America to Britain," *International Review of Retail, Distribution and Consumer Research*, 16/3: 375–94.

Shaw, G., Curth L., and Alexander, A. (2004). "Selling Self-Service and the Supermarket: The Americanisation of Food Retailing in Britain, 1945–1970," *Business History*, 46/4: 568–82.

Shin, H. Y., and Lee, Y.-I. (1995). "Korean Direct Investment in Southeast Asia," *Journal of Contemporary Asia*, 25/2: 179–96.

Smith, A. (1977 [1776]). *An Inquiry into the Nature and Causes of the Wealth of Nations*. Chicago: University of Chicago Press.

Smith, C., and Pun, N. (2006). "The Dormitory Labour Regime in China as a Site for Control and Resistance," *International Journal of Human Resource Management*, 17/8: 1456–70.

Smith, D. (1996). "Going South: Global Restructuring and Garment Production in Three East Asian Cases," *Asian Perspective*, 20/2: 211–41.

Solomon, B. (2001). *The Heritage of North American Steam Railroads: From the First Days of Steam Power to the Present*. Pleasantville, NY: Reader's Digest.

Sparks, L. (1996). "Reciprocal Retail Internationalisation: The Southland Corporation, Ito-Yokado and 7-Eleven Convenience Stores," in G. Akehurst and N. Alexander (eds), *The Internationalisation of Retailing*. London: F. Cass, 57–96.

Speer, J. K. (2002). "Sourcing in China: Firms Discuss Advantages, Issues," *Bobbin*, Jan. 1, www.apparelmag.com/bobbin/search/search_display.jsp?vnu_content_id=1431921.

Spulber, D. F. (1996). "Market Microstructure and Intermediation." *Journal of Economic Perspectives* 10/3 (Summer), 135–52.

Spulber, D. F. (1998). *Market Microstructure: Intermediaries and the Theory of the Firm*. Cambridge: Cambridge University Press.

Stern, H. (1962). "The Significance of Impulse Buying Today," *Journal of Marketing*, 26/2: 59–62.

Sternquist, B., and Kacker, M. (1994). *European Retailing's Vanishing Borders*. Westport, CT: Quorum Books.

Strasser, S. (1995). *Satisfaction Guaranteed: The Making of the American Mass Market*. Washington: Smithsonian Institution Press.

Sturgeon, T. (2002). "Modular Production Networks: A New American Model of Industrial Organization," *Industrial and Corporate Change*, 11/3: 451–96.

Sturgeon, T. (2007). "How Globalization Drives Institutional Diversity: The Japanese Electronics Industry's Response to Value Chain Modularity," *Journal of East Asian Studies*, 7/1: 1–34.

Sturgeon, T., and Florida, R. (2004). "Globalization, Deverticalization, and Employment in the Motor Vehicle Industry," in M. Kenny and R. Florida (eds), *Locating Global Advantage: Industry Dynamics in a Globalizing Economy*. Palo Alto, CA: Stanford University Press, 52–81.

Sturgeon, T., and Lee, J. R. (2005). "Industry Co-Evolution: A Comparison of Taiwan and North American Electronics Contract Manufacturers," in S. Berger and R. K. Lester (eds.), *Global Taiwan: Building Competitive Strengths in a New International Economy*. Armonk, NY: M. E. Sharpe.

Sturgeon, T., and Lester, R. (2004). "The New Global Supply-Base: New Challenges for Local Suppliers in East Asia," in S. Yusuf, A. Altaf, and K. Nabeshima (eds), *Global Production Networking and Technological Change in East Asia*. Oxford: Oxford University Press.

Sturgeon, T., and Memedovic, O. (forthcoming). "Measuring Global Value Chains: Intermediate Goods Trade, Structural Change and Compressed Development," UNIDO Working Paper, Vienna.

Sturgeon, T., Van Biesebroeck, J., and Gereffi, G. (2008). "Value Chains, Networks and Clusters: Reframing the Global Automotive Industry," *Journal of Economic Geography*, 8: 297–321.

Sturgeon, T., with Levy, F., Brown, C., Jensen, J. B., and Weil, D. (2006). "Why We Can't Measure the Economic Effects of Services Offshoring: The Data Gaps and How to Fill Them," Final Report from the MIT Industrial Performance Center's Services Offshoring Working Group, MIT Industrial Performance Center Working Paper 06-006, Sept.

Suehiro, A. (1989). *Capital Accumulation in Thailand, 1855–1985*. Tokyo: Centre for East Asian Cultural Studies.

Sum, N.-L., and Pun, N. (2005). "Globalization and Paradoxes of Ethical Transnational Production: Code of Conduct in a Chinese Workplace," *Competition and Change*, 9/2: 181–200.

Super Market Merchandising (1954). "Non Foods Jump to Major Rank," Jan., p. 7.

Supermarket News (2007). "Top Global Retailers," May 3.

Tacconelli, W., and Wrigley, N. (2009). "Organizational Challenges and Strategic Responses of Retail TNCs in Post-WTO-Entry China," *Economic Geography*, 85/1: 49–73.

Taiwan Headlines (2007). "Yue Yuen Industrial Makes Bold Outlet Expansion in China," a service of MyEGov, Aug. 30, http://english.www.gov.tw//TaiwanHeadlines/index.jsp?categid=8&recordid=79153.

Taiwan Statistical Data Book (1997). Taipei: Council for Economic Planning and Development.

Takaoka, M., and Kikkawa, T. (2004). "American Influences and Japanese Innovation in the Distribution Industry: Changes of Supermarket System from the 1950s until the 1970s," in A. Kudo, M. Kipping, and H. G. Schröter (eds), *German and Japanese Business in the Boom Years: Transforming American Management and Technology Models*. New York: Routledge, 268–82.

Tam, P. T. G. (2004). "Developing Supply Chains to Supermarkets for Small Vegetable Farmers in Vietnam," paper presented at the FAO/AFMA/FAMA Regional Workshop on "The Growth of Supermarkets as Retailers of Fresh Produce," Oct. 4–7, 2004, Kuala Lumpur, Malaysia.

Tedlow, R. S. (1990). *New and Improved: The Story of Mass Marketing in America*. New York: Basic Books.

Teece, D. (2009). *Dynamic Capabilities and Strategic Management: Organizing for Innovation and Growth*. New York: Oxford University Press.

Thailand Development Research Institute (2002). *The Retail Business in Thailand: Impact of the Large Scale Multinational Corporation Retailers*. Bangkok: Thailand Development Research Institute.

Timmer, C. P. (2003). "Food Policy in the Era of Supermarkets: What's Different?" paper presented at the FAO technical workshop on "Globalization of the Food System: Impacts on Food Security and Nutrition," Oct. 8–10, Rome.

Timmer, C. P., Falcon, W. P., and Pearson, S. R. (1983). *Food Policy Analysis*. Baltimore: Johns Hopkins University Press for the World Bank.

Tininga, R. (1992). "The Hierarchical Structure of Intermediate Markets: A New Approach to the Analysis of Trade Flow Tables," *Journal of Macromarketing*, 12/2: 55–62.

Tokatli, N., and Eldener, Y. B. (2002). "Globalization and the Changing Political Economy of Distribution Channels in Turkey," *Environment and Planning A*, 34: 217–38.

Tzeng, D., and Lang, W. Y. (2003). "Intel Aggressively Exploring the Clone Notebook Market," *DigiTimes.com*, Sept. 7, www.digitimes.com/NewsShow/Article.asp?view=Article&DATEPUBLISH=2003/07/09&PAGES=01&SEQ=1.

Tzeng, D., and Shen, S. (2005). "Wal-Mart adds FIC and Uniwill to its Value Notebook Lineup," *DigiTimes.com*, Jan. 18.

UNCTAD (2002). United Nations Conference on Trade and Development, *World Investment Report 2002. Transnational Corporations and Export Competitiveness*. New York/Geneva: UNCTAD.

UNCTAD (2004). United Nations Conference on Trade and Development, *Assuring Development Gains From the International Trading System and Trade Negotiations: Implications of ATC termination on 31 December 2004*. Note by the UNCTAD Secretariat, TD/B/51/CRP.1.

UNCTAD (2005). United Nations Conference on Trade and Development, *Impacts of the Agreement on Textiles and Clothing on FDI in and Exports from Developing Countries*. Geneva: UNCTAD, report authored by Richard Appelbaum.

US Bureau of the Census (various years). *Economic Census*. Washington: US Department of Commerce Government Publications.

USDA NASS (2007). US Department of Agriculture, National Agricultural Statistics Service, "Trends in Agriculture: Farm Population," www.usda.gov/nass/pubs/trends/farmpopulation.htm (accessed Apr. 7, 2007).

USA Today (2008). "Thousands of Bananas Wash up on Shore," www.usatoday.com/weather/storms/2007-11-07-bananas_N.htm (accessed June 19, 2008).

US Department of Transportation (2008). "US v. World Maritime Container Traffic and Gross Domestic Product: 1995–2006," www.bts.gov/publications/americas_container_ports/html/table_01.html (accessed June 19, 2008).

Useem, J. (2004). "Should We Admire Wal-Mart? Some Say it's Evil. Others Insist it's a Model of all that's Right with America. Who are we to Believe?" *Fortune*, Mar. 8.

Van Riper, T. (2007). "World's Largest Malls," Forbes.com, Jan. 9.

Vance, S. S., and Scott, R. V. (1994). *Wal-Mart: A History of Sam Walton's Retail Phenomenon*. New York: Twayne Publishers.

Varley, Pamela (1998) (ed.). *The Sweatshop Quandary: Corporate Responsibility on the Global Frontier*. Washington: Investor Responsibility Research Center.

Veblen, T. (1899). *The Theory of the Leisure Class: An Economic Study of the Evolution of Institutions*. New York: Macmillan.

Vernon, R. (1971). *Sovereignty at Bay: The Multinational Spread of US Enterprises*. New York: Basic Books.

Wade, R. (1990). *Governing the Market: Economic Theory and the Role of Government in East Asian Industrialization*. Princeton: Princeton University Press.

Wall Street Journal (1996). "Reading the Market: How a Wall Street Whiz Found a Niche Selling Books on the Internet," May 16, p. 1.

Wal-Mart (2004). "Wal-Mart Mexico," www.walmartmexico.com.mx (accessed July 14, 2004).

Wal-Mart (2007). "Mexico Operations," walmartstores.com (accessed Feb. 7, 2007).

Walsh, C. (1999). "The Newness of the Department Store: A View from the Eighteenth Century," in S. Jaumain and G. Crossick (eds), *Cathedrals of Consumption: The European Department Store 1850–1939*. Aldershot: Ashgate Publishing, 46–71.

Wang, S. G., and Zhang, Y. C. (2005). "The New Retail Economy of Shanghai," *Growth and Change*, 36/1: 41–73.

Watson, J. (2006) (ed.). *Golden Arches East: McDonald's in East Asia*, Stanford: Stanford University Press.

Weatherspoon, D., and Katjiuongua, H. (2003). "The Battle of the Supermarket Supply Chains: Produce Procurement Approaches in Zambia and South Africa," PowerPoint presentation at the FAO technical workshop on "Globalization of the Food System: Impacts on Food Security and Nutrition," Oct. 8–10, Rome.

Weatherspoon, D. D., and Reardon, T. (2003). "The Rise of Supermarkets in Africa: Implications for Agrifood Systems and the Rural Poor," *Development Policy Review*, 21: 333–55.

Whitney, C. R. (2007). "Amid the Shirts and Socks, A Concert Can Break Out," *New York Times*, June 9, 2007, sect. B, The Arts/Cultural Desk.

Whysall, P. (2005). "GEM, 1964–1966: Britain's First Out-of-Town Retailer," *International Review of Retail, Distribution and Consumer Research*, 15/2: 111–24.

Williamson, O. E. (1975). *Markets and Hierarchies: Analysis and Antitrust Implications*. New York: Free Press.

Williamson, O. E. (1979). "Transaction-Cost Economics: The Governance of Contractual Relations," *Journal of Law and Economics*, 22: 233–61.

Wilson, R. (2004). *15th Annual State of Logistics Report: Globalization*. Oak Brook, IL: Council of Logistics Management.

Winkler, H. A. (1991). *Zwischen Marx und Monopolen: Der deutsche Mittelstand vom Kaiserreich zur Bundesrepublik Deutschland.* Frankfurt am Main: Fischer.

Winter, S. G., and Szulanski. G. (2001). "Replication as Strategy," *Organization Science,* 12/6: 730–43.

Woodward, R. B. (2007). "Making a Pilgrimage to Cathedrals of Commerce," *New York Times,* Mar. 11, sect. Travel.

Worthen, B., Tuna, C., and Scheck, J. (2009). "Companies More Prone to Go Vertical," *Wall Street Journal,* Dec. 1, http://online.wsj.com/article/SB125954262100968855. html (accessed Jan. 15, 2010).

Wortmann, M. (2004). "Aldi and the German Model: Structural Change in German Grocery Retailing and the Success of Grocery Discounters," *Competition and Change,* 8/4: 425–41.

Wrigley, N., Coe, N., and Currah, A. (2005). "Globalizing Retail: Conceptualizing the Distribution Based Transnational Corporation, TNC," *Progress in Human Geography,* 29: 437–57.

Wrigley, N., and Lowe, M. (2002). *Reading Retail: A Geographical Perspective on Retailing and Consumption Spaces.* London: Arnold.

Xinhua (2007). "China's Yue Yuen 'Underperform' on Low Retail Exposure: Credit Suisse," July 26, www.quamnet.com/fcgi-bin/news.fpl?par2=2&par3=02&par4= 20070726121705361886einens.

Yamin, M., and Sinkovics, R. R. (2009). "Infrastructure or Foreign Direct Investment? An Examination of the Implications of MNE Strategy for Economic Development," *Journal of World Business,* 44/2: 144–57.

Yen, C.-H. (1998). "Wing On and the Kwok Brothers: A Case Study of Pre-War Chinese Entrepreneurs," in K. L. MacPherson (ed.), *Asian Department Stores.* Honolulu, HI: University of Hawaii Press, 47–65.

Yeo, V. (2006). "Intel Pushes for Conformity in Notebooks," *CNET News.com,* Dec. 4, http://news.com.com/Intel+pushes+for+conformity+in+notebooks/2100-1005_3-6060277.html?tag=nefd.top.

Yeung, H. W.-C. (2009). "Regional Development and the Competitive Dynamics of Global Production Networks: An East Asian Perspective," *Regional Studies,* 43/3: 325–51.

Young, J. D. (1998). "Sun Yatsen and the Department Store: An Aspect of National Reconstruction," in K. L. MacPherson (ed.), *Asian Department Stores.* Honolulu, HI: University of Hawaii Press, 33–46.

Yue Yuen (2006). Yue Yuen Industrial Holdings, Limited Factsheet, http://202.66.146. 82/listco/hk/yueyuen/factsheet/fs060206.pdf.

Yue Yuen (2007a). Yue Yuen Industrial Holdings, "Production Facilties," www. yueyuen.com/bOverview_productionFacilities.htm.

Yue Yuen (2007b). Yue Yuen Industrial Holdings, Limited Press Release, "Yue Yuen Announces FY 2006 Results," Jan. 18, www.yueyuen.com/press_file/4Q2006-press. pdf.

Yue Yuen (2007c). Yue Yuen Industrial Holdings, Limited Press Release, "Yue Yuen Announces 2007 Interim Results," June 21, www.yueyuen.com/press_file/2QFY2007-English.pdf.

Yupoong (2003). *Company Overview*, www.yupoong.co.kr/company/index.jsp.

Zanderighi, L. (2003). "Italy," in S. Howe (ed.), *Retailing in the European Union: Structures, Competition and Performance*. London: Routledge.

Zanfei, A. (2000). "Transnational Firms and the Changing Organization of Innovative Activities," *Cambridge Journal of Economics*, 24: 515–42.

Zentes, J. (1998). "Internationalisierung deutscher Discounter und französischer Hypermarchés," in J. Zentes and B. Swoboda (eds), *Globales Handelsmanagement*. Frankfurt am Main, 201–31.

Zentes, J., Morschett, D., and Schramm-Klein H. (2007). *Strategic Retail Management: Text and International Cases*. Wiesbaden: Gabler.

Zimmerman, M. (1939). *The Super Market Grows Up*. New York: Super Market Publishing Company.

Zimmerman, M. (1955). *The Super Market: A Revolution in Distribution*. New York: McGraw-Hill.

Zola, É. (1992 [1883]). *Au bonheur des dames*, trans. as *The Ladies' Paradise*. Berkeley and Los Angeles: University of California Press.

Index

Figures and tables are indexed in bold.